Canadian Municipal and Planning Law, Second Edition

by

Stanley M. Makuch
Neil Craik
Signe B. Leisk

National Library of Canada Cataloguing in Publication

Makuch, Stanley M

Canadian municipal and planning law / Stanley Makuch, Neil Craik, Signe B. Leisk. — 2nd ed.

Includes index.
ISBN 0-459-24135-4

1. Municipal corporations — Canada. 2. City planning and redevelopment law — Canada. I. Craik, Neil, 1965- II. Leisk Signe B., 1973- III. Title.

KE4904.M3 2004 342.71'09 C2004-901593-1
KF5305.M3 2004

The paper used in this publication meets the minimum requirements of the American National Standard for Information Sciences — Permanence of Paper for Printed Library Materials, ANSI Z39.48-1984.

Cover: The land use map shown on the cover was designed by Michael G. Bissett, B.A., M.A., of Cassels Brock & Blackwell LLP.

Composition: Computer Composition of Canada Inc.

One Corporate Plaza
2075 Kennedy Road
Toronto, Ontario
M1T 3V4

Customer Relations
Toronto 1-416-609-3800
Elsewhere in Canada/U.S. 1-800-387-5164
Fax 1-416-298-5094
World Wide Web: http://www.carswell.com
E-mail: orders@carswell.com

Preface

The purpose of the second edition of this book is to amplify important areas of Canadian municipal and planning law in light of the legal and policy developments that have occurred since the first edition was published. To that end, we have retained much of the structure and approach of the first edition. However, in a number of areas, significant changes in the law have occurred resulting in the expanded treatment of some areas and a refocusing of others. It must be said, that some of the issues that were discussed in the first edition in a prescriptive fashion, often under the heading "Need For Reform", have been, in the interceding years, incorporated into the law by the courts and the legislatures adopting the recommendations set out in that edition. Consequently, less explicit attention is given to "reform" as such and a greater emphasis is placed upon evaluating the current direction of the law.

As with the first edition, the approach to citing cases and referring to legislation is not intended to be encyclopedic, but rather representative, and, more importantly, conceptual. While we have seriously attempted to incorporate major developments across all provinces, particularly where there is a diversity of approaches, we have not and could not detail all changes in the law given the nature of our approach. We have also been challenged by a rapidly evolving policy setting that has required us to alter our revisions on more than one occasion. We have endeavored to incorporate developments in the law up to January 2004.

This second edition received tremendous support from Cassels Brock and Blackwell, LLP, of Toronto, where all three authors have practiced. In addition to the many students and lawyers who provided research assistance over the years, Lorraine Walters and Eleanor Smerdon generously assisted with administrative matters and preparation of the manuscript. The authors also acknowledge and thank Eran Kaplinsky for all of his excellent research assistance. Finally, the authors would like to thank staff at Carswell for their editorial and technical work on this book.

Stanley Makuch would like to thank Neil Craik and Signe Leisk for their major contributions to this second edition. Without them it would not have been completed. He also thanks many other students and lawyers who contributed to the work. Finally, his thanks go to his wife, Barbara, for her loyalty and support during the preparation of this book.

Neil Craik would like to thank his co-authors for their abundant patience, good humour and, most of all, their friendship. He also thanks his wife Janet Craik and their children, Lauren and William, for their love and support over the course of preparing this book, to whom it is dedicated.

Signe Leisk dedicates this book to her husband Jeff and their children, Madison and Morgan, and thanks them for their unwavering support, patience and encouragement. She would also like to thank Stan and Neil, whom she considers her friends and mentors.

Stanley Makuch
Neil Craik
Signe Leisk

Toronto, ON

April 2004

Contents

Table of Cases

1

Introduction

The purpose of this book, in its second edition, is to examine the structure, organization and authority of local government in Canada, particularly in urban areas. Such a goal would be unachievable if the legislation in each of the provinces and the territories governing local government required examination in detail. As a result, this book examines local government from a broad perspective, seeking to explore the underlying bases for the structure, authority and purposes of local government. It also analyzes whether those purposes have been fulfilled, and whether they have been taken into account in judicial interpretation respecting local governmental authority. The approach, therefore, is not one of repeating or describing the details of all the major legislative provisions which regulate local governments, but rather one of attempting to clarify the principles underlying local governmental structure and authority in Canada. Thus, this book is narrower in approach than one which might seek to consider virtually every aspect of the multitude of local governments and, at the same time, broader insofar as we seek to step back from the trees to look at the forest, as it were. In taking this approach, we hope to provide insights into the functioning of local government in a national context rather than simply in the context of a particular province. In this regard, the unity of Canadian municipal law has benefited considerably since the writing of the first edition of this book (in 1982) from a number of decisions from the Supreme Court of Canada addressing the nature and scope of municipal legal authority.

Although this book seeks to examine the general aspects of local government and planning authority, it is not intended to cover the entire field of municipal and planning law in a comprehensive fashion. For example, actions in contract against municipalities are not considered, nor are actions respecting labour matters. The exclusion of these issues is due to the belief that such matters are not substantially affected by being considered in a municipal context. Instead, the intention is to focus on governance issues such as the organization of municipalities, local government finance, judicial review of municipal action and its effect on municipalities, as well as the exercise of planning powers by Canadian municipalities, including provisions for citizen participation and rights to information. We have also included a more thorough discussion of the impacts of the Canadian Constitution, including the *Canadian Charter of Rights and Freedoms*, on municipal authority. It is hoped that an examination of these matters will provide, for both the lawyer and the planner, a basic understanding of the workings of local government, the constraints within which municipal decisions are made and, in particular, the planning powers of municipalities.

Indeed, it is for those who wish to practice as lawyers and planners that this book is written. Lawyers engaged in the practice of municipal law deal with actions brought by or against the municipality, and their legal education and training will generally prepare them for that task. Often, however, they may not be as well prepared to act as counsel to a municipal corporation, to prepare municipal legislation, to advise on financial matters, to assist either the municipality or the citizen with planning or other policy matters, or to advise on municipal organization or intergovernmental matters, without a greater understanding of the unique legal position of municipal governments.

Similarly, planners may be required to prepare municipal legislation and, therefore, must understand the scope of municipal authority and the organization of local government. Policy advice cannot be given in a vacuum, without the knowledge of the financial bases of municipal decision-making and the structure of local institutions. It is important for both lawyers and planners, therefore, to understand the institutional, financial and legal frameworks within which municipalities function. An understanding of the municipal planning function is also crucial, as it is one of the most important aspects of municipal authority.

While this book presents these issues from a descriptive standpoint, we also seek to situate local governments within a broader normative framework. In undertaking such an examination, it is necessary to consider first the purpose of local government. De Tocqueville, in his now famous quote, stated:

> Town meetings are to liberty what primary schools are to science. They bring it within the people's reach, they teach men how to use it and how to enjoy it. A nation may establish the government but without municipal institutions it cannot be said to have the spirit of liberty.[1]

Thus it can be argued that the purpose of local government is to foster a democratic spirit and to provide the means by which democracy can be learned. Politicians and citizens alike can gain experience at the local government level in preparation for involvement in the "serious" matters of the federal and provincial governments. This view of local government is consistent with the conclusion that municipalities are politically inferior governmental bodies reflecting their legal inferiority as recipients of delegated authority. Such an understanding of local government leads to the further conclusion that local governments need to be tightly controlled, limited in their jurisdiction and subject to numerous restrictions to prevent abuses of power. This is a conclusion that has formed much of the historic basis for

1 De Tocqueville, *Democracy in America*, vol. 1 (New York, 1953) at 60.

legislation concerning local government, as well as for judicial review of local government action in Canada. In addition, it reflects the traditional political view that the role of municipal government is concerned primarily with administration and not policy-making, and that local governments are to function as non-partisan service delivery arms of the provincial government.

An alternative and, we suggest, richer purpose for local government, however, has been postulated and is becoming more prevalent. Local government may be perceived as an important organization, the primary task of which is to reflect and provide for the needs and priorities of individuals within its community. It is within the local community where most public services are provided. The function of local government, therefore, is not only to provide those services, but to ensure local public control over the provision of those services. The "most important functions of municipal governments are their ability to identify the needs of the communities they serve and to provide services in accordance with the dictates of their consumers — the citizens."[2]

At the writing of the first edition of this book, the democratic function of local government was only beginning to emerge in legal doctrine. Since that time this position has gained considerable currency and has significantly shaped both the judicial and legislative approaches to municipal authority. The focus on the democratic role of local government has several dimensions. A central rationale for providing local governments with independent decision-making authorities is to provide for greater accountability for the delivery of services. Through the mechanism of local governments, preferences as to the desired quantity and quality of goods and services can be registered. Thus, for example, in the allocation of policing resources, local government can provide a mechanism for deciding not only the amount of funding which should be allocated to policing in comparison with other services such as day care or road repair, but also the way in which those resources which are allocated to policing should be utilized. Political decisions regarding the expenditure of funds on traffic patrols versus community relations, for example, can then be made.

It is, however, insufficient to focus solely on the political aspects of local government functions. While an important aspect of the purpose of local governments is to make political or policy decisions rather than to simply administer provincial policies, there is more to the rationale supporting local government. Its purpose must also be to ensure that political decisions reflect *local* values. Having decisions regarding public services ultimately controlled at the provincial or federal level will ensure political control and ultimate accountability at those levels. The reason for local government must be to ensure *local* control over these decisions given the assumption that values

2 Ontario, *Report of the Royal Commission on Metropolitan Toronto* (Robarts Report) (Toronto, 1977) vol. 1 at 4.

and needs regarding policing, development, day care and all local services may vary from one locality to another. This rationale is captured to a large degree by the principle of "subsidiarity" recognized by the Supreme Court of Canada in *114957 Canada Ltée (Spray-Tech, Société d'arrosage) v. Hudson (Ville)*.[3] This broad principle of governance maintains that services are best delivered by the level of government that is both effective and closest to the electorate. The requirement for effectiveness reflects a self-explanatory desire for efficiency and efficacy in service delivery, while the requirement for "closeness" to affected citizens reflects the democratic ideal that decision makers be responsive to citizen's "needs, to local distinctiveness and to population diversity."[4]

The meaningful rationale for local governments, therefore, is to provide for local decisions respecting local political matters. It is this rationale upon which local government is based and it is this rationale which suggests the need for a wide policy-making role for municipalities in the delivery of services. Municipalities, if they are to respond to local needs and desires, should be given wide jurisdiction to make local political decisions at the local level. They should, as well, be structured to encourage the making of these decisions and be given the financial tools to effect their decisions.

The analysis of Canadian municipal and planning law in this book traces the evolution of these ideas as reflected in municipal legislation and through judicial attitudes towards municipalities. In many of the areas discussed, we suggest that ambivalence remains towards the fulfillment of this rationale. Such an ambivalence is not surprising. Indeed, as suggested by the tension between effectiveness and responsiveness in the principle of subsidiarity, although there is a need for local political input, there is often a need for province-wide or nation-wide standards with which municipalities should not be able to interfere. Such standards are important in protecting minority groups and the disadvantaged and in ensuring that all citizens have certain minimum rights which may not be adversely affected by the decisions of individual municipalities. The desirability of local political control must, therefore, be balanced against the need for broad standards and safeguards. The balance has traditionally been struck very much in favour of provincial control but now appears to be shifting towards enhanced municipal authority.

The underlying perspective of the analysis in this edition will be that local governments are bodies which should make political decisions to ensure local control over the delivery of local services, and that judicial, administrative and legislative decisions should reflect that perspective. The edition endeavours to provide a basic understanding for both lawyers and planners of local government structure, organization, financing and planning powers from that point of view.

---

3 [2001] 2 S.C.R. 241 (S.C.C.).

4 *Ibid.* at 249.

2

The Organization of Municipal Government

A. INTERNAL ORGANIZATION

1. Elected Offices

In the introduction of this book, it is argued that one purpose of local government is to ensure that local needs and desires are reflected in the delivery of local services and in the formulation of policy respecting the types and levels of services that are provided. However, the internal organization and structure of municipal government has traditionally been designed to ensure proper and efficient administration of services rather than to ensure political responsiveness. The municipality, which has been defined as a "body corporate constituted by the incorporation of the inhabitants residing within the defined area upon which the legislature has... conferred corporate status, rights and liabilities...,"[1] is to function, in law, largely in a manner analogous to business corporations. Its council is comparable to a board of directors and the mayor is comparable to the chair of the board.

The assumption implicit in municipal legislation is that the members of the council share sufficiently similar values so that the structure of the council need not encourage political division or debate. Furthermore, the subject-matter of municipal authority is conceived as being less inclined to raise ideological differences — there is no Liberal, Conservative or New Democratic way to collect garbage. This may be supported by the fact that there are few established political parties functioning at the local level in Canada.[2] This non-political approach to local government can be seen in provisions for the selection and composition of councils and the committees of council, and in the role of the mayor and executive as set out in legislation in Canadian jurisdictions.

---

1 *St. Stephen (Town) v. Charlotte (County)* (1894), 32 N.B.R. 292 (N.B. S.C.) at 297, reversed (1895), 24 S.C.R. 329.

2 J.P. Boyer, "Local Elections in Canada" (Toronto, 1988) at 11-15 for a discussion of political parties at the local level.

(i) *Council*

It is the council that is clearly the most important decision-making body in a municipality. It is an elected body, and as such should be designed to ensure local input and control over local political matters. However, the development of municipal government in Canada did not reflect a strong desire to project democratic accountability into local decision-making, rather local government has its origins in more prosaic concerns respecting administrative efficiency. The first local officials in Canada, like those in England, were not elected but were magistrates of the Court of Quarter Sessions, who performed defined administrative, legislative and judicial functions.[3] In the latter part of the eighteenth century, Loyalist immigrants from the newly formed United States of America, who had enjoyed a form of local government in the New England colonies, began to place pressure on Canadian colonial authorities to create a form of local government. In 1832, the Legislature of Upper Canada acquiesced to these demands, establishing a locally elected police board in Brockville. Other local government institutions followed thereafter on a piecemeal basis, until 1849 when the first *Municipal Act* (known as the *Baldwin Act*) was passed.[4] In other provinces a similar evolution took place and by the end of nineteenth century a basic form of municipal government was in place across the country.[5] While the form of local governance had taken a democratic turn, it was still largely viewed as a vehicle for administering programs and services, not for determining policy itself, and like their quasi-judicial predecessors, municipalities also acted in judicial and legislative capacities.

In addition, late nineteenth and early twentieth century urban reform policy also emphasized the role of the municipality as administrator. Politics in local government was considered unnecessary and, indeed, undesirable. The search that local government was to undertake was simply the most efficient solution to a problem. The structure of local government reflected that view and reflected the legal status of municipality as administrative agencies.

Consequently, much of the legislative authority granted to councils remains to be exercised within the narrow confines of policies established or determined at the provincial level, so that they function to a large extent as the administrators of provincial policy. Often, welfare payments may be made or loans given by a council, but only within predetermined provincial limits. Moreover, because municipal legislative power can be exercised only by by-law or resolution passed by council, it is the council which controls the

3 Ann MacDonald, "In the Public Interest: Judicial Review of Local Government" (1983/84) 9 Queen's L.J. 62 at 88; see also C. Richard Tindal and Susan Nobes Tindal, *Local Government in Canada* (4th) (Toronto: McGraw-Hill Ryerson, 1995), Chapter 2.

4 Statutes of Canada 1848/49, 11, 12 Victoria, c. LXXX [the Baldwin Act].

5 See Tindal and Tindal, *supra* note 3, for a brief discussion of the historical development of municipal structures in each of the provinces.

legislative decisions of the municipality.[6] It alone can exercise legislative authority, a fact reinforced by the general rule prohibiting councils from sub-delegating their authority to an official or body other than council.[7] Councils therefore pass by-laws regulating everything from planning and zoning to animal control. This results in many aspects of administration being dealt with at the council level. The details of traffic regulation such as the location of parking meters and stop signs or the approval of council members to attend conferences often must be decided by councils. As discussed below, the courts have attempted to draw distinctions between a council's legislative and purely administrative functions, (allowing councils to delegate purely administrative functions) but this distinction is tenuous and difficult to operationalize.[8]

The exercise of a municipality's quasi-judicial authority can be seen in decisions affecting disputes between parties as to the passing of a zoning by-law or the granting of a municipal license. Here, the council, in making its decision, is functioning not unlike a court in an attempt to resolve a *lis inter partes* or dispute between competing parties. Of course, in determining disputes councils must also be responsive to the public interest and the concerns of their constituents. In this regard, the neutrality one might expect from a body exercising judicial-like functions may conflict with council's more democratically responsive legislative functions. For example, in enacting a zoning by-law, almost by definition a legislative function, councils are required nonetheless to afford affected parties certain procedural rights consonant with council's quasi-judicial function.[9]

In exercising these legislative, administrative and quasi-judicial powers, councils are functioning much like administrative tribunals at the federal or provincial levels of government. The legal status of municipalities as recipients of delegated authority is like that of other administrative bodies. However, unlike municipalities, most administrative bodies are not responsible to an electorate directly, but are appointed by the Lieutenant Governor-in-Council and are ultimately accountable to provincial cabinets. It is the election of municipal councils which makes them different from other administrative tribunals, and it is to the provisions for the election of councils that one can first look for evidence to support the view that councils must be politically accountable and responsive to local values.

---

6 See *The City of Winnipeg Charter*, S.M. 2002, c. 39, s. 54; *The Municipal Government Act*, R.S.A. 2000, c. M-26, s. 7 and 8; and the *Municipal Act, 2001*, S.O. 2001, c. 25, s. 5(3). Generally in Ontario, municipal councils can exercise their powers only by by-law. See also *The Municipal Government Act* S.N.S. 1998, c. 18, s. 47(1) which provides that "The council shall make decisions in the exercise of its powers and duties by resolution, by policy or by by-law."

7 *Infra*, Chapter 4.

8 *Infra*, Chapter 10 at 252-253.

9 The Supreme Court of Canada addresses this issue in *Old St. Boniface Residents Assn. Inc. v. Winnipeg (City)*, [1990] 3 S.C.R. 1170 discussed in Chapter 10

Councils are generally composed of councillors and the mayor. The election of municipal councils can be conducted either "at large," with voters across the municipality as a whole electing the entire council, or on a "ward" basis, whereby municipalities are divided into wards modelled after constituencies at the federal or provincial level of government.

The election of a council at large tends to reduce the representation of diverse political interests, and thus provides a less accurate reflection of local values. Since voters of all social-economic backgrounds are combined into one pool, elections tend to be dominated by those most likely to vote (i.e. the wealthy and better educated). Significant minority interests may, in many cases, not be strong enough to counterbalance the dominance of that particular group. On the other hand, the use of a ward system tends to produce a more diverse council, one on which minority interests are represented. This results in more vigorous debate of conflicting political views, and encourages political responsiveness. Of course, this view is predicated on the geographical concentration of people sharing the same interests. The legislation of Ontario, Manitoba and Alberta authorizes both methods of election.[10] British Columbia also calls for at-large elections;[11] but the council may divide the municipality by by-law into neighbourhood constituencies with the approval of the Lieutenant Governor-in-Council.[12] For the most part, municipalities have opted for elections based on ward representation, although rural municipalities, perhaps due to greater homogeneity, may have at-large representation. The City of Vancouver, despite its size and obvious complexity, also elects its councillors on an at-large basis.

Election on a ward basis may, however, pose a number of different problems. The way in which ward boundaries are drawn can have a profound effect on the way in which local values are reflected. The drawing of boundaries to include diverse interests, but with one dominant political group, may succeed in producing the same results as an election at large. Such was the case with "strip" wards in the City of Toronto prior to 1970. Several acts in Canada governing municipal wards now address this problem. For example, the *City of Winnipeg Charter* provides that the commission determining ward boundaries for the City shall take into account the community or diversity of interest of the population as well as the physical features of the ward.

---

10 See the *Municipal Act, 2001*, S.O. 2001, c. 25, s. 217; The *Municipal Government Act*, R.S.A. 2000, c.M-26, s. 147 and *The Local Authorities Election Act*, R.S.A. 2000, c. L-21, s. 36.

11 *Local Government Act*, R.S.B.C. 1996, c. 323, s. 36(1); *Vancouver Charter*, S.B.C. 1953, c. 55, s. 138(1).

12 *Local Government Act*, R.S.B.C. 1996, c. 323, ss. 36(2)-(6); *Vancouver Charter*, S.B.C. 1953, c. 55, s. 138(2).

An additional concern in establishing wards is the number of councillors in each ward. The *Municipal Act, 2001* (Ontario)[13] authorizes the election of more than one councillor in each ward. This use of "multi-member constituencies" also inhibits the development of a council which accurately reflects the political views of the community. This problem used to exist in the City of Toronto, when it was part of the Municipality of Metropolitan Toronto. Two councillors were elected in each ward. Sometimes a great deal of animosity existed between the two councillors who represented the same ward. Often the animosity was not the result of true political or ideological differences, but rather was due to competition for votes. Hostility between councillors results in differences that focus on petty personal concerns rather than local values. At council, the votes of such competing councillors frequently cancelled each other out, and representation of the political values of a ward was replaced by representation of personal values of councillors trying to out-manoeuvre each other. These problems led to changes in the legislation governing municipal elections in the Municipality of Metropolitan Toronto and the City of Toronto — all city and metropolitan wards then elected only a single councillor for each ward.[14]

(ii) *The Mayor*

The mayor, also referred to as the head of council, is a member of the council and the chief officer of the municipality. In addition to the role of member of council and presiding officer over council, he/she has administrative powers which include: causing the laws governing the municipality to be executed; supervising and inspecting the conduct of all officials of the municipality in the performance of their duties; causing all negligence, carelessness and violation of duty to be prosecuted and punished; and communicating from time to time to the council all such information and recommending such measures as he/she considers would benefit or improve the finances, health, security, cleanliness, comfort, ornamentation and prosperity

---

13 S.O. 2001, c. 25, s. 458, continues the composition of the council of a municipality as on December 31, 2002, which under the previous *Municipal Act*, R.S.O. 1990, c. M.45, s. 29(6), allows for the election of more than one councillor in each ward.

14 Under the *City of Toronto Act, 1997* S.O. 1997, c. 2, s. 3(1.1), as amended in 1998, changing from two councillors per ward to one ward, one councillor system under amalgamated City of Toronto. The *Halifax City Charter* likewise used to provide for the election of more than one councillor in each ward and was also changed as part of the Halifax Regional government restructuring process. Now see the *Municipal Government Act*, S.N.S. 1998, c.18, s. 10.

of the municipality.[15] This description of the mayor's power is relatively standard across the country. Despite the apparent breadth of these powers, the mayor does not have substantial legal powers beyond those of a councillor.

The actual functions of mayors are difficult to define. In general, the job has become what incumbents have made of it. There is little case law on the meaning of "chief officer" and that status does not in itself seem to confer any powers. A mayor may simply perform ceremonial duties, he or she may be active in introducing and promoting policy initiatives or the mayor may be looked upon as having a leading role in negotiating with senior levels of government. In addition to these duties, he or she may be actively involved in the administration of the municipality. In Alberta, unless council provides otherwise, the mayor acts as a commissioner on every committee in addition to any other commissioners appointed by council.[16] *The City of Winnipeg Charter* also provides for the mayor to be an *ex officio* member of each committee of council and the chair of the executive policy committee.[17]

Because the mayor has no real powers above and beyond those of other councillors, there are no specific legal duties or responsibilities that guide the exercise of the mayor's powers. However, it is now clear that in the exercise of his or her official duties, the mayor must act in accordance with the *Canadian Charter of Rights and Freedoms* and in accordance with human rights legislation. Thus, a mayor's refusal to proclaim Lesbian and Gay Pride Week was found to be a discriminatory denial of a service contrary to human rights legislation, notwithstanding the absence of any statutory authority to make such authorizations.[18] Similarly, the practice of the head of council to begin council meetings with a recitation of the Lord's Prayer was found to offend the *Charter*.[19]

A number of American cities have, over the years, developed strong "mayor" systems, in which the mayor has a great deal of independent authority (i.e the power to veto legislation, or the authority to make appointments on his/her own). The mayor in Canada, however, does not generally have such powers. He or she has no authority to veto legislation, although in some provinces he/she does have limited powers which could be used to

---

15 See also *The Municipal Government Act*, R.S.A. 2000, c. M-26, s. 154. Note that in Alberta the "chief elected official" in addition to performing the duties of a councillor; must

(a) preside when in attendance at a council meeting unless a by-law provides that another councillor or other person is to preside, and

(b) perform any other duty imposed on a chief elected official by this or any other enactment or by-law.

(2) The chief elected official is a member of all council committees and all bodies to which council has the right to appoint members under this Act, unless the council provides otherwise.

16 See for example *The Municipal Government Act*, R.S.A. 2000, c. M-26, s. 154(2).

17 S.M. 2002, c. 39, s. 58.

18 *Oliver v. Hamilton (City)* (1995), 26 M.P.L.R. (2d) 278 (Ont. Bd. of Inquiry).

19 *Freitag v. Penetanguishene (Town)* (1999), 4 M.P.L.R. (3d) 1 (Ont. C.A.).

strengthen his/her position vis-à-vis the council.[20] The mayor generally cannot make appointments on his/her own, nor does he/she have any legislative authority to reinforce his/her role as political spokesperson for the community.[21]

A mayor in Canada does not have the same political authority of a party leader at the senior levels of government. He or she is, in fact, elected at-large and, therefore, is elected by a constituency different from that of the councillors. The mayor is not elected by a majority vote of the council through the support of a group in that body. This often results in a lack of cohesive and consistent policy development. It is clear that some mayors have had the support of a large backing on council. Toronto and Montreal have both had such mayors. This appears, however, to be the exception rather than the rule and occurs in spite of the legislative structure rather than because of it. Unlike the American strong mayor system where the mayor effectively has some executive powers to guide the direction of council, mayors in the Canadian model have few real powers which enable them to perform an executive function.

The absence of any true executive powers detracts from the mayor's ability to be a strong spokesperson for the local values of the community or to influence policy directions on his or her own. The result can be a council that lacks a strong centre around which political opinion coalesces. At the senior levels of government, the executive tends to control very tightly the agenda and direction of the legislative activities of the government. This diffusion of power cannot be said to be normatively good or bad, but it is perhaps indicative of the traditional view of local government as being less overtly political and more oriented towards administrative functions. Moreover, the reality of modern local government is that legislative priorities and consistent policy directions must be set. In the absence of a strong executive function residing with the mayor, this function must be found elsewhere.

(iii) *Executive and Standing Committees*

With the exception of the now defunct use of Boards of Control, there is very little legislative support for the creation of executive bodies within council. Boards of Control themselves, which became a popular municipal reform in the early 1900's, were premised on the separation of executive and

---

20 See for example, *The City of Winnipeg Charter*, S.M. 2002, c. 39, s. 28(6); *The Municipal Act* (Manitoba) S.M. 1996, c. 58, s. 138; *Local Government Act* (British Columbia), R.S.B.C. 1996, c. 323, s. 219; *The Municipal Code*, R.S.Q. 1994, c. 27.1, s. 142.

21 S.M. 2002, c. 39, ss. 59, 61(1). Under *The City of Winnipeg Charter*, the mayor appoints the deputy mayor and the chairs of the four standing committees, all of whom sit as members of the executive policy committee which has a wide range of responsibilities. Since the mayor appoints all five members of this committee, the mayor and his or her appointees can influence its role and direction.

legislative functions, but again were rooted in the idea that municipal decision-making was a value free and largely technocratic affair.[22] The idea was to place important executive functions, such as budget setting, the dismissal of department heads and the awarding of contracts, in the hands of the Board, whose decisions could only be overturned by a two-thirds vote of council. [23] While Board members were elected, they were not responsible to council. The system, which was designed to depoliticize municipal decision-making, lead to divisiveness and stifled political debate on important issues and was ultimately abandoned.

Legislative provisions for the cities of Winnipeg, Toronto and Montreal provide for an Executive Committee, as an alternative to the Board of Control. The executive committee provided for in the *City of Toronto Act*[24] consists of the mayor and the chairs of the six community councils, who would have to be elected by their follow councillors. It is, therefore, more likely to reflect the make-up of Council. As elected executive committees must have the support of a majority of the members of the council, they are able to provide a leadership role in the development of policy for the advancement of local values.

It is important to note, however, that, like Boards of Control, such a committee is not a cabinet. It is not responsible to the council; it cannot be removed by council; its chair, the mayor, is not responsible to the council; and generally, legislative tasks cannot be delegated to it as they can be to a cabinet. The committee can exercise only those functions authorized by statute. It is, nevertheless, an improvement on the Board of Control or a system under which there is no elected executive and under which commissioners or other appointed persons serve as the executive of the municipality.

In the absence of any true executive body, the most common model for internal organization is the use of standing committees to organize and streamline the functions of the municipal council. There is little uniformity with respect to the role, number and authority of standing committees at the municipal level. Some legislation, such as *The City of Winnipeg Charter*,[25] has provisions for standing committees and leaves the particular duties to be assigned and the actual composition of the committee to be established by by-law by council. While others such as the *Municipal Act, 2001* (Ontario),[26] make no reference to standing committees. The result in Ontario has been wide variation in the number and functions of standing committees.

---

22 Boards of Control were mandatory for municipalities of a certain size in Ontario, but were also adopted by Winnipeg, Calgary and Montreal. See Tindal and Tindal, *supra* note 3 at 55-6.

23 See the *Municipal Act, 2001*, S.O. 2001, c. 25, s. 468.

24 S.O. 1997, c. 2, s. 4(1).

25 S.M. 2002, c. 39, s. 63.

26 S.O. 2001, c. 25. However, ss. 238, 242 and 283 implicitly recognize the existence of standing committees.

The standing committees of council generally have little real power. They cannot make decisions themselves because, as noted earlier, a municipality must act through its council. They can be important, however, in hearing deputations and making recommendations to the full council. Their recommendations, unlike those of the Board of Control, have no special status. Most importantly, standing committees will often determine the agenda of Council, in that any matter that is to proceed to council will most often have to pass through a standing committee.

The matters with which standing committees concern themselves may be legislative, administrative and quasi-judicial in scope. That is to say, committees may make recommendations to council concerning enactments by the council which require by-laws to regulate activity. Committees may also deal with administrative matters concerning the internal organization and functioning of the municipality's departments and staff. In this latter area of administration, committees can be empowered to act independently and departments may, in effect, work for the committee. Although this is done quite often, committees generally (for reasons discussed in Chapter 4) function as a recommending body to the council, especially on matters of any importance. Indeed, even when council meets as a "committee of the whole" (i.e. the entire council meeting as a committee) that committee must make recommendations to the formal council for final determination. In Ontario the quasi-judicial function of holding a hearing may be delegated by council to a standing committee, although a formal decision must be made by council.[27]

2. Administration

As a result of the diffuse nature of political power in municipal governments, the administrative arm of the municipality often plays an important role in providing leadership and consistency in policy development. The administrative structure of municipalities varies across Canada. Although, in all provinces municipalities are required to appoint a clerk to maintain records of council decisions, including minutes of meetings, maintaining copies of by-laws and resolutions and making the same available to the public. The clerk may be assigned other duties and in many smaller municipalities, it is the clerk who acts as the central bureaucrat within the municipal structure. In many cases, in addition to the clerk, municipalities appoint various commissioners with specific expertise to run sectors of the municipal bureaucracy, most commonly these include a treasurer, a Commissioner of Works (water and sewer), a Commissioner of Roads, a Commissioner of Planning and a Chief Administrative Officer. Ostensibly the role of officers and employees is to implement policies formulated by council and is, therefore, considered

---

27 *Municipal Act*, 2001, S.O. 2001, c. 25, s. 252.

wholly administrative in nature. This approach is evident in the Ontario *Municipal Act* which contains the following provision defining the role of the administrative arm:

> It is the role of the officers and employees of the municipality,
>
> (a) to implement council's decisions and establish administrative practices and procedures to carry out council's decisions;
> (b) to undertake research and provide advice to council on the policies and programs of the municipality; and
> (c) to carry out other duties required under this or any Act and other duties assigned by the municipality.[28]

The extent of the powers of municipal officers, the Chief Administrative Officer in particular, is usually a matter for council, but in some jurisdictions, the role of the Chief Administrative Officer appears to be significant. In Nova Scotia,[29] for example, regional municipalities, must employ a Chief Administrative Officer, as must municipalities in Alberta.[30] The council is to make general policy decisions and the administrative arm is to implement those decisions; but the councils are not to interfere in the administration of municipal government. The wording of *The Municipal Government Act* (Nova Scotia) makes this quite clear:

> (1) The chief administrative officer is the head of the administrative branch of the government of the municipality and is responsible to the council for the proper administration of the affairs of the municipality in accordance with the by-laws of the municipality and the policies adopted by the council.[31]

The Act gives the Chief Administrative Officer wide authority over the administration of the daily business affairs of the municipality including, among other things, preparing the annual budget, appointing and suspending all employees and controlling purchases required to carry on business.[32] The Council, except for the purpose of making enquiries, is bound by the Act to deal with the administrative service of the City solely through the Chief Administrative Officer.[33] This system of a strong central management was influenced by the City Manager system that was prevalent in the U.S., and appears to be premised on the view that politics should be kept out of the administration of municipalities.

The *Municipal Government Act* (Nova Scotia) is perhaps the strongest example in Canada of the attempted separation of policy and administration.

---

28 *Municipal Act*, 2001, S.O. 2001, c. 25, s. 227.

29 *The Municipal Government Act* S.N.S. 1998, c. 18, s. 28(2).

30 *The Municipal Government Act*, R.S.A. 2000, c. M-26, s. 205.

31 S.N.S. 1998, c. 18, s. 30(1).

32 *Ibid.* at s. 31.

33 *Ibid.* at s. 30(2).

In other jurisdiction such as Ontario[34] and British Columbia,[35] municipalities are not required to have a Chief Administrative Officer, but provide the office with powers to "exercise general control and management of the affairs of the municipality" in the event that a Chief Administrative Officer is appointed.[36] In New Brunswick[37] a Manager may be appointed by the municipal council and designated powers and duties by by-law or resolution. These approaches provide for a chief administrator, or one or more commissioners appointed by council, to head up the administration of the municipality and to have broad supervisory power over the various departments of the municipality. The offices of commissioner and chief administrative officer are an attempt to provide for co-ordinated administration without resorting to the hard and fast legislated divisions between policy and administration found in the City Manager System (or the Nova Scotia Chief Administrative Officer provisions).

This form of administration allows the council to determine the independence of the chief administrative officer and the amount of administrative authority that council will delegate to the chief administrator. Nevertheless, given the lack of leadership and the divided authority on municipal council, the chief administrative officer is a person who can exercise substantial influence and power. His or her power depends largely on personality but, given that the Chief Administrative Officer heads the administration of a municipality and that in many cases councillors are part-time and do not have the same access to information as the chief administrative officer, he or she is clearly in an important, and indeed, often superior, political position.

This approach to municipal structure is premised to a large degree on an irrational distinction. Municipal councils are involved, in fact, with legislative, administrative and quasi-judicial matters. It is impossible to divide these tasks and allocate them through legislation to one body or another. The difference between policy and administration can at best be viewed as the difference between wider discretion and narrower discretion. The narrower the discretion, the more "administrative" the task and the smaller the scope for making policy or political judgments.

It is important to point out that policy-making, administration and appointment of staff are inter-related and influence each other. Problems of administration influence policy, and vice versa. Both can be profoundly influenced by the staff involved. This is so at all levels of government. For example, when the Government of Canada proposes changes in income tax law in Parliament, it does so with a consideration of redistributive policies, governmental revenue requirements and the administrative needs of the De-

---

34 *The Municipal Act, 2001*, S.O. 2001, c. 25, s. 229.

35 *The Municipal Act*, R.S.B.C. 1996, c. 323, ss. 196(1) and 197, as amended by the *Local Government Statutes Amendment Act*, S.B.C. 1998, c. 34, cl. 1.

36 *The Municipal Act, 2001*, S.O. 2001, c. 25, s. 229.

37 See the *Municipalities Act*, R.S.N.B. 1973, c. M-22, ss.74(1), 75.

partment of National Revenue. Exemptions may be broadened or narrowed, tribunals established and staff changes made at least in part on the basis of the experience of civil servants administering the law.[38] Departmental staff changes, as a responsibility of government, are a proper subject for discussion in the legislature, and purely "administrative" concerns are frequently of more public concern than any bare issue of policy.

The legal basis for the internal structure of municipalities in Canada is, nevertheless, generally made on the inappropriate premise that policy can be divorced from administration. In many cases, municipalities are left with little or no discretion in structuring their administration. Thus, the political arm of council is further weakened by cutting it off to a certain extent from the administration which is a part of policy-making. At the same time, the administrative arm of municipalities is strengthened, resulting in administrators making political decisions which reflect their administrative values rather than local political values. This means that lawyers and planners working for private clients must be very aware and concerned about the role of administrators at the local level. The administrators may, in many cases, be instrumental in the approval of requests.

3. Special Purpose Bodies

A further aspect of the internal structure of municipalities is the frequent use of special purpose bodies; those numerous boards, commissions and organizations required by legislation and largely independent of municipal councils, exercise important political and administrative functions and are a further indication of the administrative nature of local government. These bodies have been mandated for a variety of purposes such as providing policing, local public health, library and transportation services, controlling planning, granting variances to zoning, or managing parks and arenas.

Special purpose bodies are mostly corporate entities, as such they have a separate legal existence from the municipality and can exercise corporate powers on their own initiative.[39] They may be appointed entirely by municipal government or by both municipal and senior government, most often the Provincial government, but in some cases, such as Port Authorities, the federal government may appoint special purpose bodies. These bodies are generally mandated by legislation, giving the municipality no option in their establishment. Special purpose bodies exercise functions that would, in their absence, likely be exercised by the council. In addition, the bodies generally are not responsible to the municipal council. Because their existence and appoint-

38 See Jaffrey and Makuch, "Local Decision-Making and Administration," A Study for the Royal Commission on Metropolitan Toronto (Toronto, 1977) at 34.

39 This is not universally the case. An example of an exception is committees of adjustment in Ontario, which are not incorporated bodies.

ment are set forth in legislation, the municipality cannot abolish the boards,[40] remove members or control in any direct way the activity of the bodies. The council may have indirect control over the bodies by providing all or part of their financial resources or by exercising the ultimate power of reappointing members. However, the relationship between council and bodies is generally structured so that the body has exclusive legal authority granted by the legislature over the matter it is given jurisdiction to control.

The case of *McAuliffe v. Toronto (Metropolitan) Commissioners of Police* is a good example of the independence that a special purpose body can have.[41] In that case, McAuliffe, a newspaper reporter, sought the release of information from the Metropolitan Toronto Police Commission under s. 19(1) of the *Municipality of Metropolitan Toronto Act*.[42] Although the Metropolitan Council was entitled to appoint two of the Board's five members, and provided most of its financing, the Court held that the Board was not bound by the provisions of the *Municipality of Metropolitan Toronto Act* and, therefore, not subject to the Act's freedom of information requirements. Both the Municipality of Metropolitan Toronto and the Board of Commissioners of Police are "creatures of statute;" the Board is neither governed by the provisions governing Council, nor is responsible to Council in any way.

The establishment of special purpose bodies can be seen to relate to both the perceived inability of municipalities to perform the specialized requirements of the service and as another attempt to keep politics out of local government. The lack of expertise rationale is dubious in light of the increased capacity of municipalities to address complex issues. However, in some cases the multi-jurisdictional nature of the service does not lend itself to municipal structures. Additionally, special purpose bodies may be resorted to where senior levels of government want to maintain uniform standards of service delivery. Although, this could also be achieved through regulatory means.

The attempt to 'depoliticize' certain services through the use of special purpose bodies is a recognition that some services should be immune from the budgetary pressures of local government. Here again the idea that underlies this rational is the distinction between policy and administrative decisions, with special purpose bodies seen as a more neutral form of policy implementation. However, this distinction is difficult to maintain and, where the municipality is responsible for the budgets of the services being overseen by special purpose bodies, there are strong reasons in favour of accountability. For example, under the *Police Services Act* in Ontario, municipalities are responsible for police budgets, but have a restricted ability to set those budg-

---

40 Municipalities in Ontario now do have the power to dissolve local boards: See *The Municipal Act, 2001*, S.O. 2001, c. 25 s. 216. However, the definition of local boards excludes school boards, police services boards, and conservation authorities. Furthermore, the power to dissolve local boards is dependent upon and subject to regulations put in place by the Minister; these have virtually eliminated the power to dissolve local boards.

41 (1975), 9 O.R. (2d) 583, 61 D.L.R. (3d) 223 (Div. Ct.).

42 R.S.O. 1970, c. 295.

ets, which are determined in the first instance by the Board and by a provincial Commission in the event of a dispute.[43] Thus, while approval of spending necessarily entails an evaluation of priorities between municipal programs, special purpose bodies are not well positioned to balance the needs of the service they are responsible for versus the other needs of the community. Accountability is further reduced by the less visible profile of many special purpose bodies.

A more sound approach would be for municipal councils, on their own initiative, to be responsible for establishing special purpose bodies. Councils should be able to determine the need for the creation of special purpose bodies, the authority of such bodies, the number and tenure of those to be appointed to them, as well as their financing.[44] After making councils legally responsible for special purpose bodies, councils could also become politically responsible for these bodies' decisions. This would end the practice of divorcing a large number of local services from the jurisdiction of local councils and granting responsibility for them to administrative agencies independent of the municipality. It would ensure that the delivery of those services was in the hands of a politically accountable local authority. In circumstances where special purpose bodies are desirable to deliver services across jurisdictions or by two levels of government, attempts must be made to match political responsibility with such matters as funding responsibility.

B. MUNICIPAL STRUCTURE

1. Introduction

Just as with the election of municipal councillors and mayors, the creation of executive and standing committees and the internal administration of municipalities, the 'external' structure or organization of municipalities is also important in determining the extent to which local government is responsive to local needs and priorities. Since the 1950s and 60s, significant changes have occurred in municipal boundaries and new municipal relationships have been forged to deal with growth and urbanization. This has led to a variety of municipal government models such as the two tier metropolitan and regional governments and urban communities in Quebec, the single tier government models such as the "Uni-City" in Manitoba, the Halifax Regional Municipality, and finally the "mega-City" of Toronto. Although each of these responses is different in structure and authority, each attempts to create new municipal structures to deal with outmoded boundaries and to increase efficiencies. In the 1950's through 1970's the reform of local government appeared to move in the direction of two tier decentralized governments, in the

---

43 R.S.O. 1990, c. P.15, s. 39.

44 See also the recommendations in the *Metropolitan Toronto First Report of the Sub-Committee on Special Purpose Bodies*, June 1989.

form of metropolitan and regional governments. Since then there has been a significant movement back towards single tier, centralized local governments, although with some important innovations. The determination as to what the structure or organization of a municipality shall be, and what services shall be delivered at which tier, is a provincial decision, often based upon financial and efficiency considerations at the provincial level, rather than responding to the needs and values of local inhabitants. To some degree this is necessary and desirable, but has consequences for local democracy.

The boundary problem is one that is common throughout Canada and it largely involves issues of finance, planning and service delivery.[45] The financial problem, which has also affected American municipalities, is a consequence of property tax being the major source of revenue for municipal governments.[46] This problem is best illustrated by the example of the City of Toronto in the early 1950's. At this time the City of Toronto was almost completely developed, and had substantial residential, commercial and industrial assessment for the property tax base. The twelve separate municipalities surrounding the city were not fully developed, and as a result had poorly developed property tax bases, yet because these suburban municipalities were in the process of experiencing rapid population growth, there was a need to expand services, such as roads, water supply, sewers and schools, which, in turn, resulted in a greater demand for revenue than the municipality on their own could raise. Thus, while Toronto had revenue sources with lower demands on them due to its substantially completed development, the separate suburban municipalities had greater demands for revenue but very limited internal sources. Under the *Municipal Act* (Ontario), each municipality's jurisdiction was limited to its own geographic area. There was little that could be done to share wealth other than through inter-municipal agreements[47] or through the already established Suburban Roads Commission.[48] A new mechanism was required to share the wealth of the City of Toronto with the suburban municipalities. Similar problems existed in other urban centres such as Winnipeg, Halifax-Dartmouth, Montreal and Vancouver.

Infrastructure and land use planning also posed difficulties in the Toronto area. Public and private transportation networks had to run beyond municipal boundaries — roads could not stop at municipal boundaries —

---

45 For an economic analysis of the boundary problem see R. M. Bird and N. E. Slack, *Urban Public Finance in Canada* 2d ed. (Toronto: Butterworths, 1993) at 30-35.

46 See Chapter 3, *infra*.

47 For instance, adjoining municipalities could enter into an agreement for the joint operation of water and sewage systems, garbage collection, hydro-electric systems, transportation systems and fire and police departments. See the *Municipal Act*, R.S.O 1950, c. 243, ss. 386(1), (4)-(5), now S.O. 2001, c. 25, s. 202.

48 A Suburban Roads Commission could be set up to direct the construction and maintenance of suburban roads. A city would be required to contribute towards expenditures made with respect to these roads. See the *Highway Improvement Act*, R.S.O. 1950, c. 166, ss. 34-42, repealed 1996, c. 1, Sch. M, s. 56.

also trunk water and sewage lines had to cross municipal lines. Moreover, economies of scale were required to construct and more efficiently operate major infrastructure projects that new growth demanded.

Finally, the need for sophisticated services in the Toronto urban area provided a further impetus for metropolitan reform. Smaller municipalities did not have the sophistication or the staff required to develop sewage treatment resources or transit services on a piece-meal basis. It was clear that a solution to these problems of finance, planning and services was needed and that existing municipal structures were not adequate to have such problems dealt with at the local level.

More recently, issues and concerns have arisen with respect to the growing size and expense of local government leading to pressure to reduce overlap between existing levels of government and to maximize the efficiency of service delivery at the local level. These developments can be seen as a move away from viewing local government as an instrument for exercising local democracy where the primary objective relates to effective and meaningful community input and a move towards a system where efficient service delivery is seen as the overriding goal. The two central models of the post-war era reflect these changes and to some degree reflect the tension between the often competing values of reflecting community values and providing the most efficient services.

2. Two Tier Models

The structure of municipal government has been reformed through time in order to address the boundary problem. One solution, which was the former trend in Canada, is to move to a two-tier structure of municipal government. Here an additional level of local government is created on a broader geographical scale, usually encompassing a number of local municipalities. Lower tier municipalities maintain their separate existence and exercise autonomous authority over a set of purely local issues, while the upper tier exercises authority over a separate set of matters which require coordination over the broader geographical area. In this way, smaller municipalities, while still retaining their individual authority, are consolidated into an upper tier government that oversees the entire region. Through the creation of this additional level of government, the delivery of services can be regulated and uniformity across the region ensured. Financial authority is divided, with the upper tier government able to levy against the area municipalities for the provision of services. In this way, the revenue problem which was faced by the former City of Toronto and the surrounding municipalities, for example, could be addressed by the consolidated tax base.

One example of this two-tier structure is the Metropolitan system of government, which has been hailed as a great innovation. In fact, it is not unlike the municipal structure established in New York City at the turn of the century.[49] Under this structure of governance, several municipalities are consolidated as a separate corporate entity for the entire area. While certain authority remains with the lower tier municipalities, the new corporate entity addresses the problem of inadequate boundaries and many of the servicing problems.[50] For example, these upper tier governments generally have the authority of an area municipality or a local board thereof, with respect to the establishment, construction, operation, and extension of a waterworks system, and to pass by-laws for regulating all aspects of supply, which is necessary to ensure a continued and abundant supply of water to the residents of the metropolitan area.[51] At the lower tier, area municipalities would be prohibited from establishing a waterworks. To ensure uniformity, the upper tier municipality is empowered to set standards for local distribution systems and to establish rates for the water supply.

The matter of sewage disposal is dealt with in the same way.[52] The upper tier municipality can have the power of a local municipality with respect to collecting and receiving sewage and land drainage from the area municipalities, and their treatment and disposal.[53] The area municipalities are left with collecting sewage from individual properties and delivering the sewage via local mains to the trunk main system operated by the metropolitan government.[54] Similar mechanisms exist for metropolitan road systems and transportation.[55] While the metropolitan municipality is principally created to deal with hard services, such as water, sewage and transportation, the upper tier government may also be given formal area municipal responsibility in the delivery of numerous other services such as policing, general welfare assistance, housing, homes for the aged, ambulances, day nurseries and homemaker and nursing services.[56]

Authority for planning is generally divided between the upper and lower tiers of government. For example, the former Municipality of Metropolitan Toronto was deemed a joint planning area for the purpose of the preparation of an official plan.[57] Once an official plan was approved by the Minister, the "subsidiary," lower-tier plans had to be amended to conform with that of the upper-tier government.[58] The Ontario *Planning Act* provides that where there is a conflict between the plans of the Metropolitan government and those of

---

49 See Weinstein, "The Effect of the Federal Reapportionment Decisions on Counties and Other Forms of Municipal Government" (1965) Colum. L. Rev. 21 at 38.

50 For example, under the *Municipality of Metropolitan Toronto Act*, S.O. 1953, c. 73, s. 2(1), the City of Toronto as well as 12 other municipalities were consolidated into a separate body corporate known as the Municipality of Metropolitan Toronto.

51 *Ibid.* at at ss. 36, 41.

52 See *ibid.* at part IV, ss. 58-73, for example.

53 *Ibid.* at s. 59.

54 *Ibid.* at s. 63.

55 *Ibid.* at parts V, VI and VII respectively.

56 For example, see the *Municipality of Metropolitan Toronto Act*, *ibid.*

57 *Ibid.* at ss. 179(1) and (2).

58 *Ibid.* at s. 179(7)(a). See also *infra*, Chapter 7.

the lower-tier municipalities, the Metropolitan plan would prevail;[59] that zoning by-laws passed by lower-tier municipalities are also required to conform to the Metropolitan official plan; and that should a lower-tier government fail to amend a by-law to conform to the Metropolitan official plan, the Metropolitan government itself was empowered to amend the by-law as required.[60]

In general, the two-tier structure can provide the financial capability required for development of a metropolitan area, and provide the hard services necessary for the region. The ability to share tax revenue across a broader geographical area had great benefit for the still developing suburban areas, as the assessment rich core could in essence subsidize growth at the periphery. This was particularly important prior to the imposition of development charges or similar schemes providing for developer financed growth. However, the ability of this governance structure to address social services is questionable. Although the limitations on municipal authority will be dealt with in Chapter 4, upper tier municipalities do not have independence in dealing with social welfare assistance[61] or even such a basic service as road construction. For example, under the *Municipality of Metropolitan Toronto Act*, the assumption of area municipal roads by Metropolitan Toronto was subject to the approval and amendment of the Lieutenant Governor in Council.[62] Under the *Public Transportation and Highway Improvement Act*, the Metropolitan Corporation had to submit for annual approval by the Minister of Transportation and Communications an estimate of expenditure for roads if it wished to obtain the provincial subsidy allocated to it for metropolitan roads.[63] Finally, under s. 89 of this Act, the council was required to make an annual report to the Minister on the progress of work on metropolitan roads.

The provincial government, therefore, had a great deal of authority over the decisions of the Metropolitan Council respecting road construction. Although it is fair to state that this authority was not exercised often, it has been used on important matters such as delaying a major and controversial urban expressway.[64] This type of provincial involvement clearly does not enhance

---

59 *Planning Act*, R.S.O. 1990, c. P.13, s. 27(4).

60 *Ibid.* at s. 27(2).

61 For example, under the *Municipality of Metropolitan Toronto Act*, R.S.O. 1990 c. M.62, s. 193, Metro was deemed to be a county for the purposes of the *General Welfare Assistance Act*, R.S.O. 1990, c. G.6. (repealed). Under this latter Act, s. 7, a municipality (which includes a county) was required to provide assistance in accordance with the regulations under the Act. This meant that Metro had to provide a minimum level of assistance in accordance with provincial rules. Under s. 194 of *Municipality of Metropolitan Toronto Act*, the Council could pass by-laws to provide additional assistance.

62 R.S.O. 1990, c. M.62, s. 75.

63 R.S.O. 1990, c. P.50, s. 88 (The act was repealed, 1996, c. 1, Sch. M, s. 60).

64 This power was exercised in connection with a proposed expressway in downtown Toronto in the 1970's (the "Spadina Expressway"). For a description of the background of this dispute, see *Spadina Expressway, Re* (1971), 1 O.M.B.R. 1 (M.B.).

the political accountability or responsiveness of municipal governments. In fact, it was used to interfere with their democratic functioning.

Another shortcoming of the metropolitan system is the lack of political accountability and responsiveness. In the former Metropolitan Toronto, this was evident in the use of non-elected special purpose bodies to deal with providing services on an inter-municipal basis.[65] As stated above, these bodies are appointed by council, but are generally structured to have exclusive legal authority by the legislature. This removes a large number of local services from the jurisdiction of local councils, and thus reduces accountability.

This lack of accountability and responsiveness is also evident within municipal councils, at both the upper and lower tier levels. If the council of the upper tier municipality is not directly elected, as was originally the situation on the former Council of Metropolitan Toronto, no one is directly and clearly responsible to the constituency for the council's actions. In addition, voter confusion can occur in determining which tier of government is responsible for what services. In 1988, reforms were made to address voter confusion between their local government and the Metropolitan government in the City of Metropolitan Toronto.[66] Metropolitan Councillors, with the exception of the mayors of the lower-tier municipalities, were elected directly from their metropolitan wards to that office. Mayors of the lower-tier municipalities, by virtue of their offices, automatically sat on both. This was to help eliminate voter confusion between the two municipal levels of government — confusion as to who sat on them and confusion as to their functions. Under the previous system — still in place in some other regional governments in Ontario — voters elected councillors only to their local council, and a certain number of these local councillors were then eligible to sit on the Metropolitan Council.[67] Aside from generating voter confusion, the previous system of indirect election also placed Metropolitan Councillors at a disadvantage in local elections, as their duties at the Metropolitan Council often forced them to neglect local concerns.

Another element of reform was that the Metropolitan Council chose its Chair from among its own members. Previously, the Chair was the only full-time member of the Metropolitan Council, but he or she was not obliged under legislation to seek election. A Chair chosen from among the Council members ensured that he or she was accountable to the Metropolitan ward from which he or she was elected, as well as to the Metropolitan Council.

After the creation of the former Metropolitan Toronto in 1953, a number of regional governments roughly based on the metropolitan model were

---

65 According to the Bureau of Municipal Research, "The 101 governments of Metro Toronto" Civic Affairs (Oct. 1968) at 6-19, there were 101 special purpose bodies in Metropolitan Toronto.

66 See *An Act to Amend the Municipality of Metropolitan Toronto Act*, S.O. 1988, c. 19.

67 In Toronto, each city ward previously elected two aldermen to City Council. The alderman receiving the higher number of votes was then selected to sit on Metro Council.

established in Ontario.[68] Created in the early 1970's, these government structures were created to address the co-ordination of services across large geographic areas and create a mechanism for sharing tax revenue. The division of functions between upper tier and lower tier municipalities followed the metropolitan model in that regional municipalities generally had jurisdiction over the provision of hard services such as transportation, water and sewer treatment (but leaving the actual delivery of services to households in local hands) and soft services, such as policing, welfare administration and housing programs. Like metropolitan government, regional municipalities do not levy taxes directly against ratepayers, but rather they pass by-laws directing lower tier municipalities to levy residents on their behalf.[69]

Unlike Metropolitan Toronto, however, regional municipalities tended to contain a more diverse mix of urban and rural areas, which lead to the provision of differentiated levies across the regional municipality. For example, under the *Regional Municipality of Ottawa-Carleton Act*,[70] the region was empowered by by-law to define one or more areas of the region as an urban transit area which in the opinion of regional council derived benefit from the provision of passenger transit. The region was further empowered to levy against one or more area municipalities that were wholly or partially in the urban transit area in order to meet the operating and capital costs of the provision of transit services. The urban service area, then, is a device to limit the sharing of burdens that regional government would bring, and a movement to a system whereby those directly receiving the benefits pay for them. Urban service areas allocate the cost of service to those areas that directly benefit, in response to the political hostility that greeted the perception that ratepayers would have to pay for services that they were not receiving.

The second way in which regional governments differ from the metropolitan model is in their special provisions for quorums. These represent an attempt to deal with the problem of domination by one municipality or group of municipalities within a regional government. The legislation provides for a quorum which requires that representatives of a minimum number of municipalities be present in order for decisions to be made.[71] These provisions do not afford protection to smaller lower tier governments in the form of a veto, but they do at least ensure that these minorities are accounted for.

One legislative innovation that addresses the requirement for greater responsiveness to local interests are the provisions in the *Municipal Act* (Ontario) which allow for the transfer of services between the upper and

---

68 In Ontario there are currently regional municipalities for the areas of Durham, Halton, Niagara, Peel, Waterloo and York, as well as the district municipality of Muskoka. Originally, there were also regional governments in Ottawa-Carlton, Hamilton-Wentworth, Haldimand-Norfolk and Sudbury, but these have since been eliminated through restructurings.

69 See *Municipal Act, 2001*, S.O. 2001, c. 25, s. 311.

70 R.S.O. 1990, c. R.14, s. 13.

71 *Municipal Act, 2001*, S.O. 2001, c. 25, s. 237.

lower tier governments.[72] Under these provisions, upper tier municipalities can assume any power currently exercised by a lower tier municipality to provide a service or facility. Conversely, lower tier municipalities can assume upper tier powers. Such a transfer of authority is effective upon a majority of votes from both upper and lower tier councils so long as the number of electors in support of the transfer in the lower tier municipalities form a majority of all of the electors in the upper tier municipality. Therefore, although the province has the authority to determine the allocation of services, this degree of flexibility allows municipalities to decide for themselves which level of government is best suited to deliver certain services and recognizes that this determination shall vary from municipality to municipality.

Another example of the two-tier system of government can be seen in the Province of Quebec, which created "urban communities" similar to metropolitan government in a number of ways.[73] Like regional governments in Ontario, urban communities are independent governments with jurisdiction over an area which includes smaller municipalities. Election to this upper-tier government is generally indirect, and its legal structure is very similar to metropolitan and regional governments. Provision is made for the protection of the minority interests of the suburban municipalities through provisions for the structure of the executive committee, which has broad overseeing powers, and the voting and quorum provisions of the council.

3. Single Tier Local Governments

Ways of encouraging municipalities to better represent and implement local values have already been suggested in this chapter. The election of councillors on a single constituency basis, the election of a mayor by the council, the establishment of an executive committee elected by council, the end of an artificial division between policy and administration, and municipal authority over special purpose bodies, would all go a long way towards serving such a goal. These approaches result in highly centralized political control over decision-making at the local level, which is the current trend in municipal organization, and another response to the boundary problem. Under the single tier structure of government, several smaller municipalities are abolished and one large, central government is created for the entire area. While the impetus for the move towards single tier government is the reduction of overlap and redundancies, these reforms minimize the input of local values at a neighbourhood community level. Therefore, along with the move towards single-tier government structures have been legislative initiatives to

72 *The Municipal Act, 2001*, S.O. 2001, c. 25, s. 188-193.

73 In the province of Quebec there are urban and regional communities in Quebec City and the Outaouais. The entire regional area of Montreal became a single municipality on January 1, 2002.

attempt to decentralize decision-making at the local level to provide for neighbourhood or community control within the municipality.

(i) *Uni-City – Winnipeg*

An important innovation in Canada in modifying metropolitan government has been *The City of Winnipeg Act, 1971*.[74] That Act abolished the two-tier level of government and established what was popularly known as the "Uni-City." The structure was single-tiered in that the government of Winnipeg is vested in one corporate body, the City of Winnipeg. The legislative powers of the City were exercised by the council, and there is, therefore, no division of legislative authority as found in metropolitan, regional or community government. The Act abolished existing lower tier governments and the new City of Winnipeg was made the successor to and the continuation of each of the area municipalities.

Under the current *City of Winnipeg Charter*,[75] the power of the City is exercised by council. Council is composed of a mayor elected at large, and one councillor for each of the 15 wards. There is no representative on a community basis required by the legislation. The City is required to have an executive policy committee which is composed of the mayor, who is the committee's chair, the chairs of the standing committees (s. 61), and any other councillor appointed by the mayor. Furthermore, since the mayor appoints all five of the members of the executive policy committee, it is possible for the mayor to develop strong political leadership. The main purpose of the executive policy committee is to formulate and present recommendations to council on policies, plans, budgets, by-laws and any other matter that affects the city as a whole.[76] The executive policy committee also co-ordinates the work for the standing committees, receives and considers their reports and recommendations, and may refer in whole or in part any report and recommendation to a standing committee or City administrator.

Under the previous legislation,[77] community committees were established, supported by residents' advisory groups, to facilitate local community input into the highly centralized political and administrative system. However, the system did not function very well,[78] perhaps because of the highly centralized and strong administrative structure found at the council level and

---

74 S.M. 1971, c. 105, now S.M. 1989-1990, c. 10.

75 *Ibid.*

76 *City of Winnipeg Charter*, S.M. 2002, c. 39, s. 62(1)(a).

77 *City of Winnipeg Act 1971*, S.M. 1971, c. 105, ss. 20-28.

78 See Siegel, "Provincial-Municipal Relations in Canada: An Overview" (1980) 23 Can. Pub. Admin. 281 at 287.

perhaps because legislation had eroded their power.[79] Therefore, these community committees were abolished under the recent legislation.

(ii) *The Halifax Regional Municipality*

The municipalities of Halifax, Dartmouth and Bedford have been eliminated and replaced by the Halifax Regional Municipality. The Act also eliminates the Halifax-Dartmouth Regional Authority. The organizational structure and the powers of the Halifax Regional Municipality are determined by the general provisions of the *Municipal Government Act* (Nova Scotia)[80] regarding regional municipalities, as well as by the specific provisions of part XXII of the Act. As in Winnipeg, this "regional" government is not a second-tier of local government, but is instead the only local government body for the former municipalities. The mayor of Halifax is elected at large. The council is composed of 23 councillors, one for each of the municipality's 23 polling districts. The 23 polling districts are also organized in four community councils. Communities are established by the municipal council, and must include the whole, or part of, at least three polling districts, with a total number of voters no less than twice the average number of electors per polling district.

The community councils consist of the councillors elected from the included polling districts. The community councils are responsible for monitoring the provision of services within the boundaries of the community and making recommendations to the "regional" council. If it is so provided in the policy establishing the community, the community councils may determine expenditures for the benefit of the community, financed by a local rate, and exercise planning powers. The success of these community councils in representing local values has not been assessed as they represent a new development.

(iii) *"Mega City" – The City of Toronto*

The evolution of Toronto continued with a radical restructuring in 1997, whereby the metropolitan government and the local municipalities were dissolved and a new single tier government was created. The new council consists of 45 members, one from each of the 44 wards, and a mayor who is elected at large.

The Act creating the new city calls for the creation of community councils composed of the members of council that represent wards within the

---

79 See for example the powers originally given in *The City of Winnipeg Act* 1971, S.M. 1971, c. 105, ss. 22(1) and (5), which were later repealed by S.M. 1977, c. 69, ss. 12 and 15.

80 S.N.S. 1998, c. 18.

community council area.[81] It should be noted that the city council has the authority to dissolve or change the composition of the community councils, although only council members can sit on a community council. The legislative powers of the community council are limited both in scope and in function. The scope of matters that can be finally decided by community councils is limited to local planning matters that are delegated under the *Planning Act* and to management of recreational facilities.[82] Other than these exceptions, none of the decisions of community council are final and must proceed to city council for final approval. Thus, community councils are in essence no more than area specific committees of council. Although, the practice has been for city council not to interfere with the decision that community councils make on purely local matters.

A problem experienced by the new city council is the sheer volume of work that the council must deal with. The single-tier structure results in council having to address everything from multi-million dollar infrastructure projects to local parking issues. In its first year council meetings generally lasted for a full three days with agendas that are literally a foot thick. Arguably, city councillors are less able to address constituency matters, potentially resulting in a loss of citizen accessibility to their local representative.

It is also questionable as to whether the amalgamation has produced the financial savings that the province anticipated. According to the three year status report on amalgamation,[83] there appears to have been an over-estimation by the province as to the amount of immediate savings that would occur as a result of efficiency gains, as well as an underestimation of the one-time and annual costs of amalgamation. However, by 2000, $136.2 million in annual savings occurred as a direct result of amalgamation, the majority of which was achieved through staff reductions.[84] The status report concludes that it is difficult to evaluate the success of amalgamation, as the amalgamation programs constitute only 27% of the city's gross expenditures, as well as the added complication of concurrent provincial — municipal services realignment.

It appears as though the reorganization of municipal government structures has come full circle. The boundary problems that led to the creation of the former City of Metropolitan Toronto are now appearing again with respect to the new Mega-City. The regional municipalities which surround the new City are experiencing rapid growth, without the developed tax base necessary for the increased demand for services. The boundaries of the City of Toronto have remained static for over 25 years, in spite of numerous changes in the areas surrounding it. Those boundaries appear to be as inadequate as the

81 *City of Toronto Act, 1997*, S.O. 1997, c. 2, s. 7.

82 *Ibid.* at s. 8.

83 *Building the New City of Toronto: Three Year Status Report on Amalgamation*, January 1998 – December 2000, <http://www.city.toronto.on.ca/cao/amalgamation__3yearstatus.htm>.

84 *Ibid.*

municipal boundaries in 1953. As far back as 1977, a study called for a co-ordinating agency for planning in the region including Metropolitan Toronto and its surrounding municipalities.[85] This was a further indication of the inadequacy and inflexibility of then existing boundaries. Although Metropolitan Toronto had argued that its boundaries should be expanded, the province refused.

While the Province of Ontario has been consolidating municipal structures on the one hand, they also created a new municipal structure to deal with supra-regional issues such as transit and economic development. The Greater Toronto Services Board (GTSB), which has now been abandoned, was created to manage the regional transit system and more nebulously to promote and facilitate co-ordinated decision-making among municipalities within the Greater Toronto Area.[86] While the GTSB proved unsuccessful, it illustrates the need for co-ordination of services across a broader area and the need to pool resources to address regional issues such as welfare and social housing. It also represented a recognition that the Greater Toronto Area functions as a single economic unit which requires a co-ordinated approach to issues such as economic development and infrastructure.

4. Other Approaches

In other provinces there have been different approaches to reforming urban governments. In New Brunswick, the approach seems largely to be one of transferring jurisdiction from the municipal to the provincial level of government.[87] In Alberta, the approach has been simply to use a traditional one-tier municipal structure covering a wide geographical area. Prince Edward Island has undertaken no reform.

The final jurisdiction to be discussed in this section, which attempted to deal with outmoded boundaries is British Columbia. Under the *Local Government Act*,[88] regional districts have been established in the province, including one for the Greater Vancouver Area. Regional districts are like metropolitan governments in that they are independent from the area municipalities. The concept was first established by the province in 1965 and there are now 29 regional districts in British Columbia.

However, rather than creating another level of government, an attempt has been made to co-ordinate governance. The Greater Vancouver Regional

---

85 Ontario, *Report of the Royal Commission on Metropolitan Toronto* (Robarts Report), (Toronto, 1977), Vol. 2 at 226.

86 The Greater Toronto Area came into existence on August 16, 1988, with the passage of Order in Council No. 2064/88. It is comprised of the City of Toronto, and the Regions of Durham, Halton, Peel and York.

87 See Siegel, *supra* note 78 at 283.

88 R.S.B.C. 1979, c. 290, s. 767. For the legislation presently dealing with the regional districts, see *Local Government Act*, R.S.B.C. 1996, c. 323, ss. 773-847.

District is a partnership of the 21 municipalities and one electoral area that make up the metropolitan area of Greater Vancouver. One municipality (Abbotsford) outside the boundaries of the regional district also participates in its parks service. The role of the Regional District is to deliver to the area's 2.0 million people, about half the population of British Columbia, essential services that are regional rather than local in nature. These services are provided on a regional basis for reasons of economy, effectiveness and fairness. Yet the system is structured so that each member municipality maintains its local autonomy and has a say in the operation of the Greater Vancouver Regional District.

The powers of a regional district in British Columbia are exercised by a board of directors. A board consists of municipal directors and electoral area directors.[89] The number of votes to which each municipality and each electoral area is entitled is generally the number obtained by dividing the population of the municipality or electoral area by the voting unit specified in the letters patent.[90] The number of directors to which each municipality is entitled is obtained by dividing the number of votes to which that municipality is entitled by five or, if otherwise specified in letters patent for the regional district, by the other number specified.[91] The chair of the regional district board is elected from amongst the directors.[92] The chair has generally the same powers and duties in relation to a regional district as the mayor of a municipality.[93]

Subject to specific limitations, a regional district may operate any service that the board considers necessary or desirable for all or part of the regional district.[94] This includes the authority to operate a service in an area outside the regional district with consent.[95] The District may also expropriate property and exercise any other power conferred upon it by the Minister.[96]

The board may, by by-law, provide for a referendum on a question regarding a service that is or may be operated by the regional district.[97] By-laws establishing local or extended services have no effect unless they receive the approval of the inspector and the assent of the electors in each participating area.[98]

---

89 *Local Government Act (1996)*, *ibid.* at s. 783(1).
90 *Ibid.* at s. 783(2)(a).
91 *Ibid.* at s. 783(5).
92 *Ibid.* at s. 792(1).
93 *Ibid.* at s. 792(5).
94 *Ibid.* at s. 796(1).
95 *Ibid.* at ss. 796(2) and 796.1.
96 *Ibid.* at ss. 798 and 799.
97 *Ibid.* at s. 797.3.
98 *Ibid.* at s. 801.

The board, like other municipalities, must prepare a budget[99] and raise funds for its needs. The Regional District does not levy taxes itself, but rather apportions the cost of the services to the participating municipalities.[100]

The system, as applied in Vancouver, has been called the "gentle imposition of metropolitan government."[101] In light of the statutory amendments previously mentioned, however, this may be an overstatement. The limitation on the functioning of the regional districts in general and the Greater Vancouver Regional District in particular means that they do not have the breadth of authority of regional government in Ontario. The lack of full jurisdiction over planning, policing, roads, and social services, for example, means that the Greater Vancouver Regional District is not able to function as a local government by exercising authority over an important range of local services. Neither is it able to make political choices respecting those services.

C. CONCLUSION

The reform of local government in Canada has taken a number of different forms, from Metropolitan government, to different types of regional authorities, to large unified cities. It seems fair to conclude that the emphasis of this reform has been the improvement of local administration through limited boundary changes and the transfer of services between levels. Much of what has motivated these reforms has been driven by the desire to improve the efficiency of service delivery with little emphasis on enhancing the capability of municipal governments to be viable political units in their own right, able to respond to local political needs and wants. Reforms increasing the political accountability of local government have occurred with respect to a small number of municipal governments. However, for the most part, local governments continue to face the problems discussed earlier, and even reformed local governments could be substantially improved.

---

99 *Ibid.* at s. 819.

100 *Ibid.* at s. 805.

101 Tennant and Zirnhelt, "Metropolitan Government in Vancouver: The Strategy of Gentle Imposition" (1973) 16 Can. Pub. Admin. 124.

3

Municipal Finance

A. INTRODUCTION

The purpose of this chapter is two-fold. First, it is to examine the political and legal limitations on the ability of municipalities to raise and spend money. Political limitations can be seen as arising from the heavy reliance by Canadian municipalities on the property tax as a major source of revenue. Legal limitations can be seen in statutory restrictions and provincial government oversight over municipal borrowing powers, restrictions, both legislative and judicial, on the use of user fees, licensing fees and the like to raise general revenue, as well as restrictions respecting capital expenditures. These limitations, both political and legal, may constrain the ability of municipalities to carry out their functions in accordance with locally determined priorities and objectives. The second aim of this chapter is to examine in greater detail the rules respecting municipal property assessment and taxation. Assessment is important not only because it affects every property owner, but also because it can affect decisions relating to development and can have an important impact on the overall equity of taxation in Canada.

Municipal revenues are derived from three major sources: 1) property and related taxes; 2) non-tax receipts, such as license and permit fees and charges for services; and 3) transfer payments from the federal and provincial governments. In 2001, it was estimated that municipal taxes, including special assessments and development charges accounted for approximately 53% of gross general municipal revenues, non-tax receipts for 23% and grants in lieu of taxes and transfers from senior levels for 16%.[1]

The most significant trend respecting the sources of municipal revenues is the dramatic decrease in funding from other levels of government, which has been reduced from just under 50% to total revenues in 1980 to 16% in 2001.[2] Of this source, amounts transferred by the provinces to their local governments are much higher than the federal transfers to the local level and, of the provincial transfers, only about 14% are general, as opposed to specific

---

1 Statistics Canada, CANSIM II, table 385-0004 online at: <http:www.statcan.ca>.

2 *Ibid.* and Canadian Tax Foundation *Provincial and Municipal Finances (1980)*, serial publication (Toronto: Canadian Tax Foundation, 1971 *et seq.*).

purpose, grants.[3] This restricts considerably the ability of local governments to establish their own financial priorities. Notwithstanding the significant decrease in support from other levels of government, municipalities have not been given significantly enlarged powers to raise revenue for their own purposes and, accordingly are still largely (and increasingly) dependent upon municipal property tax as the sole major source of municipally-controlled revenue.

B. POLITICAL AND LEGAL LIMITATIONS

1. Limited Financial Base

In most provinces, the amount of property tax to be paid by an individual is determined by a rating by-law passed by the municipal council.[4] The rate of taxation levied by the council against individual property is determined by two important factors: the total annual financial requirements of the municipality to be raised from the property tax, and the total amount of the assessed value of real property in the municipality. In order to determine the rate of taxation on real property, the amount of money to be raised by property tax is divided by the total assessed value of property in the municipality.[5] The product of this computation, the rate per dollar of assessment, or "mill rate" (or "tax rate") as it is often called, is then multiplied by the assessed value of taxable property of each individual in the municipality to determine the amount of tax for each property.

The actual formula used in determining the taxes due can vary in actual application from jurisdiction to jurisdiction and can vary according to classes of property, where legislation allows. For example, in Alberta and Ontario, municipalities have the option of applying differential tax rates for different classes of property. In Alberta, one rate may be established for non-residential property and one or more lesser rates for residential property according to classifications determined by council under s. 96 of the *Municipal Government Act*.[6] In Ontario, the tax rates are determined in relation to tax ratios

---

3 Statistics Canada and Canadian Tax Foundation, *ibid.*

4 See the *Vancouver Charter*, S.B.C. 1953, c. 55, s. 396 "as amended" (1990 c. 325.11 - all of 396 became 396(1) and they added a (2)); *The Municipal Government Act*, R.S.A. 2000, c. M-26, s. 353 and 354.

5 In Quebec's *Act Respecting Municipal Taxation*, R.S.Q., c. F-2.1, the rate of taxation is set by the Minister: s. 264.

6 R.S.A. 2000, c. M-26, s. 297 and 354. Quebec's *Act Respecting Municipal Taxation*, R.S.Q., c. F-2.1 provides for varying rates of taxation for different kinds of property such as golf courses, timber producing lands, trailers, oil refineries and agricultural operations: see ss. 211-231.4. In some instances, the parameters of the permitted tax rate are narrow, so that the municipality has little or no freedom to decide how much tax can be levied: see, for example, s. 231 dealing with taxation of trailers. A separate tax may be imposed on

that control the allowable differences between tax rates for different classes of property using the residential/farm class as the basis of comparison.[7] There are seven basic classes of property: residential/farm; multiple residential; commercial; industrial; pipe line; farmlands and managed forests.[8] The tax ratio system was created to provide a fairer property tax system, and reduce the vast differences in tax rates between the various property classes. With the creation of this system, the province established ranges of fairness for the tax ratios.[9] A municipality can alter tax ratios within the established ranges, however, if a ratio is outside the range, municipalities are required to maintain the ratio within a transitional range, and move towards the established range in subsequent years.[10]

There is a direct correlation between municipal spending, as determined by the estimates, and the property tax levied against individual properties. Unlike senior levels of government that have numerous sources of direct and indirect revenue, an increase in a municipality's spending has an overt and immediate impact on the individual taxpayer.[11] This relationship forces municipal politicians to be acutely concerned with the political impact of their decisions on property taxes; the financing of Canadian municipalities encourages municipal politicians to support decisions which do not result in increases in the property tax. High spending programs such as those involving social services are traditionally avoided.[12]

Because an increase in overall assessment will keep the tax rate and individual assessments low, municipal politicians are motivated to support planning decisions that have a positive effect on the overall balance of assessment. For example, high density development has traditionally been supported on the basis that it creates additional revenue for municipalities by increasing the assessment base and thus stabilizing or lowering the rate of taxation within a municipality or allowing more spending by council.[13]

---

businesses based on the rental value of the business: s. 232, and a surtax may be imposed on non-residential immoveable properties: s. 244.11.

7 *Municipal Act*, S.O. 2001, c. 25, s. 308(3). However, despite this section, the tax ratio for the farmlands property class and the managed forests property class prescribed under the *Assessment Act* is .25, s. 308.1(2) and (3).

8 *Assessment Act*, R.S.O. 1990, c. A.31, s. 7(2).

9 *Supra*, note 7, s. 308(8).

10 *Ibid.* at s. 308(9).

11 See Plunkett, *The Financial Structure and Decision-Making Process of Canadian Municipal Government* (Ottawa, 1972), at 53.

12 But see Alan Altshuler and Jose Gomez-Ibanez, *Regulation for Revenue: The Political Economy of Land Use Exaction* (Washington: The Brookings Institute, 1993), which demonstrates that past a "critical mass" any type of development, including commercial and industrial, is a financial burden on municipalities.

13 See Price-Waterhouse Associates *The Corporation of the Borough of York, Cost/Benefit Study on Land Use Within the Borough* (1971), and Price-Waterhouse Associates *Metropolitan Toronto Cost/Benefit Factors Relative to Large Apartment Development, Study Guidelines* (1973). Both studies indicate that high density development can be financially beneficial or at least neutral in its financial impact.

The substantial reliance that Canadian municipalities must place on the property tax results in municipal decision-making being distorted and restricted in a way that decisions of the federal and political governments are not. It may be argued that the direct relationship between spending and overt taxation is a beneficial one in that it results in a kind of fiscal discipline being imposed on municipalities and increases the transparency of spending decisions. Certainly, lower property taxes are reflective of strong local opposition to high taxation, but it may make it harder for municipalities to maintain services that benefit only a minority, such as welfare or housing programs.

Since municipalities have no other major source of revenue granted to them other than property taxes,[14] municipal decision-making is restricted on the one hand by the political limitations of the property tax and on the other by the controls found in conditional grants which make up approximately 86% of provincial transfers.[15] Through conditional payments in which funds are directed towards identified projects or programs, the provinces can substantially control a wide range of service delivery and infrastructure development decisions.

It should be noted, however, that this is not an argument that all conditional grants should be abolished. There may be need for such grants to ensure basic minimum standards; to safeguard the protection of minority groups; or to encourage new initiatives in matters of provincial concern such as housing or pollution control. To the extent that municipalities are viewed as being a service delivery arm of the provincial government, this form of financial intervention may appear appropriate. However, where municipalities function as an independent level of government greater autonomy in financial matters should be granted to match the political autonomy of municipalities.

2. Restrictions on Borrowing

Municipalities are generally obligated to raise funds sufficient to produce the amount required by the municipal spending estimates for a given year including: any debenture installments or sinking fund payments falling due; contributions to any special reserve funds; ordinary municipal expenditures; moneys required for various boards, and any other funds that it is

---

14 But see *The Provincial-Municipal Tax Sharing Act*, C.C.S.M., c. T.5, s. 2. Under this Act, the province of Manitoba allocated 2% (2.2% beginning in January 1, 1979) of its personal income tax revenues and 1% of its corporate income tax revenues as unconditional grants to municipalities on a per capita basis with supplements for municipalities with large populations or rapid population growth: Siegel, "Provincial-Municipal Relations in Canada: An Overview" (1980) 23 Can. Pub. Admin. 281 at 311. The provinces of British Columbia, Saskatchewan and Nova Scotia also have revenue sharing programs. See *Report of the Advisory Committee to the Minister of Municipal Affairs on the Provincial-Municipal Financial Relationship* (Ontario, 1991) at 70-71.

15 *Supra* note 1.

required by law to raise.[16] Canadian municipalities are prevented from budgeting for a deficit on their annual operating budgets as they are required to raise funds to meet all of their obligations falling due in a given year. They are permitted, however, to borrow money on a limited basis, principally to finance major capital projects and to finance short term operating expenditures pending receipt of property tax revenue. In all provinces, there are extensive restrictions on the municipal borrowing power.

The rationale behind such restrictions is to require the expenditures of each year to be borne by the taxation of that year so that, as far as possible, the ratepayers of one year should not be called upon to discharge the obligations accruing from a previous year. [17] This is markedly different from the rules governing other levels of government where it is not uncommon for governments to maintain deficit budgets. Underlying the municipal restrictions in this regard is a fear that municipalities cannot be trusted to exercise borrowing powers freely because they may seek favour with electors by approving politically expedient projects or otherwise incur debt irresponsibly. It is not at all clear that this fear is substantiated or that municipal councils are more apt to spend funds for short term political gains than other levels of government.

Generally speaking, each provincial government sets limits on the amount of debt that a municipality can incur and retains control over the terms upon which municipalities can borrow funds. The level of control retained by the province with respect to borrowing varies from province to province. For example, pursuant to the Alberta *Municipal Government Act*, a borrowing by-law must set out the amount to be borrowed and the purpose for which it is borrowed. The financial terms of the borrowing, as well as the sources to be used to pay the principal and interest must also be detailed in the by-law.[18] Generally, the borrowing municipality may use the borrowed sums only for the purpose set out in the by-law.[19]

Ministerial approval is required when the municipality exceeds its debt limit, which is determined in regulation by the Minister.[20] Presently, the regulations allow most municipalities to borrow up to 1.5 times their annual revenues, while the cities of Edmonton and Calgary may borrow 2 times their annual revenues — without the approval of the minister.[21]

---

16 See *Municipal Government Act*, R.S.A. 2000, c. M-26, s. 243 and 353; and the *Municipal Government Act*, S.N.S. 1998, c. 18, s. 526. However, note that in the *Toronto (City) v. Toronto (Metropolitan)* (1976), 12 O.R. (2d) 601 (H.C.), the Court held that the expenditure of funds raised by the issuing of approved debentures did not have to be included in the estimate or approved by a 2/3 vote of council as it was not to be raised by an annual levy.

17 Discussed in *Athens High School Board, Re* (1913), 29 O.L.R. 360 (H.C.).

18 The *Municipal Government Act*, R.S.A. 2000, c. M-26, s. 251.

19 *Ibid.* at s. 253.

20 *Ibid.* at s. 252; s. 271.

21 Debt Limit Regulation, A.R. 255/2000.

In Ontario, municipalities were at one time required to receive the approval of the Ontario Municipal Board prior to incurring debt, with the result that a provincially appointed Board could scrutinize municipal spending priorities. Now, however, the *Municipal Act* provides a generous exemption to the review requirements such that Municipal Board approval is not required for borrowing within prescribed debt limits provided for in the regulations.[22] This exemption provides a significant relaxation from the previous regime and allows municipalities to retain a significant degree of control over their spending priorities. The Ontario *Municipal Act* also provides for municipalities to incur short-term debt through a temporary borrowing by-law which allows municipal councils to borrow money pending receipt of uncollected taxes provided that the total amount borrowed, outstanding principal borrowed and accrued interest does not exceed 50% (from January 1 to September 30 of the year), or 25% (from October 1 to December 31), of the total estimated revenues of the municipality as set out in the budget adopted for the year.[23]

More restrictive practices can be seen in provinces such as Nova Scotia where the *Municipal Government Act* allows municipalities to borrow money in order to carry out an authority to expend funds for capital purposes, provided that authority is in an act of the legislature.[24] A municipality may also borrow money to cover the annual current expenditure of the municipality that has been authorized by the council, up to half of the sum of taxes levied by the municipalities and federal and provincial grants received or due for the previous fiscal year.[25] Such short-term borrowing does not require special approval, but all other municipal borrowing must be approved by the Minister of Housing and Municipal Affairs. Ministerial approval is generally required for any long-term commitment to pay money in an amount exceeding $100,000, including borrowing.[26] The Minister may also establish borrowing limits for municipalities for any given year.

British Columbia also places considerable restrictions on municipal borrowing power through an elaborate regulatory scheme relating to borrowing. The *Local Government Act* limits the total debt municipalities may incur at any given time to the total of 20% of the average taxable value for the municipality, and 20% of the value of the utility systems and other municipal enterprises.[27] The Inspector, a provincially appointed regulator, may increase this amount in his or her discretion.[28] A council may, under an agreement, incur a liability payable after the end of the current year, if it is not a debenture debt and the period of the liability is not longer than the reasonable life

22 *Municipal Act, 2001*, S.O. 2001, c. 25, s. 401.
23 *Ibid.* at s. 407.
24 *The Municipal Government Act*, S.N.S. 1998, c. 18, s. 66.
25 *Ibid.* at s. 84.
26 Excluding an employment or a collective agreement – see *ibid.* at s. 88(4) .
27 *Local Government Act* R.S.B.C. 1996, c. 323, s. 334.
28 *Ibid.* at s. 334(5).

expectancy of the activity, work or service under the agreement.[29] However, the council must not incur a liability for a total period of over five years until it has provided a counter petition opportunity in relation to the proposed liability.

A council may, by by-law, and without the assent of the electors or the approval of the inspector, borrow money necessary to meet current lawful expenditures in anticipation of, and not exceeding, revenue from unpaid taxes and money remaining due from other governments in that year.[30]

Without question, there is a need for some control over a municipality's ability to incur debt. Provincial governments have a constitutional responsibility for municipalities and would ultimately be responsible politically, if not legally, for defaulting municipalities. For that reason, they should be concerned about municipal spending and exercise some control over it. Nevertheless, such control need not include an evaluation of the details of municipal projects, or the wisdom and desirability of those projects. Those determinations are the very reason for the establishment of municipal government. The present system of review may result in costly delay and duplication of effort as the reviewing body reconsiders the details of projects for which funds are borrowed, and may lessen flexibility where municipalities wish to change projects after borrowing approvals have been given.

Review of municipal borrowing at the provincial level should be limited to an examination of total expenditures and the general financial capability of the municipality requesting the approval. It could even be argued that no review is necessary as the financial markets and voters at election time will be effective watchdogs of municipal borrowing, although this in turn may require enhanced disclosure requirements of municipal financial records. A further method of controlling municipal councils in the area of borrowing is the requirement of a plebiscite or the assent of the electors. But such a requirement appears to be equally unnecessary and would offer little protection to minority interests.[31]

3. Restrictions on the Imposition of Fees

As a result of the decrease in other sources of funding and the political limitations on raising further revenue through property taxes, there is an increasing reliance on municipal revenues that are derived from the imposition of fees and charges, such as license fees and user fees for various services provided by municipalities. Given the wide range of licenses, permits and services provided by municipalities and the associated fee levying authority granted therewith, it would appear that there is ample scope for municipalities to raise revenue in this manner. In Ontario, when the provincial government

29 *Ibid.* at s. 334.1.
30 *Ibid.* at s. 334.3.
31 See S. Fish, annotation to *Nepean (Township), Re* (1976), 1976 1 M.P.L.R. 220 (O.M.B.).

announced that local governments would have to bear the costs of certain programs formerly borne by the province, they also provided increased powers for municipalities to raise revenues through the imposition of fees and charges.[32] However, the ability for municipalities to raise revenues through fees is restricted in two important ways. Firstly, as statutory creations, municipal powers are limited to those powers expressly granted by statute. Secondly, as creatures of the province, municipalities are subject to the same constitutional limitations respecting taxation to which the provinces are subject.

Where these limitations have been apparent is in situations where municipalities have attempted to impose as a fee, a levy that goes beyond the cost to the municipality of administering the service or providing goods for which the fee was imposed to include a component that has as its purpose the generation of general revenue. The limitation arises because there is a legal distinction drawn between the fees and taxes.

In making this distinction, the Canadian courts have relied upon the Supreme Court of Canada's decision in *Lawson v. British Columbia (Interior Tree Fruit & Vegetable Committee of Direction)*,[33] which held that a tax is a levy which is: 1) enforceable by law; 2) imposed under the authority of the Legislature; 3) imposed by a public body; and 4) made for a public purpose. Of particular importance in this definition is that a central feature that distinguishes a fee from a tax is that a fee can only be imposed to defray the costs for providing a service or good for which it was imposed, while a tax may be imposed for the purpose of raising general revenue. Where a municipality is only authorized to impose a fee, the levy will be struck down as being beyond the statutory authority of the municipality to impose where the affect of the levy is to raise funds beyond the amount required to defray the cost of the service. That is, there must be a reasonable nexus between the fee charged and the cost of the service or goods provided. This distinction between fees and taxation was underscored more recently by the Supreme Court of Canada in *Eurig Estate, Re,* where a probate fee was found to be a tax because it raised funds in excess of the costs of the service provided, in this case, the costs of probating the will.[34]

The sharp distinction between fees and taxes means that there are limited opportunities for municipalities to raise any excess revenues through the imposition of licensing or user fees. Critical in this analysis is a careful review of the statutory provisions that authorize the imposition of the fee. In some instances, the legislative authority is broad enough to include some general revenue raising powers. For example, in the Ontario *Municipal Act,* the municipality has the right to exact a fee in the nature of a tax for the purpose of raising revenue for municipal purposes. However, even in the face of

32 *Municipal Act*, S.O. 2001, c. 25, ss. 390-400.
33 (1930), [1931] S.C.R. 357.
34 [1998] 2 S.C.R. 565.

seemingly broad powers, the courts have interpreted these powers in a strict fashion restricting municipalities to raising funds only for the purposes of defraying the cost of providing the service in question.[35] Here the courts seem to be applying the more general interpretive rule that statutes that seek to impose taxes should be interpreted restrictively and in favour of the taxpayer. In these cases, the courts held that if the province had intended for municipalities to raise revenues through user fees more explicit language should have been used.

A further and related restriction arises as a consequence of the constitutional restriction placed on the provinces, limiting provinces to imposing direct taxes only, with the imposition of indirect taxes being within the exclusive jurisdiction of the federal government. (A direct tax is defined as a tax that is demanded from the person who, it is intended or desired, should pay it.) Municipalities, as creatures of the provinces are, thus, similarly restricted to imposing taxes of a direct nature. Thus, even where the statutory authority is broad enough to allow the imposition of a tax, the imposition may still be invalid, if it is in the nature of an indirect tax.[36]

4. Restrictions on Municipal Expenditures

The principal restriction on municipal spending requires that funds be expended for municipal purposes only. Consequently, restrictions on spending tend to follow a municipality's jurisdiction to exercise power. Where a municipality has authority to pass by-laws, the power to spend funds in furtherance of the exercise of that authority is implied. It follows from this that municipal spending decisions for matters within the municipality's jurisdiction cannot be attacked on the basis that they are unreasonable. Instead, it is only where funds are expended for matters beyond jurisdiction or which are patently unreasonable that the courts will prevent such expenditures.[37]

There are, however, specific restrictions on a municipality's ability to grant so-called "bonuses." In this context, a "bonus" means a benefit conferred by council on a person that is over and above the benefits conferred on other ratepayers or inhabitants and involves a direct or indirect expenditure or forfeiture of monies owed. The *Municipal Government Act* (Nova Scotia), for example, expressly prohibits municipalities from granting a tax conces-

---

35 *Ontario Private Campground Assn. v. Harvey (Township)* (1997), 39 M.P.L.R. (2d) 1 (Ont. Gen. Div.); see also A.N. Craik, "Case Comment: O.P.C.A. v. Harvey" (1997), 39 M.P.L.R. (2d) 220.

36 *Allard Contractors Ltd. v. Coquitlam (District)*, [1993] 4 S.C.R. 371; *Ontario Home Builders' Assn. v. York (Region) Board of Education*, [1996] 2 S.C.R. 929 (S.C.C.); both discussed *infra* Chapter 6.

37 See *Nanaimo (City) v. Rascal Trucking Ltd.*, [2000] 1 S.C.R. 347 (B.C. C.A.), discussed *infra* Chapter 4.

sion or other form of direct financial assistance to a business or industry.[38] The *Municipal Act* (Ontario) provides that, "despite any Act, a municipality shall not assist directly or indirectly any manufacturing business or other industrial or commercial enterprise through the granting of bonuses for that purpose."[39]

The most important issue in analyzing whether a municipality is granting a bonus is an examination of its purpose. In doing this it is important to begin with the meaning of the word "aid." In order to determine the meaning of "aid," it is necessary to consider the purpose of this provision, which is a blanket prohibition to prevent municipalities from granting "aid" or "assistance" directly or indirectly to private entrepreneurs. While there is no case law determining the meaning of the words "aid" or "assistance" in this section, those words must clearly be interpreted in light of their statutory purpose.

It is clear that the statutory purpose of the prohibition is not to prevent private parties from obtaining benefits from municipal rezoning or undertakings. Whenever a parcel of land is rezoned or redesignated or a road is built, a subway constructed, or a public work undertaken by a municipality, there are direct and indirect benefits to private parties. Private land values in many cases may increase. Servicing costs to individuals may be reduced and private commercial activity may be encouraged. The purpose cannot be to prohibit industrial business or commercial enterprises from receiving such benefits which arise out of municipal government activity even if they receive particular benefits. Moreover, when municipal land is sold at a fair market value, one can only assume that the sale benefits the private purchaser or he or she would not have purchased the property from the municipality at a fair market value. Such a sale, however, cannot be a bonus. The mere existence of a "benefit" is insufficient to bring about a conclusion that "aid" or "assistance" is being granted.

In order for there to be a bonus, there must have been more than a mere benefit, direct or indirect, occurring to private entrepreneurs or businesses. The purpose of these provisions is to prevent municipalities from providing assistance for the purpose of assisting or helping a particular individual or business. The reason for the assistance may be to attract that business to the municipality,[40] to encourage it to expand or to give it an advantage over a competitor or indeed, for some other reason. At issue is that the purpose of the bonus is to "assist" or grant "aid" directly or indirectly to a business, commercial or industrial enterprise. If the only motivation or benefit is the securing of the business enterprise, the action is covered by the express

---

38 S.N.S. 1998, c. 18, s. 57(1). For another example, see the *Municipal Act*, R.S.B.C. 1996, c. 323, s. 182.

39 S.O. 2001, c. 25, s.106(1).

40 See *Cie immobilière Viger v. Lauréat Giguère Inc.*, [1977] 2 S.C.R. 67, which held that the improvement of land to induce a commercial enterprise to locate on that land offends the prohibition against municipal aid.

prohibition against bonuses.[41] Municipalities can undertake actions, the purpose of which is not merely to assist a commercial enterprise as such, but which in fact does give such assistance, when there is a non-business rationale for the benefit.

The nature of the enterprise is also important as the prohibition relates to "manufacturing, business or other industrial or commercial enterprises."[42] In the case of *Ontario Regional Assessment Commissioner v. Caisse populaire de Hearst Ltée*,[43] the Supreme Court of Canada examined the meaning of "carrying on a business" under the *Assessment Act*.[44] It concluded that the appropriate test is whether the activity concerned is carried on for the purpose of earning a profit or for some other preponderating purpose.

In the case of *Gilbert v. Toronto (Metropolitan)*,[45] a grant to the Stadium Corporation by Metropolitan Toronto was challenged on the basis that it was a bonus. The court held that the Stadium Corporation, which is incorporated under the *Ontario Business Corporations Act*,[46] is a provincial Crown corporation, and therefore, does not qualify as a manufacturing business or other industrial or commercial enterprise within the meaning of the *Municipal Act*.

Should a municipality wish to grant aid in spite of the prohibition against bonuses, there are some possible ways to do so. The municipality should endeavour to ensure that the granting of the aid is not merely to assist the business itself, and where possible, that the granting of the aid has a proper planning or other public rationale. The municipality may also look to private/public partnerships or public corporations to avoid the prohibition. These devices provide legitimate methods of providing assistance for proper planning or policy reasons. For example, an exception to the bonusing provisions in the Ontario *Municipal Act* is contained in s. 110(3).[47] The municipality can provide financial assistance by selling or leasing property at less than fair market value where the purchaser has entered into an agreement with the municipality for the provision of a "Municipal Capital Facility" by the purchaser. Any assistance provided by the municipality to the purchaser under this section must relate to the "Municipal Capital Facility." In addition, the municipality may also exempt the land that is the subject of an agreement under this section from municipal taxation[48] and from municipal development charges.[49]

---

41 Laux, "Municipal Bonuses and Tax Exemptions to Entice Private Development"(1987) 15 Alta. L. Rev. 234.

42 *Municipal Act, 2001*, S.O. 2001, c. 25, s. 106(1).

43 [1983] 1 S.C.R. 57, (1983), 21 M.P.L.R. 9 (S.C.C.).

44 R.S.O. 1970 c. 32, s. 7, as amended 1974, c. 41, s. 3.

45 (1984), 29 M.P.L.R. 184 (Ont. Div. Ct.).

46 R.S.O. 1990, c. B.16.

47 *Municipal Act, 2001*, S.O. 2001, c. 25.

48 *Ibid.* at s. 110(6).

49 *Ibid.* at s. 110(7).

Furthermore, under the *Municipal Act* municipalities do have general authority to make grants,[50] which are distinct from bonuses, and numerous provinces give municipalities authority to permit relief from taxation on a case by case basis. *The Urban Municipality Act, 1984,* (Saskatchewan), for example, provides that the council, "may compromise or abate the claim of the municipality for taxes... and may enter into an agreement for payment of the balance owing, ... or may refund any amount already paid."[51]

C. PROPERTY ASSESSMENT AND TAXATION

Having examined municipal finance in general, it is now appropriate to turn to the narrow issue of assessment and taxation. The financial restrictions placed on municipalities are important to lawyers and planners because such restrictions can have a major impact on decisions which either professional might be attempting to persuade a council to make. A lawyer representing a client on a development matter would want to raise the issue of impact on assessment; a planner advocating that a certain project be built should be aware of the funding available for it. Both could be involved in provincial and administrative review of the municipal decision. Similarly, the narrower, more detailed concerns of assessment and taxation are of interest to both professions. The lawyer often argues assessment appeals and the planner may well be advising on the impact of assessment and taxation on the development of a community.

In dealing with assessment and taxation there are a number of matters to consider: (a) who is liable for property tax; (b) what is assessable or taxable property; (c) what property is exempt; (d) how property is valuated; (e) whether an entity is to be taxed as a business; and (f) how appeals of assessment matters are handled. The answers to these questions are far from clear cut and vary from province to province.

1. Who is Liable for Property Tax?

Generally, at a minimum, the owners of real property are liable for taxation on that property. The *Municipal Government Act* (Alberta) makes owners, purchasers, lessees, licensees or permittees liable for taxes.[52] The *Assessment Act* (Ontario) provides that land is assessed against its owner and

50 *Ibid.* at s. 107.

51 See *The Urban Municipality Act, 1984*, S.S. 1983-84, c. U-11, s. 285 - however, see s. 285(3) for consequences of doing so. Also the *Municipal Government Act*, R.S.A. 2000, c. M-26, s. 347(1), which allows council to compromise on arrears and cancel or refund all or part of a tax levy; and the *Municipal Act, 2001*, S.O. 2001, c. 25, s. 354(2)(a), which allows forgiveness of uncollectible taxes and s. 357, which allows cancellation, reductions or refunds for a variety of reasons, an example being property damage from fire.

52 R.S.A. 2000, c. M-26, s. 331(1) and 304.

against the tenant only in certain limited circumstances.[53] An "owner" includes trustee, guardian, executor and administrator.[54]

Taxes due upon land are generally a special lien upon the property in respect of which they are payable. For example, the *Vancouver Charter*[55] states:

> 414. Real property taxes ... shall constitute a special lien upon the real property in respect of which they are payable, having preference to any claim, lien, privilege or encumbrance of any person except the Crown, and shall not require registration to preserve it.

Under the *Municipal Act* (Ontario) taxes due upon any land in Ontario may be recovered as a debt due to the municipality from the taxpayer against whom the original assessment was made and from any subsequent owner of the assessed land, and the taxes are a special lien on the land with priority over every claim except that of the Crown.[56] Alberta has a similar provision in the *Municipal Government Act* which states that taxes are the liability of any person who was or subsequently became the owner, purchaser, lessee, licensee or permittee of the land or any part thereof at the time of its assessment.[57] The section also provides that the taxes due are recoverable as a debt to the municipality and are a special lien on the land.[58]

2. What is Assessable or Taxable Property?

For the purpose of municipal taxation it is sufficient to divide property into two broad categories — real property and personal property. It is real property, including improvements on that property, that makes up almost the entire base for municipal taxation in Canada. Inclusions in that base are determined by two factors: the definition of real property and improvements found in the various provincial statutes; and the exemptions from taxation on real property that would ordinarily fall within the definition.

For example, under the *Assessment Act* (Ontario), all real property in Ontario is liable to assessment and taxation subject to certain exemptions from taxation.[59] "Land", "real property" and "real estate" are defined in s. 1 of the Act to include:

(a) land covered with water,
(b) all trees and underwood growing upon land,

53 R.S.O. 1990, c. A.31, ss. 17.1 and 17.3(1).
54 *Ibid.* at s. 17.1(2).
55 S.B.C. 1953, c. 55, s. 414.
56 S.O. 2001, c. 25, s. 349(1) and (3).
57 R.S.A. 2000, c. M-26, s. 331.
58 *Ibid.* at s. 348.
59 R.S.O. 1990, c. A.31, s. 3.

(c) all mines, minerals, gas, oil, salt quarries and fossils in and under land,
(d) all buildings, or any part of any building, and all structures, machinery and fixtures erected or placed upon, in, over, under or affixed to land,
(e) all structures and fixtures erected or placed upon, in, over, under or affixed to a highway, lane or other public communication or water, but not the rolling stock of a transportation system.

The Act also states in s. 9 that easements are to be assessed in conjunction with the land they affect. This broad definition, subject to exemptions to be discussed later, determines what property is subject to taxation in Ontario.

Other provinces have somewhat different definitions. Although the *Assessment Act* (Nova Scotia)[60] defines "assessable property" as expansively as the Ontario legislation, it has certain qualifications regarding machinery, and specifically includes mobile homes used for residential or commercial purposes, rafts, floats, houseboats and other similar devices. That Act also specifically excludes land used as public streets, roads and highways and growing or unharvested agricultural crops in or on land.[61]

In British Columbia and Alberta, the legislation also contains references to real property. Under the *Municipal Government Act* (Alberta), any property situated in a municipality, unless explicitly exempt, is subject to assessment.[62] "Property" is defined as a parcel of land, an improvement or a parcel of land and the improvements to it,[63] and "improvements" means a structure, any thing attached or secured to a structure, that would be transferred without special mention by a transfer or sale of the structure, a mobile unit and machinery and equipment.

Generally in Alberta, property is grouped as land and improvements, linear property (such as cable), farm land, machinery and equipment. Each group is separately treated.

The *Vancouver Charter* provides only that all real property in the City is liable to taxation subject to certain exemptions.[64] In the *Charter*, however, real property includes "land and every improvement thereon."[65] The definition of improvements for the purposes of the *Vancouver Charter* is found in the *Assessment Act* (British Columbia)[66] which exempts, among other things, fixtures and machinery that is not affixed for any purpose other than its own stability and that is easily moved by hand, anything intended to be moved as a complete unit in its day to day use, and production machinery, unless any

60 R.S.N.S. 1989, c. 23.
61 *Ibid.* at ss. 2(aa)(ix) and (x).
62 R.S.A. 2000, c. M-26, s. 285.
63 *Ibid.* at ss. 284 (j), (l) and (r).
64 S.B.C. 1953, c. 55, s. 396.
65 *Ibid.* at s. 2.
66 R.S.B.C. 1996, c. 20.

of these falls into the definition of "Building." There is debate with respect to what constitutes "building" and what constitutes "machinery." There have been a series of anomalous decisions with respect to this area of assessment.[67]

The courts have frequently become confused in the litigation of assessment matters, with respect to the definitions of "real property" that should be used. The courts have referred to real estate and mortgage cases where the question of "what is a fixture" is often litigated.[68] However, some courts, in assessment cases, have specifically disapproved of importing "real property" and "fixture" definitions from real estate cases. These courts have, instead, recognized that assessment legislation internally defines "real property" and that the distinction between fixtures and chattels is not directly relevant in the context of assessment.[69] The particular words of the legislation must be looked at in order to determine the definition of "real property."

It should also be noted that under the *Assessment Act* (Ontario) there is a wide exemption for machinery which would ordinarily be defined as real property under the Act.[70] The Act does not define machinery and as a result the exemption has frequently resulted in litigation.[71]

A definition of machinery and a test to determine same was formulated in the case of *London (City) v. John Labatt Ltd.*,[72] and thereafter applied in many decisions. The definitions of machinery adopted in that case were "any instruments employed to transmit force or to modify its application" or "the means and appliance by which anything is kept in action or a desired result is obtained." The test formulated to determine if the item was "machinery" was in part "does it form an integral part of the overall or general process of

---

67 See *London (City) v. John Labatt Ltd.*, [1953] O.R. 800 (H.C.); *Galloway Lumber Co. v. East Kootenay Assessor, Area No. 22* (1989), 63 D.L.R. (4th) 222 (B.C. C.A.), leave to appeal refused (1990), 68 D.L.R. (4th) vii (note) (S.C.C.); *Irving Oil Co. v. New Brunswick (Minister of Municipal Affairs)* (1975), [1977] 1 S.C.R. 310; *Metals & Alloys Co. v. Regional Assessment Commissioner, Region No. 11* (1985), 49 O.R. (2d) 289 (C.A.), leave to appeal refused (1985), 51 O.R. (2d) 64 (note) (S.C.C.); *Ciment Québec Inc. c. St-Basile Sud (Village)*, [1993] 2 S.C.R. 823; *Nabisco Brands Ltd. v. Mississauga Regional Assessment Commissioner, Region No. 15* (1988), 64 O.R. (2d) 135 (C.A.), leave to appeal refused (1989), 66 O.R. (2d) xi (note) (S.C.C.).

68 See *Canadian Imperial Bank of Commerce v. Alberta (Assessment Appeal Board)* (1992), 89 D.L.R. (4th) 20 (Alta. C.A.); *Cominco Ltd. v. Assessor of Area No. 18, Trail-Grand Forks* (1982), 19 M.P.L.R. 204 (B.C. S.C.); and *Lyons v. Meaford (Town)* (1978), 6 M.P.L.R. 245 (Ont. C.A.).

69 *Ciment Québec Inc.*, *supra* note 67; *Newfoundland Telephone Co. Ltd. v. Marystown (Town)* (1992), 93 D.L.R. (4th) 715 (Nfld. C.A.); *Nova Scotia Director of Assessment v. Nabisco Brands Can. Ltd.* (1986) 72 N.S.R. (2d) 12 (C.A.); *Trans Mountain Oil Pipe Line Co., Re* (1966), 58 D.L.R. (2d) 97 (B.C. C.A.); *Ford Motor Co. v. Ford City (Town)*, [1929] 2 D.L.R. 109 (Ont. C.A.), affirmed [1929] S.C.R. 490.

70 See the *Assessment Act*, R.S.O. 1990, c. A.31, s. 3 para. 17 for the definition of "machinery" and s. 1 for the definition of "land."

71 *Algoma Steel Corp. v. Ontario Regional Assessment Commissioner, Region No. 31* (1988), 37 M.P.L.R. 200 (Ont. H.C.).

72 *Supra* note 67.

the same person [sic] of manufacturing from raw material to a finished product."

These definitions and the test formulated out of them (the "integration test") have been severely criticized as solely determinative tests by two decisions of the Ontario Court of Appeal. In *Metals & Alloys Co. v. Ontario Regional Assessment Commissioner, Region No. 11*[73] an exemption was sought for an enclosure designed and built to contain noise and dust emitted from a shredder used in the processing of aluminum. The Court of Appeal concluded that the definition formulated in the *John Labatt's* case was inappropriate, and the integration test (i.e. the use of the item), while perhaps relevant to determine if the item was machinery, was only one criteria out of several to be examined and was clearly not paramount or determinative. Instead, the initial question asked was whether the item was a building, structure or machinery. In resolving this question, common sense was to be applied — for example: does the item look like a building? If the item is found to be a building or structure then, irrespective of its use, it is not exempt. Similarly in *Nabisco Brands Ltd. v. Mississauga Regional Assessment Commissioner, Region No. 15*,[74] where an exemption for grain silos was sought, the Court of Appeal in large part adopted the reasoning in *Metals and Alloys* and rejected the *John Labatt's* case definition of machinery. In *Nabisco* the Court went even further by indicating that the integration test had no relevance in determining if an item was a building, structure or piece of machinery.

The lack of a legislative definition of "machinery" has resulted in litigation in other provinces as well. In *Cie de papier Quebec & Ontario Ltée v. Baie-Comeau (Ville)*[75], the Court found that an electrical distribution system in a paper mill was "machinery." Although it provided electricity for some building services (eg. light, heat, fans), it was primarily used to operate production machinery. Any lines which could be identified as being used for building services were taxable. In *Director of Assessment v. Miramichi Pulp and Paper Inc.*[76] the Court found instead that the same pieces of machinery should be included in the definition of "land" by virtue of the fact that they were "affixed" and that they enhanced the building for the purpose for which it was designed or used, that is, as a mill. The problems with this last decision are two-fold. Firstly, the degree of "affixedness" or "fixture" is not relevant to the inquiry. The Court did not examine the legislative definition provided which was:

> "real property" means
>
> ...

---

73 *Supra* note 67.

74 *Supra* note 67.

75 [1988] J.Q. No. 2130 (Que. S.C.).

76 [1996] CarswellNB 104 (C.A.).

but excludes

(e)... structures other than buildings, not providing shelter for people, plant or moveable property and all machinery, equipment, apparatus and installations other than those for providing services to buildings as mentioned in paragraph (b) **whether or not the same are affixed to land and buildings**, [emphasis added][77]

Instead, the Court imported real estate definitions of real property. The Court also employed a test which appears to be incorrect: "whether machinery enhances the building for its intended use" is a test which will always be answered in the affirmative. Even production machinery not fixed to the building in any way enhances, for example, a factory. It is not, however, assessable property according to the definition provided in the legislation.[78]

Unfortunately, while the Supreme Court of Canada has frequently dealt with assessment matters, no test for determining what is machinery has been elaborated, other than the test set out in *New Brunswick (Minister of Municipal Affairs) v. Canaport Ltd.*[79] for determining whether large structures such as kilns are buildings or machines.

Another issue that has arisen is whether mobile homes should be included within the definition of lands, buildings or structures. The *Assessment Act* (Nova Scotia) defines assessable property to include mobile homes used for residential or commercial purposes.[80] The *Assessment Act* (Ontario) has no such references, but nevertheless the courts have held that mobile homes are structures and therefore "land" under the *Assessment Act.* [81] However, while mobile homes are "structures" and therefore considered land, they are not land in their own right but are rather improvements to the land they are affixed to. Therefore, even where the mobile homes are owned by tenants on the land, and therefore will not add to the sale price of the land, they are assessable against the owner of the land.[82]

However, the Saskatchewan Court of Appeal in *Melfort Danceland v. Star City (Rural Municipality)*,[83] held that a mobile home was not a "building" and, therefore, could not be assessed for property tax under *The Rural Municipality Act* (Saskatchewan), which provided for the assessment of the owner of a building situated on land belonging to another person, or not

77 *Assessment Act*, R.S.N.B. 1973, c. A-14, s. 1.

78 *Ibid.* at s. 1, s. 4(1).

79 [1976] 2 S.C.R. 599.

80 *Assessment Act*, R.S.N.S. 1989, c. 23, s. 2(aa)(vii) and see *Municipal Government Act* R.S.A., c. M-26, s. 284(j) and (h).

81 *Johnston v. Sault Ste. Marie Board of Education* (1978), 5 M.P.L.R. 129 (Ont. Div. Ct.). See also *Kelders v. Ontario Regional Assessment Commissioner, Region No. 26* (1987), 36 M.P.L.R. 12 (Ont. H.C.).

82 See *Myers v. Ontario Regional Assessment Commissioner, Region No. 32* (1991), 3 O.R. (3d) 488 (Div. Ct.).

83 [1977] 3 W.W.R. 737, 2 M.P.L.R. 205 (Sask. C.A.).

attached to the land on which it is placed. The legislature responded by including in *The Urban Municipality Act, 1989*, a provision which includes trailers, mobile homes and portable shacks within the definition of a building.[84]

3. Exemptions from Taxation

As noted earlier, the tax base of a municipality is dependent not only on the definition of land or improvement, but also by property or improvements that ordinarily would be caught by the definition but are exempted. All provinces provide for some exemptions — mandatory, discretionary or both. There is no uniformity across the country in terms of exemptions but almost all provinces exempt places of worship, federal Crown lands and provincial Crown lands. Charitable and non-profit organizations usually enjoy an exemption. In many cases, exemptions are found not in the public statutes providing for exemptions, but in private or special acts which pertain to bodies or organizations. In addition to exemptions, there are often special provisions found in legislation to lessen the burden of taxation on particular lands or individuals. Following is a discussion of the major exemptions found in the various provincial statutes.

(i) *Crown Lands*

The *Assessment Act* (Ontario) provides, as does legislation in other provinces, that Crown lands are exempt from taxation.[85] Under the Act "land owned by Canada or any Province" are exempt from taxation. However, the tenant of Crown land which is rented for valuable consideration and the owner of land in which the Crown has an interest are to be assessed in respect of the land as if the land were owned by another person.[86] Thus, the land is subject to taxation. The reason for this provision is that another entity besides the Crown is occupying the property and that entity can be taxed.

---

84 See *The Rural Municipality Act, 1989*, S.S. 1989-90, c. R-26.1, s. 267(1)(c). This section corresponds to *The Urban Municipality Act*, R.S.S. 1978, c. U-10, s. 310(4). However, now see *The Rural Municipality Act, 1989*, S.S. 1989-90, c. R-26.1, s. 2(1)(c) and *The Urban Municipality Act, 1994*, S.S. 1983-84, c. U-11, s. 2(1)(b).

85 See the *Assessment Act*, R.S.O. 1990, c. A.31, s. 3 para. 1. For examples in other provinces, see The *Assessment Act*, R.S.N.S. 1989, c. 23, s. 5(1)(a); The *Municipal Government Act*, R.S.A. 2000, c. M-26, s. 362(1)(a); The *Urban Municipality Act, 1984*, S.S. 1983-84, c. U-11, ss. 275(1); and the *Vancouver Charter*, S.B.C. 1953, c. 55, s. 396(a) and the *Crown Corporations Local Taxation Act*, R.S.N.L. 1990, c. C-40, s. 3.

86 See the *Assessment Act*, R.S.O. 1990, c. A.31, ss. 17(1) and 18. For examples in other provinces, see the *Assessment Act*, R.S.N.S. 1989, c. 23, s. 5(1)(a); *The Urban Municipality Act, 1984*, S.S. 1983-84, c. U-11, ss. 275(1)(a), 276(i); and the *Vancouver Charter*, S.B.C. 1953, c. 55, s. 396(a).

Other provinces such as Nova Scotia, Saskatchewan and British Columbia have similar provisions. The *Assessment Act* (Nova Scotia) provides that if Crown property is "occupied by any person otherwise than in an official capacity [of the Crown], the occupant shall be assessed and rated in respect thereof, but the property itself shall not be liable."[87] The difficulty under these sections is in making the determination as to whether the tenant or occupier is someone other than the Crown.

The early case of *Stinson v. Middleton (Township)*[88] placed heavy emphasis on the extent of control of the occupier vis-à-vis the Crown. The Court in *Delta Parking Systems Ltd. v. Toronto (City)*[89] followed this approach as well. Although the *Assessment Act* (Ontario) defines tenant as including an occupant and a person in possession other than the owner,[90] the Court focused on the degree of control exercised by the Crown to determine if there was a tenancy by Delta in operating a parking lot for the Crown. In the *Delta* case, the Crown had complete control in determining the rates and operation of the parking facility. The moneys collected were placed in the Crown's account. In addition, it was clear that no landlord and tenant relationship existed as there was no lease between the parties. The Court therefore concluded that the Crown was the occupier. The approach of the Court in *Delta* in focusing on control conforms with the earlier decision in *Maple Leaf Services v. Essa (Township)*.[91]

In the *Halifax Public Service Commission v. Halifax (County)*,[92] the Court held that agreements between the Public Service Commission and the Crowns of Canada and Nova Scotia indicated that the Commission was occupying property for its own purposes and not as an agent of, or in an official capacity of, the Crown.

The impact of exemptions for federal Crown lands is lessened from the point of view of local taxing authorities by the federal *Payments in Lieu of Taxes Act*[93] which provides for payments in lieu of taxes on certain federal Crown properties. Provincial statutes such as the *Municipal Tax Assistance Act*[94] in Ontario also provide for payments in lieu of taxes. The provisions vary from province to province and there is much special legislation dealing with the problem as well.

The lands of foreign governments in Canada (i.e. embassies and consulates) are generally exempt from taxation. However, the case of *Detroit*

---

87 R.S.N.S. 1989, c. 23, s. 5(1)(a).

88 [1949] O.R. 237 (C.A.).

89 [1965] 1 O.R. 380 (H.C.), affirmed [1965] 1 O.R. 660n (C.A.).

90 See the *Assessment Act*, R.S.O. 1980, c. 31, s. 1(s). Now R.S.O. 1990, c. A.31, s. 1.

91 [1963] 1 O.R. 475 (C.A.).

92 (1978), 5 M.P.L.R. 51 (N.S. C.A.), leave to appeal refused (1978) 28 N.S.R. (2d) 90 (S.C.C.). The Court referred to *Watters v. Watrous*, [1950] 2 D.L.R. 574, [1950] 1 W.W.R. 711 (Sask. C.A.) and *Mersey Paper Co. Assessment, Re* (1947), [1948] 2 D.L.R. 788 (N.S. S.C.).

93 R.S.C. 1985, c. M-13.

94 R.S.O. 1990, c. M.59.

(City) v. Sandwich West (Township),[95] held that the City of Detroit was a foreign corporation holding land in Ontario as a lessee from the Crown and was therefore liable to taxation.

(ii) *Places of Worship*

The exemption for religious properties is virtually universal but the exact form and nature of the exemption varies from province to province. Under the *Assessment Act* (Ontario), every place of worship and lands used in connection with places of worship are exempt from taxation.[96] However, land acquired for cemetery purposes but not immediately to be used is not exempt until actually used for such a purpose.[97]

In Nova Scotia, the breadth of the *Assessment Act* is similar to that of the Ontario Act and the exemption from taxation applies to:

> [E]very church and place of worship and the land used in connection therewith, and every churchyard and church burial ground and every church hall used for religious or congregational purposes exclusively save only for occasions specifically authorized by church authorities and for which no revenue in excess of one hundred dollars per annum is received...[98]

The exemption in the *Vancouver Charter* provides an exemption for real property "of which a religious organization, either directly or through trustees therefore, is the registered owner, . . . and which is set apart and in use for the public worship of God..."[99]

In the case of *Presbyterian Church Building Corp. v. Algoma Assessment Commissioner*,[100] the Court held that the exemption under the Ontario Act applied to a church building although the congregation of the church had been dissolved, the manse sold, and the church left vacant and put up for sale. The reason was that the building was still a church, was consecrated as a church and could be used again as a church. It was therefore a place of worship. The same result would appear to follow under the Nova Scotia provision, but not under the provision of the *Vancouver Charter*, because the language of the *Charter* requires the property to be "in use for the public worship of God."[101]

---

95 (1970), 10 D.L.R. (3d) 391 (S.C.C.); see also *Ogdensburg Bridge & Port Authority v. Ontario Regional Assessment Commissioner, Region No. 2* (1989), 67 O.R. (2d) 519 (H.C.).

96 R.S.O. 1990, c. A.31, s. 3, para. 3.

97 *Ibid.* See also *Municipal Government Act*, R.S.A. 2000, c. M-26, s. 362(k).

98 *Assessment Act*, R.S.N.S. 1989, c. 23, s. 5(1)(b).

99 S.B.C. 1953, c. 55, s. 396(1)(c)(iv).

100 [1973] 3 O.R. 1007 (Dist. Ct.).

101 S.B.C. 1953, c. 55, s. 396(1)(c)(iv).

In the case of *Singh v. Sudbury (City)*,[102] it was held that religious activity carried on in part of a private home by a religious community qualified that part of the home for exemption under the Ontario Act as a place of worship. Although s. 3(3)(b) of the *Assessment Act* (Ontario) provides that an exemption from taxation does not apply to lands rented or leased to a church or religious organization by any person other than another church or religious organization, in the *Singh* case, the portion of the house used by the religious community was not rented or leased to the community.

(iii) *Public Education Institutions*

Property owned by public education authorities is generally exempt from taxation. *The Urban Municipality Act* (Saskatchewan) exempts from taxation property owned and occupied by a school division.[103] The *Assessment Act* (Nova Scotia)[104] is wider in scope. Subsection 5(1)(d) exempts "the property of every college, academy or other public institution of learning with the exception of property mainly used for commercial, industrial, business, rental or other non-educational purpose." Subsection 5(1)(e) exempts every "public school house" and s. 5(1)(f) exempts all school lands.

The *Assessment Act* (Ontario) exempts educational institutions (universities, high schools, and public and separate schools) and the buildings and grounds of seminaries of learning maintained for religious or philanthropic purposes are also exempted.[105] Universities and colleges can also be exempt under the legislation establishing them.[106]

It has been held that when an educational institution applies for an exemption, the onus is on the institution to show that it is a *bona fide* educational institution, as in *Westminster College v. London (City)*.[107] In addition, the legislation and cases generally require the institution to own or occupy the property for educational purposes. However, the *Municipal Government Act* (Alberta) exempts all school buildings and lands unless they are used exclusively for activities other than school purposes.[108] The *Assessment Act* (Ontario) states that the exemption applies as long as the land is "owned, used and occupied solely" by the institution.[109]

In the case of *Donaldo Pianezza Beauty Salon v. North York (Borough)*,[110] a university rented out part of its premises to private entrepreneurs

---

102 (1975), 8 O.R. (2d) 377 (Dist. Ct.).

103 S.S. 1983-84, c. U-11, s. 275(1)(e). See also *The Municipal Government Act*, R.S.A. 2000, c. M-26, s. 362(c) and (d).

104 R.S.N.S. 1989, c. 23.

105 See the *Assessment Act*, R.S.O. 1990, c. A.31, s. 3, paras. 4 and 5.

106 See for example the *York University Act, 1965*, S.O. 1965, c. 143, s. 18.

107 [1963] 2 O.R. 25 (H.C.).

108 See *The Municipal Government Act*, R.S.A. 2000, c. M-26, s. 362, 368.

109 See the *Assessment Act*, R.S.O. 1990, c. A.31, s. 3, para. 4.

110 (1978), 19 O.R. (2d) 343, 5 M.P.L.R. 256 (C.A.).

and the properties so rented were held not to be exempt from taxation. But in *McMaster University v. Hamilton (City)*,[111] a student residence was held to be controlled and operated by McMaster University and thus exempt.

In the cases of *Edgehill School v. Windsor (Town)*[112] and *National Ballet School v. Ontario Regional Assessment Commissioner, Region No. 9*,[113] the Courts held that buildings owned by schools did not have to be used for teaching in order to gain an exemption under the respective Acts. In the latter case, the building was used occasionally for meetings of the board of directors and various committees and for a major fundraising event, while in the former case, the property was used only occasionally for sports events and was for sale as the school had moved to another location for financial reasons. In both cases, the property was not in regular use but the exemption was granted.

The Ontario Act has, in addition to exemptions for educational institutions, exemptions for seminaries of learning maintained for philanthropic or religious educational purposes.[114] As in the provisions respecting educational institutions, the property generally must be used for the purposes of the seminary in order to qualify for an exemption.[115] The Courts are prepared to give the words "seminary of learning" in ss. 3(5) and (6) a wide meaning, as in the case of *Societa Unita v. Gravenhurst (Town)*, where a children's camp which had a program of chapel activities, Italian cultural subjects, swimming, crafts and related subjects was held to be a seminary of learning.[116] While "seminary of learning" is not to be restrictively interpreted, recent decisions require the applicant for the exemption to demonstrate that the principal use of the land, objectively viewed, is as a seminary of learning. If this is not demonstrated the exemption will be denied.[117]

---

111 (1974), 1 O.R. (2d) 378 (C.A.), affirmed [1975] 1 S.C.R. v. For a similar result, see *University of Ottawa v. Ottawa (City)* (1967), [1969] 2 O.R. 382 (Co. Ct.).

112 (1979), 10 M.P.L.R. 137 (N.S. C.A.).

113 (1979), 10 M.P.L.R. 208 (Ont. H.C.).

114 *Assessment Act*, R.S.O. 1990, c. A.31 s. 3(1)5.

115 *Christian Brothers of Ireland in Canada v. Ontario Assessment Commissioner*, [1969] 2 O.R. 374 (H.C.).

116 (1978), 3 M.P.L.R. 24 (Ont. H.C.), affirmed (1978), 6 M.P.L.R. 172 (Ont. Div. Ct.). See also *Seafarers Training Institute v. Williamsburg (Township)* (1982), 19 M.P.L.R. 183 (Ont. Div. Ct.). For a contrasting result see *Gurdjieff Foundation v. Ontario Regional Assessment Commissioner, Region No. 9* (1981), 14 M.P.L.R. 303 (Ont. H.C.), where an exemption was denied because the non-profit corporation taxpayer's activities consisted of self-development through the study of mystical, philosophical teaching which had no public benefit and conveyed no communicable knowledge.

117 *Nazareth Catholic Family Life Centre of Combermere v. Renfrew Regional Assessment Commissioner* (1987), 35 M.P.L.R. 77 (Ont. Div. Ct.), leave to appeal allowed (1987), 35 M.P.L.R. xxvi (Ont. C.A.). See *Associated Gospel Churches v. Ontario Regional Assessment Commissioner, Region No.13* (1979), 9 M.P.L.R. 287 (Ont. Div. Ct.), where the Court held that the primary purpose must be a seminary for learning and education cannot be a mere by-product. See also *Western Day Care v. London (City)* (1981), 16 M.P.L.R. 35 (Ont. Co. Ct.), where a day care centre was denied an exemption under s. 3(6) as the educational aspects were a secondary purpose. See also *Augustinian Fathers (Ontario)*

(iv) *Other Organizations*

The property of a host of other organizations is also exempted under various provincial acts. For example, public hospitals are commonly exempt.[118] The breadth of these exemptions also varies from province to province. The *Vancouver Charter* states, *inter alia*, that only real property which is in actual occupation by a hospital receiving aid and is wholly used for the purpose of the hospital, or is held by the hospital for future use as a hospital site and has been designated by the Minister of Municipal Affairs and Housing, is exempt.[119]

In *Wellesley Hospital v. Ontario Regional Assessment Commissioner, Region No. 9*[120] space leased outside the hospital for a lab that formed an integral part of the hospital was exempt from taxation. However, the Ontario Act excludes from exemption the land of a public hospital when occupied by a tenant or lessee.[121] In *York Central Hospital Assn. v. Vaughan (Township)*,[122] however, a staff residence on the grounds of a hospital was exempt as an integral part of the hospital. The residents were held not to be tenants because of their lack of control over their residences.

The property of boy-scout and girl-guide organizations is often exempt. For example, the *Assessment Act* (Ontario) exempts property owned, occupied and used solely by the Boy Scouts Association or the Canadian Girl Guides Association or by any provincial or local association or other local group in Ontario that is a member of either organization or is otherwise chartered or officially recognized by it.[123]

The exemptions for particular organizations vary across Canada. *The Urban Municipality Act, 1984* (Saskatchewan)[124] exempts the buildings and lands of the Royal Canadian Legion (Saskatchewan Command), the Army, Navy and Air Force Veterans in Canada, the Disabled Veterans' Association of Saskatchewan and the Canadian Mental Health Association (Saskatchewan Division) so long as the buildings and grounds are actually used and occupied by a branch but not otherwise. Section 275(1)(m) of the Saskatchewan Act

---

Inc. v. Ontario Regional Assessment Commissioner, Region No. 14 (1985), 52 O.R. (2d) 536 (H.C.), and *Camp Grounds Assn. of Canada-Great Lakes Conference of Free Methodist Church v. Zorra (Township)* (1988), 38 M.P.L.R. 1 (Ont. Dist. Ct.) where the Courts followed the *Associated Gospel Churches* case and refused the exemption where the primary purpose, objectively viewed was not to provide a seminary of learning.

118 See for example the *Vancouver Charter*, S.B.C. 1953, c. 55, s. 396(c)(iii); the *Assessment Act*, R.S.O. 1990, c. A.31, s. 3, para. 7 and *The Municipal Government Act*, R.S.A. 2000, c. M-26, s. 362(e).

119 S.B.C. 1953, c. 55, s. 396(c)(iii).

120 (1990), 18 O.R. (3d) 383 (Div. Ct.).

121 R.S.O. 1990, c. A.31, s. 3, para. 7.

122 [1972] 1 O.R. 244 (H.C.).

123 *Assessment Act*, R.S.O. 1990, c. A.31, s. 3, para. 10. Nova Scotia has a similar provision in the *Assessment Act*, R.S.N.S. 1989, c. 23, ss. 5(1)(o) and 5(1)(p).

124 S.S. 1983-84, c. U-11, s. 275(1)(o).

contains exemptions for the Young Men's and Young Women's Christian Association and for any law school established and maintained by the Benchers of the Law Society. Both Ontario and Saskatchewan exempt agricultural organizations[125] and Ontario has an exemption for the property of children's aid societies,[126] public libraries and other public institutions — literary or scientific and agricultural or horticultural associations.[127]

(v) *Charitable Institutions*

The provisions regarding charitable institutions also vary substantially. The *Assessment Act* (Ontario) provides that land owned, used and occupied by the Canadian Red Cross Society, St. John's Ambulance Association, or any incorporated institution organized for the relief of the poor, conducted on philanthropic principles and not for the purpose of profit or gain, is exempt. In addition, the organization must be supported, in part at least, by public funds and qualifies only when the land is owned by the institution and occupied and used for the purposes of the institution.[128]

This cumbersome exemption has been considered in two important cases. In the case of *Ina Grafton Homes v. East York (Township)*,[129] the Ontario Court of Appeal held that a claim under the section must be brought strictly within the exempting words. Land vested in the United Church under a statutorily approved agreement with a charitable organization to continue to operate thereon homes for elderly and needy women who paid rents which were insufficient to cover ordinary expenses and carrying charges, did not qualify for exemption because the United Church was not organized for the relief of the poor, nor was it supported by public funds (although the provision of services in the home were publicly subsidized).

In *Stouffville Assessment Commissioner v. Mennonite Home Assn.*[130] lands used as a nursing home by an organization incorporated by the Mennonite Church, where one of the purposes of the organization was to provide home care and security for the aged, were held to be exempt, although no means test was required for the residents. The Supreme Court of Canada held that the taxpayer was essentially similar to a charitable institution organized for the relief of the poor since it could not operate for gain or profit and that

---

125 See the *Assessment Act*, R.S.O. 1990, c. A.31, s. 3(14), and *The Urban Municipality Act, 1984*, S.S. 1983-84, c. U-11, s. 275(1)(l).

126 R.S.O. 1990, c. A.31, s. 3, para. 13.

127 *Ibid.* at para. 14.

128 *Ibid.* at s. 3, para. 12.

129 [1963] 2 O.R. 540 (C.A.).

130 (1972), 31 D.L.R. (3d) 237 (S.C.C.). However, more recent decisions indicate that the applicant for this exemption must establish some economic deprivation or need, the relief from which is a part of the purpose of the institution. See for example, *LDARC Corp. v. London (City)* (1985), 29 M.P.L.R. 9 (Ont. Div. Ct.); and *London (City) v. Byron Optimist Sports Complex Inc.* (1983), 23 M.P.L.R. 10 (Ont. C.A.).

"poor" was a word of relative meaning, not only including destitute. The home was also subsidized by public funds.

In both cases, the Courts concluded that there was no community of meaning in the terms "organizations for the relief of the poor," "the Canadian Red Cross Society" and "St. John's Ambulance Association," but sought to ascertain whether the taxpayer seeking the exemption was similar to one incorporated for the relief of the poor, as that was the relevant comparison.

The *Vancouver Charter* and the *Assessment Act* (Nova Scotia) contain exemptions which are more direct. The former exempts the real property owned by an incorporated charitable institution which is in actual occupation by the institution and is wholly used for charitable purposes.[131] The latter, perhaps the most sensible of all, exempts property used directly and solely for a charitable purpose of a particular charitable organization registered as such under the *Income Tax Act* (Canada) but only if exempted by the municipal council.[132] The *Municipal Government Act* (Alberta) exempts *inter alia* property used for a charitable or benevolent purpose that is for the benefit of the general public, and owned by a non-profit organization.[133]

(vi) *Municipal Properties*

Municipal properties are exempt from taxation under the *Assessment Act* (Ontario) except when occupied by a tenant who would otherwise be taxable if the tenant owned the land.[134] This exemption for municipal properties is found in many provinces.[135] The exemption is clearly a sensible one to prevent the need for the municipality to tax itself; it has caused some difficulty in Ontario however. In the case of *Toronto Transit Commission v. Toronto (City)*,[136] the Supreme Court of Canada stated, in interpreting the municipal exemption in the Ontario Act, that legislative policy required that municipally-owned lands should not be exempt when the "lands are not devoted to purposes of the municipality but are devoted to commercial purposes." That change in purpose occurred, the Court concluded, as soon as the lands were leased by a municipality, regardless of physical occupation. As a result, although the tenant in that case had not physically occupied the property, the lands were no longer exempt because the words of s. 3(a) (now s. 3, para. 9)— "but not when occupied by a tenant or lessee" (as the Act then provided) — must be interpreted to mean "that when a tenant or lessee has a

131 S.B.C. 1953, c. 55, s. 396(c)(i).

132 *Assessment Act*, R.S.N.S. 1989, c. 23, s. 5(1)(q); the *Income Tax Act*, R.S.C. 1985, c. I-5, as amended.

133 R.S.A. 2000, c.M-26, s. 362(1)(n)(iii)(B).

134 R.S.O. 1990, c. A.31, s. 3, para. 9.

135 See for example *The Urban Municipality Act, 1984*, S.S. 1983-84, c. U-11, s. 275(1)(n); the *Vancouver Charter*, S.B.C. 1953, c. 55, s. 396(b); and *The Municipal Government Act*, R.S.A. 2000, c. M-26, s. 362(b).

136 (1971), 18 D.L.R. (3d) 68 (S.C.C.) at 73.

contractual right to occupation, whether or not he exercises that right by going into the lands and buildings or otherwise utilizing them for the development which he intends, the exemption is removed."[137] In British Columbia, where legal title is vested in a company, but the entire beneficial interest is in the municipality, the land will be exempted.[138]

(vii) *Pollution Control*

British Columbia has provided an exemption for pollution control equipment. The *Municipal Act*[139] and the *Vancouver Charter*[140] exempt any improvement or land used exclusively or primarily for the control or abatement of water, land or air pollution but, generally, only to the extent that the assessment commissioner, in his or her discretion, determines is attributable to the use of pollution abatement.[141] Alberta had similar provisions and incentives but they were repealed.[142]

In the case of *Rayonier Canada (B.C.) Ltd. v. British Columbia Assessment Authority*,[143] the British Columbia Supreme Court stated that the obvious purpose of the exemption is to provide an incentive for pollution control by way of tax relief. When the use of the equipment is primarily for a commercial purpose and pollution control is only an incidental result, the legislature did not intend tax relief to be provided. It was recognized, however, that both a commercial benefit and pollution control benefit could result and it is clear from the provision that relief is not to be excluded merely because a commercial benefit results, so long as the pollution control benefit remains primary in object and result; the purpose or intent of the user must be examined. In that case, the installation of hydraulic barkers at a saw mill was for both a pollution control and a commercial purpose, and a decision which reflected that duality was upheld.

(viii) *Exemptions and Ownership of Property*

In some statutes it is clear that in order for exemptions to arise the property must be owned by an exempted party. The *Vancouver Charter*[144]

---

137 *Ibid.* at 74. Section 3, para 9, now only refers to tenants, which is defined to include occupants and persons in possession (s. 1).

138 See *Whistler Village Land Co. v. North Shore-Squamish Valley Area Assessor* (1981), 15 M.P.L.R. 192 (B.C. S.C.).

139 R.S.B.C. 1996, c. 323, s. 339(1)(q).

140 S.B.C. 1953, c. 55, s. 396(e.01).

141 *See East Kootenay Assessor, Area No. 22 v. Westar Mining Ltd.* (1993), B.C. Stated Case 336 (S.C.).

142 See S.A. 1973, c. 42, s. 10.

143 (1979), 10 M.P.L.R. 180 (B.C. S.C.), affirmed (1980), B.C. Stated Case 127 (C.A.).

144 S.B.C. 1953, c. 55, s. 396.

often exempts property by reference to the registered owner. In other statutes exemptions are granted for the "property of" certain bodies or organizations.[145]

In the case of *Royal Ontario Museum v. Ontario Regional Assessment Commissioner, Region No. 10*,[146] the Royal Ontario Museum claimed an exemption under s. 3(14) of the *Assessment Act* (Ontario) for lands that it leased from an owner who was assessed for municipal taxation. The Court found that the words "property of" did not include a leasehold interest and held that the leasehold interest did not fall under an exemption for the property of the Museum.

Similarly, in the case of *Markham York Hospital v. Markham (Town)*,[147] lands leased for 99 years by two charities seeking an exemption were held not to be exempt. Ownership was a condition precedent for the exemption under s. 3(12) and a 99 year lease did not constitute ownership.

Where an exempting provision requires "ownership" of the property this does not necessarily mean that the entire property must be owned by the party seeking an exemption. Rather, depending on the provisions of the statute, an exemption from taxation may be granted in respect of the part of the property owned by the exemption seeker. In *Kiwanis Club of Brantford v. Brantford (City)*[148] the Kiwanis Club, an incorporated charitable institution, erected a building upon lands leased for 30 years from a conservation authority. The Kiwanis Club paid taxes with respect to the leased land but sought an exemption under s. 3(12) of the *Assessment Act* (Ontario) for the building which it had erected and for which it claimed ownership. The Court concluded that under the Act the building could be owned separate and apart from the land on which it was built, and therefore could be the subject of an exemption under s. 3(12) of the Act. The Court then held that since the lease granted the Kiwanis Club the right to remove the building at the end of the lease term, it was owned by the Kiwanis Club and an exemption was granted.

(ix) *Exceptions to Exemptions and Municipal Exemptions*

It can be seen that the exemptions found in the legislation of the provinces for the most part represent an attempt to provide aid to organizations. Certain exemptions, such as those for Crown and municipal properties, do not fall into this description and can be seen in part to be mandated by the

---

145 See for example *The Urban Municipality Act, 1984*, S.S. 1983-84, c. U-11, s. 275(1)(i), which exempts the land and improvements of certain public libraries. Similarly, the *Assessment Act*, R.S.O. 1990, c. A.31, s. 3, makes numerous references to the "property of."

146 (1976), 12 O.R. (2d) 778 (Div. Ct.).

147 (1976), 12 O.R. (2d) 238 (H.C.).

148 (1983), 44 O.R. (2d) 12 (Div. Ct.), leave to appeal refused (1984), 24 M.P.L.R. xxxvi (Ont. C.A.).

Constitution or common sense. Most exemptions are, however, the result of provincial policy although funded by the municipal tax base.

Although studies have been conducted which largely criticize the use of exemptions[149] and although some provinces have stated policies against granting further exemptions, the exemptions continue without any large degree of rationalization. The legislation does not reflect any attempt to ensure that exempted organizations benefit primarily the municipality in which they are situated, although it is the municipality which bears the burden of the exemption. There is no legislative recognition that exemptions are hidden subsidies by taxpayers that are not evaluated on any ongoing basis. The legislation generally does not grant to the municipality the ability to determine, in accordance with its own local values and priorities, which bodies it wishes to exempt. There are some, albeit few, exceptions to this general conclusion.

The *Municipal Act* (Ontario),[150] for example, provides that municipalities may pass by-laws to levy an annual tax on designated universities and colleges not exceeding $75 per year for each full time student. Similar provision is made with respect to other provincially funded institutions such as correctional institutions, training schools, public hospitals, provincial mental health facilities and facilities under the *Development Services Act*.[151]

In addition, there are provisions which give municipalities some discretion in determining exemptions. The *Municipal Government Act* (Alberta)[152] allows exemptions for certain properties unless a municipality, by by-law, authorizes an assessment to be made.

The *Assessment Act* (Ontario)[153] grants authority to municipalities to exempt or partially exempt farm lands of not less than five acres which are held and used by any one person situate in the municipality if the lands do not receive the benefit of municipal services. As well, Ontario municipalities may exempt the land of religious institutions and the Navy League of Canada, under certain conditions.[154]

---

149 See Ontario *Committee on Taxation Report* (Smith Report) (Toronto, 1967), vol. II, at 124 and Ontario *Report of the Commission on the Reform of Property Taxation in Ontario* (Blair Report) (Toronto, 1977), at 70-83. The Blair Report comes out less strongly against exemptions but suggests that generally, where granted, the municipality should retain control over the exemption.

150 S.O. 2001, c. 25, s. 323(1).

151 S.O. 2001, c. 25, s. 323(4), which provides for an annual levy on facilities governed by the *Development Services Act*, R.S.O. 1990, c. D-11.

152 R.S.A. 2000, c. M-26, s. 363(2).

153 R.S.O. 1990, c. A.31, s. 21.

154 R.S.O. 1990, c. A.31, ss. 4 and 6. See also for another example the *Municipal Government Act*, S.N.S. 1998, c. 18, s. 69 granting Council the authority to exempt persons of low income; see also the *Urban Municipality Act 1984*, S.S. 1983-84, c. U-11, ss. 275(2) and (3) which authorizes the council to exempt by by-law, in whole or in part, land, improvements or businesses in the municipality.

4. Special Provisions

Although assessment standards, such as market value provisions, are designed to ensure the equity of assessment in order that the tax burden falls uniformly on all properties, (as discussed *infra* under *Valuation of Property for Assessment Purposes*), there are many provisions that alter that uniform burden. As mentioned earlier, in Alberta it is possible to have different mill rates for different classes of property. The basic exemptions, in any case, cause a shift in the tax burden. There are numerous special provisions in legislation in all provinces that provide for shifting the burden of taxation in addition to the exemptions and provisions already discussed.

(i) *Farm Land and Golf Courses*

Farm land is regularly given special protection from local taxation. Under the *Assessment Act* (Nova Scotia),[155] it is exempt from taxation. Under the *Assessment Act* (Ontario)[156] the market value of farm land, for assessment purposes, is determined by taking into account its use only as farm land and is taxed at 25% of the residential rate.[157]

The Ontario Municipal Board in *Clark v. Peel County Assessment Commissioner*,[158] affirmed the principle that the agricultural productivity of the land should be the basis for determining the market value of farm land under the section. The purchase of land for speculative purposes would seem to be irrelevant as long as the property is used for farming. It is only when the property ceases to be used for farming purposes that it can be assessed at its full value.

The Urban Municipality Act (Saskatchewan)[159] enables municipalities to enact a by-law authorizing them to enter into agreements with the owners of land used exclusively for farming, and where the owner's principal occupation is farming, to fix the value of lands and buildings for assessment or taxation. In Alberta, farm land is assessable, but crops in all municipalities and farm buildings, including the farm house and other improvements connected with farming, are exempt.[160]

Golf courses are considered a special problem in urban areas because of their large size and their potential for development. In Ontario, local municipalities may enter into agreements with the owners of golf courses to fix the

---

155 R.S.N.S. 1989, c. 23, s. 47(1).
156 R.S.O. 1990, c. A.31, s. 19(3).
157 *Municipal Act, 2001*, S.O. 2001, c. 25, s. 308.1(3).
158 (April 8, 1970), Doc. P 9463-69 (O.M.B.).
159 S.S. 1983-1984, c. U-10, s. 239.1(1) ; if an agreement cannot be reached, or if council, upon application by the owner, fails to enter into an agreement, the owner may bring a petition to the Saskatchewan Municipal Board.
160 *Municipal Government Act*, R.S.A. 2000, c. M-26, s. 298(w) and (y).

assessment of golf courses, aside from any buildings or structures on the courses and aside from the land occupied by any buildings or structures. The buildings and structures and the land occupied by them must continue to be assessed at market value. When no agreement with respect to a fixed assessment is entered into, golf course property is taxed at market value. [161]

In the case of *Brampton Golf Club Ltd. v. Mississauga (Town)*,[162] the Ontario Court of Appeal held that golf course lands should be assessed in light of the amount paid for the land for golf course purposes. Therefore, although factors other than the actual amount paid for land for golf course purposes may be taken into account in assessing such land, it is improper to assess it on the basis of its redevelopment value. As a result, golf course lands in Ontario can be treated in their assessment in a manner similar to farm lands.

A further example of special provisions for golf courses is found in the *Vancouver Charter*, which enables the City to enter into an agreement with the owner of a golf course to fix the assessment.[163] Both the *Assessment Act* (Ontario) and the *Vancouver Charter* have provisions for foregone taxes to be recouped.[164]

(ii) *Forest Lands*

Forest lands are also given special protection from taxation. The *Assessment Act* (Ontario)[165] has special provisions for the valuation of reforested lands, wood lands and orchards. In Nova Scotia, the *Assessment Act*[166] provides for a forest property tax.

(iii) *Telephone, Telegraph, Electric, Pipeline and Railway Companies*

The property of numerous companies that operate on an intermunicipal basis and have special equipment or transmission facilities is often dealt with by special provisions. The *Assessment Act* (British Columbia), provides for regulated rates for the valuation of utility properties such as railways, pipelines, and power lines, rather than actual market value.[167]

---

161 Pursuant to O. Reg. 282/98, s. 3(1)2(vi), land used as a golf course is contained within the residential property class.

162 [1972] 2 O.R. 816, 26 D.L.R. (3d) 695 (C.A.).

163 S.B.C. 1953, c. 55, s. 395A(2), as amended.

164 S.B.C. 1953, c. 55, s. 395A(4) and (6), as amended and ss. 23(4) and (5) in the Ontario *Assessment Act*, R.S.O. 1990, c. A.31.

165 See the *Assessment Act*, R.S.O. 1990, c. A.31, s. 19(6), which states that land planted for forestation or reforestation shall not have its assessment increased as a result of the planting. See also s. 19(7), (8) and (9).

166 R.S.N.S. 1989, c. 23, s. 47, as amended.

167 R.S.B.C. 1996, c. 20, s. 21.

In the *Assessment Act* (Ontario), s. 24(4) provides for special valuation for structures, substructures, nails, ties, poles and wires of a transportation system, s. 25 governs pipelines, s. 27 public utilities, and s. 30 railways, while s. 3(21) of the Act covers telephone and telegraph companies.

D. THE VALUATION OF PROPERTY FOR ASSESSMENT PURPOSES

1. Market Value

In theory, market value appears to be the basis for assessment in Canada. Generally, the acts governing assessment require assessment to be at market value or a percentage thereof. The *Assessment Act* (Ontario), mandates that land shall be assessed at its current value or average current value, which is, in relation to land, the amount of money the fee simple, if unencumbered, would realize if sold at arm's length by a willing seller to a willing buyer.[168] This standard of exchange is the same as that found in the Ontario Act prior to 1968 when it referred to "actual value." The terms "market value" and "actual value" are synonymous, according to *Office Specialty Ltd. v. Ontario Regional Assessment Commissioner, Region No. 14.*[169] Although the current Act now refers to "current value," it is clear from the definition that it is also synonymous with market value and actual value.

The *Assessment Act* (British Columbia) requires the assessor to determine the "actual value" of land and improvements.[170] *The Urban Municipality Act* (Saskatchewan) refers to "fair value."[171] The *Assessment Act* (Nova Scotia) refers to "market value."[172]

The market value principle has been widely accepted because it provides an easily understood and applicable gauge for measuring the comparative worth of properties. Almost every developed country in the world uses some form of market value assessment, particularly with respect to residential properties.[173]

There is a great deal of difficulty in determining the market value of properties. The uniqueness of property causes difficulties in translating the market value of one property, as evidenced by a sale, into a criterion for estimating the market values of other properties. Although a single family

---

168 R.S.O. 1990, c. A.31, s. 19(1) and s. 1.

169 (1974), [1975] 1 S.C.R. 677.

170 R.S.B.C. 1996, c. 20, s. 18.

171 S.S. 1983-84, c. U-11, s. 238(1). See *Managerial Services Ltd. v. Regina (City)* (1980), 14 M.P.L.R. 82 (Sask. C.A.), for a consideration of fair value under s. 311. Among other things, the Court held that the assessor was wrong in not considering the effect of zoning controls when determining fair value.

172 R.S.N.S. 1989, c. 23 s. 42(1).

173 Joan Youngman and Jane Malme, *An International Survey of Taxes on Land and Buildings* (Boston: Kluwer Law and Taxation Publishers, 1994).

residence may be easily categorized according to value, this is much more difficult with respect to industrial and commercial property.[174]

A second problem is that actual sale prices may not reflect market value. Pressure exerted on either the buyer or the seller in an expropriation; a non-arm's length transaction; the financing of the sale; a temporary fluctuation in the market; or the particular knowledge of those in the market may create an inaccurate picture in terms of market value.

In order to circumvent these problems some provinces have set out legislative and administrative guidelines for the determination of market value. The *Municipal Government Act* (Alberta) provides that each assessment must reflect the characteristics and physical condition of the property on December 31st of the year in which the assessment is prepared, and the valuation standard set out in the Regulations for that property. The Minister of Municipal Affairs may make regulations establishing valuation standards for property, respecting procedures for preparing or adopting assessments and respecting the allowance of depreciation on machinery and equipment.[175]

The Urban Municipality Act, 1984, (Saskatchewan) specifies that in determining fair value "the assessor shall take into consideration and be guided by the present use, location and zoning of the land and any other condition or circumstance affecting its value, other than interim development controls; and any profitable use that may reasonably be made of the land; and any applicable formula, rule or principle set forth in a manual prepared for the assessors by the Assessment Management Agency and established as a manual by order of the agency."[176]

In Ontario, current value is calculated on June 30 for a taxation year before 2005, at the land's current value for the taxation year.[177] In 2005, the current value will be the average of the land's current value for the taxation year and the land's current value for the previous taxation year. After 2005, the average of the land's current value for the taxation year and the land's current value for each of the previous two taxation years will be calculated. In gradually moving to an average current value based upon three taxation years, the goal is to control some of the problems with a market value system as described above, such as temporary fluctuations in the market.

In the absence of legislative or administrative formulas, in addition to an actual recent sale of the property,[178] a number of methods have been

---

174 See *Office Specialty Ltd.*, *supra* note 169; *Empire Realty Co. v. Metropolitan Toronto Assessment Commissioner*, [1968] 2 O.R. 388 (C.A.); and *Foxhead Inn Ltd. v. Regional Assessment Commissioner (Region No. 18)* (1977), 2 M.P.L.R. 66 (O.M.B.).

175 R.S.A. 2000, c. M-26, s. 289 and 322.

176 S.S. 1983-84, c. U-11, s. 238(4), as amended.

177 *Assessment Act*, R.S.O. 1990, c. A. 31, s. 19.1(1) and s. 19.2(1).

178 *Ontario Regional Assessment Commissioner, Region No. 11 v. Nesse Holdings Ltd.* (1984), 27 M.P.L.R. 253 (Ont. Div. Ct.), affirmed (1986), 54 O.R. (2d) 437 (C.A.), leave to appeal refused (1986), 58 O.R. (2d) 128 (S.C.C.), where the Divisional Court stated that the "recent free sale of subject property is generally accepted as the best means of establishing market value of that property."

accepted by the courts to determine market value. Those methods are: the comparative sales method, the income capitalization method and the cost replacement method.

The comparative sales method is the most desirable method of determining market value because it utilizes open market sales to estimate the market value of comparable properties. Under this method, the property being assessed is compared with the characteristics of similar properties in a sample of sales. Differences such as use, surrounding neighbourhood, age, quality, design and services are taken into account and adjustments are made to the market values of the properties in the sales sample so that the properties are comparable to the property being assessed. The adjusted market values of the sample properties are then used to provide an estimated market value or assessment for the property being assessed. This method, however, has the difficulty of having to acquire market data for comparative sales and having to make the appropriate adjustments, as in the case of a unique office building[179] or in the case of a manufacturing building for which there is no comparable market.[180]

A second method of assessing properties that is linked to market data is the income capitalization technique. This technique involves determining the price which the revenue-producing possibilities of the properties will command. In applying the income capitalization technique, the net income of the property is capitalized into an estimate of market value by calculating the present worth of the future income to be produced by the property.

Under the cost replacement method, market data on material costs and wage rates are used to provide a cost estimate of a hypothetical property that is an acceptable substitute for the property to be valued. The market value estimate of the structure is based on a comparison with the hypothetical substitute's replacement cost, less depreciation. Added to this is an estimate of the market value of the site to obtain a total market value estimate. The assumption built into this technique is that a buyer will not pay more for a property than it would cost him to acquire another property that was an acceptable substitute.

The cost replacement method is often used because it eliminates the problem of a lack of suitable market data although it is difficult to reflect the real replacement cost of older or unique buildings using this method. This method is also inappropriate where market data establishes that no one is willing to purchase the assets at anything close to replacement cost and the owner cannot be taken as willing to replace the assets at cost because of economic and functional obsolescence.[181]

---

179 *Montreal (City) v. Sun Life Assurance Co.* (1951), [1952] 2 D.L.R. 81 (Canada P.C.).

180 See *Office Specialty Ltd., supra*, note 169.

181 See *Swan Valley Foods Ltd. v. British Columbia (Assessment Appeal Board)* (1978), 6 M.P.L.R. 53 (B.C. S.C.). See also *Canso Seafoods Ltd. v. Canso (Town)* (1980), 13 M.P.L.R. 284 (N.S. C.A.), where the Court rejected an assessment based on replacement cost less depreciation on the grounds that the building was unsuitable for the owner.

The case of *Montreal (City) v. Sun Life Assurance Co.*[182] stated that any of the following five methods are appropriate to reach a market value figure: a recent free sale of the property; recent free sales of identical properties in the same neighbourhood and market; recent free sales of comparative properties (the comparative sales method); the price which the revenue-producing possibilities of the properties will command (the income capitalization technique); and finally, the depreciated replacement cost method. Regardless of the method used, it is required that the result approximate the market value of the property.

The Court in that case held that, in determining the market value, the assessor must take into account the present owner as a possible purchaser of the property. The assessor must attempt to determine what the owner would be willing to pay for the property if he were entering the market for a building to meet his requirements, or what he would be willing to expend in erecting a building in place of that which is being assessed. This view was upheld in the cases of *Office Specialty Ltd. v. Ontario Regional Assessment Commissioner, Region No. 14*[183] and *Swan Valley Foods Ltd. v. British Columbia (Assessment Appeal Board).*[184]

2. Equity

One of the purposes of the use of standards such as market value, fair value, or fair actual value is to ensure equity among taxpayers. Such a uniform standard of assessment will ensure that the property tax burden is not disproportionately assigned to a specific class or area of properties. Moreover, if market value or a similar standard is used then all properties are assessed equally and fairly because they will not have been assessed beyond their present worth.

In reality, however, market value assessments have not always been used. For example, in Ontario different classes of properties have historically been overvalued or undervalued in comparison to their real market value. As stated in the *Report of the Commission on the Reform of Property Taxation in Ontario*,[185] "Assessment values of industrial and commercial property are still seen to be higher than those of residential property; apartments are assessed at higher values than are single residential buildings." Moreover, as the Report indicated, historically there have been inequities in assessment among properties in the same class. The new tax system in Ontario has attempted to address these issues.

---

182 [1950] S.C.R. 220, affirmed (1951), [1952] 2 D.L.R. 81 (Canada P.C.).

183 *Supra*, note 169.

184 *Supra* note 181.

185 See Blair Report, *supra* note 149, vol. II at 17.

In 1996, The Report of the GTA Task Force[186] identified three types of problems with the previous system of property taxation:

(1) inequities within classes of property;

(2) inequities between classes of property; and

(3) inequities between municipalities.

The inequities within classes are the ones that give rise to appeals; inequities between municipalities are seen as driving businesses out of the expensive city core and into surrounding municipalities with lower assessment rates. The Task Force's proposed solution to the assessment ills in the Greater Toronto Area was, in part, to re-assess all property in the Greater Toronto Area on an "actual value" basis. While it was stated above that Actual Value Assessment (AVA) and Market Value Assessment (MVA) are synonymous, the Task Force set out some differences between the systems.

AVA provides greater stability — the system averages values over a three year period, it is updated annually (using a computer model) and land and buildings are assessed separately and buildings are valued on current use. MVA on the other hand, is supposed to use values for a single year but updates those values (by reassessing) only every four years (so that if your assessment year coincides with a market peak, that value is used for four years, long after the market has corrected itself) and also includes speculative value in assessments.

AVA is also supposed to provide greater reliability than MVA. While MVA is based on sale values of individual properties, AVA establishes base rates for 15 different "quality classes" province-wide and adjusts for the specifics of the home (or other building) (i.e. size, amenities). Assessments would be produced centrally, using "across the board" criteria, rather than locally and at the discretion of different provincially appointed assessors. The AVA method is also touted as putting in place more equitable assessment. In AVA the methods and criteria are the same province-wide, while in MVA different methodologies and different tax base years may be used in different municipalities. With the uniform imposition of AVA, taxpayers can more readily compare their assessment values with those of similarly situated property owners — with the MVA, it is currently more difficult to compare assessed values within a class, and between similar classes in different municipalities.

The AVA system has been used in Vancouver for over a decade and has met with great success. Only about 2 to 3% of the assessment base is appealed annually and of those only 10% are successful. Generally, the system has a high rate of acceptance.

---

186 Greater Toronto: Report of The GTA Task Force; January 1996, at 73-96.

With the creation of the current value system of property taxation, the creation of taxation ratios with fairness ranges, as well as the creation of the Municipal Property Assessment Corporation (MPAC), which is responsible for all property assessments in Ontario, the province of Ontario has sought to adopt the recommendations of the Golden Task Force. With municipalities in Ontario being forced to rely more and more on the property tax to fund municipal budgets, a solid and equitable assessment base is a must.

While it can be argued that the introduction of real market value or actual value in assessment may obviate the need for equity provisions as found in the court decisions and statutes,[187] the relationship between equity and market value, and which is the most important principle, has been an issue the courts have struggled with.

In the case of *Managerial Services Ltd. v. Regina (City)*,[188] the Court was interpreting *The Urban Municipality Act* (Saskatchewan), which stated in part that "the dominant and controlling factor in the assessment of land and buildings shall be equity."[189] In applying this provision the Court found that uniformity of assessment was the primary goal of assessment and that fair value was secondary to it. Similarly, in the case of *British Pacific Building Ltd. v. Alberta (Assessment Appeal Board)*,[190] the Court held that assessment of improvements, in the absence of regulations under s. 6 of *The Municipal Taxation Act*,[191] was governed by s. 7(2), which required fair actual value to be determined "in a manner that is fair and equitable with the level of value prescribed for use in determining the fair actual value of other improvements." A decision which did not reflect market value but which was fair and just in proportion to the value at which like improvements were assessed was therefore upheld.

The Ontario *Assessment Act* provides that reference shall be had to the value at which similar lands in the vicinity are assessed.[192] This has been interpreted as being a secondary consideration, such that it is more important to determine the correct current value than to create equity.[193] The Ontario

187 See *Empire Realty Co.*, *supra* note 174, which held that, when an assessor departed from market value as a standard, the onus was on the assessor to demonstrate that the assessment was fair and equitable to the taxpayer in that it resulted in the same distribution of the tax burden as would have been maintained if the assessments had been made strictly as required by the Act.

188 (1980), 14 M.P.L.R. 82 (Sask. C.A.).

189 R.S.S. 1978, c. U-10, s. 311, now S.S. 83-1984, c. U-11, s. 238(2).

190 (1973), 37 D.L.R. (3d) 314 (Alta. C.A.), affirmed (1974), 42 D.L.R. (3d) 318 (S.C.C.). See also *Strathcona No. 20 (County) v. Alberta (Assessment Appeal Board)* (1995), 89 W.A.C. 300 (C.A.).

191 R.S.A. 1980, c. M-31. As we have seen, however, the new Alberta *Municipal Government Act* has put in place a new assessment program designed to eliminate such problems.

192 R.S.O. 1990, c. A.31, s. 44(2).

193 See *Pierce v. Ontario Property Assessment Corp. Region No. 3*, [2000] O.A.R.B.D. No. 774 (Q.L.); see also *Dobsi v. Ontario Property Assessment Corp., Region No. 07*, [2000] O.A.R.B.D. No. 447, para 17.

Divisional Court held that where "there is good evidence of market value, as shown by a recent arm's length sale, the concept of equity and fairness amongst the taxpayers would ordinarily be satisfied."[194] The court has also emphasized that the new assessment regime aims to focus on the correctness of the current value. However, given the mandatory language used in s. 44(2) of "shall," it is the duty of the Court to have reference to the value at which similar lands in the vicinity are assessed.[195]

E. BUSINESS TAX

Businesses in all Canadian provinces pay some form of extra tax beyond that imposed on residential properties. The purpose of such a tax is to aid in shifting the burden of taxation from residential uses to business or commercial uses. Since businesses can deduct the payment of this tax as a business expense in calculating income tax[196] (while ordinarily a homeowner or residential tenant cannot make any such deduction), the burden of the tax is not generally excessive and its desirability is strengthened.

There are a number of bases upon which the business tax is imposed: rental value; personal property; square footage; storage capacity; assessed value of real property; and flat rate.[197] In Alberta, municipalities have options in choosing the base applied. In the Greater Toronto Area "commercial property" may be subject to additional provincial taxation under the *Commercial Concentration Tax Act*.[198]

In Alberta, the *Municipal Government Act* empowers municipalities to charge a business tax on the "gross annual rental value" of occupied premises.[199] It has been held that gross rental value should be calculated from the point of view of the owner or landlord of the property and that, in so doing, payments made on property taxes should not be considered. Payments for insurance, janitorial service and costs of utilities are similarly not relevant to value from the point of view of an owner and thus should not be considered in calculating gross rental value. Improvements added by the tenant which are fixtures that become part of the realty are relevant in determining the value of property but temporary and removable things which will continue

---

194 *Viva v. Ontario Property Assessment Corp.* (2001), 145 O.A.C. 358 (Div. Ct.).

195 *Krugarand Corp. v. Ontario Property Assessment Corp., Region No. 09*, [2002] O.J. No. 4727 (Div. Ct.).

196 *Income Tax Act*, R.S.C. 1985, c. 1 (5th Supp.), s. 9.

197 Karen Treff and David B. Perry, *Finances of the Nation: A Review of Expenditures and Revenues of the Federal, Provincial and Local Governments of Canada* (Toronto: Canadian Tax Foundation, 1998) at 6.16.

198 R.S.O. 1990, c. C.16.

199 R.S.A. 2000, c. M-26, s. 374(1)(b)(i). See also *The Municipal Assessment Act*, C.C.S.M., c. M226, s. 28; *Vancouver Charter*, S.B.C. 1953, c. 55, s. 280. While the Ontario *Assessment Act*, R.S.O. 1990, c. A.31, s. 7, previously provided for an additional "business assessment," this has been repealed.

to be owned by the tenant are not matters to be considered with regard to business tax.[200]

There are two main problems that arise in a consideration of the business tax: fixing the meaning of "carrying on a business, commercial or industrial undertaking" (depending on the exact wording of the legislation); and determining "who is carrying on the business."

1. Meaning of "Carrying on Business"

With respect to the first matter, the courts in a number of provinces appear to be moving towards a test of whether, in light of all the circumstances, the activity was a true commercial activity. In the case of *Forest Industrial Relations Ltd. v. Vancouver (City)*,[201] the British Columbia Supreme Court considered an appeal by Forest Industrial Relations Ltd. (F.I.R.) from a decision that it was carrying on a business. F.I.R. was incorporated pursuant to the *Company Act* (British Columbia)[202] and its membership consisted of 120 organizations which were engaged in the forest industry or related businesses and which entered into a subscription agreement for services. The services consisted primarily of representing subscribing members in all labour relations matters. The company also assisted members in interpreting federal and provincial statutes and regulations, carrying out job evaluations and rate determination studies and negotiations in connection with certain wage rates. However, it did not make a profit, no dividends had ever been declared, it was exempted from income tax as a non-profit organization and it provided its services to members at cost.

The Court held, following *Windsor-Essex County Real Estate Board v. Windsor (City)*[203] that the test with respect to liability under the *Vancouver Charter*[204] was whether the activity in question was a truly commercial activity and not whether there had been an intent to make profit. F.I.R. was properly assessed for business tax as its activities were truly commercial although they were managerial rather than operational or productive in nature. The performance of the functions on a cost rather than profit basis did not alter their commercial nature.

The test for "carrying on business" appears to be shifting from one of merely examining the preponderate purpose of the occupants to one of determining the nature of the activity carried on. In the case of *R. v. Victoria*

---

200 *Hudson's Bay Co. v. Calgary (City)* (1979), 10 M.P.L.R. 153 (Alta. T.D.), reversed (1980), 12 M.P.L.R. 88 (Alta. C.A.).

201 (1978), 7 M.P.L.R. 1 (B.C. S.C.), affirmed (1979), 10 B.C.L.R. 180 (C.A.).

202 R.S.B.C. 1979, c. 59.

203 (1974), 6 O.R. (2d) 21, 51 D.L.R. (3d) 665 (C.A.), leave to appeal refused (1976), 1976 CarswellOnt 895 (S.C.C.).

204 S.B.C. 1953, c. 55, s. 280.

(City),[205] the Court explicitly rejected the preponderate purpose test. In determining whether the Crown was carrying on business, the Court rejected the view that the purpose of all government activity was serving the public and stated that the Crown's activity must be examined in totality. The Court recognized that the Crown was often engaged in private sector activity and that it was appropriate that it be liable to certain taxes while involved in those activities.[206] This problem, in the absence of express legislation, may be resolved by the decision of the Supreme Court of Canada in *Ontario Regional Assessment Commissioner v. Caisse populaire de Hearst Ltée* in which the Supreme Court held that the appropriate test is not whether an activity is of a commercial nature but whether its preponderate purpose is the making of a profit.[207]

2. Determining Who is Carrying on the Business

In *Saga Canadian Management Services Ltd. v. Ottawa (City)*[208] the Court dealt with the issue of whether the applicant, which provided food services, was carrying on a business or merely managing a business under a master-servant relationship. In seeking to determine the issue, the Court examined the degree of control exercised by the owner of the premises, the ownership of the equipment, the risk of loss and the chance of profit.

The Court in *Saga* also pointed out that there must be occupancy or use of the land for the purpose of carrying on business although that use need not be exclusive. There need only be a right to occupy or use the land without someone else, such as the landowner, having a simultaneous right to carry on the same business in the same location. In short, for liability for business assessment there must be an occupation sufficiently exclusive to enable the occupier to carry on the commercial activity. In *Saga*, the Court found that, although the owners of the premises used by Saga for the business purposes of providing food services had a right to use those premises, that right did not interfere with Saga's occupancy for those business purposes.

In *Casco Terminals Ltd. v. Vancouver (City)*,[209] the British Columbia Court of Appeal distinguished the *Saga* case and stated that exclusiveness, paramountcy or dominance of a taxpayer's use of a property is not conclusive of liability for business tax. The liability for tax turned on whether the

205 (1979), 10 M.P.L.R. 264 (B.C. C.A.).

206 See also McNairn *Governmental and Intergovernment Immunity in Australia and Canada* (Toronto, 1977), at 163, where it is argued that the Crown, when engaging in a commercial activity, should be subject to business tax. The Crown should not receive the hidden subsidies that business tax exemptions would provide.

207 [1983] 1 S.C.R. 57.

208 (1977), 16 O.R. (2d) 65 (H.C.). See also *Delta Parking Systems Ltd. supra* note 89, and *Mowat v. Lorne Murphy Foods Ltd.* (1971), [1972] 1 O.R. 559 (C.A.) and *Toronto (Metropolitan) v. Thompson* (1984), 25 M.P.L.R. 88 (Ont. H.C.) on this issue.

209 (1978), 8 B.C.L.R. 177 (C.A.).

occupation or use is such as to render it liable for assessment. In this case, the respondents were independent contractors handling goods on piers owned by the National Harbours Board, a Crown corporation. The court stated that the words "occupying or using" should not be applied literally, but rather so as to reach practical and sensible solutions in each case. The respondents worked on the board's piers, but could not be said to occupy or use the property for the purpose of carrying on business.

Another issue, and one related to the question of which business is being carried on and for what purpose, is whether and in what circumstances a subsidiary or related corporation will be found to be occupying or using their premises for the purposes of and in connection with the business of the parent or related corporation.

This issue arose in the case of *Aluminum Co. of Canada v. Ontario Regional Assessment Commissioner, Region No. 5*[210] where the court had to determine whether the manufacturing company which owned the land, or the "related" but legally separate research and development company, was the proper party for assessment purposes. In that case, the choice of party was significant, as the tax rate for research firms was substantially lower. The Court looked to the fact that the research firm was the "sole occupier" of the site, that it was legally independent of the manufacturing company, that it was independent business-wise and that the business carried on was not the same as that of the parent. The Court concluded that the research firm was the proper party to be assessed, and at the lower rate.

The area of business assessment, like municipal taxation and assessment generally, is closely controlled at the provincial level of government. The decisions are generally narrow and technical.[211] There is little opportunity for municipalities to use their one independent source of revenue to play a substantial policy role or to use assessment and taxation to further municipal goals. Municipalities are, of course, unable to amend provincial legislation after judicial pronouncements on assessment or taxation. Although the revenue is independent in that municipalities levy the tax, the base, scope and the burden of taxation is generally in the hands of provincial governments.

There have been many suggestions for reform of this situation. A municipal income tax, a share of the provincial income tax revenue, transfers of revenues from various sources of taxation, a municipal sales tax and provincial municipal funding agreements are all examples of suggestions to improve on the existing situation which has resulted in municipalities being "puppets on a shoestring."[212]

---

210 (1984), 26 M.P.L.R. 1 (Ont. H.C.), affirmed (1986), 54 O.R. (2d) 249 (Div. Ct.). For a contrary result see *Seagram (Seagrams) Distillers (Ontario) Ltd. v. Ontario Regional Assessment Commissioner, Regions Nos. 9 & 10* (1986), 54 O.R. (2d) 289 (Div. Ct.), affirmed (1988), 1988 CarswellOnt 1948 (S.C.C.).

211 The case of *R. v. Victoria (City)*, *supra* note 205 is a desirable exception to this trend.

212 See Canadian Federation of Mayors and Municipalities, *Puppets on a Shoestring: The Effects on Municipal Government of Canada's System of Public Finance* (Ottawa, 1976).

It must be recognized that, given the legal inferiority of the municipal level of government and the lack of municipal constitutional status, nothing can be done to guarantee municipalities a truly independent and viable source of revenue without change to the current system. The value of local government being able to respond to local needs and desires must be recognized and municipal financial independence must be made possible in order to reach that goal.[213]

F. APPEALS

Various routes of appeal exist among the provinces. In Ontario, under the *Assessment Act*,[214] there are basically two routes. Section 46(1) provides that the municipality, assessment corporation or any person assessed may apply to the Superior Court of Justice for the determination of any matter relating to the assessment, except a matter that could be the subject of a complaint under subs. 40(1) or a determination that lands are conservation lands for the purposes of paragraph 25 of subs. 3 (1). Under s. 46(4), there is a further right of appeal to the Divisional Court.

Under the other route, the purpose is to ensure the administrative integrity of the assessment roll. The initial complaint is to the Assessment Review Board and it must concern either that the current value of the person's land or another person's land is incorrect; the person or another person was wrongly placed on or omitted from the assessment roll; the person or another person was wrongly placed on or omitted from the roll in respect of school support; the classification of the person's land or another person's land is incorrect; or for land, portions of which are in different classes of real property, the determination of the share of the value of the land that is attributable to each class is incorrect.[215] Under s. 43.1(1), the decision of the Assessment Review Board can be appealed to the Divisional Court, with leave of the Divisional Court, on a question of law. Section 44 provides that all appeals under this route permit the Assessment Review Board or the court to "reopen the whole question of assessment so that omissions from, or errors in the assessment roll may be corrected, and the amount for which the assessment should be made, and the person or persons who should be assessed therefor may be placed upon the roll, and if necessary the roll of the municipality, even if returned as finally revised, may be opened so as to make it correct in accordance with the findings made on appeal."

Nova Scotia also has an approach with two routes. Its administrative tribunal route involves a regional assessment appeal court with a further

---

213 It is clear that all sources of municipally controlled revenue have not been covered here. Other important sources of municipal revenue are lot levies, development charges and the imposition of fees for rezoning. These are discussed in Chapter 6.

214 R.S.O. 1990, c. A.31.

215 *Ibid.* at s. 40 (1).

appeal to the Nova Scotia Utility and Review Board.[216] Alberta's system is similar. A complaint must be made to a municipal assessment review board, from which an appeal lies to the Municipal Government Board.[217] In British Columbia, property assessment review panels review property assessments. Property owners may appeal decisions made by a property assessment review panel to the Assessment Appeal Board and further to the Supreme Court of British Columbia.[218] In Saskatchewan, the Saskatchewan Municipal Board hears appeals from the Boards of Revision.[219] The New Brunswick *Assessment Act* provides for both a referral to the Director of Assessment and an appeal to the Regional Assessment Review Board.[220] Appeals from the Boards of Revision in Manitoba go either to the Municipal Board, if the issue is one of amount of assessment, or to the Court of Queen's Bench, if the issue is one of liability.[221]

The lines of divergence in the appeal routes indicate the constitutional element involved. Only the "section 96 courts" (courts appointed by the federal governments) have final binding power for taxation — that is, liability issues.[222] Very clear words in a statute are generally required before provincial tribunals can be seen as having jurisdiction to hear preliminary questions of liability, although they may be empowered to make preliminary judicial determinations to discharge their administrative duties.[223]

216 *Assessment Act*, R.S.N.S. 1989, c. 23, ss. 62-97, as amended.

217 The *Municipal Government Act*, R.S.A. 2000, c. M-26, ss. 454 and 460.

218 *Assessment Act*, R.S.B.C. 1996, c. 20, ss. 31, 32, 43, 50, 64 and 65.

219 *The Urban Municipality Act, 1984*, S.S. 1983-84, c. U-11, ss. 251 and 260.

220 *Assessment Act*, R.S.N.B. 1973, c. A-14, ss. 25 and 27.

221 *The Municipal Assessment Act*, C.C.S.M., c. M-226, ss 56(1) and 56(2).

222 *Constitution Act*, 1867, (U.K.) c. 3, s. 96.

223 See *Downtown Church Workers' Assn. v. Ontario Regional Assessment Commissioner, Region No. 7* (1978), 5 M.P.L.R. 261 (Div. Ct.), affirmed (1979), 28 O.R. (2d) 662 (note) (C.A.), at 266, 269 [M.P.L.R.]; but see *Ontario Regional Assessment Commissioner, Region 23 v. Coombs* (1986), 19 O.M.B.R. 196 (Div. Ct.) where the majority of the Court held that the Ontario Municipal Board had jurisdiction to determine if the occupier was "carrying on a business" and therefore liable for business assessment.

4

The Exercise of Municipal Authority and Judicial Review

A. INTRODUCTION

The purpose of this chapter and the two subsequent chapters is to examine the exercise of municipal authority and the legal constraints placed on municipalities in the exercise of their powers. These constraints are constitutional, legislative and judicial in origin and include restraints imposed by the *Canadian Charter of Rights and Freedoms.*[1] They arise from the Constitution and the legally inferior status of municipal governments. As delegates of provincial power, municipalities are in no way sovereign and must receive their authority from provincial legislatures. In this respect, municipalities are in law no different in status from other provincial delegatees and, likewise are restricted to exercising only those powers that are granted to them by the legislature. However, unlike most other delegates of provincial powers, municipalities are directly accountable to the electorate under the system of municipal elections. This critical difference raises the issue as to whether municipalities should be accorded greater freedom in the exercise of their authority in order to pursue local objectives.

Legislation granting authority to municipalities tends to be detailed, placing narrow limits on what municipalities can do, and severely restricting the scope of municipalities to initiate policy. This legislative approach towards municipalities has been paralleled by a similar judicial approach. There are many judicial doctrines that limit the authority of municipalities to function as autonomous levels of government. Doctrines such as "express authority," "the rule against delegation" and "paramountcy of provincial policy" all limit the ability of municipal councils to function as complete legislative bodies. Restrictions on municipal authority and the judicial review of that authority coupled with the structural and financial limitations discussed earlier have traditionally resulted in local governments that function largely as administrators of provincial policy.

---

1 Schedule B to the *Canada Act 1982* (U.K.) 1982, c. 11.

As discussed below, the courts have recently begun to apply a more purposive approach towards the interpretation of municipal legislation suggesting a more flexible judicial attitude towards municipal policy making. Provincial legislatures have also shown signs of providing municipalities with a broader scope of powers, through such initiatives as extending so-called "natural person powers" to municipalities. This deferential attitude towards municipal policy making powers is based partly on the recognition of the democratic legitimacy of local governments.

B. THE EXERCISE OF MUNICIPAL POWERS

Municipalities, as corporate entities, can only exercise their powers through the corporate acts of council, usually through the passing of a municipal by-law or by council resolution. The difference between a by-law and resolution is one of formality. By-laws, before they can become effective, must be authenticated by being sealed and signed by the head of council and the clerk of the municipality. By-laws are usually employed when council wants the enactment to have a continuing regulatory effect, whereas a resolution is a statement of council's intent respecting specific circumstances. The choice of method to employ depends largely upon the statutory requirements of the jurisdiction and is left to the discretion of council.

In Ontario, for example, the *Municipal Act* expressly provides that the powers of council are to be exercised by by-law, unless otherwise provided.[2] The failure to enact a by-law where one is required results in there being no valid corporate act. Despite this seemingly straightforward direction, the courts have established certain exceptions to this requirement beyond those permitted by statutory provisions. In particular, the discharge of a statutory duty, the appointment or dismissal of employees and matters of everyday occurrence or matters of unimportant or trifling character, have been found not to require the enactment of by-laws.[3]

If the legislative intent of requiring certain acts to be exercised by way of by-law were to ensure that council exercise its authority with appropriate care and deliberation, then a consideration of the gravity of the enactment and its potential impact on the electorate would be more fitting. In this regard, the courts have also attempted to draw a distinction between administrative and legislative acts of council, with only the latter requiring the passing of a by-law.[4] Unfortunately, this distinction is difficult to establish and in this context appears to be somewhat circular in that a legislative act of council is the passing of a by-law and to determine whether a by-law needs to be passed with reference to its legislative character is not helpful. It is also questionable

2 For example, see *Municipal Act, 2001*, S.O. 2001, c. 25, s. 5(3).

3 *Apex Auto Supply Co. v. Hamilton (City)* (1925), 28 O.W.N. 265 (H.C.); *MacKay v. Toronto (City)* (1919), [1920] A.C. 208 (Canada P.C.) at 213-14.

4 *Passmore v. St. Marys (Town)* (1984), 47 O.R. (2d) 262 (H.C.).

whether such a distinction is justified by the wording of the Ontario statute. These judicial constructions are an indication of the court's reluctance to invalidate the acts of municipal council where their intent is clear simply on the basis of a lack of formality.

Given the understandable judicial reticence in defeating the express intent of Council, Ontario would be wise to adopt the approach taken by jurisdictions, such as Alberta and Manitoba, where the legislation provides that unless a by-law is expressly required, a resolution is sufficient to bind council.[5] This approach essentially leaves the decision as to the mode of exercise of its powers to Council.

Council itself must exercise the powers of granted to it, unless there is a specific statutory provision allowing for the delegation of powers. Thus, for example, the indoor management rule,[6] which provides that certain corporate officers may bind a business corporation *vis à vis* a third party, notwithstanding a lack of formal authorization, does not apply to municipalities.[7] There may be other procedural requirements, such as the giving of notice, the proper conduct of meetings and the appropriate publication or promulgation of by-laws, as may be set out in the legislation. Furthermore, it is a general requirement of the exercise of municipal powers that those powers be exercised in good faith and in the interests of the inhabitants of the municipality. As discussed below, the judicial approach to applying these various doctrines has a dramatic impact on municipal policy making powers.

C. LEGISLATIVE RESTRICTIONS AND PROVINCIAL CONTROL

The ability to provide services and make regulations regarding the provision of services is an integral aspect of government. The ability to develop policy respecting service delivery can be important only in the context of relatively wide powers to decide what services are to be delivered and the method by which delivery is to occur. That is, the ability to deliver a service is of diminished importance in responding to local concerns, if senior levels of government with respect to the particular service have already formulated policy. Indeed, the ability to govern is of decreasing value to the extent that such ability is narrowed by policies and decisions already made.

The municipal-provincial relationship with respect to the delivery of services can be seen as a spectrum. At one end of the spectrum, the municipality has near complete authority to determine policy and set priorities within a wide area of jurisdiction without interference from senior levels of govern-

---

5 *Municipal Government Act*, R.S.A. 2000, c. M-26, s.180; *Municipal Act*, S.M. 1996, c. 58, C.C.S.M. c. M225, s. 81.

6 See *Business Corporations Act*, R.S.O. 1990, c. B.16, s. 19.

7 *Collins v. Renfrew Hydro-Electric Commission*, [1947] O.R. 477 (H.C.), affirmed (1947), [1948] O.R. 29 (C.A.).

ment. Coming closest to this end of the spectrum are certain American jurisdictions where municipalities are given wide grants of power protected by state constitutions. Within those grants of power, municipalities are supreme and are viewed as legislative bodies responsible for their own decisions. In this regard, municipalities operate as a true level of government, restricted in their actions only by constitutional constraints.[8]

This model, often referred to as the "home rule" model, can be viewed as coming closest to enabling municipalities to best reflect local values and needs, at least on a purely majoritarian basis. Its principal advantages are that it allows municipalities the freedom to adopt the structure and function of local government that is best suited to the requirements of the municipality, it prevents senior levels of government from engaging in partisan political interference, and allows municipalities to determine the nature and scope of municipal services in accordance with local needs.

At the other end of the spectrum, the municipality is primarily an administrative arm of the province with very limited ability to initiate policy or "legislation" independently. Policy decisions are made at the provincial level through provincial acts and regulations with little scope for policy initiative at the municipal level. This approach would also carve out areas of jurisdiction from municipal councils and place them with special purpose bodies. Municipalities, in exercising their authority under such an approach, would essentially be exercising administrative powers, responsible for the implementation of superior legislation already enacted at the provincial level, but not for the creation of policy at the local level. At this end of the spectrum, the municipality lacks autonomy and is an agent of the provincial government.

It is clear that the models of local government adopted in Canada at the turn of the nineteenth century come closer to municipal governance at this latter end of the spectrum. Many of the structural and financial limitations remain reflective of this narrow view of local government autonomy. Since municipal councils, under this model, exercise their discretion within narrowly defined boundaries, municipal decision making tends to be more technocratic and "non-political." This model allows for centralized control over policy issues that affect geographic areas beyond municipal boundaries or that require uniform standards or practices. The need for at least some broader based oversight is evident in the coordination problems associated with the rise of metropolitan areas over the last half century.[9]

In between these two poles is a third approach that allows for a fair degree of latitude with respect to municipal authority for making policies respecting service delivery and regulation while ensuring that the senior levels of government also have input in the process either through the establishment of minimum standards, provincial intervention in restricted situations where

---

8 Discussed in Osbourne M. Reynolds, *Jr. Handbook of Local Government Law,* 2d ed. (St. Paul, Minn.:West Group, 2001) at ss. 35-37.

9 Discussed in Chapter 2, *supra.*

it perceives guidance to be necessary, or restricting the wide municipal policy role in certain matters. The challenge here is, of course, determining the level of autonomy that should be granted to municipalities and the basis for imposing stricter provincial controls in particular areas.

In assessing these models in a Canadian context, it is clear that Canadian municipalities are not subject to home rule and have no constitutional status, and are not at all likely to have such status conferred upon them.[10] Furthermore, the "home rule" experience in America suggests that unadulterated local self government is not without its problems. The "home rule" system has led to ongoing disputes between state and local governments over state and municipal responsibilities and the courts are still struggling to differentiate between these roles.[11] There have been significant instances of local government mismanagement and corruption which goes unchecked by state legislatures. Moreover, in the absence of guidance from senior levels of government metropolitan and inter-municipal co-ordination has also been problematic.[12]

In Canada, it can be seen that provincial controls are desirable in some matters to maintain minimum standards. It may be appropriate for provincial controls, direct or through special purpose bodies, to provide a check against local government excesses and can, therefore, be important in protecting against financial mismanagement or abuses of minority rights. If one views library, welfare or child services as benefits for particular interest groups which the majority in a given community might wish to reduce, then it would seem desirable to make such a decision a difficult one to implement in order to protect those minorities from the local majority whose paramount concerns might be roads, garbage, or sewage collection.[13] In short, provincial control and regulation can provide for checks and balances within the governmental system (and ensure that there will be reasonable compromises and trade-offs) by reducing the ability of councils to respond to short term pressures, particularly those related to the reduction or maintenance of property tax levels.

On the other hand, a system of tight provincial oversight is clearly based on the false premise that many local decisions are of an objective, "non-political" nature. Decisions to build roads instead of transit systems, or to provide day care services, but not homeless shelters are political decisions and not objective or expert decisions. Where council's ability to reflect local political choice is restricted through tight provincial control, either directly through regulatory instruments or indirectly through, for example, the system

10 For example, a federal government committee (chaired by Judy Sgro, Lib. M.P.) immediately ruled out any constitutional changes when examining possible steps to improve the development of Canadian cities. *Globe and Mail*, August 8, 2001 "Who speaks for the cities? The premiers sure don't. Canada's cities are in decline and need new political tools to save themselves" Jane Jacobs and Alan Broadbent.

11 Reynolds, *supra*, note 8 at §§ 38-43.

12 *Ibid.* at 111.

13 *Ibid.* at 70.

of conditional grants, it gives a false sense of accountability. The concerns respecting the protection of minority rights remain important, but are often mitigated by the "log-rolling" and compromise that occur in larger municipalities.[14]

A highly centralized system of local government policy making also defeats the democratic goal of local governments being able to respond to the particular needs and values of local communities. This goal is often described as the principle of "subsidiarity," and has recently been recognized by the Supreme Court of Canada where the principle was described as follows: "This is the proposition that law-making and implementation are often best achieved at a level of government that is not only effective, but also closest to the citizens affected and thus most responsive to their needs, to local distinctiveness and to population diversity."[15] Thus, to the extent a service can be effectively and efficiently delivered at the local level, the authority to make determinations respecting service delivery should reside at that level, being closer to the electorate.

While the need to balance municipal autonomy with some restricted central government oversight is widely acknowledged, the experience in Canada with determining the appropriate roles and responsibilities between levels of government has been confusing and unprincipled. For example, the 1996 Report of the Greater Toronto Area Task Force notes that in Ontario numerous reports prepared over the last 30 years have recommended the disentanglement of municipal and provincial services, but the result has been increasing duplication, inefficiency and a lack of accountability.[16]

One such report, undertaken for the Royal Commission on Metropolitan Toronto, indicated that "the relationship between the province and the municipalities in Metropolitan Toronto is one in which the province oversees or controls virtually all major services."[17] Of the 131 services reviewed in the study, only 30 could be exclusively assigned to the municipal level as services for which the municipality sets standards and provides for municipal delivery and administration. Thirty-eight matters could be viewed as being under the authority of special purpose bodies, which in turn were responsible to the province since the province set the standards. Thirty-three were categorized as being administered by the municipalities under the supervision of the province, which set standards for the service.[18] Moreover, it could be argued that many of those 30 matters assigned exclusively to the municipalities were relatively unimportant: removing ice and snow free of charge; regulating heat

---

14 "Log-rolling" is the political practice of trading one's support for a particular initiative for reciprocal support on another issue.

15 *114957 Canada Ltée (Spray-Tech, Société d'arrosage) v. Hudson (Ville)*, [2001] 2 S.C.R. 241, at 249.

16 Greater Toronto: Report of the GTA Task Force (Golden Report), January 1996.

17 See Jaffrey and Makuch, "Local Decision-Making and Administration", A Study for the Royal Commission on Metropolitan Toronto (Toronto, 1977) at 72.

18 *Ibid.*

in residential premises; dog licensing and controlling nuisances. The "downloading" of services from provincial governments to local municipalities has seen municipalities assume financial responsibility over matters such as welfare payments and social housing, notwithstanding the income redistributive aspect of these services. Arguably, because the province draws from a much larger income pool, it is better able to redistribute resources.[19]

If one applies the principle of subsidiarity to the distribution of powers, a more principled result would emerge. Municipalities would be responsible for those services that are clearly of local interest and where determination of local preferences is important. Because inter-regional and income redistributive services cannot be most effectively delivered at the local level, provincial governments should have primary responsibility for these services. The advantage of the subsidiarity principle is that it is flexible and can evolve with the requirements of government without being completely *ad hoc* and thereby sacrificing accountability.

D. JUDICIAL REVIEW

It is clear that Canadian municipalities have no status of their own, no inherent jurisdiction, and even no right to exist except by virtue of provincial fiat. There was no municipal representation or involvement in the formulation of the *British North America Act*. Indeed the only reference to municipalities in that Act is a provision placing them under provincial jurisdiction.[20] Municipalities are, therefore, from a historical perspective, both legally and constitutionally inferior bodies under the jurisdiction of the province. They have no constitutional protection whatsoever against provincial laws that change their structures, functions and financial resources without their consent.[21] The municipality is "wholly a creature of the [provincial] legislature, it has no abstract rights — it derives all powers from statute. . ."[22]

A municipality's legally inferior position places it in a very different position from senior levels of government, in that, at the provincial or federal level, government decisions are only subject to review from a constitutional standpoint. In all other respects, they are sovereign. Municipalities, on the other hand, as entities with a defined jurisdictional sphere, are required to act within their appointed jurisdictional limits and failure to do so may result in the courts quashing the municipal action as being *ultra vires*, or beyond its legal competence. As a result of this status, there has been a great amount of

---

19 Report of the GTA Task Force, *supra* note 16.

20 *Constitution Act, 1867*, 30 & 31 Victoria c. 3, s. 92(8) (formerly the *British North America Act, 1867*).

21 See *East York (Borough) v. Ontario (Attorney General)* (1997), 34 O.R. (3d) 789 (Gen. Div.), affirmed (1997), 36 O.R. (3d) 733 (C.A.), leave to appeal to S.C.C. dismissed [1998] 1 S.C.R. vii.

22 *Smith v. London (City)* (1909), 20 O.L.R. 133 (Div. Ct.).

judicial consideration of the scope of municipal powers in the context of challenges to the exercise of municipal authority as being *ultra vires*, that is, beyond their jurisdiction.

In this regard, there have been two quite distinct approaches to the interpretation of municipal legislation in Canada. Traditionally, the courts have adopted a narrow, interventionist approach to the review of municipal decision-making, treating municipalities no differently than other statutory bodies exercising a delegated authority. In other instances, the courts have adopted a more expansive approach in which the courts appear to have recognized the distinct democratic attributes of municipal decision making and are more prepared to examine statutory grants of power from a purposive perspective.[23]

1. Restrictive Interpretation – The Express Authority Doctrine

As a result of this inferior legal position, the courts have traditionally interpreted statutes respecting grants of power to municipalities narrowly. This approach may be described as "Dillon's rule" (as it was set out in *Dillon on Municipal Corporations)*, or the "express authority doctrine," which states that a municipality may exercise only those powers expressly conferred by statute, those powers necessarily or fairly implied by the expressed power in the statute, and those powers essential to, and not merely convenient for, the effectuation of the purposes of the corporation.[24] In the event of some reasonable doubt as to the existence of a municipal power, the approach was to resolve the doubt against the municipal corporation.[25]

This approach can be traced historically from the origins of local government in England and from administrative bodies created by royal prerogative with powers mostly exercised by non-elected officials, such as magistrates or Justices of the Peace. In this regard, the only recourse available to an aggrieved citizen was through the courts. Given the lack of democratic accountability, the courts understandably took a more active role in overseeing the actions of local decision makers. As a consequence, as one author notes:

> The courts exercised a broad, supervisory jurisdiction in the nature of appellate review and had a direct role in defining and shaping local government authority. They exercised a wholesale judgment on the "reasonableness" of the actions of

---

23 *Rogers v. Toronto (City)* (1915), 33 O.L.R. 89 (H.C.) at 91.

24 See *Ottawa Electric Light Co. v. Ottawa (City)* (1906), 12 O.L.R. 290 (C.A.), at 299, where Dillon, *Commentary on Municipal Corporations*, 4th ed. was quoted with approval by the Ontario Court of Appeal.

25 *Ottawa Electric, ibid.* at 299.

these bodies and, by evolution of the decisional law, defined the limits of their powers.[26]

This pro-interventionist approach has resulted in the courts espousing a strict interpretation approach to the exercise of municipal authority. The Ontario Court of Appeal articulated this approach in *Merritt v. Toronto (City)*, stating, "Municipal corporations, in the exercise of the statutory powers conferred upon them to make by-laws, should be confined strictly within the limits of their authority, and all attempts on their parts to exceed it should be firmly repelled by the Courts."[27] The Supreme Court of Canada voiced a similarly restrictive view in *Sun Oil Co. v. Verdun (City)*, where Fauteux J., states that "municipalities derive their legislative powers from the provincial Legislature and must, consequently, frame their by-laws strictly within the scope delegated to them by the Legislature."[28] In an early example of this approach to municipal authority, provincial legislation which enabled a municipality to produce, manufacture, use or supply electricity was found not to enable that municipality to purchase electricity in order to use and supply it.[29] Similarly, authority in the *Vancouver Charter* to regulate noises was found not to enable the City to prohibit noises between certain hours notwithstanding the existence of the following power: "The Council, in addition to the powers specifically allotted to it, shall have power to do all such things as are incidental or conducive to the exercise of the allotted powers."[30]

Perhaps the most interesting examples are those relating to the interpretation of the wide plenary powers granted to municipalities, which have been viewed by the courts as having very little effect. The *Vancouver Charter*, for example, provides that the "Council may provide for the good rule and government of the City."[31] Such a provision, in the absence of established rules of statutory construction, arguably would grant to the City wide control over local matters. Similar "omnibus" or residual power provisions appear in provincial legislation across the country.[32] For example, the *Municipal Act* (Ontario) contains a general grant of power to municipalities which states that "a municipality may regulate matters not specifically provided for by this Act or any other Act for purposes related to the health, safety and well-

---

26 Ann MacDonald, "In the Public Interest: Judicial Review of Local Government," 9 Queens L.J. 62 at 90.

27 (1895), 22 O.A.R. 205 (C.A.) at 207.

28 (1951), [1952] 1 S.C.R. 222 at 228.

29 See *Ottawa Electric, supra*, note 24.

30 See *Pride Cleaners & Dyers Ltd., Re* (1964), 50 W.W.R. 645, 49 D.L.R. (2d) 752 (B.C. S.C.).

31 S.B.C. 1953, c. 55, s. 189.

32 *Municipal Government Act*, R.S.A. 2000, c. M-26, ss. 3(c) and 7; *Local Government Act*, R.S.B.C. 1996, c. 323, s. 249; *Municipal Act*, S.M. 1996, c.58, C.C.S.M. c.M225, ss. 232 and 233, *Municipalities Act*, R.S.N.B. 1973, c. M-22, s.190(2); *Cities, Towns and Villages Act*, R.S.N.W.T. 1988, c.C-8, ss. 54 and 102; *Municipal Act, 2001*, S.O. 2001, c. 25, s. 102; *Cities and Towns Act*, R.S.Q., c. C-19, s. 410(1); *Municipal Act*, S.Y. 1998, c. 19, s. 271.

being of the inhabitants of the municipality."[33] This provision has been interpreted as granting virtually no power at all.

In the leading case on this matter, *Morrison v. Kingston (City)*,[34] the Court stated that very few subjects falling within the ambit of local government are left to the general provisions of the section in question. In addition, the Court stated that matters of "health" are generally dealt with by provincial legislation affecting health, and that "morality" is generally dealt with in the *Criminal Code*, so that these areas are removed from the sphere of municipal legislation. The Court further held that the power to legislate for the "welfare" of the inhabitants is too vague and general to admit of definition, and may mean so much that it probably means very little.[35] It cannot include powers that are otherwise specifically given, nor can it be taken to confer unlimited and unrestrained power.

2. Expansive Interpretation — Benevolent Construction

The opposing approach to the interpretation of municipal legislation is often described as being one of "benevolent construction" and is exemplified by the following passage from *Hamilton Distillery Co. v. Hamilton (City)*:

> In interpreting this legislation I would not desire to apply the technical or strict canons of construction sometimes applied to legislation authorizing taxation. I think the sections are, considering the subject matter and the intention obviously in view, entitled to a broad and reasonable if not, as Lord Chief Justice Russell said in *Kruse v. Johnson*, [1898] 2 Q.B. 91 (Eng. Div. Ct.), at p. 99, "a benevolent construction," and if the language used fell short of expressly conferring the powers claimed, but did confer them by a fair and reasonable implication, I would not hesitate to adopt the construction sanctioned by the implication. [36]

A further early articulation of a more liberal approach to the interpretation of municipal powers is found in *Howard v. Toronto (City)*, where the Ontario Court of Appeal stated, "The question of the relative balance of convenience or detriment to different persons is a matter which the Legislature has committed to the consideration and determination of the municipal council, and their judgment on that question, if *bona fide* exercised in what they believe to be the public interest, will not be interfered with by the court. . ."[37]

---

33 S.O. 2001, c. 25, s. 130.

34 (1937), [1938] O.R. 21, 69 C.C.C. 251, [1937] 4 D.L.R. 740 (C.A.). See also *Trumble v. Kapuskasing (Town)* (1986), 57 O.R. (2d) 139, 32 D.L.R. (4th) 545 (H.C.), additional reasons at (1986), 34 D.L.R. (4th) 545 at 560 (Ont. H.C.).

35 The recent amendments to the *Municipal Act, 2001* removed "welfare" from this general grant of power.

36 [1907] 38 S.C.R. 239.

37 (1928), 61 O.L.R. 563 (C.A.), at 575.

3. The Emergence of a Rational Approach

The result of these two approaches to municipal legislation was a significant degree of conceptual confusion and inconsistency in the interpretation of municipal legislation. Consider the following examples. In *Christie Taxi Ltd. v. Doran*,[38] the Ontario Court of Appeal held that the power to regulate taxi cabs did not include a power to regulate the financial arrangements between owners and cab drivers. Metropolitan Toronto Council enacted a by-law which made it an offence for owners to require their taxi drivers to pay into an accident fund or other such fund. The court reasoned that in order for a by-law to be considered valid legislation under the *Municipal Act*, a by-law must regulate and govern the manner in which the business is carried on. As the sole purpose of this by-law was to regulate financial arrangements, it was *ultra vires* the municipality.

A similar approach was taken by the Ontario Court of Appeal in *Stadium Corp. of Ontario v. Toronto (City).*[39] In that case, City Council passed a by-law that purported to prohibit the use of exotic animals in circuses in the City. The authority for such a by-law was claimed to arise under a general grant of power which permits municipalities to pass by-laws for "prohibiting or regulating the keeping of animals...."[40] The Court declared the by-law invalid on the basis that the power to regulate the keeping of animals under the *Municipal Act* did not extend to regulating in the interests of animal welfare since the legislature had assigned this aspect of animal regulation to the SPCA under the *Society for the Prevention of Cruelty to Animals Act*. Moreover, a power to regulate circuses was not granted under this section but rather under the *Municipality of Metropolitan Toronto Act* to Metropolitan Toronto. In these cases, the Courts appear to be ignoring the ordinary meaning of the statutory language, which at the very least requires the Court to justify its strict approach with reference to some principle beyond the express authority doctrine (an essentially circular argument).

The use of more liberal approaches has also lacked a degree of analytical rigor. An illustrative example is found in the case of *E. & J. Murphy Ltd. v. Victoria (City)*,[41] where the British Columbia Supreme Court upheld a by-law of the City of Victoria which, in order to preserve certain historical buildings, prevented the demolition of certain buildings, prohibited construction on certain lands and revoked demolition permits, notwithstanding the

38 (1975), 10 O.R. (2d) 313 at 319, 26 C.C.C. (2d) 569 (C.A.). See also *R. v. Pennylegion* (1975), 8 O.R. (2d) 707, 24 C.C.C. (2d) 141 (Co. Ct.), where the power to regulate kennels was held not to include the power to regulate dogs in kennels; and *Calgary Hotel Assn. v. Calgary (City)* (1983), 23 M.P.L.R. 158 (Alta. Q.B.) where the power to licence, regulate and control the taxi business did not include the power to prohibit taxi brokers from entering into exclusive concession agreements.

39 (1993), 12 O.R. (3d) 646, 14 M.P.L.R. (2d) 229, 101 D.L.R. (4th) 614 (C.A.).

40 *Municipal Act*, R.S.O. 1990, c. M.45, s. 210(1).

41 (1976), 1 M.P.L.R. 166, 73 D.L.R. (3d) 247 (B.C. S.C.).

absence of any specific authority to do so. The exercise of power was instead justified on the basis of provisions of the *Municipal Act*, which provided that, notwithstanding any other provisions of that Act, when powers vested in the council are inadequate to deal with an emergency, the council by two-thirds vote may declare that an emergency exists and exercise all powers as are necessary to effectively deal with the emergency.[42] Likewise, in the case of *Fonent Properties Ltd. v. Vancouver (City),* the Court upheld a by-law which prohibited landlords from entering into rental agreements which exceeded 20 years in length. The Court, while implicitly acknowledging the requirement for legislative authority, found that since the enabling legislation authorized the municipality to "prohibit" the licensee from carrying on its business, it had the power to prohibit tenancy agreements of specified durations.[43]

The point here is not that the results of any of these cases were necessarily unjust, but that the courts failed to examine the legislation granting the power or the by-law passed under the legislation from the viewpoint of the purpose of the legislation. By-laws were not examined in the context of the reason for the legislative provision purporting to grant the authority to pass them — the problem that the legislator intended to overcome by granting the power is not considered. The reason for the emergency power was not considered in the *Murphy*[44] case, nor was the reason for the power to supply electricity considered in the *Ottawa Electric*[45] case.

It seems that the courts had adopted an arbitrary, if not irrational, approach to interpreting municipal powers — irrational because the case law loses any element of predictability in the absence of a reasoned discussion of the purposes for the legislation, the granting of authority and the by-laws passed under it. A narrow and literal interpretation is found in most of these cases but the basis for any rational understanding of that interpretation in the context of the legislation and power exercised is not. Without a rational discussion of the objectives and purposes of the enabling legislation, and discussion of the manner in which the municipal by-law attempts to attain the legislative objectives, the courts cannot, in a principled way, fulfill their stated role of determining the scope of municipal authority.

It would seem appropriate for the courts to assume the existence of a rational purpose for legislation granting power to municipal governments,

---

42 *Local Government Act*, R.S.B.C. 1996, c. 323, s. 250 (formerly s. 218(2) at the time of the case in question).

43 (1990), 49 M.P.L.R. 223, 45 B.C.L.R. (2d) 338 (S.C.); see also *Nash v. London (City)* (1995), 26 M.P.L.R. (2d) 24 (Ont. Gen. Div.), additional reasons at (1995), 26 M.P.L.R. (2d) 24 at 34 (Ont. Gen. Div.) which held that a by-law prescribing a 15-minute grace period prior to the towing of a motor vehicle fell within the regulatory power granted by the *City of London Act*, 1989, which included the right to regulate towing, including issues of time and place.

44 See *supra* note 41.

45 See *supra* note 24.

and therefore to examine the power granted and the by-law in the context of that purpose. The courts should examine the section in question, surrounding sections, and, indeed, the whole statute.[46] The Court in the *Murphy*[47] case could have at least considered the meaning of the word "emergency" in its legislative context in order to ascertain if there were limits upon it. For example, an "emergency" may be restricted to physical disasters or cases of imminent physical harm by virtue of its legislative context. This might have been a sensible interpretation as the power was found in a section granting incidental powers and enabling municipalities to petition the Lieutenant-Governor for additional powers.

In *Morrison v. Kingston (City)*[48] the Court stated that the word "welfare" was so vague as to have no meaning. That appears to have been an abdication of the judicial role of giving meaning to the word in its legislative context. Surely there was wide room for a finding that "health" and "welfare" granted authority over the purely local aspects of unspecified matters pertaining to the health and well-being of the community not set out in the Act. In the *Pride Cleaners*[49] case a narrow interpretation of "regulation" was taken so as to exclude the power to prohibit certain activity during certain hours. This is an interpretation that is common in the municipal field.[50] The interpretation makes little sense given the purpose of the power to regulate nuisances and the fact that regulation is virtually impossible without some prohibition. One must wonder if such an approach would have been followed if the Lieutenant-Governor-in-Council were exercising the power. [51] In *Ottawa Electric*,[52] the simple holding that the power to supply electricity does not include the power to purchase electricity to supply it, indicates the tendency of the Court to merely adopt a narrow and literal interpretation without analysis and without substantial discussion of the possible parameters of the power in question. In *Morrison*, the Court stated that the municipality, in regulating slot machines, could not regulate their use or possession. This ignored the fact that the regulation of these and other devices may well warrant regulation of the persons possessing or using them. The purpose of licensing is partly to protect individuals who are making use of services from fraud, poor quality and danger that is unknown to them because of their lack of knowledge regarding the service itself and the person delivering the service.[53]

---

46 See Driedger, *Construction of Statutes*, 2nd ed. (Toronto; Butterworths, 1983) at 105; and *R. v. Varga* (1979), 27 O.R. (2d) 274, 12 M.P.L.R. 278, 106 D.L.R. (3d) 101 (C.A.) where Wilson J.A. (as she then was) in dissent used such an approach.

47 See *supra* note 41.

48 See *supra* note 34.

49 See *supra* note 30.

50 See *Toronto (City) v. Virgo* (1895), [1896] A.C. 88 (Canada P.C.) where there was also an attempt to distinguish between prohibition and regulation.

51 (1902), 188 U.S. 321.

52 See *supra* note 24.

53 J. Bossoms, S. Makuch and J. Palmer, *Municipal Licensing* (U of T Press, June 1984).

The *Christie Taxi*[54] case provides another example of the courts making a conclusion that the regulation of the financial relationship between the owners and drivers of taxis is beyond municipal competence, without stating any reasons for that conclusion. The courts' shortcut of restricting municipal powers (and on occasion upholding them), without examining in detail the legislative context and the reasons why a particular power should or should not be upheld is problematic — the simple desire to protect individual rights from "untrustworthy" local government interference is not enough "reason" in itself.

In the cases referred to, there would appear to be a number of legitimate concerns. One has already been discussed — lack of examination of the purpose of the grant of power in the legislative context and whether the municipal by-law fits that purpose. A second concern is the impact that the exercise of the power has on procedural rights and safeguards. Does the exercise of the general power mean that a particular process required under a specific grant of power can be avoided? The courts would seem to be a most appropriate body to examine this question. A third concern is the extent to which the power interferes with the basic legal regime of the province. Does the exercise of the municipal power mean that basic principles of law in torts, property or contracts are being altered within the municipality? The courts need to carefully and subtly balance the need for provincial uniformity in civil law and civil rights, and the need for differences among communities and variations in values within the province if municipalities are to perform their real function.

Another issue that could be raised is whether the power exercised by the municipality interferes substantially with persons living outside of the municipality. Local governments are limited in jurisdiction to their own geographic territory.[55] Where a decision creates externalities, such as zoning that could restrict ownership to residents of a particular municipality, the courts will likely require express power because of the inability of those residing outside the municipality to have any influence on the decision of the council.

As a result of the courts' approach in interpreting detailed legislative provisions governing municipal action, and the legislature's failure to implement legislation counteracting this judicial approach, municipalities have very little authority from a legal point of view to initiate policies or to act independently of their provincial governments. Specific authority must be found in legislation before any action can be taken. In this way, courts treat municipalities not as elected responsible governments but rather as administrative agencies. They cannot act without provincial sanction. Policies or

54 See *supra* note 38.

55 See *Hatch v. Rathwell* (1909), 12 W.L.R. 376 (Man. C.A.). See also the *Municipal Act, 2001*, S.O. 2001, c. 25, s. 19, which confines the jurisdiction of municipal councils to the municipalities they represent unless otherwise specified.

initiatives cannot be undertaken to provide new services without authorizing legislation. For example, provincial legislation has been requested by municipalities in the past for the funding of information centres, for the regulation of handcrafted wares for sale on sidewalks, to create bus lanes, to purchase a theatre and to provide free snow shovelling for elderly persons within a municipality. In terms of policy development, the province examines the policy initiatives of municipalities and evaluates and approves them by the passing of enabling legislation.

One early example of the courts adopting a rational approach is *Ottawa (City) v. Royal Trust Co.*,[56] where the Supreme Court of Canada, in determining that a by-law taxing certain classes of buildings was *intra vires,* examined the by-law in light of the purpose of the legislation to tax new buildings, and the enlargements of existing buildings, to pay for the upgrading of services required as a result of the construction.

More recently, the courts, particularly the Supreme Court of Canada, have recognized the distinct democratic nature of municipal government and in a series of decisions have, without abandoning the requirement for express authority for the exercise of municipal powers, indicated a more purpose based approach to the interpretation of municipal enabling statutes. In *R. v. Greenbaum*[57] and *R. v. Sharma,*[58] the Supreme Court of Canada struck down municipal licensing by-laws on two grounds: discrimination and statutory empowerment. In determining whether the by-laws had been validly enacted under applicable statutes, Mr. Justice Iacobucci quotes with approval the above cited passage from the *Hamilton Distillery*[59] case, and continues:

> A court should look to the purpose and wording of the provincial enabling legislation when deciding whether or not a municipality has been empowered to pass a certain by-law.[60]

Where by-laws are susceptible to more than one interpretation, the Court held that it should select the interpretation that fits within the parameters of the empowering provincial statute. This part of the decision supports the thesis that the "rational purpose approach" to municipal by-laws is modifying the "express authority approach." However, the Court in *Greenbaum* also relied upon the express authority doctrine, stating that courts must be vigilant in ensuring that municipalities do not impinge upon the civil or common law rights of citizens in passing *ultra vires* by-laws.[61]

Accordingly, in order to determine whether the by-law was authorized by the *Municipal Act*, the Court in *Greenbaum* first considered the wording

56 [1964] S.C.R. 526, 45 D.L.R. (2d) 220.
57 [1993] 1 S.C.R. 674.
58 [1993] 1 S.C.R. 650.
59 *Supra* note 36.
60 [1993] 1 S.C.R. 674 at 688.
61 *Supra* note 57.

and the purpose of the by-law itself. It found that the purpose was to prevent encumbrances and obstructions on the sidewalks, and found that such a purpose was not authorized by the provision of the *Municipal Act*, which empowers municipalities to pass by-laws for prohibiting or regulating the obstructing or encumbering of highways.[62] The Court found that the by-law in question was overly broad, since it referred to exposing articles on sidewalks that might not encumber or obstruct the sidewalk. Further, since the by-law did not expressly refer to "sales," it was not authorized by the section empowering a local municipality to prohibit or regulate sales on highways. Finally, the by-law was said not to fall within s. 102 of the *Municipal Act*, the omnibus provision, which provides for the general power to regulate for health, safety, morals and welfare of the inhabitants of the municipality.[63] This section did not apply because the Court found that the licencing power in this instance was authorized elsewhere, albeit without the specific powers under consideration, and the residual powers in s. 102 could not be used to enlarge a specifically granted power. For all the above reasons, then, and taking an approach which utilized both the "express authority" doctrine and the "purposive approach" the Court found that the licensing by-laws did not fall within the powers granted by any of the applicable statutes.

The next case where the Court considered the scope of municipal powers was in *Shell Canada Products Ltd. v. Vancouver (City)*.[64] In this case, the City of Vancouver resolved not to do business with the appellant oil company until its parent had divested itself of its business interests in South Africa. Here the impugned resolution was again struck down. Speaking for the majority, Sopinka J. rejected the City's argument that the resolution fell within the omnibus provision found within the *Vancouver Charter* on the basis that the resolution in question was not passed for a municipal purpose. In particular, it was the majority position that the residual power could not be resorted to for "matters external to the interests of the citizens of the municipality."[65]

In many respects, the majority decision appears to advocate a fairly narrow reading of municipal enabling statutes. Indeed, Iacobucci J. includes in his reasons a strong policy basis in favour of court intervention, stating:

> There is good reason to encourage municipalities to act within their statutory powers. An absence of judicial review would leave some ratepayers without an effective remedy. The suggestion that the only remedy is at the polls is of no value to the minority, who would be left with no remedy, and Council could continue to enlarge its statutory powers as long as it was able to retain its

62 *Municipal Act*, R.S.O. 1990, c. M.45, s. 314(1).

63 *Ibid.* at s. 102.

64 [1994] 1 S.C.R. 231,(1994), 20 M.P.L.R. (2d) 1 (S.C.C.).

65 *Ibid.* at 22 [M.P.L.R.].

majority support. The public policy in favour of restricting a municipality to its statutory powers exists as much for the minority as for the majority.[66]

Nevertheless, the Supreme Court does appear to attach importance to reviewing the purpose of specific grants of power and in this case looked to the objects of the municipality itself, in finding that the resolution did not further those objectives, being related to a matter outside of the municipality's territorial boundaries. Arguably, in coming to this conclusion, the majority takes a rather narrow view of the objects of local government, preferring to see the purpose of local government being restricted to matters having a direct impact on the citizens.

Perhaps the most expansive articulation of the broad approach is found in the dissent judgment in *Shell Canada Products Ltd. v. Vancouver (City)*, where McLachlin J. states:

> Recent commentary suggests an emerging consensus that courts must respect the responsibility of elected municipal bodies to serve the people who elected them, and exercise caution to avoid substituting their views of what is best for the citizens for those of municipal councils. Barring clear demonstration that a municipal decision was beyond its powers, courts should not so hold. In cases where powers are not expressly conferred but may be implied, courts must be prepared to adopt the "benevolent construction" which this Court referred to in *Greenbaum*, and confer the powers by reasonable implication. Whatever rules of construction are applied, they must not be used to usurp the legitimate role of municipal bodies as community representatives.[67]

McLachlin J. goes on to discuss, from a policy perspective, the desirability of a purposive approach over a narrow, interventionist approach, making particular reference to the democratic nature of local government. In particular, a benevolent construction, "adheres to the fundamental axiom that courts must accord proper respect to the democratic responsibilities of elected municipal officials, and the rights of those who elect them. This is important to the continued healthy functioning of democracy at the municipal level. If municipalities are to be able to respond to the needs and wishes of their citizens, they must be given broad jurisdiction to make local decisions reflecting local values."[68]

Unlike the majority, McLachlin J. sees the role of local government from a broad perspective:

> The term "welfare of the citizens", it seems to me, is capable of embracing not only their immediate needs, but also the psychological welfare of the citizens as members of community who have an interest in expressing their identity as

66 *Ibid.* at 19 [M.P.L.R.].
67 *Ibid.* at 32 [M.P.L.R.].
68 *Ibid.* at 32 [M.P.L.R.].

> a community. Our language recognizes this: we speak of civic spirit, of city pride. This suggests that City Council may properly take measures related to fostering and maintaining this sense of community identity and pride. Among such measures may be found community expression of disapproval or approval of different types of conduct, wherever it is found.[69]

Based on this expanded view on the role of local government in Canadian society, McLachlin J. found that the resolution was proper and within the powers of the City to pass. Thus, while there was apparent agreement on the bench regarding the need for a purposive approach, there remained a divergence of opinion as to how broadly drawn the objects of local government should be interpreted.

The court had the opportunity again to consider the question of the interpretation of municipal statutes in *Nanaimo (City) v. Rascal Trucking Ltd.*[70] In this case, a municipal resolution declaring a pile of soil a nuisance pursuant to s. 936 of the *Municipal Act* (British Columbia) was challenged for want of authority. Here, the Supreme Court unanimously held that municipal legislation "be constructed purposively in their entire context and in light of the scheme of the Act as a whole with a view to ascertaining the legislature's true intent." Interestingly, the Court in *Nanaimo* quotes with approval parts of McLachlin J.'s dissent judgment in the *Shell* case in support of its finding that *intra vires* decisions should only be reviewed if patently unreasonable. Arguably, McLachlin J. was moving towards an even more generous threshold in *Shell*, suggesting municipal decisions, including jurisdictional questions, should only be disturbed in "clear cases."[71] The distinction between *ultra vires* and *intra vires* decisions was, in McLachlin J.'s mind, a slippery one whereby "courts disguise an assessment for reasonableness in the cloak of a review for *vires*."[72] She criticizes her colleague, Sopinka J. for doing just that. He states, on the one hand, that the reasonableness of the resolution was not at issue. Yet, on the other hand, the basis of his decision, as McLachlin J. points out, was that the resolutions fell outside the interests of the electorate. Thus, jurisdiction is defined to a large degree by defining the interests of the citizens. An entirely rational approach may look at who is in the best position to identify those interests. For McLachlin J., council was in a better position to determine that a moral stance on apartheid was in the best interests of the community.

A similar analysis as that done in the *Shell* case, was again undertaken by the Supreme Court in *114957 Canada Ltée (Spray-Tech, Société d'arrosage) v. Hudson (Ville)*.[73] In this case, the impugned by-law sought to regulate the use of pesticides by limiting their use to agricultural and other

69 *Ibid.* at 37 [M.P.L.R.].
70 [2000] 1 S.C.R. 342, (2000), 9 M.P.L.R. (3d) 1 (S.C.C.).
71 *Supra* note 64.
72 *Ibid.* at 41 [M.P.L.R.].
73 *Supra* note 15.

essential uses, but prohibiting pesticides for residential (lawncare) uses. In upholding the by-law under the omnibus provision contained in the *Cities and Town's Act*[74], the Court distinguished *Greenbaum* on the basis that in the *Spraytech* case the municipality was not seeking to expand the ambit of a specific power by recourse to the general omnibus provision. Furthermore, the Court maintained, as it did in *Shell*, that the by-law must be passed for a municipal purpose. However, unlike *Shell*, the purpose by-law in this case was found to fall within the legitimate health promotion component of the enabling legislation. In this regard, the majority found that accepted principles of international environmental law, namely the precautionary principle, helped "inform the contextual approach to statutory interpretation and judicial review."[75]

In a concurring, but separate decision, LeBel J., seeks to reassert the limitations to which the omnibus clause can be resorted to in order to justify municipal actions. Acknowledging that the residual power was intended to allow municipalities to address through their legislative powers unforeseen circumstances, LeBel J. continues:

> Nevertheless, such a provision cannot be construed as an open and unlimited grant of provincial powers. It is not enough that a particular issue has become a pressing concern in the opinion of a local community. This concern must relate to problems that engage the community as a local entity, not a member of the broader polity. It must be closely related to the immediate interests of the community within the territorial limits defined by the legislature in a matter where local governments may usefully intervene.[76]

Thus, the question respecting judicial review becomes one of defining those limits. To some degree provincial legislatures will have to grapple with the extent to which they want to include express language defining such limits. However, the judiciary will continue to play an important role in this regard. To the extent judges see local government as something more than a mere delegate of statutory powers and acknowledge the democratic legitimacy of municipal council, municipal policy making may benefit. In this regard, it is significant that the Supreme Court in *Spraytech* gave judicial recognition to the principle of subsidiarity.[77] For in determining the scope of municipal interests and purposes this concept provides the basis for a principled approach to this exercise.

---

74 R.S.Q., c. C-19, s. 410(1).

75 *Supra* note 15 at 266, quoting from *Baker v. Canada (Minister of Citizenship & Immigration)*, [1999] 2 S.C.R. 817, at 861.

76 *Ibid.* at para 278.

77 *Supra* note 75 (*Baker*).

E. OTHER JUDICIAL TECHNIQUES

In determining the legality of municipal enactments, the courts have developed a number of other principles to evaluate municipal actions. The doctrines of unreasonableness, discrimination, bad faith and uncertainty are closely akin to the "express authority" approach in that they are used by the courts as a means of determining whether a municipality has exceeded its jurisdiction. As the application of the strict express authority doctrine recedes in Canadian law and is replaced by a more liberal, purposive approach, one would expect a corresponding liberalization or perhaps, rationalization, of these related principles. However, as discussed below, while the courts appear to be moving towards a broader interpretation in favour of the exercise of municipal powers generally, a stricter approach remains entrenched within some of these specific doctrines.

1. Unreasonableness

Historically the courts tended to take a more encompassing view of their power to review municipal actions that included not only reviewing the jurisdiction of municipalities to make certain enactments, but also reviewing the reasonableness of those enactments. This approach is exemplified in the English case of *Roberts v. Hopwood.*[78] Here the authority of a municipality to set wages for municipal employees was challenged by the District Auditor when the council in question failed to reduce wages in the face of a reduction of the cost of living. The House of Lords determined that the council's failure to consider the cost of living was unreasonable and, therefore, illegal. There was no question of the council's authority to set wages, but their decision, which took into consideration certain social objectives, was overturned nevertheless. The House of Lords essentially substituted its own view of what was relevant citing the need for fiscal responsibility and criticizing the municipal council for being "guided in preference by some eccentric principles of socialistic philanthropy or by a feminist ambition."

This kind of judicial review severely restricts the ability of municipalities to engage in any meaningful policy making of their own and clearly fails to recognize the democratic legitimacy of local governments. This broad supervisory role assumed by the courts may have been appropriate and necessary when local decision makers were not accountable to the citizens, but as local governments evolved into democratic institutions, the justification for this kind of judicial interference evaporated. This evolution of local government structure was recognized in the seminal English case, *Kruse v. Johnson.*[79] This case involved a challenge to a by-law that prohibited public singing

78 [1925] A.C. 578 (U.K. H.L.).
79 [1898] 2 Q.B. 91 (Eng. Div. Ct.).

on the grounds that such a prohibition was unreasonable. The court, after reviewing the historical context of judicial review for unreasonableness, went on to state:

> But, when the Court is called upon to consider the by-laws of public representative bodies clothed with ample authority which I have described, and exercising that authority by the checks and safeguards which I have mentioned, I think the consideration of such by-laws ought to be approached from a different standpoint. They ought to be supported if possible. They ought to be, as has been said, "benevolently" interpreted, and credit ought to be given to those who have to administer them that they will be reasonably administered.[80]

The court goes on to consider the circumstances under which interference may be warranted, stating that a by-law could be unreasonable and invalid if it involved "such oppressive or gratuitous interference with the rights of those subject to them as could find no justification in the minds of reasonable men." The basis for the doctrine was set out as "Parliament never intended to give authority to make such rules; they are unreasonable and *ultra vires.*"[81] Thus, the justification for review is not lack of reason, but rather, lack of jurisdiction.

The Canadian courts similarly recognized the importance of not interfering with the decisions of duly elected councils on the grounds of reasonableness. For example, the Ontario Court of Appeal framed the matter as follows:

> What is or is not in the public interest is a matter to be determined by the judgment of the municipal council; and what it determines, if in reaching its conclusion it acted honestly and within the limits of its powers, is not open to review by the Court. . ..[82]

Notwithstanding this recognition by the courts, the legislatures have also found it necessary to enact specific statutory language expressly prohibiting the overturning of the by-laws on the grounds of unreasonableness. For example, in Ontario, the *Municipal Act* provides:

> A by-law passed by a council in the exercise of any of its powers and in good faith shall not be open to question, or be quashed, set aside or declared invalid either wholly or partly, on account of the unreasonableness or supposed unreasonableness of its provisions or any of them.[83]

---

80 *Ibid.* at 99.

81 *Ibid.* at 100.

82 *Supra* note 37 at 575.

83 *Municipal Act, 2001*, S.O. 2001, c. 25, s. 272.

Similar provisions have been enacted in other jurisdictions.[84]

Despite these statutory enactments, the Courts have from time to time overturned municipal by-laws on the basis of unreasonableness. In *R. v. Bell*,[85] the Supreme Court of Canada considered a zoning by-law that restricted the use of residential dwellings to individuals or families. "Family" was defined as a group of two or more persons living together and interrelated by bonds of consanguinity, marriage or legal adoption. The majority of the Court cited examples of potentially inequitable applications of the by-law and found it to constitute "oppressive or gratuitous interference with the rights of those subject to them as could find no justification in the minds of reasonable men." It was therefore unreasonable and *ultra vires*. This case relies on *Kruse v. Johnson*[86] and clearly bases its decision on its view that the legislature could not have intended to give municipalities the power to zone with reference to occupants.

In this regard, the *Bell* decision is in keeping with the Supreme Court's later decision in *Nanaimo*[87] where the Court held that *intra vires* decisions could only be reviewed on the basis of patent unreasonableness. This standard is no doubt derived from administrative law decisions that have used the same standard of review for judicial review of tribunal decisions in the face of a privative clause. In this case, the statutory provision contained in the *Municipal Act* was held not to apply because the by-law was adopted under a different statute. There is certainly an argument to be made that such a prohibition applies to all municipal by-laws regardless of the source of their authority.

2. Discrimination

A subcategory of the doctrine of "express authority," the courts also use the doctrine of discrimination to interpret and invalidate municipal by-laws. In essence, absent the express grant of power to classify or sub-classify within a by-law, the courts generally find that the authority conferred by the legislation does not include the power to provide different rules or regulations for different categories of individuals or groups. Where this occurs the court will set aside the by-law on grounds of discrimination, on the theory that the legislature could not have intended to establish a sub-legislative mandate to make such rules.[88] In this respect, the rule against discrimination is clearly a specific application of the more general express authority doctrine. Discrimination in the municipal sense must be distinguished from discrimination in

84 See *The Municipal Government Act*, R.S.A. 2000, c. M-26.1 s. 539; *The Municipal Government Act*, S.N.S. 1998, c. 18 s. 189.

85 [1979] 2 S.C.R. 212.

86 [1898] 2 Q.B. 91 (Eng. Div. Ct.).

87 *Supra* note 70.

88 *R. v. Donald B. Allen* (1975), 11 O.R. (2d) 271, 65 D.L.R. (3d) 599 (Div. Ct.).

the human rights sense. In the municipal context, the concern is simply one of the "ambit of delegated power."[89] That is, by-laws may only sub-classify for the purpose of different treatment under the by-law where authorized by legislation.

The basic principle, which is well established, is stated with clarity by Schroeder J.A. delivering the judgment of the Court of Appeal in *S.S. Kresge Co. v. Windsor (City)*:

> The right given to a municipality to regulate a trade or business does not give it the power to discriminate. The general principle governing the exercise of such a regulatory power is stated by Middleton, J.A. in *Forst v. Toronto (City)* (1923), 54 O.L.R. 256 (C.A.) at 278: — when the municipality is given the right to regulate, I think that all it can do is to pass general regulations affecting all who come within the ambit of the municipal legislation. [90]

In *Bunce v. Cobourg (Town)*[91] the Ontario Court of Appeal dealt with a by-law regulating the closing hours of shops. The by-law prescribed hours during which shops must be closed and further prescribed exceptions for certain classes of stores, including shops which specialized in "small manufactured articles of small value used in personal or household adornment, candy, soft drinks, ice cream, newspapers, periodicals, magazines and similar articles." The by-law was passed pursuant to authority given to municipalities to require the closing of "all or any class or classes of shops." The Court suggested that under the *Municipal Act*, "class" was to be determined by reference to the species of merchandise, not to the size of the articles. The Court found that municipal council had no power to subdivide the "class" and make one subdivision of shops subject to the by-law and the other not. Shopkeepers in the municipality selling merchandise of the same type, kind or species must be treated alike. It was, therefore, discriminatory for the municipal council to permit shopkeepers who dealt only in "small articles" to remain open for business without any restrictions as to hours, but require shopkeepers who dealt in "small articles" but also with larger articles of that same type to close for specified hours.

Similarly, in the case of *R. v. Donald B. Allen Ltd.*,[92] the Court applied the *ultra vires* doctrine, and held that the municipality did not have the authority to establish a sub-classification of car washes according to whether the car wash was within 500 feet of a residential area. The municipality, in short, could not discriminate among different types of car washes.

In *R. v. Varga*[93] a by-law provided for the early closing of retail service stations but provided an exemption for full service stations. The majority of

---

89 *Supra* note 64 at 42 [M.P.L.R.].
90 [1957] O.W.N. 154 (C.A.) at 158.
91 [1963] 2 O.R. 343 (C.A.).
92 *Supra* note 88.
93 *Supra* note 46.

the Court of Appeal held that the municipality had gone beyond its powers and had discriminated against certain sub-classes of service stations in the retail gasoline industry by limiting the members of the class who could apply for exemptions. The majority held that the by-law clearly discriminated against the small service stations by allowing their competitors, who happen to be equipped to provide additional service, to sell gasoline at retail stations 24 hours a day.

The traditional rule, that the power to make by-laws does not include that of enacting "classification" provisions unless the enabling legislation so provides, was confirmed by the Supreme Court of Canada in *Fountainhead Fun Centres Ltd. c. Montréal (Ville).*[94] In that case, the municipality had passed a by-law prohibiting amusement halls from permitting people under the age of 18 years onto the premises.

Justice Beetz, speaking for the Court, noted that the by-laws which are discriminatory are rendered invalid even though the distinction on which they are based is perfectly rational or reasonable, and conceived and imposed in good faith without favoritism or malice. Therefore, if by-laws are unequal in operation between different classes and are based on perfectly rational or reasonable grounds, they may be declared invalid if express authority for such regulation is not found.

The Court embarked on the traditional analysis of determining whether the enacting legislation expressly or by necessary implication provided the municipality with authority to regulate classes of individuals by age. The Court recognized that authority to make distinctions based on age of children and adolescents would be useful to the City in exercising its general powers, and especially in exercising its power to adopt policing by-laws, but however useful or convenient such an authorization might be, the Court was not persuaded that the City could exercise such powers.

The Court found that in the absence of express provisions to the contrary or implicit delegation by necessary inference, the sovereign legislature has reserved to itself the important power of limiting the rights and freedoms of individuals in accordance with such fine distinctions as age. This principle, the Court stated, "transcends the limits of administrative and municipal law. It is a principle of fundamental freedom."[95]

The principle was reaffirmed in the *Sharma* decision where the Supreme Court quashed a municipal by-law that treated freestanding street vendors differently from those who owned or occupied abutting property.[96] The Supreme Court also considered the issue of discrimination in the *Spraytech*[97] case where it was argued that the by-law regulating pesticides was discrimi-

94 [1985] 1 S.C.R. 368, 29 M.P.L.R. 220, 18 D.L.R. (4th) 161 at 404-405 [S.C.R.].

95 *Ibid.* at 413 [S.C.R.].

96 *Supra* note 58. See also *Roy v. Ottawa (City)* (1995), 29 M.P.L.R. (2d) 117 (Ont. Gen. Div.), additional reasons at (1995), 29 M.P.L.R. (2d) 117 at 130 (Ont. Gen. Div.) for another discussion concerning statutory authorization for discrimination in municipal by-laws.

97 *Supra* note 15.

natory because it treated owners of agricultural properties differently from the owners of residential properties. Here the Court found that the distinction made, although not expressly provided for, was valid as it was found to be necessarily incidental to the exercise of the power in question.

It is difficult to reconcile the *Spraytech* decision with its predecessors in that the statutory power in question was a general power to enact by-laws for the health and general welfare of the municipality. Very clearly the distinction between agricultural and residential land owners was a reasonable and rational one, but arguably allowing the use of pesticides for agricultural uses was a political choice and not "absolutely necessary" (to use the words of the Supreme Court in the *Fountainhead Fun Centres*[98] case) to the exercise of those powers. The Court's approach to discrimination in *Spraytech* is much more in keeping with the emerging broad, purposive approach towards the interpretation of municipal enabling legislation. Which is to say, the Court recognized that the purpose behind the by-law was to restrict pesticide use in cases where the use was related to aesthetics, as opposed to situations where the use of pesticides was undertaken for reasons relating to agricultural production or the elimination of in plants or insects that constitute a danger to human beings. What seems to be important is not whether there is express language authorizing every distinction made by local government, but rather that the distinctions made have a rational basis that is in keeping with the objectives of the overall grant of power.

In some cases involving discrimination, the results reached and the need for such a doctrine are readily accepted. The courts as protectors of individual rights do not want municipalities classifying by personal characteristics or playing favourites amongst various property owners or individuals by regulating on an individual basis. So certainly the underlying rationale for the doctrine, namely the prevention of municipal abuse of power by classifying in an arbitrary manner, makes sense and has merit.

Had the courts in earlier decisions applied the same approach as the Supreme Court in *Spraytech*, very different results may have arisen. For example, in the *Allen* case[99] the Court struck down a sub-classification for car washes within 500 feet of residential areas. Arguably, the classification was a rational one relating to the purpose of regulating the hours of such establishments. There is a rational distinction to be drawn between car washes within 500 feet of residential areas and those beyond 500 feet. Ones within 500 feet can cause problems like noise and traffic that could interfere with the residential neighbourhood. There is no reason why the same hours should be imposed on car washes far from residential areas.

---

98 *Supra* note 94.

99 *Supra* note 88.

Similarly, in *Fountainhead Fun Centres*[100] the Supreme Court of Canada, while acknowledging that the by-law was rationally connected to the authorized legislative objectives of preventing juvenile crime and the commercial exploitation of children, struck down a by-law which attempted to reach those objectives because it classified by age. Drawing distinctions based on such criteria as age, the Court indicated, was reserved to the province, and was not, in the absence of express authority, to be entrusted to municipal government. This, the Court stated, was a principle of fundamental freedom that transcended the limits of administrative and municipal law. What is lacking, however, is a principled discussion of why it is that municipal governments should not, in the absence of express authority, be found to have jurisdiction to draw rational and reasonable classifications to achieve authorized legislative purposes. Certainly when a by-law is both rationally and reasonably connected to authorized legislative objectives it is arguable that it is not discriminatory. Implicit in the decision is simply the fact that the courts do not wish to entrust such power to municipal government.

Yet seen from a broad perspective, local decision makers can be seen as being in a better position to make these distinctions. There is no reason the power to determine, for example, whether gas stations in different locations or certain types of retail outlets should be subject to differing regulation, should be reserved for senior levels of government. It is likely that local decision makers may in fact be in a better position to make distinctions that are reflective of local values without being arbitrary. Presumably, if the courts follow the *Spraytech* approach, arbitrary distinctions shall be in all likelihood struck down as not furthering the legislative intent of the enabling provisions.

3. Bad Faith

Another basis for challenging municipal decisions is that they are made in "bad faith." An allegation of "bad faith" is another method by which the issue of impartiality can be addressed. Bad faith can obviously mean wrongdoing on the part of Council, and an attempt by members to gain personal advantage. However, the term "bad faith" can also characterize conduct which is unreasonable, arbitrary and without the degree of fairness, openness and impartiality required of a municipal council particularly when dealing with planning powers.[101]

---

100 *Supra* note 94, whether the drawing of rational and reasonable distinctions based on other criteria, for example, the type of business, will be afforded the same measure of protection by the Supreme Court of Canada remains to be seen.

101 See *Howard v. Toronto (City)*, 61 O.L.R. 563, [1928] 1 D.L.R. 952 (C.A.); *Kuchma v. Tache (Rural Municipality)*, [1945] S.C.R. 234, [1945] 2 D.L.R. 13; *Cadillac Development Corp. v. Toronto (City)* (1973), 1 O.R. (2d) 20, 39 D.L.R. (3d) 188 (H.C.); and *Luxor Entertainment Corp. v. North York (City)* (1996), 31 M.P.L.R. (2d) 149 (Ont. Gen. Div.).

The rationale underlying the bad faith doctrine goes back to the general rule that municipal councils can only exercise their powers for legitimate municipal purposes for the benefit of the inhabitants of the municipality. In cases where the evidence demonstrates a lack of candor or impartiality on council's behalf, the courts have been willing to draw a negative implication that such behavior indicates an ulterior purpose not related to the legitimate purpose of power granted.

The leading Ontario case, *H.G. Winton Ltd. v. North York (Borough)*[102] is a good illustration of the application of this doctrine. Here, a pre-existing zoning by-law allowed for lands to be used for church purposes. However, when a religious group wished to establish a temple on these lands, the municipality, influenced no doubt by public hostility to the proposal, enacted a rezoning preventing the use. The zoning by-law was successfully attacked on the basis of bad faith. In particular, the evidence showed that the by-law in question was not based on valid planning principles, the by-law was essentially aimed at one property, and clearly represented unfair and unequal treatment.

Care must be taken to distinguish bad faith from unreasonableness, for only the former will result in the invalidation of a by-law. Unreasonableness may be evidence of bad faith, but it should not result in the quashing of a by-law. Thus, in order to succeed in attacking a by-law for bad faith, some evidence of improper motives needs to be brought forward. Thus, in *Equity Waste Management of Canada Corp. v. Halton Hills (Town)*,[103] the Ontario Court of Appeal refused to quash an interim control by-law, even though questions were raised whether the by-law was passed, not for planning reasons, but in order to appease ratepayers. Addressing this issue, Laskin, J. held that, in such circumstances, courts should generally exercise restraint, respecting the legislative and democratic function of council (quoting McLachlin J. in *Shell*).

A related basis upon which by-laws may be attacked is the doctrine of improper or impermissible purpose. As discussed above, this was the basis of the majority decision to quash the City of Vancouver's anti-apartheid resolution in *Shell*.[104] In the *Shell* case, the Supreme Court of Canada examined the scope and purpose of the authorizing provision and determined that the resolution was not passed for a valid municipal purpose. Unlike the bad faith doctrine, where a municipal enactment may *prima facie* appear valid (such as passing a zoning by-law), but loses its validity due to the improper motives of Council, a by-law which is passed for an improper or impermissible purpose is simply *ultra vires*, regardless of council's motives. What takes the bad faith by-law outside the scope of municipal powers is the judicial

102 (1978), 20 O.R. (2d) 737 (Div. Ct.).
103 (1997), 40 M.P.L.R. (2d) 107 (Ont. C.A.).
104 *Supra* note 64.

assumption that by-laws passed for some ulterior purpose could not have been intended by the legislature.

4. Uncertainty and Vagueness

A municipal by-law may also be found invalid on the basis of vagueness or uncertainty, the test for which is where a reasonably intelligent reader (or well-intentioned citizen) cannot ascertain the meaning or application of the by-law.[105] There is a duty on the municipal council to express the meaning of a by-law with certainty so that every citizen may understand the by-law in order to comply with it.[106]

The judicial approach to this doctrine, and the application of the "reasonable reader" test, is crucial, for if a narrow approach similar to the "express authority doctrine" were taken then the ambiguity that, in general, accompanies legislation could result in the "wholesale" invalidity of municipal by-laws.

It is clear that vagueness in law is undesirable and that municipal by-laws should make clear what is required for compliance. Predictability, it must be agreed, is not only a value to be sought in judicial decision-making but also in municipal legislating, so that it is appropriate that by-laws should be struck down for lack of clear standards. But that is only one side of the argument. Senior levels of government often set nebulous standards, to be developed on a case-by-case basis, because detailed standards are impossible to articulate in advance. It is expected that these vague standards will be given form over time as decisions are made. Policy is often developed in such a manner by telecommunications boards, transport boards and liquor licence boards. The decisions of those boards create the real standards which the legislature was unable to articulate in advance. This is an important tool in policy development which municipalities are unable to utilize. For them, all standards must be clearly set out in advance regardless of limited knowledge and the possibility of changing circumstances.

5. Conflict with Superior Legislation

Municipal by-laws, although validly authorized, may still be found *ultra vires* if they conflict with provincial legislation. This rule essentially follows

105 *R. v. Sandler*, [1971] 3 O.R. 614, 21 D.L.R. (3d) 286 (C.A.); *Hamilton Independent Variety & Confectionery Stores Inc. v. Hamilton (City)* (1982), 20 M.P.L.R. 241, 143 D.L.R. (3d) 498 (Ont. C.A.); *538745 Ontario Inc. v. Windsor (City)* (1988), 64 O.R. (2d) 38, 49 D.L.R. (4th) 108, 37 M.P.L.R. 1 (C.A.), leave to appeal refused (1988), 65 O.R. (2d) x (S.C.C.); and *Bayfield (Village) v. MacDonald* (1997), 39 M.P.L.R. (2d) 63 (Ont. C.A.), leave to appeal refused (1997), 226 N.R. 397 (S.C.C.).

106 See *Hamilton Independent Variety & Confectionery Stores Inc.*, *ibid.* at 506-507; and *Veri v. Stoney Creek (City)* (1995), 26 M.P.L.R. (2d) 312 (Ont. Gen. Div.) at 317.

the more general rule respecting delegated legislation that subordinate legislation in conflict with its enabling legislation or other legislation from a senior level of government will be invalid.[107] The rationale for this rule is that subordinate legislation cannot in effect amend superior legislation. Consequently, where there is a conflict, the superior legislation is paramount.

There have been two distinct judicial approaches to determining what constitutes a conflict. Not coincidentally, these approaches mirror the differing approaches taken by the courts respecting conflicts between provincial and federal legislation as a matter of constitutional law. The traditional approach can be described as one of pre-emption. That is, where a senior level of government has enacted comprehensive legislation in a particular field, it is said to have occupied the field, leaving no room for a subordinate body to legislate itself.[108]

For example, in *Union Gas Ltd. v. Dawn (Township),* the Court struck down a zoning by-law which attempted to control the manner in which natural gas lines were laid out in the township.[109] The Court examined the by-law and its enabling legislation and then examined the *Ontario Energy Board Act* to determine whether or not the matter or area regulated by the municipality was to be exclusively covered under the *Ontario Energy Board Act.*[110] The Court, in light of the statutory scheme of this Act, which comprehensively dealt with the production, distribution, transmission and storage of natural gas and further provided that the "Act and the regulations prevail over any by-law passed by a municipality," found that the matters regulated by the municipality were under the exclusive jurisdiction of the Ontario Energy Board and not subject to the legislative authority of municipal councils under the *Planning Act.*

Similarly in *Ontario (Attorney General) v. Mississauga (City),*[111] the Court of Appeal held that municipal by-laws that prohibited the burning of PCBs were invalid because a Ministry official had issued a certificate of approval authorizing the burn under provincial legislation. The Court found that there was a conflict between the municipal by-law and the provincial legislation — the *Environmental Protection Act*, and the by-law was ruled *ultra vires.* This overturned the lower court decision that held that the by-law enhanced the provincial legislation.

In coming to this conclusion, Morden J.A. proposed the following test to determine whether or not there is a conflict between a by-law and provincial legislation:

---

107 Jones and de Villars, *Principles of Administrative Law* (Toronto: Carswell, 1994) at 113.

108 See *Johannesson v. West St. Paul (Rural Municipality)*, [1951] 4 D.L.R. 609 (S.C.C.).

109 (1977), 15 O.R. (2d) 722, 2 M.P.L.R. 23, 76 D.L.R. (3d) 613 (Div. Ct.); and see also *Minto Construction Ltd. v. Gloucester (Township)* (1979), 23 O.R. (2d) 634, 8 M.P.L.R. 172, 96 D.L.R. (3d) 491 (Div. Ct.); *Propane Gas Assn. of Canada Inc. v. North Vancouver (City)* (1989), 42 M.P.L.R. 29 (B.C. S.C.) on the issue of pre-emption.

110 R.S.O. 1990, c. O-13.

111 (1981), 33 O.R. (2d) 395 (C.A.).

> If the competing pieces of legislation are intended to advance the same policy and the provision in the statute covers the same ground as the by-law in a way to give rise to the interpretation that the statutory provision is intended "completely, exhaustively or exclusively", [to express] what [shall be] the law governing the particular conduct...to which its intention is directed then there is a case of conflict... If, in covering the same ground the subordinate legislation works at cross purposes to the provincial statute, then the case for conflict is reinforced.

The Court, however, qualified its analysis and attempted to restrict the scope of conflict by indicating that the principles of accommodation which have developed in cases involving federal-provincial areas of conflict could be utilized in cases of municipal-provincial conflict, and that great care should be taken before a properly enacted by-law is to be found inoperative.

The following year, the Supreme Court of Canada, in *Multiple Access Ltd. v. McCutcheon,*[112] unequivocally ruled that duplication is not an appropriate test for the invocation of the doctrine of paramountcy, preferring instead to declare a provincial enactment invalid only in cases of direct inconsistency. Notwithstanding this case, when the issue arose before the Ontario Court of Appeal in the case of *Superior Propane Inc. v. York (City),*[113] the Court ignored its earlier direction to have recourse to the principles developed respecting federal/provincial conflicts, and re-affirmed its decision in *Ontario (Attorney General) v. Mississauga (City).*[114] However, in the *Superior Propane* case there was no direct inconsistency, rather the municipal by-law, which enacted certain set backs and size restrictions relating to propane storage and dispensing facilities, contained similar but more stringent standards. Because the competing enactments were found to be passed for similar purposes, the court held that the laws were at cross-purposes. This approach took a very narrow view of the scope of the municipality's zoning power, under which the by-laws passed, which arguably may have required a more stringent standard to address issues such as nuisance and safe separation of uses, than that required by the provincial scheme.

A strikingly different approach to the issue of conflict is set out in the decision of the British Columbia Court of Appeal in *British Columbia Lottery Corp. v. Vancouver (City).*[115] In this case, the City of Vancouver passed a zoning by-law prohibiting the operation of video lottery terminals and slot machines in the City. However, the *British Columbia Lottery Corp.*, acting

---

112 [1982] 2 S.C.R. 161.

113 (1995), 23 O.R. (3d) 161 (C.A.). See also *382671 Ontario Ltd. v. London (City) Chief Building Official* (1996), 32 M.P.L.R. (2d) 1 (Ont. Gen. Div.), leave to appeal refused (1997), 1997 CarswellOnt 1024 (C.A.) which held that the deeming provision in a zoning by-law that all non-conforming uses constituted legally permitted uses was in operative conflict with s. 34(9)(a) of the *Planning Act*, R.S.O. 1990, c. P.13.

114 *Supra* note 111.

115 (1999), 169 D.L.R. (4th) 141 (B.C. C.A.).

pursuant to the *Lottery Corporation Act*,[116] enacted a regulation authorizing anyone who carried on business in British Columbia to enter into an agreement with the Lottery Corporation for the operation of Video lottery terminals and slot machines. In determining that the city by-law was valid, the court, citing the *Multiple Access* case, held that there was a move away from the compartmentalizing of powers between governments and, as such, a conflict should only be said to arise where there is actual repugnancy. That is, where compliance with one standard would result in noncompliance with the other.[117]

The Supreme Court of Canada in the *Spraytech* case endorsed this approach, where both the provincial government and the municipal by-law in question sought to regulate the use of pesticides.[118] The Court's acceptance of a pluralist approach to regulation is consistent with the Court's purposive approach to interpreting municipal powers. While municipalities remain inferior bodies, where they are regulating within the scope of their authority, they are in a better position to respond to local concerns. If a local response has the impact of creating a more stringent standard in that municipality, that is a policy decision that should be respected.

A more problematic aspect of the rule respecting conflict with superior legislation is where a municipal by-law is said to conflict with the purpose of provincial legislation. The leading case in support of this rule is *Ottawa-Carleton (Regional Municipality) v. Marlborough (Township)*.[119] In this case, a municipality, in concert with some landowners, devised a scheme whereby certain lands would be conveyed to the municipality, while the owner retained abutting lands, the effect of which was to subdivide land without the approval of the land division committee. The court quashed the resolutions enacting this scheme partly on the basis that the scheme, while complying with the letter of the law, was "inconsistent with the general policy of law as embodied in paramount legislation." In this instance, the scheme circumvented the requirements for certain approvals prior to the subdivision of land. While the result in this instance appears to be a just one, the reasoning allows for fairly broad judicial intervention with little guidance. It should be noted that the court found that the conveyances themselves were not effected for a municipal purpose and on that basis the scheme could have been defeated.

The Ontario Court of Appeal relied on the *Marlborough* decision in the *Barrick* case,[120] where a municipal restructuring proposal was quashed by the courts on the basis that it was structured to avoid the full participatory process called for under the *Municipal Act*. Interestingly, while the rationale for the decision was that the scheme was contrary to provincial policy as embodied

116 R.S.B.C. 1996, c. 279.

117 [1982] 2 S.C.R. 161.

118 *Supra* note 15 at para. 36-42.

119 (1974), 42 D.L.R. (3d) 641 (Ont. H.C.), affirmed (1974), 50 D.L.R. (3d) 68n (Ont. C.A.).

120 *Barrick Gold Corp. v. Ontario (Minister of Municipal Affairs & Housing)* (2000), 51 O.R. (3d) 194 (C.A.).

in the legislation, the provincial government in this case approved the scheme. Additionally, much of the so-called "provincial policy" was contained in regulations, which are also subordinate legislation. Distilling a binding policy from provincial legislation is at best imprecise and difficult for municipalities to predict. It is also hard to reconcile the approach in *Barrick* with the Supreme Court's determination that by-laws should only be quashed in the case of direct conflict.

6. Delegation

The limitations on municipal power are exacerbated by the rule against sub-delegation. "*Delegatus non potest delegare*," is the Latin maxim which the courts use to prevent bodies which themselves exercise a delegated authority from sub-delegating that authority to other bodies or persons. Here again the rule is closely related to the "express authority" doctrine in that the courts in determining the validity of a delegation of power by a municipal council will look for an express grant of authority to delegate that particular power. In the absence of an express authority to sub-delegate, there is presumption against it. The maxim is not unshakeable but rather, as previously discussed with respect to "express authority," discrimination and other principles of review, has been used by the courts as a device for interpreting statutes which grant authority to bodies, organizations, or individuals.[121] In requiring that a delegate exercise the power it is granted, this rule seeks to ensure that democratic accountability is not compromised by having wide discretionary powers being exercised by unelected officials.[122]

As a result, municipalities need specific authority where municipal employees or other public officials are exercising discretionary powers.[123] The general restrictions on delegation do not apply only to municipal officers or employees, but will also apply to committees of council. For example, the early case of *Simon v. Gastonguay*[124] struck down an attempted delegation of a power to remove certain buildings by Halifax City Council to its Committee on Works. Similarly, the case of *Davies v. Forest Hill (Village)*[125] clearly indicates that authority cannot be granted by council to groups within the community. In the *Davies* case, the council by-law set out regulations regarding the construction of swimming pools on residential properties. Included in these regulations was a provision that before an individual could construct a swimming pool it was necessary to have the consent in writing

121 See *Reference re Regulations (Chemical) under War Measures Act (Canada)*, [1943] S.C.R. 1, 79 C.C.C. 1, [1943] 1 D.L.R. 248 at 33-4 [S.C.R.], and Willis, "Delegatus non potest delegare" (1943) 21 Can. Bar. Rev. 257 at 257 .

122 *R. v. Holmes* (1942), [1943] 1 D.L.R. 241 (Ont. Co. Ct.) at 247.

123 *Vic Restaurant Inc. v. Montreal (City)* (1958), 17 D.L.R. (2d) 81 (S.C.C.).

124 2 M.P.R. 470, [1931] 2 D.L.R. 75 (N.S. C.A.).

125 (1964), [1965] 1 O.R. 240, 47 D.L.R. (2d) 392 (H.C.).

of all registered property owners within one hundred feet of the pool. The Court held the by-law invalid as it delegated to neighbouring property owners the authority to decide if a pool should be constructed.

The rule against sub-delegation is not absolute. There is a general recognition that requiring a delegate of power to exercise all aspects of that power is not feasible from a governance standpoint. In this regard, the courts have used the distinction between a municipality's legislative, quasi-judicial and administrative functions as a basis by which to assess the permissibility of a particular sub-delegation. Administrative authority, the courts have stated, may be delegated.[126] Without undertaking a detailed analysis of "administrative authority," it is sufficient to state that where the authority being granted by a municipality involves tasks or decisions which do not adjudicate or determine rights, and where the task or decision does not involve the exercise of a great deal of discretion, policy or legislative action on the part of the body receiving the authority, then the delegation has generally been held to be valid.[127] However, the lines between these functions are not at all clear. The result of the courts' interpretations of the nature of the authority being delegated, and thus when authority may be sub-delegated, are confusing.

Two cases may serve as illustrations. In one, *R. v. Sandler*,[128] the Court said that a by-law passed by the City of Toronto purporting to enable the fire chief to inspect fire protection equipment in any premises and to make such orders for the installation, repair or replacement of fire protection equipment as deemed necessary was invalid because only the municipality was authorized, under the *Municipal Act* (Ontario),[129] to make regulations for the prevention of fires. The Court stated that the legislature could not have intended that the municipality could evade its responsibilities for making regulations by substituting the judgment of a non-elected fire department official for its own.

The case of *R. v. Campbell*[130] offers a contrast to the *Sandler*[131] case because in the *Campbell* case a City of Toronto municipal by-law provided that no one could hold or take part in any public meeting or similar gathering in a park without approval of the time and place being given in advance by the Commissioner of Parks. The issue was again whether the City Council was delegating authority granted to it to regulate parks under the *Public Parks Act*[132] (Ontario) to the Commissioner. The Court held that the authority granted by the City was merely administrative. The Court also stated that it

126 See *R. v. Campbell* (1962), [1963] 2 O.R. 149, [1963] 2 C.C.C. 283, 38 D.L.R. (2d) 579 (C.A.).

127 *Ibid.*

128 *Supra* note 105.

129 See the *Municipal Act*, R.S.O. 1990, c. M.45, s. 210(31) – (52).

130 See *supra* note 126.

131 See *supra* note 105.

132 R.S.O. 1980, c. 417, s. 11, formerly R.S.O. 1960, c. 329, s. 11.

would be an undue burden for the Council to specify all the situations and regulations respecting the use of parks for meetings, and so it was appropriate for the Commissioner to do so.

Why councils must specify regulations for fire equipment but not for the use of parks is a mystery. Both cases involved the conflicting interest of the rule against delegation on the one hand and the facilitating of reasonable administration on the other. In the *Sandler*[133] case, the problems from the point of view of administration were the need for flexibility, the need to have different standards for different buildings, and the need to tailor requirements to specific fire hazards that would vary depending on age, material, number of stairwells, structure and height of buildings. The concern of the Court, of course, was that persons should know in advance what rules affect them and that those rules should apply uniformly. This case saw the triumph of the rule of law value over that of administration and perhaps efficiency. The resulting uniform regulations might well impose standards which would be higher than necessary in some instances.

In the *Campbell*[134] case, the same conflict can be seen. It appears reasonable from an administrative point of view to give the Commissioner of Parks some flexibility in permitting activities in parks. Meetings have to be scheduled and conflicts in timing sorted out. This cannot be completely regulated by Council. Balanced against this was the freedom of individuals to hold meetings in public areas and the importance of dealing with that freedom fairly and uniformly. However, once the Court concluded an administrative discretion was being granted, it examined the matter no further.

The traditional distinction between administrative, quasi-judicial and legislative functions has been discarded with respect to determining the procedural protections that attach to a decision.[135] Part of the move away from viewing the different functions of a municipality in a formalistic manner was based on the acknowledgement that these functions are difficult to differentiate. The distinction is still useful from a conceptual point of view, but in practice the courts should be looking beyond this distinction to more functional criteria. In this regard, it would be beneficial to consider, *inter alia,* the nature of the interests at stake, the extent to which the discretion is qualified; who is exercising the discretion, i.e. is it exercised by an elected official or can the decision be appealed to council, and the impacts on the ability of the municipality to efficiently and effectively administer the scheme in the absence of the sub-delegation.

---

133 *Supra* note 105.

134 *Supra* note 126.

135 *Old St. Bonifice Residents Assn. Inc. v. Winnipeg (City)* (1990), [1990] 3 S.C.R. 1170, 46 Admin. L.R. 161, 2 M.P.L.R. (2d) 217, [1991] 2 W.W.R. 145, 75 D.L.R. (4th) 385, Discussed in Chapter 10, *infra.*

7. Fettering of Discretion

A final restriction on the ambit of municipal powers related to the rule against delegation is that a municipality cannot fetter its legislation discretion by committing to exercise (or not exercise) its legislative powers in a prescribed manner. Because a delegated statutory power must be exercised by the person upon whom the power has been conferred, the ability to exercise that power must not be constrained by the adoption of an inflexible policy either through contractual means or in some other fashion.[136]

In the absence of an express power authorizing municipalities to enter an agreement which would have the effect of divesting or restricting its legislative powers, such agreements are *ultra vires*. Thus, a municipality that agrees to zone lands in a particular fashion in exchange for certain concessions or amenities to be provided by a landowner will be void. The public policy rationale behind this rule relates to the principle that requires municipalities to exercise their powers in the best interests of the citizens of the municipality. If through a contractual arrangement a municipality is prevented from exercising its legislative powers, a municipality may be prevented from exercising its powers in the public interest.

An interesting application of this rule was considered by the Supreme Court of Canada in *Pacific National Investments Ltd. v. Victoria (City)*.[137] In this case, the City of Victoria entered into an agreement with a developer whereby the developer would provide certain public improvements to the lands based on an agreed upon zoning and subdivision arrangement which was duly enacted by the municipality. After the developer had carried out these improvements and had partially completed the development of the lands in question, there was significant public concern respecting aspects of the development scheme. As a consequence, Council downzoned some of the lands. The developer sued for damages based on an implied term in the contract requiring the municipality to maintain the agreed upon zoning. The Supreme Court, in a split decision, reaffirmed the rule against the fettering of discretion and further held that indirect fettering, in this case, an implied term that compensation would follow any downzoning, was also illegal. The minority held that the municipality had the authority to enter into an agreement which provided for compensation as part of the municipality's wider authority to contract.

It is important to note that the rule against fettering only relates to a municipality's legislative powers and the Supreme Court draws a distinction between contracts entered into as part of the municipality's business or proprietary functions and those relating to its legislative functions. Thus, a municipality may be able to bind successor councils under a purchasing arrangement. The distinction between legislative and other functions will not

---

136 Jones and de Villars, *supra* note 107 at 168.

137 [2000] 2 S.C.R. 919, reconsideration refused (2001), 2001 CarswellBC 523 (S.C.C.).

always be apparent as almost any arrangement will require the municipality to enact by-laws or pass resolutions. Even business commitments of a long term nature may have the indirect effect of limiting a municipality's ability to react to issues of public policy. Notwithstanding the difficulty of this distinction, it is a valid distinction from a public policy standpoint, allowing municipalities to engage in beneficial long term arrangements without derogating to a significant degree their ability to enact by-laws as circumstances dictate.

F. CONCLUSION

Since the first edition of this book many of the concerns documented have begun to be addressed by the courts. In particular, the rigid adherence to the express authority doctrine at the expense of a more rational, purpose based approach has been largely dispensed with. The general rule respecting the scope of municipal authority has been consistently formulated as follows: "Municipalities have only those powers expressly conferred on them, powers necessarily following from these, or powers essential to municipal purposes."[138] This articulation of the rule is not in form different from the express authority doctrine as set out as "Dillon's Rule" in *Ottawa Electric Light Co.*[139] However, the strict application of this rule has been tempered by the courts' acceptance of the appropriateness of adopting a broad and purposive approach to the interpretation of municipal legislation. A good example of the application of this approach was the Supreme Court of Canada's consideration of the issue of discrimination in the *Spraytech*[140] case, where the court upheld the distinction made in the by-laws between residential and agricultural uses of pesticides with reference to the purpose of the health and welfare power, concluding that a denial of the agricultural exception would be at cross purposes to the overall intent of the health and welfare clause and, thus, the distinction was necessary to the exercise of the power. There may, of course, be instances where a distinction cannot be supported by the legislation, if, for example, the pesticide ban only applied to one geographic area within the Town, but so long as the acceptability of such distinctions is made with reference to the overall legislative context, the decisions are less likely to appear arbitrary.

The broader approach has resulted in the courts taking into consideration the context in which municipal decision-making and policy setting occurs, with particular reference to the democratic elements of local government. Moreover, the principle of subsidiarity, which suggests that local governments are best suited to make policy decisions on matters of local interest, is

---

138 *Ibid.* at 942.

139 *Supra* note 24.

140 *Supra* note 15.

beginning to enjoy some currency as a basis to determine the scope of municipal authority. This may lead the courts to consider more probingly questions relating to a municipal government's democratic legitimacy. For example, should the traditionally low voter participation rates in municipal elections be a relevant consideration in assessing municipal autonomy in the exercise of their powers? Likewise, to what extent should municipalities be required to consider and protect minority rights in their formulation of policy? These are unquestionably valid considerations. However, the rational approach which is now emerging is capable of assessing these claims in the context of the particular decision under review.

Despite the move away from a strict interpretation of municipal powers, there remain clear limits to municipal authority from both a legal and policy perspective. For example, the courts have maintained that a purposive approach should only apply to expressly conferred powers.[141] As a result, municipalities, when faced with a novel situation not yet contemplated by municipal legislation, may still face significant jurisdictional limits to the exercise of their powers. In this regard, it must be remembered that municipal legislation across Canada is largely drafted with specifically enumerated powers, regulating in considerable detail the particular areas in which municipalities may legislate. While this problem may be alleviated to some degree by a more expansive approach to the interpretation of municipal omnibus clauses, these clauses are not wholly open ended and the Courts have been careful to state that omnibus clauses cannot be used to expand the scope of an existing specific authority.[142]

Provincial legislatures have responded to this issue in a variety of ways. In Alberta, the legislature has amended the *Municipal Government Act* to include the granting of "natural person powers" to municipalities.[143] Ontario has enacted similar legislation.[144] The intent of this provision is to provide municipalities with the same broad powers that are enjoyed inherently by natural persons. To some degree this amendment inverts the traditional authority analysis by providing municipalities with the freedom to acquire and dispose of property and to contract, subject only to the express limitations contained within the Act. The utility of this approach remains to be seen, although it is noteworthy that in subsequent decisions respecting municipal authority in Alberta, the courts have not used the natural person powers to justify an expansion of powers beyond those contained in the specific provision of the *Municipal Government Act*. It should be noted that notwithstanding the inclusion of natural person powers, the *Municipal Government Act* still contains very detailed and specific language respecting particular powers. Thus, there remain restrictions on the disposal of real property, on investment,

---

141 *Supra* note 137 at 942.

142 *Supra* note 15 at 259-261.

143 *Municipal Government Act*, R.S.A. 2000, c. M-26, s. 6.

144 *Municipal Act, 2001*, S.O. 2001, c. 25, s. 8.

borrowing and the ability to control profit corporations. Very clearly, natural person powers cannot serve to enlarge a municipality's legislative authority since the ability to pass by-laws or to issue permits and licenses falls outside the scope of natural person powers.

A more useful tool also contained in the *Municipal Government Act* is the conferring of jurisdiction to pass by-laws in respect of broadly defined areas such as, "the safety, health and welfare of people and the protection of people and property," "transport and transportation systems," "nuisances" and "business activities."[145] Likewise, in Ontario, the legislative scheme refers to "spheres of jurisdiction" in which municipalities will have plenary authority to enact by-laws within those "spheres of jurisdiction," subject to conflict with legislative instruments of senior levels of government and other conditions and restrictions contained within the Act.

In addition, the Ontario *Municipal Act, 2001* and the Alberta *Municipal Government Act* contain explicit interpretive directions which affirm the right of municipal councils to govern as they consider appropriate and "to respond to present and future issues in their municipalities."[146] These broad powers are still subject to any specific by-law passing powers contained within the Act, but they are not to be read down in light of the specific powers (i.e. in the same fashion that the Supreme Court has read down omnibus clauses in light of specific provisions).[147] The use of broadly defined powers and explicit direction for the interpretation of those powers accords with the judicial trend towards viewing municipal governments as democratic institutions deserving of sufficient autonomy to reflect the values and needs of municipal inhabitants.

145 *Ibid.* at s. 7.

146 *Ibid.* at s. 9.

147 R.S.A. 2000, c. M-26, s. 10; S.O. 2001, c. 25, s. 15.

5

Municipal Liability in Negligence

A. INTRODUCTION

Municipalities are increasingly called upon to perform a wide variety of functions to fulfill their legislative responsibilities. As their involvement in our daily affairs grows, there is a corresponding risk of harm to individuals through the negligent actions of municipal officials or employees. Individuals who have suffered a loss as a result of municipal activities can seek political solutions to their problems, but political redress may often be ineffective, particularly where the harm suffered is directed towards one or two persons, (who are less likely to mobilize broad political support to address their losses). There are other avenues to attack the exercise of municipal powers, such as judicial review of municipal action, discussed above. However, when economic or physical harm results from the exercise of these powers, public law judicial review will not provide a sufficient basis for negligent actions, which are often taken within a municipality's jurisdiction, and even where the impugned conduct lies outside a municipality's jurisdiction, damages to compensate the harmed individual are generally not available as a public law remedy. As a consequence, persons who suffer damages as a result of wrongful municipal activities most often seek their remedies through private law causes of action, such as negligence.[1]

In order to establish liability in negligence on the part of a municipality, a plaintiff must, of course, establish the essential elements of the tort, namely, a duty of care owed by the municipality, a breach of the standard of care and damages. However, because a municipality's duties are definable in public law, different considerations will arise with respect to municipal liability. Tort liability may be seen as another form of judicial review of municipal actions, in the sense that the courts are called upon to determine the boundaries of appropriate municipal behavior, except these boundaries are drawn with

---

1 There are other common law sources of municipal liability such as nuisance, trespass, assault and liability in contract. A consideration of these issues is beyond the scope of this chapter, but see Boghosian and Davison, *The Law of Municipal Liability in Canada* (Toronto: Butterworths, 1999); Hillel David, ed., *Thomson Rogers on Municipal Liability* (Toronto: Canada Law Book Inc., 1997).

reference to private law standards of reasonableness, as opposed to public law considerations, such as jurisdiction or bad faith.

Determining the scope and nature of these elements requires the court to define the types of relationships and conduct for which liability can be imposed and to establish the standards to be applied to that conduct. However, unlike private actors, municipalities are involved in a range of governmental functions, such as exercising legislative, quasi-judicial and administrative powers, which significantly complicate the application of private law remedies to municipal activities. Like the application of public law remedies to municipal decisions, there are compelling public policy reasons to limit judicial intervention in the policy-making functions of local government. Consequently, it is not surprising that in the sphere of private law, an attempt has been made to circumscribe the limits of judicial intervention with the *bona fide* exercise of statutory powers by municipalities.

In an action against a municipality for the negligent exercise of its powers, the courts are potentially called upon to measure decisions authorized by statute against an objective standard of reasonableness. Yet decisions in the arena of politics are often value-laden reflections of local opinion, which have traditionally been evaluated through the electoral and not the judicial process. As discussed in relation to the public law standards of review, one of the reasons why *intra vires* municipal decisions have not been reviewed on a reasonableness standard is that, through the creation of local government, we have chosen to have elected representatives or their delegates make these types of decisions, even if they are unreasonable. This position is supported by the separation of powers and the supremacy of Parliament in substantive policy matters.[2] Judicial evaluation of political decisions on a standard of reasonableness offers the courts an opportunity to substitute their views for those of the legislature or its delegates, including municipalities, and as such may be seen as incompatible with the democratic objectives of local government.

As a result of the foregoing considerations, there has been a traditional reluctance on the part of the courts to hold public authorities to the same standards of tort liability as those governing private persons. However, as the sphere of public activities broadened, a general exception to liability in tort became untenable. The essential tension that both the courts and legislature must grapple with in this regard is the need to protect the public from the negligent activities of public authorities, while minimizing judicial interference with the policy making functions of those same public authorities.

In recognition of the tensions inherent in the judicial review of governmental decision-making through actions in negligence, legislatures, courts

---

2 Legislative supremacy and institutional incompetence have been offered as the substantive basis for immunizing governmental decision from a review through actions in negligence. See Cohen; Feldthusen at 290; and Cohen and Smith at 7 and 8, all *infra* note 3.

and commentators[3] have addressed the question of when and whether it is appropriate for the courts to review a decision of a public authority, its employees or officers through an action in negligence.[4] Because the law in the U.K. and the U.S. has influenced and is likely to continue to influence Canadian law on these issues, it is helpful to understand the law as it has evolved in these jurisdictions.

B. THE DEVELOPMENT OF PUBLIC AUTHORITY LIABILITY

1. The United Kingdom

Governmental immunity in England originated in the notion of sovereign immunity, which prevented the King from being sued in his own court. This broad immunity was extended to all levels of government, including local governments.[5] However, liability for negligence against public authorities, including municipalities, has been accepted in the U.K. courts on a restricted basis since the late eighteenth century,[6] with the courts being reluctant to impose liability against public authorities in a manner equal to individuals, particularly in the area of the discretionary exercise of statutory powers. One early distinction the courts made was between the exercise of statutory duties and statutory powers. In the exercise of a statutory duty, a general duty in private law could be found because the public authority had an obligation to act. However, statutory powers that authorized the carrying out of activities, but did not mandate them, could not give rise to a duty of care in the absence of some special duty owed to the plaintiff.[7] Given that a vast area of municipal activity falls within the category of statutory powers, this formulation provided a broad immunity from liability for municipal

---

3 See: Cohen, "The Public and Private Law Dimensions of the UFFI Problem: Part II," (1983-84) 8 Can. Bus. L.J. 410; Feldthusen B., *Economic Negligence*, 2nd ed. (Toronto: Carswell, 1989) at 281-328; Hogg, *Liability of the Crown*, 2nd ed. (Toronto: Carswell, 1989) at 121-140; Makuch, "Municipal Immunity from Liability in Negligence" in Steel and Rodgers-Magnet (eds.), *Issues in Tort Law* (Toronto: Carswell, 1983); Shibley, "Liability of Public Authorities in Negligence" (1983) Law Society of Upper Canada, Special Lectures, *Torts in the 80s*, 255; Smillie, "Liability of Public Authorities in Negligence" (1985) 23 U.W.O.L Rev. 213; Cohen and Smith, "Entitlement and the Body Politic: Rethinking Negligence in Public Law" (1986) 64 Can. Bar Rev. 1.

4 Some commentators have suggested that the traditional law of negligence is incapable of dealing with many types of governmentally caused harms and other methods of compensating for governmentally caused harms have been offered. Compensation schemes based on invalidity, risk and entitlement have been proposed. For a discussion of these schemes see Hogg *supra* note 3 at 113.

5 See Cohen and Smith, *supra* note 3 at 2; *Russell v. Men of Devon* (1788), 2 Term Rep. 667, 100 Eng. Rep. 359.

6 Cohen and Smith, *supra* note 3 at 2; *Mersey Docks & Harbour Board v. Gibbs* (1866), 11 H.L.C. 686 (U.K. H.L.).

7 *Kent v. East Suffolk Rivers Catchment Board*, [1940] 4 All E.R. 527 (H.L.).

activities, particularly with regard to the acceptance of novel claims arising out of an expanding role for public authorities. A further distinction relied upon was that between "nonfeasance" and "misfeasance," imposing liability only where a positive act was negligently undertaken (misfeasance), but not where a public authority simply failed to act at all, notwithstanding that it had the power to do so (nonfeasance).

This theory of immunity was substantially altered by the House of Lords in the case of *Anns v. Merton London Borough Council*.[8] In *Anns*, the issue at hand, as a preliminary question of law, was whether, in the exercise of the statutory power of inspection, a local authority could be under a private law duty of care. In holding that the public authority could be under such a duty of care, the dichotomy between statutory duties and statutory powers was no longer to be determinative of immunity or liability. Rather, to determine if a public authority could, in addition to being under a public law duty, be under a private law duty of care, a two step approach was proposed. First, one determined if, within the factual and statutory context, there was the necessary proximity between the public authority and the individual so as to give rise to a duty of care, i.e. forseeability. Secondly, assuming there was forseeability, the immunity or potential liability of the public authority would depend on the nature of the challenged act or omission. Considered policy decisions, for example, those involving the allocation of resources, if taken within the grant of statutory discretion, could give rise to no private law duty of care. Purely operational acts or omissions being the practical implementation of these policy decisions that involved no discretion, such as inspections according to specified guidelines, could give rise to a private law duty of care. Operational acts or omissions involving the exercise of discretion, for example, discretion as to the time and matter of the inspection and the techniques to be used, could only give rise to private law duty of care, if they were taken outside of the delegated discretion.

The *Anns* case involved the statutory power to inspect buildings to ensure their compliance with adequate standards of construction. There was no positive duty to inspect, but in this case the local authority had passed by-laws providing for a system of inspection. The plaintiffs alleged that either the inspection was not carried out or it was not carried out without due care because a subsequent investigation showed that the foundation of the building in question was not set deep enough into the ground. The defendant Council argued that since there was no positive obligation to carry out an inspection, it followed that there could not exist a duty to carry out an inspection with due care. In the court's view, while the local authority was under no obligation to carry out inspections under the relevant legislation, it was under an obligation to "give proper consideration to the question whether they should inspect or not."[9] In rejecting the defendant's argument, the House of Lords

8 [1977] 2 All E.R. 492 (H.L.).

9 *Ibid.* at 501.

held that the Council, having made the policy decision to create a system of inspection, owed a duty to implement that policy with reasonable care. The difficulty in distinguishing between policy decisions on the one hand, and operational decisions on the other, was not lost on the court and Lord Wilberforce noted that the distinction was probably one of degree.[10]

The implication of this decision was to open up the whole range of municipal activities undertaken pursuant to discretionary powers to liability based in the first instance on questions of forseeability of harm and then, if a *prima facie* duty is found, upon whether the decision in question fell outside the scope of exempted policy decisions.

A more difficult aspect of the decision was the court's determination that in order to be properly immune from liability, a decision made at the operational level would have to be a *bona fide* exercise of the discretionary powers. Thus, it appears that there may be wide immunity from liability at the implementation stage, provided the steps taken are *bona fide*. It is not clear what the court meant by *bona fide* in this context, although Lord Wilberforce suggests that the decision would need to be *intra vires*. It seems that the court wanted to ensure that municipalities, at a minimum, take into consideration relevant matters that have larger policy implications. The requirement for *bona fides* appears to extend beyond technical decisions. Consequently, the defendant was liable in *Anns* for failing to properly consider its responsibilities towards public safety when it decided not to exercise its powers of inspection.

More recently, the U.K. courts have moved away from the reliance of the two part test in *Anns*, in favour of a more contextual and functional determination of whether it is just and reasonable to impose a duty of care on a public authority. The primary question to be resolved in determining this issue is whether in light of the statutory and factual context there exists between the public authority and the individual harmed such a close and direct relationship as to place the public authority under a duty of care to the individual in the exercise of its statutory obligations.[11]

In resolving this issue, the U.K. courts have generally not been inclined to impose a duty of care on a public authority in the exercise of its statutory powers. The approach, which begins with a careful analysis and weighing of all relevant competing considerations, is that "the law should develop categories of negligence incrementally by analogy with established categories."[12] The relevant considerations that are examined, aside from the necessary ingredient of foreseeability of harm, include: whether the harm was caused by a third party and if so to what degree the public authority controlled the

---

10 *Ibid.* at 500.

11 *Yuen Kun Yeu v. Hong Kong (Attorney General)*, [1987] 2 All E.R. 705 (Hong Kong P.C.) at 712; *Davis v. Radcliffe*, [1990] 2 All E.R. 536 (P.C.).

12 *Rowling v. Takaro Properties Ltd.*, [1988] 1 All E.R. 163 at 172; *Murphy*, *infra*, note 19 at 915; and *Davis*, *ibid.* at 540.

third party;[13] whether a special relationship, which generally involves individualized reliance, existed between the public authority and the harmed individual;[14] a determination of the party for whose benefit the public authority was acting;[15] the purpose of the legislation and what statutory obligations it imposed;[16] the effect of imposing a duty of care on the public authority;[17] the nature and type of discretion exercised by the public authority;[18] and the type of loss occasioned.[19] The resort to these considerations has tended to weigh against the imposition of a duty of care on the public authority. This approach then, while not using immunity terminology can be said to effectively provide a public authority with a wide immunity from actions for the negligent exercise of statutory obligations.

2. The United States

The evolution of the law in the U.S. has followed a similar trajectory; starting with a broad immunity for federal and state governments, as well as municipal governments,[20] but moving away from the rule of complete immunity to a more qualified immunity for local governments. In this regard, there are three basic doctrines that U.S. courts have utilized to limit or immunize municipal governments from liability in negligence. The first doctrine applied in many states, and often referred to as the "duty to all, duty to no-one" rule, is utilized in situations where an individual attempts to hold the governmental entity liable for the negligent performance of a statutory duty that is owed to the general public, for example, policing or fire protection. This doctrine is also referred to as the "government function / specific function" dichotomy. Generally, absent a special relationship, which requires the claimant to demonstrate detrimental reliance and an individualized relationship with the governmental entity, the municipality will be under no duty of care to the injured party in relation to the exercise of a general government function. The rationale offered in support of the doctrine's application is that actions in negligence against a municipality in the performance of these public functions would interfere with governmental operations and subject munic-

13 *Yuen, supra* note 11 at 711 and 713; *Davis, supra* note 11 at 541.

14 *Yuen, ibid*; *Hill v. Chief Constable of West Yorkshire*, [1988] 2 All E.R. 238 (H.L.) at 243; *Davis, supra* note 11 at 541.

15 *Ibid.*

16 *Yuen, supra* note 11 at 713.

17 *Rowling, supra* note 12.

18 *Yuen, supra* note 11 at 713; *Davis, supra* note 11 at 541; *Hill, supra* note 14 at 240.

19 *Davis, supra* note 11 at 541; *Murphy v. Brentwood District Council*, [1990] 2 All E.R. 908 (H.L.).

20 Discussed generally in Bouchard, "Government Liability in Tort", (1924) 34 Yale L.J. 1; early cases include *Cohens v. Virginia*, 19 U.S. 264 (1821) and *Reeside v. Walker*, 52 U.S. 272 (1850); as applied to a municipality see *Mower v. Inhabitants of Leicester*, 9 Mass. 247 (1812).

ipalities to an overwhelming burden.[21] This is a difficult test to apply given the breadth of these competing functions and the inherent difficulties in disentangling a municipality's public and private functions.

Under the next two doctrines, the court reviews the nature of the decision or action taken by the municipality and categorizes it. Depending on the category of the activity, the municipality may be immune from an action in negligence. Under the first of these doctrines, the municipality will be immune from liability for "governmental" (mandatory, public, essential) activities, but potentially liable for "proprietary" (private, corporate, commercial) activities.[22] For example, activities of the police or fire fighters, though carelessly performed, are usually considered governmental and as a result the municipality is immune from liability. On the other hand, if the municipality operates a utility for which fees are charged, this is analogous to private enterprise (usually considered proprietary), so that the municipality may be liable in negligence for the operation of this activity.[23]

While this approach may be less coarse grained than the "duty to all, duty to no-one" rule, looking more specifically at the various functions of public actors, on the whole, the distinctions, tests and various results arising from this distinction have been severely criticized,[24] with the U.S. Supreme Court stating, in rejecting the application of this doctrine to claims against the federal government:

> It would push the courts into the non-governmental / governmental quagmire that has long plagued the law of municipal corporations. A comparative study of the cases in the 48 states will disclose a clear and irreconcilable conflict. More than that, decisions of each state are disharmonious and disclose the inevitable chaos of courts trying to apply a rule of law that is inherently unsound.[25]

The final doctrine utilized may be referred to as the "discretionary function immunity doctrine." This doctrine is used by a majority of jurisdictions in the U.S. to immunize federal, state and municipal governments from actions in negligence. The basic rule is that a public entity acting within the

---

21 For a comprehensive discussion and critique of the public duty doctrine see MacMillan, "Government Liability and the Public Duty Doctrine" (1987) 32 Vill. L. Rev. 505. See also Kiely, *Modern Liability Recovery in the 90's* (New York: John Wiley and Sons, 1990) at 153 - 227 for a discussion of the doctrine and its application to a wide variety of governmental functions.

22 See: *Bailey v. City of New York*, 3 Hill 531 (1824) and *Owen v. City of Independence*, 445 U.S. 622, 100 S.Ct. 1398 (1980) for discussion of this doctrine as well as a discussion of the discretionary function immunity doctrine.

23 *Prosser and Keeton on the Law of Torts*, 5th ed. (St. Paul, Minn.: West Publishing Co.,1984) at 1053.

24 Speiser, Krause and Gans *The American Law of Torts* (Rochester, New York: The Lawyers Co-operative Publishing Co., 1985) Vol. 2 at 48-61.

25 *Indian Towing v. United States*, 350 U.S. 61 (1955).

scope of its authority is not liable for discretionary policy acts or omissions, but may be liable in tort when acting in a ministerial or operational capacity.[26]

The doctrine appears to have originated in the interpretation of a statutory exception in the *Federal Tort Claims Act*, 1946,[27] preserving the immunity for:

> Any claim based upon an act or omission of an employee of the government, exercising due care, in the execution of a statute or regulation whether or not such statute or regulation be valid, or based on the exercise or performance or the failure to exercise or perform the discretionary function or duty on the part of a federal agency or an employee of the government, whether or not the discretion involved be abused.[28]

The breadth and scope of this exception was clarified by the U.S. Supreme Court in *Berkovitz By Berkovitz v. United States*[29] where the Court held that the discretionary function exemption did not bar claims alleging that a U.S. government agency negligently issued a license to a polio vaccines manufacturer and negligently released a particular non-conforming vaccine lot. In determining whether or not the exemption applied, the Court stated that it was the nature of the conduct, rather than the status of the actor, that governed whether the exemption would apply in a given case. On examining the nature of the challenged act, the court must first consider whether the action is a matter of choice for the government entity or its acting delegate. Where the agency or employee must follow a prescribed course of action, the discretionary function exemption does not apply.

Even where the challenged conduct involved an element of judgment, the court must still determine whether the judgment is of the kind the exemption was designed to protect. As the rationale for the discretionary function exemption was to "prevent judicial second-guessing of legislative and administrative decisions grounded in social, economic and political policy through the medium of an action in tort," the exemption properly construed only protects government actions and decisions based on considerations of public policy.[30]

Most state courts have also recognized the discretionary exception and have acknowledged that its purpose is to preserve the separation of powers and prevent unwarranted judicial intervention with legislative and executive

26 Kiely, *supra* note 21 at 155; see also "The Demise of the Discretionary Exemption to Sovereign Immunity" (1989) 18 Stetson L. Rev. 615.

27 See 28 U.S.C.

28 *Ibid.* s. 2679(a).

29 108 S.Ct. 1954 (1988). See also *United States v. S. A. Empresa de Viacao Aerea Rio Grandense (Varig Airlines)*, 467 U.S. 797 (U.S. Cal., 1984); *Dalehite v. United States*, 346 U.S. 15 (U.S. Tex. 1953); *Indian Towing, supra* note 25; and *Blessing v. United States*, 447 F.S. 1160.

30 *Supra* note 27 at s. 1959.

actions under the guise of tort claims.[31] Defining discretionary functions, however, has proved to be a difficult task, with some state courts distinguishing between planning and operational functions, and others distinguishing design activities from maintenance or ministerial tasks. Because very few governmental actions can be neatly categorized, the use of catch phrases has proved problematic,[32] and some state courts have turned to the rationale underlying the need for the immunity, and have indicated that it is basic policy decisions that are to be immunized.[33] For example, one court set out the rationale in the following terms:

> Liability cannot be imposed when condemnation of the acts or omissions relied upon *necessarily* brings into question the propriety of governmental objectives or programs or the decision of one who, with the authority to do so, determined that the acts or omissions involved should occur or that the risk which eventuated should be encountered for the advancement of governmental objectives.[34]

In this regard, some courts have adopted a preliminary test consisting of the following four questions to determine whether the discretionary exception to liability should apply:

1. Does the challenged act, omission or decision necessarily involve a basic governmental policy, program or objective?
2. Is the questioned act, omission or decision essential to the realization or accomplishment of the policy, program or objective as opposed to one which would not change the course or direction of the policy, program or objective?
3. Does the act, omission or decision require the exercise of basic policy evaluation, judgment and expertise on the part of the governmental agency involved?
4. Does the governmental agency involved possess the requisite constitutional, statutory or lawful authority and duty to do or make the challenged act, omission or decision?[35]

If all four questions are answered affirmatively, then the governmental conduct is deemed to be discretionary. A large number of state legislatures have adopted a statutory discretionary exemption similar to that found in the federal legislation, and as a result interpretation given to the federal legislation

---

31 *Supra* note 26, "Demise of the Discretionary Exception to Sovereign Immunity" at 621, 622.

32 *Ibid.* at 622.

33 See for example: *Johnson v. California*, 447 P.2d 352 (1968); *Wedgeworth v. Harris*, 592 F. Supp. 155 at 163; *Japan Airlines v. State*, 628 P.2d 934 at 936; *Nusbaum v. Blueworth County*, 422 N.W.2d 713 at 718; see also *Evangelical United Brethren Church v. State*, 407 P.2d 440 (1965) and *Department of Health and Rehabilitative Services v. Yamuni*, 529 So. 2d 258.

34 *Evangelical United Church, ibid.* at 445, quoting Peck, 31 Wash. L. Rev. 207.

35 *Ibid.* at 445.

has been given significant weight to the interpretation of the state discretionary exemption.

C. PUBLIC AUTHORITY LIABILITY IN CANADA

The starting place for the modern law of municipal liability in Canada begins with the acceptance of the *Anns* test into Canadian law as a result of the Supreme Court's decision in *Nielsen v. Kamloops (City)*.[36] Like the *Anns*[37] case, the *Kamloops* case involved a claim against a municipality for failure to carry out a building inspection with due care. In considering whether liability could be imposed against a public authority in relation to its discretionary power, the Supreme Court held that the potential liability or immunity of a public authority is to be determined in accordance with the two stage approach set out in *Anns*. The Supreme Court stated the test as follows:

1) Is there a sufficiently close relationship between the parties, (the local authority and the person who has suffered the damage) so that, in the reasonable contemplation of the authority, carelessness on its part might cause damage to that person? If so,
2) Are any considerations which ought to negate or limit (a) the scope of the duty and (b) the class of persons to whom it is owed or (c) the damages to which a breach of it may give rise?

It is within this second stage that the court considers whether there are statutory, common law, public law, or policy considerations that operate to immunize the public authority or restrict the scope of the duty. In this case, the municipality carried out an inspection, noted defaults and issued a stop work order, but took no further steps to ensure compliance with the order. The failure in this case was not the decision not to take further steps, but rather that the municipality failed to give due consideration whether further steps should be taken. Thus, the decision to do nothing fell outside the proper limits of the statutory discretion and, consequently attracted liability. Interestingly, there was no finding of bad faith *per se*, rather the finding was that the decision taken was not *bona fide*, as it was not made with due care.

There are two areas of ambiguity in the approach adopted in the *Kamloops* case. First, the dividing line between policy and operational decisions is very difficult to discern. Certainly, the judges in minority were of the view that the failure in question involved a decision whether to commence enforcement proceedings, a decision which only council could take and which involved policy considerations. The majority, on the other hand, characterized the decision as being of an operational nature, even though it involved dis-

36 [1984] 2 S.C.R. 2.
37 *Supra* note 8.

cretion, but determined that the discretion had not been properly exercised and was not, therefore, immune from liability. This leads to the second area of ambiguity; determining the standard upon which a discretionary decision shall be found to be improperly exercised. It seems that the Supreme Court wants to inject a consideration of reasonableness in determining whether a decision should be subject to liability. The Supreme Court, in its discussion of whether discretion was properly exercised, states, "Where the question whether the requisite act should be taken has not even been considered in good faith, it seems clear that for that very reason, the authority has not acted with reasonable care."[38] By conflating the considerations of policy/operation and reasonableness, the Supreme Court obscures the basis for the immunity in the first place. Policy decisions should be immune precisely because they are not amenable to considerations of reasonableness. These issues respecting the policy/operation dichotomy and the *bona fide* exercise of discretion were central considerations in the Supreme Court's decisions in three subsequent decisions, *Just v. British Columbia,*[39] *Brown v. British Columbia (Minister of Transportation & Highways)*[40] and *Swinamer v. Nova Scotia (Attorney General),*[41] which define the Canadian law as it currently stands. While none of these decisions involve a municipal defendant, the scope of liability for public authorities that these cases delineate apply equally to local government decisions and activities.

In *Just*, the appellant's vehicle was stopped in a line of traffic on a major highway in a mountainous region of British Columbia. A large boulder fell from the slope above the highway and struck the appellant's vehicle, seriously injuring the appellant and killing his daughter. The appellant sued the province in negligence, alleging that the system developed to prevent rockfalls and the manner in which it was implemented were negligent.

The province was under no statutory duty to maintain the highway, but had exercised its statutory powers to implement a maintenance system.[42] The system developed to implement the governmental decision to prevent rockfalls had not been the subject matter of a written policy statement or directive, but rather the British Columbia Department of Highways, which had the authority to maintain provincial highways, including the prevention of rockslides, had created a Rock Work Section and its engineers were responsible for rock stabilization inspections on the highway. The practice of these engineers had been to make visual inspections from the highway unless there

38 *Supra* note 36 at 24.

39 [1989] 2 S.C.R. 1228.

40 (1994), 112 D.L.R. (4th) 1 (S.C.C.).

41 [1994] 1 S.C.R. 445.

42 *Supra* note 39. The province had however abrogated sovereign immunity and was subject to liabilities as though it were an ordinary person. In the context of the maintenance of highways the legislation provided that it was not subject to any greater liability than that of a municipality. The case then clearly sets out the common law parameters of a municipality's liability in negligence for the maintenance and inspection of its roads.

was evidence of or history of rock instability in the area in which case the engineers would climb the slope for a closer inspection. The engineers would then submit their findings and recommendations to a District Highway Manager, who in turn would submit a requisition for a rock scaling crew whose purpose was to perform remedial work on the slopes.[43] The slope in question had been visually inspected from the highway on a number of occasions, but had not been the subject matter of a close inspection because the rock work crew did not deem it to be a priority.[44]

The primary issue at all levels of court was whether the decisions as to the system of inspection and remediation were decisions of policy or operations. In the lower courts, it was held that the challenged decisions were ones of policy and immune from review by the court.[45] The majority of the Supreme Court of Canada overruled the lower courts and held that the decisions regarding the system of inspection and remediation were operational in nature and, therefore, reviewable through an action in negligence. The matter was accordingly sent back for trial on the issue of whether the government's system met the appropriate standard of care.[46]

In coming to this conclusion, the Court provided analysis and general guidelines on how to distinguish between "true" policy decisions and operational ones. The analysis commences with the general proposition, supported by the legislative abrogation of sovereign immunity,[47] that a public authority will be subject to a duty of care as though it was an ordinary individual except where it is making political decisions that are not amenable to any objective standard of review. These types of decisions the Court suggests are ones based upon social, political or economic factors.[48]

Therefore, as a general guideline, the Court proposed that policy decisions are ones which "involve or are dictated by financial, economic, social or political factors or constraints," while operational decisions, which can be evaluated on objective standards are "merely the product of administrative direction, expert or professional opinion, technical standards or general standards of reasonableness."[49]

These general guidelines, which are to be used to distinguish between policy and operation appear to have been dispositive of the issue in this case,[50]

---

43 *Supra*, note 39 at 1232, 1233.

44 *Ibid.* at 1254.

45 (1986), [1987] 2 W.W.R. 231 (B.C. C.A.), affirming [1985] 5 W.W.R. 570 (B.C. S.C.).

46 *Supra* note 39 at 1247, Justice Sopinka dissenting.

47 In this case, s. 2 of the *Crown Proceeding Act*, R.S.B.C. 1979, c. 86.

48 *Supra* note 39 at 1239-42. See also: *Ryan* v. *Victoria (City)* [1999] 1 S.C.R. 201, (1999), 50 M.P.L.R. (2d) 1 (S.C.C.), for a discussion of the "scope" of the duty of care which can be limited by broad policy considerations such as efficiency and economic fairness or on specific principles of law which operate in particular circumstances.

49 *Supra* note 39 at 1242.

50 *Ibid.* at 1246. The usefulness of using these criteria to distinguish between governmental decisions that are reviewable and those that are not has been questioned, on the basis that

but are not necessarily dispositive in all cases, for it is only "true" policy decisions that are immune from actions. Distinguishing "true" policy decisions, from other types of decisions introduces a further unspecified standard of reasonableness into the analysis.[51] In addition, the majority appears to draw a distinction between decisions that are made at a high level and those made at a low level.

At a high level, to constitute a "true" policy decision immune from liability, the public authority must make its decision in a reasonable manner, which constitutes a *bona fide* exercise of discretion. What this means is unclear, though a considered decision based on the availability of funds appears to satisfy the test.[52] In the context of a decision concerning inspections, the public authority must make a considered policy decision whether to implement an inspection system, and if a system is implemented, it must be a reasonable one in all the circumstances.[53]

Decisions taken at a lower level, for example by the inspectors themselves, as to how and when the inspections are to be conducted, may also constitute "true" policy decisions, if they are considered decisions, based on, for example, the availability of resources, and the public authority establishes that the decision taken at this level was a reasonable one in light of the surrounding circumstances.[54]

If, however, decisions regarding when to inspect, or what particular system is to be utilized, are not considered decisions taken on a reasonable basis, such as availability of funds, but rather arise as a matter of practice,[55] or on the basis of technical or scientific opinion, then they will not constitute "true" policy decisions, but will instead be found to be operational decisions, which can be reviewed through an action in negligence.[56]

It therefore appears that in order to constitute a "true" policy decision, a public authority, upon being granted discretionary statutory powers, must, acting in a "reasonable" manner, consider whether to act pursuant to a power, and if it does so, the system or method adopted to implement a decision must be a "reasonable" one in all the circumstances. Unreasonable decisions, it is implied, will not constitute a *bona fide* exercise of discretion, and will not be considered true policy decisions. Moreover, when the discretionary decision-making authority is delegated to lower level officials, the public authority must establish that the decision taken was a reasonable one in all the circumstances.

---

operational decisions cannot be divorced from financial, social or political factors. See Feldthusen, *Economic Negligence, supra*, note 3 at 307.

51 *Ibid.* at 1242-43.

52 *Ibid.* at 1242-43.

53 *Ibid.* at 1242.

54 *Ibid* at 1243.

55 *Laurentide Motels Ltd. c. Beauport (Ville)*, [1989] 1 S.C.R. 705.

56 *Supra*, note 39.

This analysis appears to necessitate a judicial review of both high and low level governmental decisions, even those based on political factors, such as the allocation of resources, to determine whether the decision taken was reasonable in all the circumstances. It is not clear what this standard of reasonableness amounts to or whether it is appreciably different from a consideration of the standard of care.[57]

These same issues were addressed again by the Supreme Court in two decisions heard and decided at the same time. In *Brown v. British Columbia (Minister of Transportation & Highways)*, the policy in issue was the decision by the municipality to operate its summer road maintenance routine in November. As a consequence, there were fewer on duty workers working reduced hours, a fact that may have resulted in an icy condition not being remedied sooner. In denying liability, the court determined that the level of maintenance service to be provided was a policy decision. The Court clarified two important aspects of the *Just* decision. Firstly, the Court maintained that true policy decisions are not necessarily high level decisions, but can be made at all levels of authority.[58] It is the nature of the decision itself that is relevant, not the position of the person who makes the decision. Secondly, the court distinguishes between determining whether a decision is *bona fide* and whether it is reasonable, employing a higher standard to show the former. It is suggested that the decision must be "so irrational or unreasonable as to constitute an improper exercise of governmental discretion."[59] The decision may likewise be attacked "where the policy decision is shown to have been made in bad faith or in circumstances where it is so patently unreasonable that it exceeds government discretion."[60]

Taking these two clarifications together, it follows that the standard for determining the *bona fide* exercise of discretion should apply equally to both high level and low level decision makers. As a result, the discussion in *Just* that low level discretionary decisions should be reasonable in all the circumstances should be rejected in favour of a standard of patent unreasonableness.

The patently unreasonableness standard set out in *Brown* is more in keeping with the original rational for providing immunity from liability for policy decisions. For example in *Kent v. East Suffolk Rivers Catchment Board*, the basis for such immunity was stated to be as follows:

---

57 While the scope of the inquiry into the legality of high level decisions appears to have expanded beyond earlier pronouncements by the Court, (see *Nielsen, supra* note 36 at para. 68 where the majority indicated that "inaction for no reason or inaction for an improper reason cannot be a policy decision taken in the bona fide exercise of discretion") the inquiry's parameters are at least theoretically restricted to the issue of whether the decision was a *bona fide* exercise of discretion. The inquiry into low level policy decisions does not appear to even be theoretically restricted to this inquiry. These decisions must be reasonable in all the circumstances.

58 *Supra* note 40 at 16.

59 *Ibid.* at 11.

60 *Ibid.*

> . . .it must be remembered that when Parliament has left it to a public authority to decide which of its powers it shall exercise, and when and to what extent it shall exercise them, there would be some inconvenience in submitting to the subsequent decision of jury, or judge of fact, the question whether the authority had acted reasonably, a question involving the consideration of matters of policy and sometimes the striking of a just balance between the rival claims of efficiency and thrift.[61]

The inappropriateness of reviewing *intra vires* decisions by municipalities on a standard of reasonableness has been unequivocally determined in relation to public law judicial review in the *Nanaimo* case.[62] While the remedies invoked obviously differ, the underlying principle regarding freedom from review based on the supremacy of parliament and the separation of powers is the same. Consequently, a standard for review that is common to both public and private law is a sound judicial approach. Clearly, an *ultra vires* decision will not necessarily give rise to liability in negligence, but an exercise of discretion that is beyond the bounds of delegated authority should not rightly have the benefit of an immunity from review, as it is not a decision for which such protection is to be extended.

In *Swinamer v. Nova Scotia (Attorney General),*[63] the claim also concerned a highway accident. In this case, the plaintiff struck a falling tree. The highway department had a system of inspecting trees and removing trees that posed a serious risk. Trees were marked for removal in the vicinity of the tree in question, but, on the evidence, a layperson would not be able to tell the particular tree in question posed a threat before it fell. In the court's analysis, the decision respecting the nature of the tree inspection routine was a policy decision and consequently there was an exception to the general duty to maintain highways.

It is difficult to reconcile *Swinamer* and *Just* on the facts presented in each case. Both cases involved public authority decisions placing limitations on the extent of an inspection program and as such raised budgetary considerations. Additionally, in both cases, there was no evidence that the impugned decisions were exercised in bad faith or were patently unreasonable. However, insofar as the court in *Just* required that low level discretionary decisions be reasonable in the surrounding circumstances, it was open to the court to consider the reasonableness of the inspection system. Whereas, in *Swinamer* the more restrictive standard of review, prevented the courts from disturbing the decision in the absence of a patently unreasonable exercise of discretion.

---

61 (1939), [1940] 1 K.B. 319 (Eng. C.A.) at 388.

62 *Nanaimo (City) v. Rascal Trucking Ltd.* [2000] 1 S.C.R. 342, (2000), 9 M.P.L.R. (3d) 1 (S.C.C.). See discussion *supra* at chapter 4 at 92.

63 *Supra* note 41.

D. CONCLUSION

The current formulation of the law of negligence in Canada remains centered on the two part test first articulated in *Anns*. Given the broad scope of determining a *prima facie* duty based on forseeability, there has been a strong emphasis on the distinction between policy and operational decisions in order to define limits to a municipal duty of care. However, this distinction has long been recognized as being inherently difficult to work with since a wide range of decisions taken by a public official, whether taken at a high or low level, will to some degree involve or be dictated by policy considerations, such as resource constraints. The manner of implementing policy decisions, cannot, except perhaps at a purely mechanical level, be divorced from the political considerations that gave rise to the decision to implement the scheme. Any official who is delegated the task of developing and implementing the scheme of inspection will not only be designing the scheme and its standards on the basis of expert opinion, but also on the basis of the policy considerations which have been communicated to him or her. The degree or scope of policy making may be small but it will exist nonetheless in many practical implementation decisions.

One can see, therefore, that the policy-operational dichotomy is at best a continuum, with clear demarcation possible only at the extremes.[64] Identifying decisions at either end of the spectrum is relatively easy. In between these two extremes clarity disappears and decisions taken will, to a greater or lesser extent, involve policy. This identification problem manifests itself most clearly when discretionary decisions are taken by those involved in the practical implementation of a scheme. Weighing the policy/operational components of such decisions is an extremely difficult task. Therefore, a line based on the competing tensions of immunity and liability has to be drawn. There are some indications suggesting that the courts should move away from the policy/operational dichotomy as the central determinant for public au-

64 The difficulty in drawing the distinction was acknowledged in *Nielsen supra* note 36 at 23, 25, 26. See also *Anns supra* note 8 at 500. Professor Cohen argues that the policy/operational categorization is artificial and unworkable and suggests that it would be preferable to commence the analysis on this issue by asking whether the allegation of negligence is one that is appropriate for judicial review and develop variables to assist in the inquiry. Professor Cohen offers several interdependent variables relevant to this determination which include: 1. Is there a pre-existing standard of conduct against which the government's behaviour can be judged?; 2. Was the decision a routine one?; 3. Was there a great degree of discretion involved in the decision?; 4. What type of interest was involved?; 5. Was the injury deliberate or unintentional?; 6. What was the nature of the government activity which was alleged to have been negligent?; 7. What was the status of decision maker?; 8. Can the wrong be pinpointed to one party?; 9. Was it an individualized wrong?; 10. Did the decision involve resource allocation?; and 11. Was there individualized or institutional reliance present? Cohen provides a useful discussion on how these variables can be utilized in resolving the issue; "The Public and Private Law Dimensions of the UFFI Problem: Part II", *supra* note 3 at 420 and 421.

thority liability. For example, Justice Sopinka states that the "court may wish to reconsider at some future time the continued usefulness of this test [the policy/operation distinction] as an exclusive touchstone of liability."[65] In addition, the Canadian approach is increasingly at odds with the more contextual and functional approach found in recent U.S. and U.K. court decisions. The emphasis in these jurisdictions is to look at the particular circumstances of the impugned decision to determine whether an immunity from liability would be in keeping with the underlying rationale for providing such an exemption. The Canadian courts may benefit from taking a similar functional approach, which could be articulated as follows.

1. Is there a legislative duty to act? In cases where there is a legislative duty to act, there is no need to determine a private duty of care with reference to forseeability, rather the courts look straight to the question of whether there is a breach of the standard of care.
2. In cases where the municipality is exercising a discretionary statutory power, an initial consideration should be whether the decision in question is justiciable. Non-justiciable decisions would be those decisions at the extreme end of the policy/operational dichotomy. For example, decisions that are an exercise of legislative or quasi-judicial powers, should simply not be subject to judicial review, so long as they are *bona fide*, (i.e. they are not patently unreasonable or made in bad faith). Some high level administrative decisions may also fall in the category of non-justiciable decisions, but the threshold for this category should be high. In these instances, the courts should not be exercising judicial review, regardless of the question of forseeability.
3. This leaves the broad category of exercises of statutory power that still involve some degree of discretion. In these cases, a more contextual approach may be warranted. Clearly, for liability to be found, the harm would have to be foreseeable, but the court may want to look beyond the policy/operational dichotomy to other factors such as third party involvement, the existence of a special relationship giving rise to reasonable reliance, the nature of the damages suffered, and the effect of imposing liability, and the statutory purpose of the powers in question.

In considering these latter factors, the Courts must bear in mind the broader objectives of public authority immunity. In many cases, decisions respecting the allocation and use of scarce public resources, the nature and scope of a particular government program or policy will be a reflection of local values and reviewable through other democratic processes. While such an approach may appear to invite instrumentalism, careful consideration of

65 *Brown, supra* note 40 at 4.

a broad range of relevant factors should ultimately lead to a more principled and predictable approach to municipal liability.

6

Constitutional Review

A. INTRODUCTION

Municipalities, as creatures of the provincial legislature, are subject to the same constitutional restrictions placed upon the provincial legislature and other organs of the provincial government. These constraints take two principal forms; those arising from the constitutional division of powers pursuant to ss. 91 and 92 of the *Constitution Act,*[1] and those arising from the application of the *Canadian Charter of Rights and Freedoms*.[2] Municipalities themselves, as a distinct level of government, have no constitutional recognition as such. The only mention in the Constitution (in ss. 92(8), (9)) is to delegate legislative authority respecting "Municipal Institutions" to the provincial legislatures and to provide provincial authority for licensing fees for municipal purposes. Consequently, unlike some American state constitutions, where municipalities are given an autonomous sphere of authority, no such independence exists within the Canadian constitutional framework. Thus, there are no independent constitutional limitations on the power of provincial legislatures to make wholesale changes to municipal structures, including the power to determine the very existence of municipalities, contrary to the wishes of the municipality. Thus, despite efforts by aggrieved parties to overturn municipal restructuring initiatives, the courts have been unsympathetic to arguments based on municipalities having some explicit or implied constitutional recognition that would constrain in any manner provincial powers to enact restructuring legislation.[3]

In light of the fact that municipalities have no autonomous constitutional status of their own, it is perhaps not surprising that in most respects judicial review of municipal activities on constitutional grounds does not differ from the assessment of constitutionality of other government activity. There is no defined area of municipal constitutional law *per se*. However, in the broader context of looking at the scope of the exercise of municipal powers, constitutionality remains a fundamental consideration for both provincial legisla-

---

1 R.S.C. 1985, Appendix II, No. 5.

2 *Amendment Act*, R.S.C. 1985, c. 31 (1st Supp.).

3 *East York (Borough) v. Ontario (Attorney General)* (1997), 43 M.P.L.R. (2d) 155 (Ont. C.A.), leave to appeal refused [1998] 1 S.C.R. vii; *Ville de Baie D'Urfe v. Quebec*, [2002] R.J.Q. 1589.

tures drafting municipal legislation and for municipal councils in exercising those powers. In this regard, this chapter is not intended to be an exhaustive cataloguing of constitutional constraints on the exercise of municipal power, rather the aim is to examine the impact of these constraints by looking at a number of areas where municipal activities commonly give rise to constitutional concerns.

B. DIVISION OF POWERS

As noted, s. 92(8) of the Constitution gives the provinces the exclusive authority to enact legislation in respect of municipal institutions. While s. 92(8) clearly assigns to the provinces the authority to create and regulate municipalities, it was not immediately clear whether s. 92(8) by itself, could be used as an independent source of provincial power or whether the powers conferred on municipalities had to arise under a separate head of provincial jurisdiction under s. 92. In considering this question, the Privy Council, in *Ontario (Attorney General) v. Canada (Attorney General),* held that the constitutional authority for most municipal activities must be found outside of s. 92(8). Which is to say that the provinces cannot act outside the scope of their authority under s. 92 by delegating powers to municipalities and justifying the exercise of these powers under s. 92(8). In the words of the Privy Council:

> Since [confederation] a provincial legislature cannot delegate any power which it does not possess; and the extent and nature of the functions which it can commit to a municipal body of its own creation must depend upon the legislature authority which it derives from the provisions of s. 92 other than No. 8.[4]

The courts have on occasion upheld municipal legislation relating to the establishment and alteration of municipal institutions on the basis that the province has the authority to legislate in relation to "municipal institutions." In this regard, legislation imposing conditions of disqualification from municipal office was upheld as a valid exercise of power under s. 92(8),[5] as was legislation providing for municipal electricity utilities.[6] Similarly, a provincial scheme restructuring and amalgamating a number of municipalities was held to be *intra vires* as the pith and substance of the provincial law related to municipal institutions, notwithstanding the law's incidental effects on matters under federal jurisdiction.[7] More recently, the Ontario Court of Appeal reaffirmed that s. 92(8) conferred upon provincial legislatures the power to create municipal bodies, amalgamate such bodies and establish their geo-

---

4 [1896] A.C. 348 (Canada P.C.) at 364.

5 *Samson v. Drolet* (1927), [1928] S.C.R. 96.

6 *Smith v. London (City)* (1909), 20 O.L.R. 133 (Div. Ct.).

7 *Ladore v. Bennett*, [1939] A.C. 468 (Ontario P.C.).

graphical boundaries.[8] Thus, the general rule in *Ontario (Attorney General) v. Canada (Attorney General)*, requiring constitutional jurisdiction beyond s. 92(8) for provincial legislatures to confer powers on municipalities, remains intact. However, s. 92(8) may be used to resolve constitutional questions that directly impact the establishment, restructuring or internal governance issues respecting municipalities. The obvious rationale for such a rule is to prevent provincial legislatures from indirectly encroaching on federal powers by delegating matters of federal jurisdiction to municipalities and justifying the exercise of power under s. 92(8). However, given the breadth of powers under the provincial heads of power such as property and civil rights, and matters of a local nature, much of the authority regarding the traditional scope of municipal activities resides with the province.

In determining the constitutionality of either municipal legislation enacted by the province or of municipal by-laws, a principal consideration will be how the instrument in question is characterized, or in constitutional parlance, the "pith and substance" of the enactment. In this regard, the courts are required to classify the matter subject to legislation. Thus, in the well known case of *Johannesson v. West St. Paul (Rural Municipality)*, the Supreme Court struck down both provincial legislation and a by-law enacted thereunder, where the express purpose of the legislation was to allow municipalities to license and regulate the erection of aerodromes, which was a matter of exclusive federal jurisdiction and, therefore, *ultra vires* the province.[9]

In some instances an area of legislative authority may be found to have a double aspect, which is to say that it is an area of regulation in which both the provincial and federal legislatures may validly enact laws. For example, in *Hamilton Harbour Commissioners v. Hamilton (City)*,[10] the area of land use regulation within a harbour was found to have a double aspect. Thus, a municipality was allowed to pass a by-law affecting land use within a harbour so long as the by-law did not explicitly attempt to regulate or control matters relating to "shipping and navigation," (a matter of federal jurisdiction). However, the Court went on to hold that the Harbour Commissions, pursuant to their Act, were also permitted to enact land use regulations relating to shipping and navigation. In the event of a direct conflict, the rule of federal paramountcy would result in the municipal by-law having no effect.

The determination of constitutionality in relation to the division of powers follows in essence a two-stage process.[11] The first step is to determine

---

8 See *East York*, *supra* note 3.

9 (1951), [1952] 1 S.C.R. 292.

10 (1978), 21 O.R. (2d) 459 (C.A.).

11 In the municipal context, this two stage process is referred to explicitly in *Ontario Adult Entertainment Bar Assn. v. Metropolitan Toronto (Municipality)* (1997), 42 M.P.L.R. (2d) 1 (Ont. C.A.), leave to appeal refused (1998), 49 C.R.R. (2d) 188 (note) (S.C.C.) at 9 [M.P.L.R.], following the Supreme Court's decision in *Rio Hotel Ltd. v. New Brunswick (Liquor Licensing Board)*, [1987] 2 S.C.R. 59.

whether the subject matter of the legislation is exclusively federal or provincial, or whether the subject matter is an area where both levels of government may legitimately enact legislation (double aspect). Where provincial or municipal legislation falls within an area of exclusive federal jurisdiction, the impugned legislation cannot stand. If, however, the subject matter falls within an area of "bijurisdictional responsibility,"[12] then it is necessary to determine whether the provincial or municipal enactment conflicts with validly enacted federal jurisdiction. In the event of a direct conflict, the federal legislation takes precedence pursuant to the doctrine of paramountcy. The test for a direct conflict in a constitutional context requires that compliance with one instrument would result in breach of the other.[13] This stringent test for conflict is consistent with the test for conflict between municipal and provincial instruments, and reflects a similar judicial attitude that favours multi-jurisdictional regulation so long as the result is rational and without contradiction. In the case of *114957 Canada Ltée (Spray-Tech, Société d'arrosage) v. Hudson (Ville),*[14] the Supreme Court of Canada puts forward the principle of subsidiarity, which suggests that law-making and law-implementation are often most effective at the level closest to the people. In the context of environmental regulation, the Supreme Court recognized the importance of action at all levels of government, a point that informs the Court's position in the *Spraytech* case.

Following this line of decisions, it is now clear that even where municipal legislation or by-laws impose stricter standards than those imposed by validly enacted federal legislation, the local enactments will be allowed to stand.[15] The paramountcy doctrine only applies where the subject matter has a double aspect and a direct conflict exists.

While the Supreme Court of Canada takes a deferential approach to local decision-making in connection with potential conflict in regulatory matters, the Court is less accommodating of provincial and municipal enactments that affect undertakings under federal jurisdiction. This often arises in the context of the application of municipal rules of general application to undertakings or activities under federal jurisdiction. In contrast to a case like *Johannesson,*[16] where the pith and substance of the impugned legislation and by-law was found to be related directly to an area of exclusive federal jurisdiction, in many cases the pith and substance of the by-law clearly falls within an area of exclusive provincial jurisdiction, such as a general land use by-law. In such cases, the by-law will be considered *intra vires*, but may be read

12 This term was utilized by the Supreme Court in *114957 Canada Ltée (Spray-Tech, Société d'arrosage) v. Hudson (Ville)*, [2001] 2 S.C.R. 241 at 268.

13 *Ibid.* at para 34; see also *Multiple Access Ltd. v. McCutcheon*, [1982] 2 S.C.R. 161 at 187 re the "express contradiction test."

14 *Supra* note 12.

15 *Ontario Adult Entertainment Bar Assn., supra* note 11 at 10.

16 *Supra* note 9.

down so as to exclude any application to the federal undertaking.[17] The circumstances under which this may happen were traditionally restricted to instances where the municipal enactment had the effect of "sterilizing" the federal undertaking. More recently, the courts have imposed a less stringent test and required that the provincial or municipal enactment cannot "affect a vital part of the management and operation of the undertaking."[18] This rule has been found to exclude the application of provincial and municipal building code regulations and fees to airport construction, to prevent the application of development charges to airport construction, as well as prevent the application of municipal land use restrictions to airports, aerodromes and the like.[19] Unlike, the principle of paramountcy, there is no requirement for conflict or inconsistency, nor does the federal government have to have entered the legislative field. One exception to this doctrine arises where a law indirectly affects a federal undertaking. In such cases, the threshold for invalidity shall be sterilization.[20]

The earlier and more stringent test of sterilization is more consistent with the deferential approach found in the direct conflict test. While maintaining some minimum level of immunity from provincial and municipal regulatory authority is necessary to protect the core of federal authority over certain undertakings, this doctrine of interjurisdictional immunity has been criticized for creating an unclear distinction between allowable provincial and municipal regulation under the pith and substance doctrine and improper interference under the interjurisdictional immunity principle.[21] One could perhaps draw a distinction between a by-law that prohibits the establishment or critically impairs the operation of a federal undertaking, with a by-law that seeks to impose local standards for construction, for example. At a minimum, some onus should be placed on the federal government to demonstrate how a locally imposed rule impairs a federal activity.

Another area of recurring constitutional difficulty is in relation to municipal forms of revenue raising. Under the constitutional division of powers, the provinces are restricted in their taxation powers to imposing taxes of a direct nature only, as per s. 92(2), as opposed to the federal government,

---

17 In the aeronautics field see *Orangeville Airport Ltd. v. Caledon (Town)* (1976), 11 O.R. (2d) 546 (C.A.); *Walker v. Ontario (Minister of Housing)* (1983), 41 O.R. (2d) 9 (C.A.), leave to appeal refused (1983), 51 N.R. 398n; *Venchiarutti v. Longhurst* (1992), 10 M.P.L.R. (2d) 179 (Ont. C.A.).

18 *Greater Toronto Airports Authority v. Mississauga (City)* (2000), 16 M.P.L.R. (3d) 213 (Ont. C.A.), leave to appeal refused (2001), 274 N.R. 196 (note) (S.C.C.).

19 Other areas of exclusive federal jurisdiction that often come into conflict with municipal regulation include telecommunication installations such as telephone poles, underground wires, and cellular installations. A recent controversy regarding the right to regulate the installation of fiber optic cable within municipal rights-of-way illustrates the difficulties municipalities may face arising from constitutional considerations.

20 *Irwin Toy Ltd. c. Quebec (Procureur général)*, [1989] 1 S.C.R. 927.

21 See Hogg, *Constitutional Law of Canada*, 4th ed. (Toronto: Carswell, 1997), Chapter 15.8(e).

which may also impose indirect taxes. Additionally, s. 92(9) of the *Constitution Act* provides that the provinces may make laws in relation to "Shop, Saloon, Tavern, Auctioneer, and other Licenses in order for the raising of Revenue for Provincial, Local, or Municipal Purposes." This section raises the possibility that provinces and municipalities may impose indirect taxes in the form of license fees. Thus, insofar as provincial legislatures have provided municipalities with the means of raising revenue, such schemes must fall within the provincial revenue raising powers as being either a form of direct taxation or falling within s. 92(9).

The distinction between direct and indirect taxation that the courts have adopted is based on the definitions provided by John Stuart Mill:

> A direct tax is one which is demanded from the very person who it is intended or desired should pay it. Indirect taxes are those which are demanded from one person in the expectation and intention that he shall indemnify himself at the expense of another.[22]

The approach of the courts in using Mill's formulation has been to look at the likelihood or ability of a person against whom a tax was imposed on to pass that tax on to another. Thus, where the tax was related to a unit of a commodity and imposed in the course of its manufacture, the tax will, as a general rule, cling as a burden to the unit, and as a result, be considered indirect in nature.[23] Although taxes on property, including municipal property taxes, are considered to be direct taxes, even when they are imposed against landlords (who would presumably pass the costs on to tenants).[24] More controversial are municipal fee and charges schemes. For example, in *Allard Contractors Ltd. v. Coquitlam (District)*, a municipal by-law that imposed a license fee based on the volume of material extracted from a gravel pit was held to be a form of indirect taxation since volumetric fees would likely cling to the commodity in question. However, the court went on to consider whether the fees imposed could be permitted under a different head of provincial jurisdiction, holding that because, in this case, the fees went to defray the costs of the overall regulatory scheme (to regulate gravel pits), the fees were ancillary to a valid provincial regulatory scheme.[25] Similarly, the educational development charge scheme in Ontario whereby certain capital costs relating to school facilities where imposed against development in the form of a charge related to new construction, was upheld as being ancillary to the provincial

---

22 John Stuart Mill, *Principles of Political Economy* (New York: D. Appleton, 1983), Vol. 2 Book V, Chapter 3, s. 1 as quoted in *Ontario Home Builders' Assn. infra* note 26.

23 *Allard, infra*, note 25.

24 *Germain c. Montreal (Ville)*, [1997] 1 S.C.R. 1144, referring to *Ontario Home Builders' Assn., infra* note 26.

25 *Allard Contractors Ltd. v. Coquitlam (District)*, [1993] 4 S.C.R. 371.

land use planning scheme.[26] Again in this case, although the impost was found to be an indirect tax, the court found that the purpose of the by-law was to defray the overall cost of the regulatory scheme. Although it should be noted that the court draws the scheme in extremely broad terms, being the system of land use planning in Ontario and those costs included the capital costs of education related infrastructure required as a result of new development.

In neither of the above cases did the Supreme Court have to consider whether a similar scheme, but whose purpose was to raise revenue of general purpose, would be a valid exercise of provincial powers. However, subsequent to these cases, in *Eurig Estate, Re* the Supreme Court considered another provincial scheme relating to probate fees where it was clear that the intent of the fee was to raise general revenue, as opposed to merely defraying the costs of the regulatory scheme.[27] In this case, the court held that the raising of revenue through such a scheme was not allowed, as there was not a sufficient nexus between the fee in question and the scheme.[28] Which is to say, because the charge must be justified under a power other than the taxing power, being an indirect tax, the purpose of the impost must relate to defraying the costs of the scheme itself and not for raising general revenue. As a result of this case, it is clear that municipal fees that cannot demonstrate some reasonable relationship to the costs of the regulatory scheme are likely to be found *ultra vires*.

The test in *Eurig Estate, Re* was applied by the Ontario Court of Appeal in a case involving a fee imposed in connection with a sign by-law.[29] In this case, the Court held that because the evidence demonstrated that the fees were directed to the costs of administering the city's sign regulation program, the fee was validly imposed. The court correctly rejected an argument by the appellant that the fees had to defray the costs of services that were of direct benefit to the payors, in favour of a broader view that in order to qualify as fees, there simply had to be a demonstrable connection between the fee and the program. In this case, the fees objected to were small relative to the overall costs of the program and did not vary with respect to the value of the sign in question. The court's approach was one of apparent deference that is in keeping with the notion that municipalities should be granted "reasonable leeway" in determining the quantum of fees.

---

26 *Ontario Home Builders' Assn. v. York (Region) Board of Education* [1996] 2 S.C.R. 929, (1996), 35 M.P.L.R. (2d) 1 (S.C.C.).

27 [1998] 2 S.C.R. 565.

28 *Ibid.* at 578-579.

29 *Urban Outdoor Trans Ad v. Scarborough (City)* (2001), 52 O.R. (3d) 593, 16 M.P.L.R. (3d) 241 (C.A.).

C. THE CANADIAN CHARTER OF RIGHTS AND FREEDOMS

1. Introduction

The *Canadian Charter of Rights and Freedoms* (the *Charter*) enacted in 1982[30] constitutionally guarantees the rights and freedoms set out therein. Its purpose is to constrain governmental action that has the purpose or effect of infringing or limiting the exercise of those rights or freedoms. The constitutional guarantees are not, however, absolute. They are subject to such reasonable limits as can be demonstrably justified in a free and democratic society.[31] Laws that are inconsistent with the *Charter* are, to the extent of that inconsistency, of no force or effect[32] and governmental action or legislation that infringes the guaranteed rights or freedoms may lead to other remedies including damages.[33] As discussed below, municipal government legislation will be subject to the constraints of the *Charter* as well. The *Charter* offers one more avenue for the review of municipal decision-making and the exercise of municipal statutory authority.

The nature of the review will of course depend on the scope of the *Charter's* application to municipal government, the definition of the rights and freedoms contained in the *Charter* and the scope of protection offered and the potential justification of these infringements under s.1 of the *Charter*. Again, rather than attempting a comprehensive review of the implications of *Charter* review for local government, the purpose of this section will be restricted to briefly discussing the general principles of *Charter* application and interpretation, and examining some of the topical issues in the context of municipal government.

2. General Principles

The methodology for determining whether a right or freedom has been infringed has been set out by the Supreme Court of Canada in several early decisions.[34] Simply stated it involves a two-step inquiry.

First, the person alleging an infringement of a protected right or freedom, besides establishing that he or she enjoys the right or freedom in question,[35] has the onus of establishing that the legislation or governmental action either

30 Part 1 of the *Constitution Act, 1982* [enacted by the *Canada Act, 1982* (U.K.) c. 11]; proclaimed in force April 17, 1982, s. 15 proclaimed in force April 17, 1985.

31 *Ibid.* at s. 1.

32 *Ibid.* at s. 52.

33 *Ibid.* at s. 24(1) and 2.

34 *R. v. Big M Drug Mart Ltd.*, [1985] 1 S.C.R. 295; *R. v. Oakes*, [1986] 1 S.C.R. 103.

35 See for example *Irwin Toy Ltd. c. Quebec (Procureur général)*, [1989] 1 S.C.R. 927 where the Court concluded that corporations are not included within the definition of "everyone" in s. 7 of the *Charter* and therefore, except perhaps when charged with an offence, cannot invoke its protection.

by its purpose or by its effect violates an interest protected within the definition of the right or freedom and that the violation of the protected right or freedom was caused by a governmental entity subject to the *Charter*.

The approach taken by the Courts in defining the scope of the right or freedom in issue and whether it protects against the alleged violation has been described in a series of cases as a "purposive approach." The *Charter* right in question is to be interpreted and defined in light of the interests it is meant to protect.[36] The Courts have used various sources including, for example, U.S. and European jurisprudence, academic articles, law reform commission materials, and sources of international law to help define the purpose of *Charter* rights and the interests they are meant to protect.

Once the purpose of the right or freedom has been determined, the court then determines whether the purpose or effect of the legislation (or governmental action) infringes the right or freedom as defined. If an infringement is found, the second step of the inquiry commences and the onus then shifts to the government to establish that the infringement is justified under s. 1 of the *Charter*. To justify the infringement, the government must establish that the limit imposed is prescribed by law,[37] and that it constitutes a reasonable limit within a free and democratic society.

The basic test for determining if the infringement is reasonable was set out in the case of *R. v. Oakes*.[38] This also involves a two-stage test, with the second stage being a proportionality test to which there are three components. In the first stage the government must establish that the legislation or governmental action addresses a pressing and substantial objective. If it does, then the proportionality test commences and the government must establish: 1) a rational connection between the legislation and the pressing and substantial objective; 2) that the legislation impairs the right as little as possible in achieving that objective; and 3) that there is proportionality between the effects of the measures which are responsible for limiting the *Charter* right or freedom and the objective which has been identified as of a sufficient importance.

This test, if strictly applied, would be exceedingly difficult to meet and in recognition of this difficulty the Supreme Court of Canada has emphasized that the nature of the s. 1 test is to be flexible with the stringency of its application depending on the circumstances.[39]

---

36 *R. v. Big M Drug Mart, supra* note 34.

37 On what constitutes "prescribed by law" see *R. v. Thomsen*, [1988] 1 S.C.R. 640; *R. v. Hebert*, [1990] 2 S.C.R. 151; and *Comité pour la République du Canada - Committee for the Commonwealth of Canada v. Canada*, [1991] 1 S.C.R. 139, reconsideration refused (May 8, 1991), Doc. 20334 (S.C.C.).

38 *Supra* note 34.

39 *R. v. Videoflicks Ltd.*, [1986] 2 S.C.R. 713; *Irwin Toy, supra* note 35.

3. Application of the *Charter* to Municipal and Local Government Institutions

The application of the *Charter* is governed by s. 32 of the *Charter*. Section 32 provides:

> This Charter applies:
>
> (a) to the Parliament and Government of Canada in respect of all matters within the authority of Parliament ...;
> (b) to the Legislature and Government of each Province in respect of all matters within the authority of the Legislature of each Province.

That s. 32 makes no mention of the municipal level of government is consistent with the overall constitutional non-recognition of local government. However, s. 32 very clearly extends the application of the *Charter* to "all matters within the authority of the Legislature of each Province." Thus, the inferior status of municipalities was considered determinative of the issue of whether the *Charter* applied to municipal by-laws in the case of *McCutcheon v. Toronto (City)*[40] where the Court concluded:

> Municipalities, though a distinct level of government for some purposes, have no constitutional status; they are merely "creatures of the legislatures", with no existence independent of the Legislature or government of the province. Hence, just as the provincial Legislatures and governments are bound by the *Charter*, so too are municipalities, whose by-laws and other actions must be considered, for the purposes of s. 32(1), as actions of the provincial government which gave them birth.[41]

The reasoning and result in *McCutcheon* were considered by the Ontario Court of Appeal in the case of *McKinney v. University of Guelph*,[42] where the issue was whether the *Charter* applied to the mandatory retirement policies and employment contracts of various universities. While not disagreeing with the result in *McCutcheon*, the Court reached a similar conclusion on the basis of different reasoning and stated:

> While we do not disagree with the conclusion that a municipality is subject to the *Charter*, our approach would differ somewhat. The fact that municipal corporations are "creatures of the Legislature" is not determinative. It is the function that they were created to perform that is. "Creatures of the legislature" do not automatically become accountable to the *Charter*: they remain accountable to their "creator". Ordinarily, it is their "creator" which would attract the

---

40 (1983), 147 D.L.R. (3d) 193, 41 O.R. (2d) 652 (H.C.); see also *Hardie v. Summerland (District)* (1985), 24 D.L.R. (4th) 257, 68 B.C.L.R. 244 (S.C.).

41 (1983), 41 O.R. (2d) 652 (H.C.) at 663.

42 (1987), 63 O.R. (2d) 1, 46 D.L.R. (4th) 193 (C.A.), affirmed [1990] 3 S.C.R. 229.

> reach of the *Charter*, but municipal corporations differ from other statutory corporations in that they are incorporated by government to perform a governmental function; a function that the provincial government could and often does perform itself. As such, they can be considered "a distinct level of government" to use Linden J.'s phrase, or "a branch of Government" to use that of McIntyre J. in *Dolphin Delivery, supra*. But it is the function for which they are incorporated that gives them this status and not the mere fact that they are incorporated and have their authority to act bestowed upon them by their incorporating statute.[43]

The Court of Appeal's decision not to extend *Charter* application to universities was upheld by the Supreme Court who adopted a similar function based test for determining the scope of s. 32 of the *Charter*. The issue of *Charter* application to municipalities was only peripherally considered by the Supreme Court of Canada in *McKinney*, where LaForest J., speaking for two other members of the Court, expressly refused to provide an opinion on whether the decision in *McCutcheon* was correct, but stated that if the *Charter* did cover municipalities, it was because "municipalities perform a quintessential governmental function. They enact coercive laws binding on the public generally, for which offenders may be punished."[44]

This functional approach was applied by the Supreme Court in direct relation to municipalities in *Godbout c. Longueuil (Ville)*.[45] Here the issue before the Court was the legality of a condition of employment imposed by a municipality that required municipal employees to reside within the municipality as a condition of their continued employment. The lower courts, in considering the application of the Canadian *Charter* (the appellant also argued the condition violated the Quebec *Charter*), held that the *Charter* did not apply because what was at issue was the exercise of non-governmental pow-

---

43 (1987), 46 D.L.R. (4th) 193 (C.A.), affirmed [1990] 3 S.C.R. 229 at 216 [D.L.R.]. The Ontario Court of Appeal at 204 seems to take an approach that requires: (1) the determination of whether the *Charter* applies to the entity; and then (2) whether the *Charter* right applies to the specific action taken by the entity. It is unclear whether this analysis is unique to s. 15(1) of the *Charter* which provides equality rights by reference to "the law" and therefore requires some definition of "law." In this regard see also *O.E.C.T.A. v. Essex (County) Roman Catholic Separate School Board* (1987), 36 D.L.R. (4th) 115 (Ont. Div. Ct.), leave to appeal refused (1988), 39 C.R.R. 384 (note) (S.C.C.).

44 *McKinney v. University of Guelph*, [1990] 3 S.C.R. 229. See also *Dolphin Delivery Ltd. v. R.W.D.S.U., Local 580*, [1986] 2 S.C.R. 573 at 602 where McIntyre J. said the *Charter* could possibly apply to municipal by-laws.

45 [1997] 3 S.C.R. 844. Numerous appellate decisions have implicitly accepted that the *Charter* applies to municipal by-laws, most notably *Ramsden v. Peterborough (City)*, [1993] 2 S.C.R. 1084. See also *R. v. Bichel* (1986), 32 M.P.L.R. 91 (B.C. C.A.); *Information Retailers Assn. of Metro. Toronto. Inc. v. Metro. Toronto (Mun.)* (1985), 52 O.R. (2d) 449 (C.A.); *Alcoholism Foundation of Manitoba v. Winnipeg (City)* (1990), 49 M.P.L.R. 1 (Man. C.A.), leave to appeal refused (1991), 4 M.P.L.R. (2d) 60n (S.C.C.); and *Cheema v. Ross* (1991), 82 D.L.R. (4th) 213 (B.C. C.A.).

ers, i.e. the power to privately contract.[46] The Supreme Court, in a divided decision, unanimously determined that the residency requirement was illegal. The majority of the Justices limited their analysis to the incompatibility of the agreement with the Quebec *Charter* and did not offer an opinion with regard to the application of the Canadian *Charter*. However, Justice LaForest (with L'Heureux-Dubé and McLachlin concurring) gave extensive consideration to the question of *Charter* application in a municipal context and while strictly *obiter*, his findings are clearly relevant and probably will be determinative of future controversies.

Relying on the *McKinney*,[47] *Harrison*,[48] *Stoffman*,[49] and *Douglas*[50] cases, LaForest draws a distinction between entities that are governmental in nature and those entities that are created by legislation and may receive some government funding, but are nonetheless non-governmental (such as universities). In determining that s. 32 contemplates application of the *Charter* to entities other than those explicitly set out in s. 32, LaForest notes that insofar as certain entities are created and controlled by the Legislatures and carry out government function on their behalf, were the *Charter* not to apply to such entities, then "the federal government and the provinces could easily shirk their *Charter* obligations by conferring certain of their powers on other entities and having those entities carry out what are, in reality, government activities or policies."[51] In determining that a municipality is an entity that is 'governmental' in nature, LaForest notes that in addition to deriving their existence and authority from the provinces, municipal councils are democratically elected, they have a general taxing power and are empowered to make and administer laws.[52]

Having determined that the *Charter* generally applies to municipalities, LaForest goes on to discuss whether the *Charter* applies to all of the activities of municipalities. Here, LaForest states that the "particular modality" by which a municipality imposes its policies should not impact the application of the *Charter*, rather any act by an entity that is governmental in nature is necessarily a public act.[53] Consequently, for LaForest at least, the *Charter* has pervasive application over all aspects of municipal activities.

The pervasive nature of *Charter* application in a municipal context was demonstrated in connection with a challenge to a practice by the mayor of a municipality to commence council meetings with a recitation of the Lord's

46 [1989] R.J.Q. 1511 (Que. S.C.), reversed [1995] R.J.Q. 2561 (Que. C.A.), leave to appeal allowed (October 3, 1996), Doc. 24990 (S.C.C.), affirmed [1997] 3 S.C.R. 844.

47 *Supra* note 42.

48 [1990] 3 S.C.R. 451.

49 [1990] 3 S.C.R. 483.

50 [1990] 3 S.C.R. 570.

51 *Supra* note 45 at 878-879.

52 *Ibid.* at 881-882.

53 *Ibid.* at 884-885.

Prayer.[54] In determining that such a practice did attract the application of the *Charter*, notwithstanding the fact that there was no by-law, official policy or other instrument implementing the practice, the Ontario Court of Appeal held that the Mayor's authority to conduct council meetings was clearly derived from the *Municipal Act* and as such was government conduct subject to *Charter* review and remedies under s. 24(1) of the *Charter*. On this basis, the practice of certain officials to engage in certain ceremonial behavior such as making proclamations, flying flags and the like, although not specifically authorized, would also be subject to *Charter* scrutiny.[55]

It is clear from the forgoing that there is no attitude of judicial deference towards municipal activities that may be subject to *Charter* scrutiny. This is clearly consistent with the judiciary's approach to the application of the *Charter* to other governmental entities. Moreover, as discussed below, this approach is also consistent with the Supreme Court's attention to democratic values in other areas of judicial review. A commitment to democratic values may require deference in favour of a duly elected body in the context of determining the scope of jurisdiction under a particular legislative provision. However, adherence and respect for the rights and freedoms set out in the *Charter* form the core of Canada's democratic values and, as a consequence, the promotion and preservation of these rights enhance local democratic values.

4. Specific Rights and Freedoms

As municipalities legislate and administrate within their expanding sphere of statutory jurisdiction, the potential for their infringing the guaranteed rights and freedoms of their residents is likely to increase. The judicial resolution of these allegations of *Charter* infringements will depend on how these rights and freedoms are defined and whether any infringements can be justified under s. 1 of the *Charter*. In many instances, as the law develops, it will be relatively simple to resolve these issues. In other instances, however, the nature of the alleged *Charter* infringements will render the issues more difficult to resolve because of the need to achieve a delicate balance between the rights of the individual and the objectives of the government. The areas most likely to involve such balancing, at least in the municipal context, appear to involve freedom of religion (s. 2(a)), freedom of expression (s. 2(b)), the right to life, liberty and security of the person (s. 7), the right to be secure against unreasonable search or seizure (s. 8) and the right to equal protection and equal benefit of the law without discrimination (s. 15(l)). These rights and freedoms will therefore be briefly discussed.

---

54 *Freitag v. Penetanguishene (Town)* (1999), 4 M.P.L.R. (3d) 1 (Ont. C.A.).

55 Although not a *Charter* case, in *Oliver v. Hamilton (City)* (1995), 26 M.P.L.R. (2d) 278 (Ont. Bd. of Inquiry), the failure of the Mayor and Council to proclaim Gay and Lesbian Pride Week attracted liability under Ontario's Human Rights legislation.

(i) *Section 2(a): Freedom of Conscience and Religion*

In two decisions, the Supreme Court of Canada defined, in part, the purpose and potential scope of freedom of religion. In *R. v. Big M Drug Mart Ltd.*[56] the majority of the Court made the following statements in defining freedom of religion under the *Charter*:

> The essence of the concept of freedom of religion is the right to entertain such religious beliefs as a person chooses, the right to declare such religious beliefs as a person chooses, the right to declare such religious beliefs openly and without fear of hindrance or reprisal, and the right to manifest religious belief by worship and practice or by teaching and dissemination. But the concept means more than that.
>
> Freedom can primarily be characterized by the absence of coercion or constraint. If a person is compelled by the state or the will of another to a course of action or inaction which he would not otherwise have chosen, he is not acting of his own volition and he cannot be said to be truly free. One of the major purposes of the *Charter* is to protect, within reason, from compulsion or restraint. Coercion includes not only such blatant forms of compulsion as direct commands to act or refrain from acting on pain of sanction, coercion includes indirect forms of control which determine or limit alternative courses of conduct available to others.

In *R. v. Videoflicks Ltd.*[57] the majority of the Court indicated that unless the legislative or administrative burden is trivial or insubstantial, legislative or administrative action which increases the cost of practicing or otherwise manifesting religious beliefs could be contrary to s. 2(a) of the *Charter*.

In the municipal context, Sunday shopping laws are often the subject of *Charter* scrutiny. While such laws are often enacted by senior levels of government, authority to determine local exemptions has been delegated to municipalities. Even where such legislation has been found to be enacted for a secular purpose (as a secular day of common pause), the legislative effects must be assessed. In one such case, it was found that a requirement that a retailer declare his or her religion in order to qualify for an exemption was not more than a trivial or insubstantial effect.[58]

The secular purpose behind common pause days stands in contrast to the overt religious act of opening council meetings with the Lord's Prayer in the *Freitag* case. Here the court found that the purpose of the activity was to impose a specifically Christian moral tone contrary to s. 2(a). As the purpose was contrary to the *Charter*, the practice could not be justified under s. 1.[59]

---

56 *Supra* note 34 at 295.

57 *Supra* note 39.

58 *Peel (Regional Municipality) v. Great Atlantic & Pacific Co. of Canada* (1991), 4 M.P.L.R. (2d) 113 (Ont. C.A.), leave to appeal allowed [1991] 3 S.C.R. x.

59 *Supra* note 54 at 16.

Given the potential scope of freedom of religion, a further difficult issue is whether a municipality that seeks to prohibit or regulate the construction or use of buildings in specified zones for religious purposes or religious instruction purposes will be in violation of s. 2(a) of the *Charter*.

In the U.S., this issue has given rise to a wide body of jurisprudence and numerous academic articles.[60] In Canada however, this issue has only been expressly considered in one case. In the case of *Milton (Town) v. Smith,*[61] the Town had passed a zoning by-law prohibiting the use of properties in a residential area for school purposes. The by-law effectively restrained the use of a church for a church-sponsored day school that taught traditional subjects, as well as giving religious instruction. The church members alleged that the prohibition violated their freedom of religion and conscience.

In brief reasons the trial judge concluded that neither in its purpose nor in its effect did the by-law constitute a violation of s. 2(a), but that even if it did it was a reasonable limit demonstrably justified in a free and democratic society.

The court's analysis on the effect of the by-law and whether it was justified under s. 1 does not bear close scrutiny — it consists only of a statement that there was no discriminatory purpose in the enactment of the zoning by-law. The issue, however, was whether the prohibition against teaching religious instruction on that location constituted a direct or indirect burden upon the church members' freedom of religion. In part, the effect of the zoning by-law was to prohibit the church from holding classes and teaching religious subjects. In essence, it was a government constraint on the manifestation of religious beliefs and although it was location specific, this did not necessarily render the burden trivial. Establishing a school at another location could increase the cost of manifesting one's belief. The relocation of the school would probably require the religious group to either purchase or lease another property and, therefore, incur added expenses. This, in effect, could reduce the congregation's ability to teach its religious beliefs to others or even its own children.

The fact that there might have been other areas of the municipality where the school could be located, while perhaps relevant to an inquiry under s. 1 of the *Charter*, could not be said to change the effect of the zoning by-law. If such a burden is to be tolerated, the municipality should have the onus of demonstrating that the prohibition against religious instruction is demonstrably justified in a free and democratic society.

---

60 For a discussion of the jurisprudence, see for example: Reynolds, L., "Zoning The Church: The Police Power Versus The First Amendment" (1985) 64 B.U.L. Rev. 767; Note, "Land Use Regulation and the Free Exercise Clause" (1984) 84 Colum. L. Rev. 1562; Comment, "Zoning Ordinances Affecting Churches: A Proposal For Expanded Free Exercise Protection" (1984) 132 U. Pa. L. Rev. 1131.

61 (1986), 32 M.P.L.R. 107 (Ont. H.C.). See as well *Hutterian Brethren Church of Eagle Creek Inc. v. Eagle Creek (Rural Municipality No. 376)* (1982), [1983] 2 W.W.R. 438, 21 M.P.L.R. 108 (Sask. C.A.).

(ii) *Section 2(b): Freedom of Thought, Belief, Opinion and Expression, including Freedom of the Press and Other Media of Communication*

This freedom, and in particular freedom of expression and freedom of the press, has been recognized by the Supreme Court of Canada in several decisions as central to a free and democratic society.[62] The purposes underlying freedom of expression have been summarized as follows:

(1) seeking and attaining the truth;
(2) participation in social and political decision making; and
(3) individual self-fulfillment and human flourishing.[63]

The approach to be taken in determining whether a violation of the guarantee of freedom of expression has occurred was outlined in *Irwin Toy Ltd. c. Quebec (Procureur general).*[64] First, one determines whether the activity at issue falls within the sphere of conduct protected by the guarantee. Activity which does not convey or attempt to convey a meaning, and thus has no content to be expressed, or which conveys a meaning but through a violent form of expression, is not within the protected sphere of conduct.

If the activity falls within the protected sphere of conduct, the second step in the analysis is to determine whether the purpose or effect of the government action is to restrict freedom of expression. Where the government has aimed to control attempts to convey a meaning either by directly restricting the content of expression or by restricting a form of expression tied to content, the government's purpose trenches upon the guarantee. Where the government aims only to control the physical consequences of a person's conduct, its purpose does not trench upon the right to free expression. In determining this issue the question becomes: does the mischief consist in the meaning of the activity or the purported influence that meaning has on the behaviour of others, or does it consist, instead, only of the direct physical result of the activity? If the government's purpose is not to restrict free expression, the plaintiff can still claim that the effect of the government's action was to restrict his or her expression. To make this claim the plaintiff must at least identify the meaning being conveyed and how it relates to the pursuit of truth, participation in the community, or individual self-fulfillment and human flourishing.

Given the broad scope of this freedom, some categories of municipal by-laws have been and will likely continue to be challenged as violating freedom of expression. For example, by-laws regulating the sale and display of erotic books and magazines,[65] the location and licensing of adult video

---

62 See for example: *Edmonton Journal v. Alberta (Attorney General)*, [1989] 2 S.C.R. 1326; *Irwin Toy Ltd., supra* note 35.

63 *Irwin Toy, supra* note 35 at 976.

64 *Ibid.*

65 *Information Retailers Assn., supra* note 45.

stores,[66] the location and erection of signs,[67] prohibiting lap dancing in adult entertainment parlours,[68] and municipal conflict of interest legislation prohibiting municipal councillors from attempting in any way to influence the council[69] have been challenged as violating s. 2(b) of the *Charter*. On the other hand, in *Cheema v. Ross*,[70] the British Columbia Court of Appeal held that a municipal noise control by-law did not infringe s. 2(b) either generally or as enforced against an individual attempting to use a sound amplification system to voice his political opinions. There was no infringement because the by-law was not aimed at restricting the exercise of the right to peaceful public persuasion, and its effect was not to deprive the listener of the true meaning of the appellant's message, but merely to control the volume of his voice.

An illustration of the kind of expression that was held not to be in the sphere of conduct protected by the guarantee was provided in *Stadium Corp. of Ontario Ltd. v. Toronto (City)*.[71] There, the Ontario Divisional Court found that a by-law prohibiting the keeping of exotic animals, which was intended to regulate circuses and other shows involving exotic animals, did not infringe s. 2(b) of the *Charter*, since the applicant had not established that there was any constitutionally protected message communicated through the medium of exotic animal shows or through exotic animals in circus acts.

A more difficult issue, however, is to what extent a municipality or municipal institution can prohibit people from expressing themselves on municipal property. In essence, the question is: does freedom of expression include the right of access to a public or municipal forum for the purpose of exercising the right of expression?

This issue has arisen in several contexts. In many cases the issue has been whether a municipality can regulate or prohibit the location of newspaper boxes on municipal property. In *Canadian Newspaper Co. v. Victoria (City)*,[72] the City rejected the newspaper corporation's application to place

---

66 *913719 Ontario Ltd. v. Mississauga (City)* (1996), 33 M.P.L.R. (2d) 171 (Ont. Gen. Div.), affirmed (1998), 47 M.P.L.R. (2d) 42 (Ont. C.A.), leave to appeal refused (1999), 123 O.A.C. 200 (note) (S.C.C.).

67 *R. v. Pinehouse Plaza Pharmacy Ltd.*, [1991] 2 W.W.R. 544 (Sask. C.A.); *Ramsden v. Peterborough (City)*, *supra* note 45; *Nichol (Township) v. McCarthy Signs Co.* (1997), 39 M.P.L.R. (2d) 96 (Ont. C.A.); *Canadian Mobile Sign Assn. v. Burlington (City)* (1997), 34 O.R. (3d) 134 (C.A.), leave to appeal refused (1998), 50 C.R.R. (2d) 376 (note) (S.C.C.); *Stoney Creek (City) v. Ad Vantage Signs Ltd* (1997), 149 D.L.R. (4th) 282 (Ont. C.A.); *Urban Outdoor Trans Ad v. Scarborough (City)* (2001), 16 M.P.L.R. (3d) 241 (Ont. C.A.).

68 *Ontario Adult Entertainment Bar Assn. v. Metropolitan Toronto (Municipality)* (1995), 29 M.P.L.R. (2d) 141 (Ont. Div. Ct.), affirmed (1997), 42 M.P.L.R. (2d) 1 (Ont. C.A.), leave to appeal refused (1998), 49 C.R.R. (2d) 188 (note) (S.C.C.).

69 *Stubbs v. Greenough* (1984), 25 M.P.L.R. 26 (N.S. T.D.).

70 *Supra* note 45.

71 (1992), 10 O.R. (3d) 203 (Div. Ct.), reversed on other grounds (1993) 12 O.R. (3d) 646 (C.A.). But see *R. v. Butler* [1992] 1 S.C.R. 452 (S.C.C.) for a broader consideration of what constitutes expression.

72 (1989), [1990] 2 W.W.R. 1 (B.C. C.A.), affirming (1987), 46 D.L.R. (4th) 695 (B.C. S.C.).

newspaper vending boxes on municipal property because it had a policy of prohibiting the placement of such boxes on municipal property. This policy was alleged to violate s. 2(b) of the *Charter*. The Court concluded that, because the policy was not aimed at restricting expression and the newspaper corporation had other means of distributing its newspapers, there was no infringement of s. 2(b).

In contrast, in *Canadian Newspaper Co. c. Québec (Ville) (Directeur des services de la voie publique & de la circulation routière)* [73] the Court concluded that a zoning by-law prohibiting the placement of newspaper vending boxes on public property was contrary to s. 2(b) of the *Charter* in that it prohibited the distribution of newspapers. Furthermore the prohibition was not justified under s. 1 of the *Charter*.

In *Edmonton (City) v. Forget*[74] the Court concluded that a by-law which *inter alia* prohibited the placement of any poster on utility poles and other structures owned by the City was in violation of s. 2(b) and could not be saved by s. 1 of the *Charter*. The Court, following the procedure outlined by the Supreme Court of Canada in *Irwin Toy*,[75] concluded that the placing of posters, in this case to advertise a meeting to discuss an important political issue, was within the sphere of conduct protected by s. 2(b) of the *Charter* and that a person was entitled to use public property to exercise the right of expression unless that exercise seriously interfered with the use of the public property by the City or other individuals. While the purpose of the by-law was not to restrict expression, it clearly had the effect of limiting a means of communication that was both effective and inexpensive. The prohibition therefore constituted a violation of s. 2(b). On the s. 1 analysis the Court concluded that the City had not proved that an absolute prohibition was necessary to obtain its goal of preserving aesthetic values and protecting public property and that its complete prohibition was, therefore, not justified under s. 1.[76]

The leading case on the issue of the exercise of freedom of expression on "public governmental property" is that of the *Comité pour la République du Canada-Committee for the Commonwealth of Canada v. Canada*.[77] In *Commonwealth,* members of a group were at Dorval Airport in Montreal distributing pamphlets and discussing the Committee's aims and objectives with the members of the public. They were ordered by the Airport Manager

---

73 (1986), 36 D.L.R. (4th) 641 (Que. S.C.).

74 (1990), 1 M.P.L.R. (2d) 214 (Alta. Q.B.); see also *Ramsden v. Peterborough (City), supra* note 45, where the Supreme Court of Canada held a similar by-law provision to be invalid and the infringement failed to meet the s. 1 test because it was overly broad in its effect and was therefore disproportionate to its objectives.

75 *Supra* note 35.

76 The Supreme Court of Canada reached a similar conclusion regarding a similar by-law in *Ramsden v. Peterborough (City), supra* note 45.

77 *Supra* note 37.

to cease these activities because they were contrary to governmental regulations prohibiting advertising or solicitation in the airport.

The issue before the Supreme Court of Canada was the extent to which s. 2(b) of the *Charter* guaranteed freedom of expression on state-owned property. The members of the court were unanimous in concluding that the order requiring the Committee members to stop distribution and discussion was contrary to s. 2(b) of the *Charter* and that the infringement was not justified under s. 1. Unfortunately, three different approaches were taken with respect to the resolution of this issue.[78]

Lamer C.J., in whose analysis two other members of the Court concurred, took an approach that balanced the interests of the individual in expressing herself or himself in a place suitable for such expression and the interests of government (society and public) in the effective operation of the governmental property. The government's rights of ownership, however, were not in themselves authority justifying prohibition of the exercise of freedom of expression. Lamer C.J. indicated that an individual will only be free to communicate in a place owned by the state if the form of expression he or she uses is compatible with the principal function or intended purpose of that place. If it is not, then it is not within the sphere of expression protected under s. 2(b). If it is, then the onus shifts to the state to justify the particular forum prohibition under s.1 of the *Charter*.

McLachlin J. took a different approach. Following the guidelines enunciated in *Irwin Toy*[79] she stated that the first step was to determine whether the government's purpose in imposing the forum restriction was to regulate the content of the expression or merely regulate its consequences regardless of its content. Where the forum restriction is aimed at the content, the infringement of s. 2(b) is established and the analysis proceeds to s. 1 of the *Charter*. Where the restriction is content-neutral, the claimant may establish a violation by establishing a link between her or his self-expression in that forum and one of the purposes that underlie the guarantee of free expression. These values, McLachlin J. suggests, are clearly linked to the use of places such as streets and by-ways which, by tradition or analogy thereto or by designation, have been dedicated to public expression for purposes of discussing political or social or artistic issues. The approach taken by L'Heureux-Dubé J. appears to be primarily definitional. If the plaintiff, under the guidelines proposed in *Irwin Toy*,[80] establishes that the purpose or effect of the forum restriction infringes freedom of expression, then an infringement is made out and the government must justify the forum restriction under s. 1 of the *Charter*.

---

78 The more recent Supreme Court of Canada decision on freedom of expression, *Ramsden v. Peterborough (City)*, *supra* note 45, did not clarify which, if any, of the approaches taken in *Commonwealth* was the most appropriate

79 *Supra* note 35.

80 *Ibid.*

Justice Iacobucci considered these three approaches in *Ramsden v. Peterborough (City)*.[81] He found that it was not necessary to determine which of the three approaches should be adopted in that case, since regardless of which approach is chosen, it is clear that postering on some public property is protected s. 2(b).[82] Whichever approach is ultimately adopted it is clear that municipal restrictions as to the use of public property for the exercise of expression cannot be solely justified on the basis of ownership rights, and given that the streets and by-ways of the municipality are generally compatible with many forms of expression and have been traditionally associated with or designated for use in public expression, restrictions on the use of this forum, whether it be newspaper distribution or postering, will normally require justification under s. 1 of the *Charter*.

In discussing the test under s. 1 of the *Charter* in a case involving a signs by-law, the Ontario Court of Appeal noted that in applying the minimal impairment component of the proportionality test, it was not necessary for the law to be the optimal solution, impairing as few rights as possible, rather a law will met the objectives of s. 1 if it "falls within a range of reasonable alternatives."[83]

(iii) *Section 7: The Right to Life, Liberty and Security of the Person*

Section 7 of the *Charter* provides:

> Everyone has the right to life, liberty and security of the person and the right not to be deprived thereof except in accordance with the principles of fundamental justice.

The primary issue with respect to this constitutional guarantee is the meaning of "liberty." The Supreme Court of Canada has stated that this section must be read in light of the values reflected in the *Charter* as a whole, and has held that:

> On the one hand, liberty does not mean unconstrained freedom. . .. Freedom of the individual to do what he or she wishes must, in any organized society, be subjected to numerous constraints for the common good. The state undoubtedly has the right to impose many types of restraints on individual behaviour, and not all limitations will attract *Charter* scrutiny. On the other hand, liberty does

---

81 *Supra* note 45 at 1096-1100.

82 *Ibid.* at 1100. See also: *Canadian Mobile Sign Assn. v. Burlington (City)* (1994), 24 M.P.L.R. (2d) 154 (Ont. Div. Ct.), affirmed (1997), 34 O.R. (3d) 134 (C.A.), leave to appeal refused (1998), 50 C.R.R. (2d) 376 (note) (S.C.C.) at 158 [M.P.L.R.], which applied the approach taken by Lamer C.J.C. at 157 of *Commonwealth* to find that there is no constitutional protection afforded to the mobile signs on public property.

83 *Urban Outdoor Trans Ad, supra* note 67, quoting *RJR-Macdonald Inc. c. Canada (Procureur général)*, [1995] 3 S.C.R. 199.

> not mean mere freedom from physical restraint. In a free and democratic society, the individual must be left room for personal autonomy to live his or her own life and to make decisions that are of fundamental personal importance.[84]

The Supreme Court has gone further in stating that liberty means "only those matters that can properly be characterized as fundamentally or inherently personal such that, by their very nature, they implicate basic choices going to the core of what it means to enjoy individual dignity and independence."[85]

In order for there to be a violation of s. 7, two conditions must be met: (1) a breach of one of the s. 7 interests of life, liberty or security of the person; and (2) the law (or by-law) that is responsible for the breach must violate the principles of fundamental justice. The latter has been interpreted to contain a substantive component respecting the end sought to be achieved and not merely the process carried out.[86] This involves balancing the right asserted by the individual and the collective interest in restricting that right.[87]

Given the importance of this *Charter* right, s. 7 challenges to municipal by-laws are seldom successful. This is because to turn municipal regulatory restrictions, such as a by-law limiting the height of fences, into *Charter* violations would "trivialize the fundamental values protected by the *Charter*."[88] Furthermore, s. 7 does not encompass property rights, which was deliberately excluded when the *Charter* was enacted. This also greatly limits application to municipal decisions, which often concern and affect property rights. For example, the decision to build a land-fill site for waste disposal may diminish the use and enjoyment of land of neighbouring property owners, but this would not constitute a violation of s. 7.[89]

Where s. 7 rights may come into play in the municipal context is in regard to municipal authority to license and regulate businesses.[90] While s. 7 does not extend to pure economic rights, the right to earn a livelihood has received some *Charter* protection. Dickson, C.J. stated in *Reference re Public Service Employee Relations Act (Alberta)* that:

> Work is one of the most fundamental aspects in a person's life, providing the individual with a means of financial support and, as importantly, a contributory role in society. A person's employment is an essential component of his or her sense of identity, self-worth and emotional well-being. Accordingly, the conditions in which a person works are highly significant in shaping the whole

---

84 *B. (R.) v. Children's Aid Society of Metropolitan Toronto* (1994), [1995] 1 S.C.R. 315 at 368; see also *R. v. Morgentaler*, [1988] 1 S.C.R. 30, for a discussion of the scope of the right.

85 *Godbout c. Longueuil (Ville)*, *supra* note 45 at 893.

86 *Reference re s. 94(2) of the Motor Vehicle Act (British Columbia)*, [1985] 2 S.C.R. 486.

87 *Godbout c. Longueuil (Ville)*, *supra* note 45 at para 76.

88 *Dorval (Ville) v. Provost* (1994), 29 M.P.L.R. (2d) 131 (Que. C.A.).

89 *Manicom v. Oxford (County)* (1985), 52 O.R. (2d) 137 (Div. Ct.).

90 For example, s. 150 of the Ontario *Municipal Act, 2001*, S.O. 2001, c. 25.

> compendium of psychological, emotional and physical elements of a person's dignity and self respect. [91]

The interference with this right must be great in order to justify application of the *Charter*. It has been held that the interference with the right to pursue a profession or occupation must result in serious psychological harm in order for s. 7 to be engaged.[92] Therefore, in order for s. 7 to apply, municipal licensing or regulation of a business must be to the extent that the right to pursue the profession is prohibited, and not merely add additional costs or other burdens, and the deprivation must have a serious effect on the psychological integrity of the claimant.[93]

However, where the licensing or regulation of a business interferes with mobility rights, s. 7 may again be engaged. In *Godbout c. Longueuil (Ville)*,[94] the Supreme Court of Canada considered a municipal resolution requiring all new permanent employees to reside within its boundaries. While the majority of the Court decided the case on the basis of an infringement of s. 5 of the Quebec *Charter* and, therefore, did not consider the application of the Canadian *Charter*, Justice LaForest (L'Heureux-Dubé and McLachlin concurring) held that the right to choose where to establish one's home falls within the scope of the liberty interest protected by s. 7 of the *Charter* as it is a "quintessentially private decision going to the very heart of personal or individual autonomy."[95] Following Justice LaForest's decision, the Alberta Court of Queen's Bench similarly declared the residency requirement of a City of Red Deer by-law invalid, which required a license to be purchased by anyone in the date or escort business.[96] In order to obtain the license, applicants had to reside in the city for six months. Such a by-law could not be justified under s. 1, as the objective of preventing an influx of prostitutes on special occasions was unjustified and based upon speculation.

(iv) *Section 8: The Right to be Secure Against Unreasonable Search or Seizure*

One of the primary purposes of the constitutional guarantee to be secure against unreasonable search or seizure is to protect the individual's reasonable expectation of privacy.[97] The Supreme Court of Canada has set out three basic zones or areas of privacy, namely, spatial or territorial privacy (for

91 [1987] 1 S.C.R. 313, para 91.

92 *United Taxi Drivers' Fellowship of Southern Alberta v. Calgary (City)* (2002), 30 M.P.L.R. (3d) 155 (Alta. C.A.), reversed 2004 CarswellAlta 355 (S.C.C.).

93 *Ibid.* at para 157.

94 *Supra* note 45.

95 *Ibid.* at para 66.

96 *Vaugeois, Re* (1999), 169 D.L.R. (4th) 744 (Alta. Q.B.).

97 *Canada (Director of Investigation & Research, Combines Investigation Branch) v. Southam Inc.*, [1984] 2 S.C.R. 145.

example the home), privacy of the person, and privacy in relation to information.[98] The determination of whether a reasonable expectation of privacy exists involves both a subjective inquiry, into whether the individual exhibited an actual expectation of privacy, and an objective inquiry, into whether the expectation is one that society is prepared to recognize as reasonable.

Section 8 protects only against "unreasonable" searches or seizures. A search is reasonable if it is authorized by law, if the law itself is reasonable and if the manner in which the search is carried out is reasonable.[99] The test for unreasonableness involves a balancing between the individual's privacy interest and the governmental interest in invading that privacy to advance governmental or public goals. The primary focus, however, is the impact of the search on the individual.[100] How this balancing is to be done and what will, therefore, constitute a reasonable search or seizure appears to depend on whether the search is in the context of criminal or quasi-criminal legislation or in the context of a regulatory statute.[101] In the criminal law context a search, except where it is not feasible to obtain prior authorization, will be *prima facie* unreasonable, unless prior authorization (usually in the form of a warrant) is obtained. Where no prior authorization is obtained, the onus, at least in the criminal search context, shifts to the state to demonstrate the reasonableness of the search.

In the context of regulatory legislation the reasonableness of the search or seizure will depend on the nature of the legislative provisions and how closely they resemble criminal law, the expectation of privacy interest and the degree of intrusion by the state.[102] Municipalities exercise a wide variety of inspection powers. In some jurisdictions there are statutes that permit such municipal inspections to be conducted without prior authorization and without reasonable grounds to suspect non-compliance with a by-law.

In *R. v. Bichel*[103] the municipality passed a by-law authorizing a building inspector to inspect residential property at all reasonable times to ascertain whether building and zoning by-laws had been complied with. The Court, in upholding the by-law, held that a distinction was to be drawn between searches in the context of a criminal investigation and inspections in the context of ensuring compliance with building or zoning by-laws. The Court, rather than focusing on where the search was to take place, namely the home, (where both the subjective and objective expectations of privacy are extremely high), concentrated on the regulatory nature of the inspection, its focus on health and safety and the limited scope of the search. Given these

---

98 *R. v. Dyment*, [1988] 2 S.C.R. 417.

99 *R. v. Collins*, [1987] 1 S.C.R. 265.

100 *Southam, supra* note 97.

101 *Thomson Newspapers Ltd. v. Canada (Director of Investigation & Research)*, [1990] 1 S.C.R. 425; and *R. v. McKinlay Transport Ltd.*, [1990] 1 S.C.R. 627.

102 *Ibid.* See also *Johnson v. Ontario (Minister of Revenue)* (1990), 73 D.L.R. (4th) 661 (Ont. C.A.).

103 *Supra* note 45.

factors the Court concluded that prior authorization was neither feasible nor required. The by-law was, therefore, held to be reasonable and thus consistent with s. 8 of the *Charter*.

The same sort of analysis can be found in *Perry v. Vancouver (City)*,[104] where the Court, in its analysis with respect to the validity of a by-law which allegedly was an unreasonable search, looked at context as a major component of the framework for determining validity. While the lower court had struck down the by-law, the Court of Appeal found that a reasonable expectation of privacy does not entitle a person who provides a private space for a private activity, (in this case a private viewing booth for adult movies), to be free from regulatory interference. The Court stated that:

> If conditions of privacy change, then expectations of privacy must change with them. And the reasonableness or unreasonableness of a search or seizure will also change.[105]

The Supreme Court of Canada considered the difference between regulatory searches and criminal searches in *Comité paritaire de l'industrie de la chemise c. Sélection Milton*,[106] where it held that a lower standard applies to regulatory searches. This approach was applied by the Ontario Court of Appeal in a municipal context, where that Court upheld a by-law and warrantless search by a municipal official undertaken for the purpose of determining whether land was being used for illegal storage of waste materials.[107] The Court noted that it is the nature of administrative searches that they occur without a prior reasonable belief in a violation, and as such reasonable and probable grounds are not a requirement to establish reasonableness.

(v) *Section 15(1): The Right to Equality Before and Under the Law*

Section 15(1) of the *Charter* provides:

> Every individual is equal before and under the law and has the right to the equal protection and equal benefit of the law without discrimination and, in particular, without discrimination based on race, national or ethnic origin, colour, religion, sex, age or mental or physical disability.

The provision spells out four basic rights: (1) the right to equality before the law; (2) the right to equality under the law; (3) the right to equal protection of the law; and (4) the right to equal benefit of the law.[108]

---

104 (1994), 19 M.P.L.R. (2d) 280 (B.C. C.A.), leave to appeal refused (1994), 24 M.P.L.R. (2d) 320 (note) (S.C.C.), reversing (1990), 1 M.P.L.R. (2d) 69 (B.C. S.C.).

105 *Ibid.* at 285.

106 (1994), 91 C.C.C. (3d) 315 (S.C.C.).

107 *Orillia (City) v. Nicol* (1997), 41 M.P.L.R. (2d) 1 (Ont. C.A.).

108 *Andrews v. Law Society (British Columbia)*, [1989] 1 S.C.R. 143.

The purpose of s. 15 of the *Charter* is to ensure equality in the formulation and application of the law; the promotion of equality entails the promotion of a society in which all are secure in the knowledge that they are recognized at law as human beings equally deserving of concern, respect and consideration.

While this provision seeks to promote equality under the law, it is not intended to eliminate all distinctions. Rather s. 15(1) of the *Charter* is designed to prevent discriminatory distinctions, namely those based on the grounds enumerated in s. 15 and those analogous to them.

Discrimination has been defined by the majority of the Supreme Court of Canada in *Andrews v. Law Society (British Columbia)* as:

> a distinction, whether intentional or not but based on grounds relating to personal characteristics of the individual or group, which has the effect of imposing burdens, obligations, or disadvantages on such individual or group not imposed upon others, or which withholds or limits access to opportunities, benefits, and advantages available to other members of society. [109]

The Supreme Court of Canada, in *Law v. Canada (Minister of Employment & Immigration)*,[110] gave a brief history of s. 15(1) jurisprudence in order to provide guidelines for the courts as to the proper approach to equality analysis. A court called upon to determine a discrimination claim is to make three broad inquires:

> (1) Does the impugned law (a) draw a formal distinction between the claimant and others on the basis of one or more personal characteristics, or (b) fail to take into account the claimant's already disadvantaged position within Canadian society resulting in substantively differential treatment between the claimant and others on the basis of one or more personal characteristics?
> (2) Is the claimant subject to differential treatment based on one or more enumerated and analogous grounds?
> (3) Does the differential treatment discriminate, by imposing a burden upon or withholding a benefit from the claimant in a manner which reflects the stereotypical application of presumed group or personal characteristics, or which otherwise has the effect of perpetuating or promoting the view that the individual is less capable or worthy of recognition or value as a human being or as a member of Canadian society, equally deserving of concern, respect, and consideration?[111]

The existence of a conflict between the purpose or effect of an impugned law and the purpose of s. 15(1) is essential for a discrimination claim.[112] In determining whether there is such a conflict, or determining a relevant com-

---

109 *Ibid.* at 174.
110 [1999] 1 S.C.R. 497.
111 *Ibid.* at 547-552.
112 *Ibid.*

parison group for the analysis, a contextual approach is to be used. Factors to be considered, from the perspective of a reasonable person in similar circumstances to the claimant, include:

(1) pre-existing disadvantage, stereotyping, prejudice, or vulnerability experienced by the individual or group at issue;
(2) correspondence, or lack thereof, between the ground or grounds on which the claim is based and the actual need, capacity, or circumstances of the claimant or others;
(3) the ameliorative purpose or effects of the impugned law upon a more disadvantaged person or group in society; and
(4) the nature and scope of the interest affected by the impugned law.[113]

Having regard to these basic principles, it appears clear that municipal by-laws or zoning by-laws that expressly draw distinctions based on the grounds enumerated in s. 15 of the *Charter*, or analogous to, will be unconstitutional unless justified under s. 1. Discrimination in the context of the *Charter* should be distinguished from discrimination as a ground for judicial review of municipal action generally. The latter involves the making of distinctions not contemplated by the authorizing legislation, while the former conforms more to our ordinary understanding of the term discrimination, as being treatment based on personal characteristics having a detrimental effect. Because discrimination under s. 15 relates to personal characteristics, s. 15 rights are only extended to natural persons.

In *Alcoholism Foundation of Manitoba v. Winnipeg (City)*[114] the City passed zoning by-laws to regulate group homes for the aged, convalescent or disabled persons, inmates discharged from penal institutions or in transit waiting for full release and persons recovering from alcohol or drug addiction. The Court concluded that the City had zoned on the basis of those grounds enumerated in s. 15(1) of the *Charter* and that the by-laws were therefore contrary to s. 15(1) of the *Charter*. Since no evidence was presented on the issue of s. 1 they were not justifiable infringements.

Similarly in *R. v. Music Explosion Ltd.*[115] the Manitoba Court of Appeal struck down a by-law which provided:

> No person licensed to operate an amusement device shall permit any minor under 16 years of age to play or operate any amusement device within his control unless such minor provides the written consent of his parent or guardian. . .

113 *Ibid.*

114 *Supra* note 45.

115 (1990), 59 C.C.C. (3d) 571 (Man. C.A.).

The Court concluded the by-law discriminated upon a prohibited ground, namely age, and was therefore contrary to s. 15(1) of the *Charter*.

A more difficult issue is whether a zoning by-law which has the effect of precluding an economically disadvantaged group in our society from the benefits of affordable housing would constitute a violation of s. 15(1) of the *Charter*. The issue has arisen on numerous occasions in the U.S. where a low cost housing sponsor seeks to build needed housing for the community's lower income population.[116] Discrimination against public housing tenants has been considered in *Dartmouth / Halifax (County) Regional Housing Authority v. Sparks*.[117] The Court held that the provisions of the *Residential Tenancies Act*,[118] which drew a distinction between public housing tenants and private sector tenants, such that a benefit extended to the latter was denied the former, violated s. 15(1). Discrimination was found on the basis of race, sex and income, as blacks, women and social assistance recipients form a disproportionately large percentage of tenants in public housing and on the waiting list for public housing. Given that public housing tenants were found to be a group analogous to those persons or groups specifically referred to by the characteristics set out in s. 15(1), based on the combined effect of several enumerated grounds, it is foreseeable that municipal by-laws which effect access to affordable housing may be challenged under s. 15 of the *Charter*.

In a licensing context, the Alberta Court of Queen's Bench considered whether a municipal lottery scheme for the licensing of taxi-cabs was contrary to s. 15, on the basis that it favoured existing license holders.[119] In partially upholding the scheme, the Court held that in order for a violation under s. 15 to be found based on an analogous ground, the following elements should be considered:

(1) whether the quality in question is a deeply-held personal characteristic;
(2) whether this characteristic is immutable;
(3) whether the group to which the individual belongs can be said to have suffered from historic disadvantage or systemic discrimination;
(4) whether this group can be characterized as a "discrete and insular minority"; and

---

116 See for example *Huntington Branch, N.A.A.C.P. v. Town of Huntington*, 844 F.2d 926, affirmed per Curiam, 109 S.Ct. 276 (1988), rehearing denied 109 S.Ct. 824 (1989); *United States v. City of Parma*, 494 F. Supp. 1049, affirmed 661 F.2d 562, cert. denied 456 U.S. 926 (1982); and see also note "Housing Discrimination", (1989) 6 Touro L. Rev. 137.

117 (1993), 101 D.L.R. (4th) 224 (N.S. C.A.), reversing (1992), 112 N.S.R. (2d) 389 (Co. Ct.).

118 R.S.N.S. 1989, c. 401, ss. 10(1), (6), (8), 25.

119 *United Taxi Drivers' Fellowship of Southern Alberta v. Calgary (City)*, *supra* note 92.

(5) whether any assistance can be drawn from the listed categories in s. 15(1).

In considering the application of these elements to the case before it, the Court held that neither being or not being a taxi driver nor not holding a taxi-cab license were accepted grounds for discrimination. However, the Court continued insofar as the lottery scheme was restricted to license holders issued prior to a certain date, there was an indirect form of discrimination based on age.

Very clearly, in this regard, s. 15 violations need not be direct and need not be based on explicit distinctions set out in the impugned instruments. Systemic discrimination arising from a seemingly neutral law will fall within the scope of *Charter* coverage. In this regard, municipal legislators must be cogniscent of the effects of by-laws and other municipal policies and should, therefore, take steps to inform themselves of possible discriminatory impacts.

7

Planning and Plans

A. INTRODUCTION

The purpose of the chapters on planning is to provide an introduction to legal mechanisms for land use planning in Canada. The focus is on municipal planning because it is that level of government which has traditionally been the most important in the planning process. Some reference, however, will be made to both provincial and private methods of land use control. It is important for both the lawyer and the planner to understand the legal tools used in municipal planning — municipal development plans, zoning by-laws and development control by-laws — and the limitations on those tools. The protection of property rights through nonconforming uses, judicial orders requiring the issuance of building permits, rights to information, appeal processes and judicial review are fundamental to a full understanding of planning. It is also necessary to examine planning in the critical perspective of the earlier chapters of this book. In that regard, the appropriate roles of municipalities, provincial governments, and appeal tribunals are also given consideration as they relate to the planning system in Canada.

B. THE NATURE OF PLANNING

Traditionally, planning has been seen as an attempt to bring rationality to decision-making respecting future physical development. The assumption of much planning legislation is that if problems are studied, investigated and analyzed the right solution will be found. The desire for rationality grew largely out of a recognition that the increasing complexities of city building could result in inefficient uses of resources unless properly coordinated. For example, sanitary systems, roads and other major municipal infrastructure had to be built with reference to both future demand and location. In the U.S., the mid-nineteenth century sanitation reform movement required comprehensive schemes in order to address broad social goals relating to public health. Similarly, the City Beautiful Movement at the turn of the century resulted in the expansion of comprehensive planning initiatives aimed at improving the physical amenities and attractiveness of American cities.[1]

---

1 Discussed in Juergensmeyer and Roberts, *Land Use Planning and Control Law* (St. Paul: West Law, 1998), at 16-20.

Despite acknowledgement that comprehensive planning was a desirable social goal, general antipathy regarding interference with private enterprise lead to many early planning documents having a non-legal, advisory function. For example, the City of Chicago developed a long-range plan for the Chicago region, with wide ranging suggestions for improvements to public spaces, transportation and street networks, as well as areas of commercial activity. The plan was adopted by the city's planning advisory commission, but its implementation was wholly dependant upon the political will of the City Council.[2] The relationship between planning and zoning, and consequently, the legal status of plans, remains as a continuing source of controversy in the U.S. today.[3]

The notion of planning as a rational process is nicely captured by Frederick Law Olmstead:

> We must cultivate in our minds and in the minds of the people the conception of the city plan as a device or piece of. . .machinery for preparing, and keeping constantly up to date, a unified forecast and definition of all the important changes, additions, and extensions of the physical equipment and arrangement of the city which a sound judgment holds likely to become desirable and practicable in the course of time, so as to avoid as far as possible both ignorantly wasteful action and . . . inaction in the control of the city's physical growth. It is a means by which those who become at any time responsible for decisions affecting the city's plan may be prevented from acting in ignorance of what their predecessors and their colleagues in other departments of city life have believed to be reasonable contingencies.[4]

In Canada, this belief in the rationality of planning is evident in the descriptions of the purpose of municipal plans found in provincial planning legislation. The *Municipal Government Act* of the province of Alberta contains the following statement of its purpose with respect to Planning and Development:

> [T]o provide means whereby plans and related measures may be prepared and adopted
>
> (a) to achieve the orderly, economic and beneficial development and use of land and patterns of human settlement, and
> (b) to maintain and improve the quality of the physical environment within which patterns of human settlement are situated...[5]

2 *Ibid.* at 21.

3 For a discussion of the recent American case law, see *supra* note 1 at 33-39.

4 Proceedings of the Third National Conference on City Planning, Philadelphia, 1911, quoted in Juergensmeyer and Roberts, *Land Use Planning and Development Regulation Law*, (St. Paul, Minn.: West Group, 2003), at 22.

5 R.S.A. 2000, c.M-26 as amended, s. 617.

The assumption of this Act and other planning legislation is that there is an accepted and understood standard of what is "orderly," "economic," and "beneficial" development and that the "improvement of the quality of the physical environment" is an objective process. It is, in part, for this reason that planning legislation in Manitoba requires development plans to:

> be prepared on the basis of studies and surveys of land use which are appropriate for the district, municipality, or jurisdiction, and may include agriculture, forestry, wildlife, mineral extraction, population growth, the economic base of the area, its transportation and communication needs, public services, social services, the capacity of the natural resources and environment to accommodate development, and any other matter related to the present or future physical, social or economic factors relevant to the preparation of the plan..[6]

The requirement in planning legislation for various studies and research to be done reinforces the view of planning as a rational decision-making process. The highly technical and scientific approaches are premised on the idea that planning is more in the nature of a value neutral, objective enterprise, where there are right and wrong answers to planning problems.

To support the rationality of planning decisions, the preparation of plans is often allocated to a body isolated from the political process. In Ontario, planning boards were for some time responsible for the preparation of all plans at the local municipal level.[7] Historically, it was these boards that were responsible for undertaking the requisite studies, preparing and recommending a plan for adoption by the municipal council. A plan had to be approved by a majority vote of all the board's members.[8] The Act furthermore had provisions for a gradual changeover in the membership of the board to prevent sudden political shifts.[9] This process ostensibly was to keep politics out of planning and to help ensure a rational process. While under current legislation, municipal councils are responsible for the preparation of plans, council may still appoint an advisory body.[10] Similar advisory bodies are found in most provinces. Generally these bodies have the authority to undertake studies and assist in the preparation of plans. A similar rationalistic assumption also underlies the use of quasi-judicial administrative tribunals, such as the Ontario Municipal Board, to oversee municipal planning decisions.

Although the assumption of planning legislation in Canada has traditionally been that planning is a rational process, and although that assumption, (as will be discussed later under administrative review) permeates much of the decision-making in Canadian planning, increasingly there is an acknowledgement that much of the essence of planning is politics.

---

6 *Planning Act*, R.S.M. 1987, c. P80, s. 25(3).
7 *Planning Act*, R.S.O. 1980, c. 379, s. 4.
8 *Ibid.* at s. 12(2).
9 *Ibid.* at s. 4.
10 *Planning Act*, R.S.O. 1990, c. P. 13, s. 8.

There are no absolutes in planning any more than there are in an act. True, it may be possible to project some remote ideal environment that would win general approval. But in our pluralistic and increasingly complicated society, it is virtually impossible to reach a consensus on specific and detailed proposals of land use.[11]

There is no right or wrong answer to whether an urban expressway should be constructed, for example. Those who live in the inner city and those whose neighbourhoods will be devastated by the expressway will be opposed to it, and for good reason. Those residents who use the expressway to reach offices in the inner city will be in favour (and for good reason) because it will facilitate their driving to work. Studies and research are important to indicate such matters as the best method of construction, the cost of construction, the cost to the urban and natural environment, and the real saving in travel time, if any, but they cannot tell us which group is right or wrong in wishing to have its own interests served.

The construction of an apartment building similarly may serve the interests of those seeking accommodation and not those who already have single-family dwellings in the area of construction. The battle over construction may well be structured and phrased in terms of public interest in preserving neighbourhoods, preserving amenities, adding to the tax base and providing needed accommodation, but the reality behind such rhetoric is the competing and divergent interests and values of those in the community.

It may be that at any given time, one value system — that of progress, growth and building — may prevail, as it appeared to do in Canada in the 1950's and 60's, but that value system is clearly no longer dominant (if it ever was) and conflicts constantly arise. "Thus the planning process as it actually functions today is not a technical exercise but rather a war among various interests competing for benefits;"[12] planning is the process whereby those benefits are allocated.

The choice between competing policy objectives or the decision to allocate benefits and resources to one group in society and not another cannot be resolved in some neutral, dispassionate fashion. The extent to which provincial planning legislation places primary responsibility for the preparation of plans in the hands of politically accountable municipal councillors is a recognition of planning's political nature. Moreover, because the decisions made have a profound impact on the character and nature of a local community, and deal with the details of land uses and the environment, it is clear that power over land uses should, for the most part, rest at the local level.

Since planning decisions have the effect of allocating benefits by determining what individuals can do with their property, it is clear that the planning

---

11 Greenspan and Vaughan "How the Zoning Game is Played: A Look at Land Use Procedures" (1972) 6 L. Soc'y Gaz. 50 at 50.

12 *Ibid.* at 51.

process itself is integral. Care must be taken to ensure adequate notice, hearings and access to information, so that decisions affecting an individual's property are made in a "fair" way in accordance with the rule of law. The centrality of process is recognized within the fabric of much of the provincial planning legislation. A stated purpose of the Ontario *Planning Act* is "to provide for planning processes that are fair by making them open, accessible, timely and efficient."[13] Likewise, the Nova Scotia *Municipal Government Act* includes as part of its purposes to "establish a consultative process to ensure the right of the public to have access to information and to participate in the formulation of planning strategies and by-laws, including the right to be notified and heard before decisions are made pursuant to this Part."[14]

The difficulty that permeates the Canadian system of planning is the reconciliation of these competing visions of planning. On the one hand, planning has been viewed as a rational exercise best approached through technocratic and expert solutions respecting matters such as population forecasting, engineering, urban design and infrastructure needs analysis. On the other hand, significant elements of planning decisions are reflections of local policy choices and allocations of benefits and burdens requiring local political accountability and in the case of interference with property and other vested rights, the need for fairness. This latter requirement, in particular, has lead to a strong judicial and quasi-judicial role in planning decisions through the protection of process rights of affected landowners. The tendency to "judicialize" planning decisions is by no means restricted to process issues, and in many provinces the substance of municipal planning decisions is also subject to some form of appellate review, reflecting the rationalist notion that planning decisions may be right or wrong, as opposed to being reflections of political preferences.

Thus, there are two important and to some degree opposing themes in the current Canadian planning regime. One is to leave decision-making to local municipal politicians because they are the best suited to make decisions respecting the allocation of benefits, and reflecting particular values. The other is to "judicialize" and formalize the system and provide for appellate review because planning affects property rights and proper decisions may be objectively determined. These two approaches arise out of the basic nature of planning and are reflected in the allocation of planning powers, the extent and nature of these powers and their appellate review.

---

13 *Planning Act*, R.S.O. 1990, c. P. 13, s. 1.1(d).

14 *Municipal Government Act*, S.N.S. 1998, c. 18, s. 190(c).

C. THE ROLE OF SENIOR LEVELS OF GOVERNMENT

1. The Federal Government

As discussed in the section addressing constitutional limitations to municipal authority, the provinces are the principal level of government with jurisdiction over matters relating to planning, a subject matter that generally falls within the provinces exclusive jurisdiction over property and civil rights and over matters of a merely local or private nature in the province.[15] The central exceptions to this rule arise in relation to federal undertakings and other matters under federal jurisdiction, such as harbours and airports.[16] In relation to these matters, it is not uncommon for the federal government to enact land use regulations addressing these items. For example, under the *Canada Marine Act*, port authorities are required to develop "a detailed land-use plan that contains objectives and policies for the physical development of the real property and immovables that it manages, holds or occupies and that takes into account relevant social, economic and environmental matters and zoning by-laws that apply to neighbouring lands."[17] The contents of such a land-use plan, which include prohibiting certain uses and structures, are similar to municipal planning and zoning documents.[18] Moreover, the legislation protects non-conforming uses and has minimum process requirements, such as notice and the right to make representations.[19] The effect of these provisions is to provide for a self-contained planning regime on federal port lands. A similar approach is used with respect to airports, where the federal cabinet may enact zoning regulations for the purposes of controlling land-uses in the vicinity of airports.[20] Another area typical of federal involvement with the land use planning process beyond federal undertakings involves the federal government's fisheries jurisdiction. Where development proposals may impact on a fisheries habitat under federal jurisdiction, approvals from the federal Department of Fisheries and Oceans is required and is usually integrated into the municipal approvals process.[21] Generally speaking, while the federal government's role in respect of planning is limited, given the federal government's ability to impose specific land use requirements in areas under its jurisdiction, development professionals must be alert to the possibility of federal planning rules where projects have the potential to interfere with matters under the federal government's control.

---

15 *Constitution Act, 1867*, U.K., 30 & 31 Victoria, c. 3, ss. 92(13),(16).

16 *Hamilton Harbour Commissioners v. Hamilton (City)* (1978), 21 O.R. (2d) 459 (C.A.); *Johannessson v. West St. Paul (Rural Municipality)* (1951), [1952] 1 S.C.R. 292.

17 *Canada Marine Act*, S.C. 1998, c. 10, s. 48(1).

18 *Ibid.* at s. 48(2).

19 *Ibid.* at s. 48(4),(5).

20 *Aeronautics Act*, R.S.C. 1985, c. A-2, as amended, s. 5.4.

21 *Fisheries Act*, R.S.C. 1985, c. F-14 , as amended, s. 35.

2. The Provincial Government

While all provinces recognize the primacy of the municipal role in land use planning, most jurisdictions also recognize that there remains a number of core provincial interests in planning matters which require continued and direct provincial involvement in land use planning decisions. The construction of a major highway or power plant, or the concentration of office buildings in one municipality can have social, economic and environmental effects in areas beyond municipal boundaries. Similarly, the refusal to allow the use of land for hospitals, low-income housing, or transportation facilities can prevent the establishment of uses which are needed by those who have no access to the local government making the decision. There can be a divergence among the interests of municipalities, just as there is among individuals, in planning decisions.

The most pervasive aspect of provincial involvement in the planning process, (beyond enacting the legislation providing for the planning regime itself), is the provincial government's role as the overseer or approval authority of municipal official plans. In a majority of provinces, a municipal official plan is not effective until it is approved by the provincial government.[22] In some cases, while the Minister may not exercise direct approval authority, it has powers to direct amendments to the plan that are in the public interest.[23]

The province of Ontario, for example, has provincial, as opposed to local, planning powers under the *Ontario Planning and Development Act*.[24] Under the Act, the Lieutenant-Governor-in-Council may approve a development plan for a defined planning area of the province. The purpose of the Act is to enable the definition of a planning area beyond municipal or regional boundaries. Once such a plan is approved, "no municipality or local board having jurisdiction over the area covered by the plan ... and no ministry, shall undertake any public work, any improvement of a structural nature or any other undertaking within the area covered by the development plan that conflicts with the plan and no municipality or planning board having jurisdiction in such area shall pass a by-law for any purpose that conflicts with the plan."[25] In addition, the Act provides for the development plan to prevail over local provisions in the event of a conflict between it and local plans or

22 Provincial approval of official plans is required in Newfoundland, Nova Scotia, Prince Edward Island, Ontario, Manitoba and Saskatchewan. See for example *Planning Act*, R.S.O. 1990, c. P.13, s. 17; *Urban and Rural Planning Act, 2000*, S.N.L. 2000, c. U-8, s. 24; and *Planning Act*, R.S.M. 1987, c. P80, s. 30.

23 *Local Government Act*, R.S.B.C. 1996, c. 323, s. 874.

24 S.O. 1994, c. 23, Schedule A.

25 *Ibid.* at s. 13.

zoning by-laws.[26] This power has been exercised in relation to significant environmental features that extend over a multitude of municipal boundaries,[27] and protect major provincial infrastructure projects.[28]

In addition, all planning in Ontario must conform to provincially set "policy statements" and identified areas of provincial interest— giving the province more control than ever over planning. The Minister of Municipal Affairs has extensive supervisory jurisdiction in the field of planning under the *Planning Act*.[29] The Minister, municipalities, local boards, planning boards, and the Ontario Municipal Board are to have regard for various provincial interests in carrying out their responsibilities under the Act.[30] Once a statement of policy is properly issued, all municipalities and others responsible for planning decisions are to ensure that in exercising any authority that affects any planning matter, planning decisions "shall have regard to" provincial policy statements.[31] Where the Minister is of the opinion that a matter of provincial interest set out in a policy statement is, or is likely to be, affected by an official plan, he or she can initiate an amendment to the plan.[32] Official plans must receive approval from the approval authority — either the Minister, the regional council or the district council.[33] The Minister may also exercise the powers of a municipality in the manner of zoning regulation with respect to any land in the municipality and his or her order supersedes existing by-laws.[34]

Other provinces have similar mechanisms. The *Municipal Government Act* (Nova Scotia), for example, enables the Governor-in-Council to adopt statements of provincial interest that are necessary to protect the interests of the province in the use and development of land.[35] Municipal planning documents must thereafter be reasonably consistent with the statements of public interest.[36] If in the Minister's opinion they do not, the Minister can request an amendment, failing which, the Minister may, by order, establish an interim planning area, and regulate or prohibit development to protect the provincial interest.[37] The Minister must approve the planning documents where they appear to affect a provincial interest, are not reasonably consistent with an

26 *Ibid.* at s. 14. Note that Ontario also controls land use through the *Niagara Escarpment Planning and Development Act*, R.S.O. 1990, c. N.2, the *Oak Ridges Moraine Conservation Act, 2001*, S.O. 2001, c. 31, and the *Planning Act*, R.S.O. 1990, c. P.13, ss. 17(6) and (7).

27 Such as the Niagara Escarpment, and Oak Ridges Moraine.

28 Such as the Parkway Belt.

29 *Planning Act*, R.S.O. 1990, c. P.13, s. 17 (6) and (7).

30 *Ibid.* at ss. 2 and 3. But see Bill 26, An Act to Amend the Planning Act, which provides that planning decisions shall be consistent with provincial policy.

31 *Ibid.* at s. 3(5) as amended.

32 *Ibid.* at s. 23.

33 *Ibid.* at s. 17(1), (2), (3) and (4) as amended.

34 *Ibid.* at s. 47.

35 *Municipal Government Act*, S.N.S. 1998, c. 18, s. 194.

36 *Ibid.* at s. 198(1).

37 *Ibid.* at s. 198(2) and (3).

applicable statement of public interest, appear to conflict with law, or conflict with provincial subdivision regulations.[38]

Similarly, the Alberta *Municipal Government Act* allows the Lieutenant-Governor-in-Council, on the recommendation of the Minister, to establish land use policies with which municipal plans and land use by-laws must subsequently be consistent.[39] In British Columbia, the Minister, if he or she believes that a plan or by-law is contrary to the public interest of the province, may request the council to amend the plan or by-law. If the council fails to do so the Minister, with the prior approval of the Lieutenant-Governor-in-Council, can order that it be altered. The order of the Minister is final and binding.[40] As well, the *Agricultural Land Reserve Act*[41] empowers a provincial commission to prepare a plan of lands that are to be reserved for agricultural uses, and lands so designated cannot be used for other than agricultural uses without the Commission's authority. The Commission's plans supersede municipal plans and must be approved by the Lieutenant-Governor-in-Council.

The retention of significant authority by the provinces over planning matters is a reflection of the need to provide common or at least co-coordinated policy responses that extend beyond municipal boundaries. The protection of the natural environment is a prominent provincial objective that is commonly addressed through provincial policies. Similarly, matters relating to housing, major infrastructure and the protection of agricultural and other natural resources are also the subject of provincial planning policy, reflecting the broader public interest in the management of these areas. While the use of direct provincial planning authority, policy statements and approval over municipal plans place much authority in the hands of the provinces, these approaches tend to allow for considerable local autonomy in implementing provincial policy objectives. In many cases provincial planning authority tends to be more abstracted, setting broad policy goals and leaving the details to local decision-makers.

In many respects the relationship between the various levels of government in planning matters can be seen as a top-down approach, with the senior levels articulating broad policies and objectives, which in turn provides the direction for regional and local municipal planning documents. Given the broad and often a-contextual nature of provincial planning policies, conformity with provincial documents is interpreted very loosely. Not surprisingly, policy objectives expressed at this level may be at cross-purposes with one another. For example, environmental objectives may conflict with social and economic objectives. Some attempts to balance these objectives may be suggested, such as "sustainable economic development," but largely this has

38 *Ibid.* at s. 208.

39 *Municipal Government Act*, R.S.A. 2000, c. M-26, as amended, s. 622.

40 *Local Government Act*, R.S.B.C. 1996, c. 323, s. 874.

41 R.S.B.C. 1996, c. 10.

been left to municipal governments. Given the ability of local governments to implement broad policies with a known context, municipalities are in a better position to assess the relative impacts and effectiveness of various policy options and thereby take into account local preferences and needs. What's good for Goose Bay is not necessarily good for Gander.

If the prevailing legislative approach is characterized by broad provincial policies coupled with considerable autonomy at the local level to implement the policies, the judicial approach reflects a similar ethos. As discussed in more general terms in Chapter 4, conflict between provincial legislation and municipal legislation has gone from deference to provincial initiatives to a narrow interpretation of conflict based on the "impossibility of dual compliance" test first articulated in the *Multiple Access Ltd. v. McCutcheon* case.[42] In the planning area, cases such as *Union Gas Ltd. v. Dawn (Township)*,[43] holding that the regulation of the location of gas lines was a provincial matter that municipalities could not regulate even in the absence of conflict, and *Bubas v. Saanich (District)*,[44] where the policy of provincial legislation respecting land severances was found to be paramount to that of the Official Community Plan Policy of the municipality, will need to be re-assessed in light of the Supreme Court's decision in *114957 Canada Ltée (Spray-Tech, Société d'arrosage) v. Hudson (Ville)*.[45]

An example of the court's approach with respect to the intersection of municipal planning initiatives and provincial legislation post-*Spraytech* is the decision of the Ontario Court of Appeal in *Goldlist Properties Inc. v. Toronto (City)*.[46] In this case, the City of Toronto adopted an official plan policy discouraging condominium conversions, which was found to be illegal by the Ontario Municipal Board partly on the grounds that the policy conflicted with provincial housing legislation, which allowed condominium conversions, on the basis that the policy and legislation were at cross purposes. In overturning the Board's decision, the Court of Appeal upheld the decision of the Divisional Court determining that the City had broad policy making powers under the *Planning Act,* and quoting significantly from the *Spraytech* decision, further held that conflict only arises where compliance with one enactment results in breach of the other. The court characterized the *Spraytech* decision as emphasizing "the importance of enhancing local decision-making and avoiding narrow and technical readings of municipal powers."[47] In other words, in the planning field, municipalities should be given broad autonomy to exercise their discretion to formulate policy that is best suited to their own community needs and values.

---

42 [1982] 2 S.C.R. 161.

43 (1977), 2 M.P.L.R. 23, 15 O.R. (2d) 722, 76 D.L.R. (3d) 613 (Div. Ct.).

44 (1988), 41 M.P.L.R. 54 (B.C. S.C.).

45 See Chapter 4 at 105.

46 (2003), 2003 CarswellOnt 3965 (C.A.).

47 *Ibid.* at para 57.

3. Provincial Planning Boards

Provincial planning boards also play an important role with respect to planning, and can be seen as another example of provincial control over municipal planning decisions. Many provinces have provincial boards which hear appeals of decisions made (or not) by municipal councils.[48] The Nova Scotia Utility and Review Board hears appeals respecting development permits, plans of subdivision, land-use by-laws, and development agreements.[49] In Alberta, in certain situations identified in the *Municipal Government Act*,[50] subdivision appeals may be made to the Municipal Government Board. In Saskatchewan, the Municipal Board hears certain appeals under the *Planning and Development Act*,[51] as is the case in Manitoba. However no provincial board in Canada has the jurisdiction over planning-related matters as extensive as the Ontario Municipal Board.

The Ontario Municipal Board (OMB) had its historical origin in 1897, when the Office of the Provincial Auditor was established to supervise account-keeping by municipalities. In 1906 it became the Ontario Railway and Municipal Board pursuant to the *Ontario Railway Act*,[52] and the *Ontario Railway and Municipal Board Act*.[53] The purpose of the Board was to resolve disputes between municipalities and companies responsible for railways, and later suppliers of utilities. Over time, more and more areas of jurisdiction were granted to the Board, which became the Ontario Municipal Board in 1932, until the Board came to exercise jurisdiction under approximately 100 public statutes and more than 80 private statutes for individual municipalities. However, most of its work is with respect to the *Planning Act*.[54] At one time, prior Board approval was required for official plans, zoning by-laws, and plans of subdivision. Although this has been replaced with the jurisdiction to hear appeals only, local planning decisions remain subject to its review anytime someone wishes to challenge them.[55]

Where the legislation provides for an appeal to a provincial board, these hearings are generally *de novo*,[56] which means that each appeal is considered

---

48 See in Manitoba, the *Municipal Board Act*, C.C.S.M. c. M240 and the *Planning Act*, C.C.S.M., c. P80; in Saskatchewan see the *Municipal Board Act*, S.S. 1988-89, c.M-23.2 and the *Planning and Development Act, 1983*, S.S. 1983-84, c. P-13.1; see also the *Nova Scotia Utility and Review Board Act*, S.N.S. 1992, c.11.

49 *Municipal Government Act*, S.N.S. 1998, c.18, s. 247.

50 S.A. 1994, c. M-26.1.

51 S.S. 1983-84, c. P-13.1.

52 *The Ontario Railway Act*, 1906, S.O. 1906, c. 30.

53 *The Ontario Railway and Municipal Board Act*, 1906, S.O. 1906, c. 31.

54 R.S.O. 1990, c. P.13.

55 See J. Chipman, *A Law Unto Itself* (Toronto: University of Toronto Press, 2002) for a greater discussion of the history of the Ontario Municipal Board.

56 See *Mississauga Golf & Country Club Ltd., Re*, [1963] 2 O.R. 625 (C.A.), at 630. Except for the Nova Scotia Utility and Review Board, which applies a standard of reasonableness. See discussion *infra*.

from the beginning as if no decision has previously been made. Neither the *Ontario Municipal Board Act*,[57] nor the Ontario *Planning Act*[58] set out any criteria or standard for the review of a municipal decision. Where a planning appeal body is established to review municipal decisions outside of standards set out at the local level through a municipal plan, the Board is replacing the political judgment of the local municipality with its own. The exercise of such authority results in the final decision-making with respect to zoning, planning, demolition control and development agreements resting at the provincial and not the municipal level, although it is the latter body which may be most visible and appear to be the most politically responsible and which, as indicated earlier, can best represent local values.

Planning decisions are for the most part value judgments about how a community should grow and develop. Planning decisions are wise or foolish, good or bad for the most part, not because of some objective truth, but rather because of the values and interests which individuals or groups espouse. Planning is fundamentally a political process which must depend on political compromise to ensure balance and harmony. Moreover, it is polycentric or multi-faceted in nature – that is, a decision to do or not to do one thing has a ripple effect throughout the community. A decision, for example, not to build an expressway has a great effect on what should be done instead to alleviate transportation problems. The result of the review of planning decisions by administrative tribunals is, therefore, a limitation on municipal authority and indeed a retention of that authority at the provincial level.

There has been a growing concern by local politicians regarding the role of the OMB, and even calls for its abolition.[59] This concern has heightened as a result of a desire to improve the status of municipalities by granting them more access to finance, more authority over local matters and more freedom from appellate review. This seems to be the trend in the other provinces, as the authority of provincial boards, where they exist at all, is being limited. However, the review of decisions made by democratically elected bodies, be they parliament, legislatures or councils, by appointed tribunals, be they courts or the Board, is not "per se" undemocratic and contrary to political values. Review by appointed tribunals such as courts or administrative bodies such as the OMB can be very beneficial and bring about healthy tensions in government decision-making. As stated by J.A. Kennedy, a former Chairman of the OMB:

> In the municipal field the same searchlight of public scrutiny does not exist as in the provincial field of government. There is no organized opposition to the government, seeking to expose maladministration, and the theory of ministerial responsibility does not exist. . .

57 R.S.O. 1990, c. O.28, as amended.

58 R.S.O. 1990, c. P.13, as amended.

59 See Chipman, *supra* note 55.

> In the light of the wide areas of power exercised by local government authorities. . .it would appear that an Ombudsman. . .would perform a useful service in the process of municipal government. Many times the author has perpetrated something in the nature of a pun by pointing out that the first three letters of Ombusdman are OMB (the letters used in headlines to refer to the Board). However, it is essentially true that in so many matters, including planning, the Board acts as an Ombudsman before the fact, so to speak. It provides a forum in which all parties can be heard after due notice in an adversary proceeding and objective appraisal made in the light of all the circumstances as threshed out at a full, open hearing.[60]

In any democratic political system based on the rule of the majority, there is a concern for individual and minority rights. The OMB can be seen as performing a similar function in planning as the courts do in applying the *Charter* to protect minority interests. Governments, especially municipalities with their authority to regulate the use of land, can affect the rights of individual property owners (which are not protected by the *Charter*). The possibility of an appeal to the Board arguably raises the bar higher in terms of review, analysis and justification for planning decisions. Knowing that decisions may be appealed to the OMB can ensure that municipal planning opinions and decisions are defensible from a professional point of view and that all appropriate analysis of an application has been carried out.

A task force comprised of GTA and Hamilton elected officials and municipal staff was created to prepare a report to the Attorney General and the Minister of Municipal Affairs and Housing recommending reform of the OMB.[61] The Task Force rejected advocating the abolition of the OMB, as this would not adequately provide for the rights and remedies of aggrieved parties when a municipal council acts improperly, arbitrarily or outside of its jurisdiction. While the courts could play this role, the Task Force felt that the OMB possesses planning expertise which could not easily be replaced by the courts. The OMB has more experience, knowledge and awareness regarding planning matters than the courts, which obviously deal with a very wide variety of matters, and the cost of appealing to the OMB for an individual, developer or ratepayer, are less than appealing to the courts. Individual ratepayers and ratepayer groups are not normally subject to a cost award, which would deter many potential litigants. Furthermore, the mere fact that the OMB is not bound by the rules of evidence, makes the OMB much more accessible to those without legal counsel and expert witnesses. Were the OMB to be abolished, review of municipal decisions would still occur. It seems clear that in a province like British Columbia, where there is no planning appeal from municipal decisions, that many more appeals are taken

60 Kennedy, "Some Observations on Planning Law" (1970), Law Society of Upper Canada Special Lectures, Series 1970, at 162.

61 "Recommendations for Reforming the Ontario Municipal Board and Ontario's Planning Appeal Process" Report of the GTA Task Force on OMB Reform, March 7, 2003.

to the courts than in Ontario. It is difficult to argue that such appeals are more expeditious, less costly, or more sensitive to a municipal council's authority.

The main recommendation of the Task Force was to change the OMB process into a true appeal or review mechanism, rather than simply a hearing *de novo*.[62] The Task Force advocates that an applicant's rights of appeal should only arise where a municipal council makes a clearly improper or unreasonable decision or deprives the parties of their rights to natural justice. This idea of injecting a reasonableness standard into the OMB process is not an original one. In 1977, the Planning Act Review Committee recommended that the OMB become more of an appeal board, with appeals from parties who object to a council's decision, or its failure to reach a decision, permitted only on the grounds that the council acted unfairly or unreasonably, or that it acted or failed to act on the basis of information or advice that was incorrect or inadequate.[63] This recommendation was rejected by the province in its formulation of the new *Planning Act*.[64] Instead, the province gave the OMB the power to dismiss appeals without a hearing if, based upon the information before it, the grounds of appeal are found to be insufficient.[65] In this regard, s. 52 of the *Ontario Municipal Board Rules of Practice and Procedure* provides for the dismissal without a hearing in the event that the notice of appeal does not disclose any apparent land use planning ground; the appeal is not made in good faith, is frivolous or vexatious, or is only for the purpose of delay; or the appellant did not make oral submissions at a public meeting, or provide written submissions before the decision appealed, without a reasonable explanation. This provision arguably provides a standard of review, that of land use planning, and results in saving of the OMB's time in avoiding frivolous appeals.

The Nova Scotia Utility and Review Board applies a form of reasonableness standard in its consideration of decisions of Council. Pursuant to ss. 250(1) and 251(2) of the *Municipal Government Act*,[66] appeals are restricted to situations where the decision of council does not reasonably carry out the intent of the municipal planning strategy, and the burden is on the aggrieved person to prove on a balance of probabilities that it does not. This has been interpreted as a limit on the jurisdiction of the Board to review municipal decisions.[67] In *Heritage Trust of Nova Scotia v. Nova Scotia (Utility & Review Board)*, the Court of Appeal stated that:

---

62 *Ibid.* at 7.

63 Report of the Planning Act Review Committee, June 1977.

64 White Paper on The Planning Act, Government of Ontario, May 1979.

65 *Ibid.* at 13.16.

66 S.N.S. 1998, c. 18.

67 *Heritage Trust of Nova Scotia v. Nova Scotia (Utility & Review Board)* (1994), 128 N.S.R. (2d) 5 (C.A.), leave to appeal refused (1994), [1994] S.C.C.A. No. 142, 23 M.P.L.R. (2d) 313n; *Bennett v. Kynock* (1994), 131 N.S.R. (2d) 334 (C.A.), leave to appeal refused (1995), [1994] S.C.C.A. No. 367, 26 M.P.L.R. (2d) 319n; *Mahone Bay Heritage & Cultural Society v. 3012543 Nova Scotia Ltd.* (2000), 190 D.L.R. (4th) 712 (N.S. C.A.).

> In reviewing a decision of the municipal council to enter into a development agreement, the Board. . .cannot interfere with a decision if it is reasonably consistent with the intent of the municipal planning strategy. A plan is the framework within which municipal councils make decisions. The Board is reviewing a particular decision; it does not interpret the relevant policies or by-laws in a vacuum. In my opinion, the proper approach of the board to the interpretation of planning policies is to ascertain if the municipal council interpreted and applied the policies in a manner that the language of the policies can reasonably bear.[68]

This test is the same for the Court of Appeal, which hears appeals of the Board on the basis of questions of jurisdiction or law.[69] It should be noted that leave is not required for an appeal from the Nova Scotia Utility and Review Board to the Court of Appeal.[70] The consideration of whether the Board erred in its determination of "reasonably carrying out the intent of the municipal planning strategy," is considered a legal issue going to the jurisdiction of the Board, therefore providing increased opportunity for appeals to the Court of Appeal.

It could be argued that to create a standard of unreasonableness in Ontario is contrary to s. 272 of the *Municipal Act*,[71] which provides that a by-law passed in good faith is not open to review because of the unreasonableness or supposed unreasonableness of the by-law. If the OMB were to make a preliminary determination of the right to an appeal purely based on whether a municipality has acted reasonably, rather than on the planning merits of any decision, s. 272 of the *Municipal Act* could be violated. Furthermore, providing a legal standard for an appeal to the OMB could create an issue of law upon which to appeal to the Divisional Court,[72] thereby increasing the number of appeals to the courts. As can be seen from the experience in Nova Scotia, the determination as to whether the Board erred in determining reasonableness has been held to be an issue of law and jurisdiction.

While the existence of the OMB, and other provincial planning boards, can be seen as the imposition of provincial control over local planning matters, it does play an important role in protecting individual rights, increasing the quality of decision making by creating a healthy tension between the OMB and municipalities, and provides a more efficient and accessible remedy than the courts.

---

68 *Ibid.* at para 99.

69 *Utility and Review Board Act*, S.N.S. 1992, c. 11, s. 30.

70 *Ibid.*

71 S.O. 2001, c. 25.

72 *Ontario Municipal Board Act*, R.S.O. 1990, c. O.28, s. 96.

D. THE MUNICIPAL AND REGIONAL PLAN

1. Introduction

At the local level, the policy document setting out the framework for future development of the municipality is referred to in a variety of ways, most commonly as an Official Plan (P.E.I. and Ontario) or a Development Plan (Alberta, Manitoba, Saskatchewan). While the nomenclature varies from jurisdiction to jurisdiction, the fundamental purpose and content of the plans are fairly consistent across the country. The purposes of such a plan include providing a framework for the environmental, social and economic development within a municipality; to guide future development decisions, to identify critical problems and opportunities with respect to development of land, to set forth timing, patterns and characteristics of future growth, and to establish means of implementing the plan. While the primary focus of all development plans is to direct the physical growth of the municipality, it is not unusual for development plans to contain detailed policies on social (i.e. housing, healthy communities), environmental and economic (usually economic development, promoting a stable tax base) matters. The New Brunswick Act even includes a mandatory requirement for a five year capital budget for the physical development of the municipality,[73] showing the close relationship between planning and municipal finance.

The required content of municipal plans varies from province to province. In some provinces such as Manitoba[74] and Newfoundland[75] the plan is required to provide detailed information while in other provinces such as Ontario the plan "may contain a description of the measures and procedures proposed" to obtain its objectives.[76] Plans may be vague and contain general invocations for a "safe and livable downtown" or may be comprised of detailed regulations regarding the nature of physical development of the city. Generally, at a minimum, plans include a map setting out the general land use pattern that the municipality desires — residential, commercial and industrial, and the appropriate densities for those land uses. Major roads, parks, and transportation facilities are also indicated. The text describes in some detail how future physical development is to occur in conformity with the map.

All jurisdictions contain process requirements that must be fulfilled prior to either the adoption or approval of the plan. At a minimum, public notice of the plan and opportunity to make representations with respect to the contents of the plan is to be given. In some jurisdictions, there is a mandatory requirement for the municipality to consult experts and carry out certain

73 *Community Planning Act,* R.S.N.B. 1973, c. C-12, s. 23(5)(c).

74 *The Planning Act*, R.S.M. 1987, c. P80, s. 25(4).

75 *Urban and Rural Planning Act, 2000,* S.N.L. 2000, c. U-8, s. 13.

76 *Planning Act*, R.S.O. 1990, c. P.13, s. 16(1) as amended.

studies.[77] These procedural requirements underscore the dualist nature of planning documents as both expressions of local values and the product of rational study.

The requirement for plans is now mandatory in a number of provinces, including Alberta, and Quebec. In other jurisdictions, while not mandatory, the minister may require that a plan be produced.[78] The power to initiate the production of a plan, or an amendment thereto is generally reserved for council itself. In Ontario, the *Planning Act* specifically provides that third parties may request council to amend its plan and upon such a request Council is obligated to hold a public meeting. Where Council fails to adopt the requested amendment, this decision may be appealed to the Ontario Municipal Board.[79] This effectively places ultimate control over the plan outside of the hands of council, since at any time a landowner may seek amendments to the plan, and if unsuccessful, may ask a provincially appointed tribunal member to overrule council. Thus, both the agenda and the ultimate decision are potentially outside of Council's control.

The legislative origins of official plans can be traced to the *Standard City Planning Enabling Act* of 1928.[80] This American federal legislation called for the preparation and adoption of planning documents, the contents of which were to provide for the physical development of the territory governed by the local government.[81] The plan was to indicate patterns of development well into the future — it was the "static end state" towards which the municipality was to grow over time. The legal effect of the plan was, however, ambiguous at best.[82] In particular, because the Master Plan under the *Standard City Planning Enabling Act* was not considered binding and had not been equated with the requirement for a "comprehensive plan" under the *Standard State Zoning Enabling Act*, the requirement that zoning "be in accordance with a comprehensive plan" has been interpreted as simply requiring internal consistency and rationality within the ordinance itself.[83] The question of the legal effect of planning documents is significantly clearer in Canada, but is not without controversy.

2. The Legal Effect of the Plan

In all provinces a plan is given legal effect. The nature and extent of the effect varies from province to province and largely depends on the relevant

77 In Manitoba, *The Planning Act*, R.S.M. 1987, c. P-80, s. 25(2)(3); in New Brunswick, *Community Planning Act*, R.S.N.B. 1973, c. C-12, s. 23(2).

78 See for example, New Brunswick, *ibid.*, at s. 23(1)(b).

79 *Planning Act*, R.S.O. 1990, c. P.13, s. 22.

80 See the *Standard City Planning Enabling Act, 1928*, ss. 6 and 7, reprinted in American Law Institute, *A Model Land Development Code, Tentative Draft No. 1* (Philadelphia, 1968).

81 *Ibid.* at 224.

82 See Haar, "In Accordance With a Comprehensive Plan," (1955) 68 Harv. L. Rev. 1154.

83 *Kozesnik v. Township of Montgomery*, 131 A.2d 1 (1957).

planning legislation and judicial construction thereof. The most common effect of a plan is to restrain the municipality in the exercise of its powers rather than to directly control land uses.

Under the *Planning Act* in Ontario, for example, there is no provision for the plan to regulate land uses directly. Rather, where an official plan is in effect, "no public work shall be undertaken and ... no by-law shall be passed for any purpose that does not conform therewith."[84] The effect of the plan is, therefore, limited to restricting municipal action. As the Court stated in *Southwold (Township) v. Caplice*,[85] an official plan in Ontario is little more than a statement of intention and is not an effective instrument in restricting the use of land. The *Vancouver Charter* provides that "the Council shall not authorize, permit or undertake any development contrary to or at variance with the official development plan" and that "it shall be unlawful for any person to commence or undertake any development contrary to or at variance with the official development plan."[86]

Besides restricting the municipality in the exercise of its powers, the adoption of a plan may impose positive obligations on a council. While plans do not obligate councils to carry out any particular projects set out in the plan[87] the adoption of a plan may require the municipality to implement the plan by passing conforming by-laws.[88] In Saskatchewan and Nova Scotia these by-laws must be passed concurrently with the adoption of the plan.[89] Under the *Land Use Planning and Development Act* of Quebec, a municipality must implement a regional development plan by adopting a planning program consistent with the objectives of the development plan.[90] Upon the adoption of the planning program the municipality must, within 90 days, adopt for its whole territory a zoning by-law, subdivision by-law and building by-law which must conform to the planning program and regional development plan.[91]

While the effect of most plans is to restrain the municipality in the exercise of its powers, the plans, be they regional or local, may also directly regulate land use or have a substantial impact on land use. Under the *Planning Act* of Manitoba "[n]o development shall take place unless (a) the development conforms with an adopted zoning by-law and this Act; (b) the development generally conforms with an adopted development plan; and (c) a

84 R.S.O. 1990, c. P.13, s. 24(1).

85 (1978), 22 O.R. (2d) 804, 94 D.L.R. (3d) 134, 8 C.E.L.R. 11 (Div. Ct.), leave to appeal refused (1978), 8 C.E.L.R. 11n (Ont. Div. Ct.). See also *Woodglen & Co. v. North York (City)* (1984), 26 M.P.L.R. 40 (Ont. Div. Ct.), leave to appeal refused (1984), 12 C.L.R. xli (Ont. C.A.).

86 S.B.C. 1953, c. 55, s. 563.

87 See for example the *Municipal Government Act*, S.N.S. 1998, c. 18, s. 217(2).

88 See for example the *Community Planning Act,* R.S.N.B. 1973, c. C-12, s. 34(1).

89 *Planning and Development Act, 1983*, S.S. 1983-84, c. P-13.1, ss. 45 and 67; *Municipal Government Act*, S.N.S. 1998, c.18, s. 219(1).

90 *Land Use Planning and Development Act*, R.S.Q., c.A-19.1, s. 33.

91 *Ibid.* at s. 102.

development permit has been issued for the development by a board, where the land is within a planning district, or a council."[92] Under the *Planning and Development Act* of Saskatchewan a basic planning statement or development plan is "binding on the municipality and all other persons, associations or other organizations and no development shall be carried out that is contrary" to these plans.[93] The *Vancouver Charter* provides that the Council cannot authorize, permit or undertake any development contrary to or at variance with the official development plan and that "it shall be unlawful for any person to commence or undertake any development contrary to or at variance with the official development plan."[94] It may be argued, therefore, that in contrast to planning Acts generally, in these jurisdictions plans alone may operate to control land uses. However, even in these jurisdictions it is envisaged that the plan will be implemented through the passing of by-laws or regulations.[95]

The scheme of planning legislation, therefore, is that a plan setting out the goals and policies for municipal physical land uses is legally approved. That plan is then brought to fruition by other land use regulations — zoning, development control and subdivision control — and by municipal undertakings in conformity with the plan.[96]

Municipal and regional plans, therefore, are generally more important in their regulation of municipal decisions than in their direct control of land uses as they prohibit municipal action that is contrary to or in conflict with the plan. The efficacy of such prohibitions depends on two factors: the actual substance of the plan and the interpretation of the prohibitions found in the various statutes.

As discussed earlier, plans can be so vague and nebulous as to have little effect on municipal decision-making.[97] Such plans not only run counter to the traditional rationale for municipal plans in that they do not prevent *ad hoc* decision-making but they also run contrary to the view that the plan is a "quasi-constitutional" document[98] which is to protect the citizens of the municipality, particularly property owners, from unwarranted and poorly con-

---

92 *Planning Act*, R.S.M. 1987, c.P-80, s. 38.

93 *Planning and Development Act, 1983*, S.S. 1983-84, c. P-13.1, ss. 50 and 62.

94 R.S.B.C. 1953, c. 55, s. 563.

95 In both Manitoba and Saskatchewan councils must enact by-laws implementing the relevant plan.

96 *Vancouver Charter*, R.S.B.C. 1953, c. 55, s. 563(1). See also *Community Planning Act*, R.S.N.B. 1973, c. C-12, as amended, ss. 18(7), 27 and 81; *Urban and Rural Planning Act, 2000*, S.N.L. 2000, c. U-8, s. 29.

97 In some provinces, such as Ontario, regional plans are often particularly prone to this weakness, partly because in terms of policy-making regional authorities occupy an awkward position between local or area municipalities and the province.

98 Bossons *Reforming Planning in Ontario: Strengthening the Municipal Role* (Toronto, 1978), at 94.

sidered or rapid changes. The plan, therefore, should be a stabilizing device, but it may not always fulfill that function.[99]

In many instances, the plan requires provincial approval[100] before coming into effect and some require other approval procedures as well.[101] The plans are more difficult to change than the land use regulations that must conform to them. The result, it is argued, is that an insubstantial plan invalidates the protective aspect of a plan's function and fails to limit or structure the discretion of the municipal council in passing land use regulations. The merit of the protective function is that the plan can be very useful as a political document to assail or support municipal decision-making. Since the plan sets out the rationale for municipal decisions, it can indicate clearly the political choices the municipal council is making and the reasons for those choices. A plan which sets out clear policies for neighbourhood preservation, for example, or clearly states that no urban expressways are to be built, is clear evidence of the political choice made with respect to these matters. In such a plan changes in the political choice will necessitate changes in the plan as well.

3. Conformity and Plans

The impact of plans can also be affected by the interpretation given to the provision of the planning legislation which requires conformity with the plan or which prohibits decisions contrary to or at variance with the plan. In practice these words have been interpreted rather liberally by the courts although their interpretation cannot be divorced from the substance of the plan itself. In the case of *Cadillac Development Corp. v. Toronto (City)*,[102] the Court dealt with the problem of conformity between land use regulations and the official plan. In this instance the official plan designated certain lands as high density residential, which would allow the construction of high-rise apartment buildings. The municipal council passed a zoning by-law, the effect of which was to remove an existing low density restriction and to allow the construction of high rise apartments. A municipal election then occurred and the subsequent council repealed the amendment and returned the zoning to its original low density provision. The by-law returning the zoning to low density was subsequently attacked in part because it did not conform to the official plan.

---

99 *Ibid.* at 9.

100 See for example the *Planning Act*, R.S.O. 1990, c. P.13, s. 17(1); and *The Planning and Development Act, 1983*, S.S. 1983-84, c. P-13.1, s. 46.

101 For example, in Ontario, the approval authority may, at the request of any person or public body, refer the plan to the Ontario Municipal Board. See the *Planning Act*, R.S.O. 1990, c. P-13, s. 17(24) as amended, and the *Municipal Government Act*, R.S.A. 2000, c. M-26, s. 636.

102 (1974), 1 O.R. (2d) 20, 39 D.L.R. (3d) 188 (H.C.).

In rendering its decision, the Court stated that an official plan represented a policy or program having legislative effect governing the area to which it applied and explained that an official plan is not immutable and does not have the effect of implementing policy outlined by it. In keeping with the discussion, the Court stated:

> Nor is there ... any requirement that the Council set about implementing the Official Plan; what the Act does is, by s. 19, [now s. 24] to place limits on the passing of future by-law's affecting the area to which the plan relates in that they must conform to it. Thus it is ensured that as the municipality develops purposefully or otherwise, the legislative changes through the by-laws necessary to allow land development to proceed are gradually channeled in the direction of implementing the policy set out in the Official Plan. Thus a municipal council that wishes to give effect to the Official Plan or any part of it is free to proceed ... under s. 35 [now s. 34,] to pass zoning by-laws but a council that wishes to permit development that conflicts with the policy of the plan is restrained and must first have recourse to the cumbersome machinery for amending the plan and the meticulous scrutiny it entails.[103]

Further, the Court, after examining the provisions of the official plan regarding high density residence areas, stated:

> The effect of these provisions and the Official Plan generally as I see it, is to permit the Council (but not require it) to designate and authorize the use of high density residence areas where this is contemplated by the policy of the Official Plan. The underlying problem is the need to move from the established and more normal situation where low density exists to the situation where economic and social necessity and pressures dictate more concentrated use of real property. These pressures usually arise from decisions made by private owners and developers and the scheme of the plan is to accommodate the desire of private initiative as well as public decision to increase density to a more efficient, economic use of land while at the same time controlling it so as to provide a reasonable balance between categories and orderly development of the community. The criteria for each category are expressed in terms of maximum density. The Council could not therefore by by-law permit a density that exceeds the maximum indicated in the Official Plan for the area concerned. This would not conform with the Official Plan.
>
> But it does not follow that Council is precluded from providing for a lower density than that recommended by the Official Plan for the category of residence area concerned. The Council may refrain altogether from zoning as high density residence area, an area or part of an area that the plan recommends for such use. It might wish on the other hand to provide for much lower densities on the outer perimeter of a high density residence area so as to ease the transition from the adjacent low density area by providing for graduated stages of heights and densities. I do not think it can be said that to place a limit on some part of a

103 *Ibid.* at 28.

> recommended high density residence area that would conform to a low density residence area criterion is a failure to conform with the plan. So far as high density residence areas are concerned the scheme is permissive not mandatory, up to the maximum density prescribed.
>
> If therefore the purpose of the repealing By-law is to reinstate or impose a density of 0.6 in respect of the ... site, I hold that this is not a purpose that does not conform with the Official Plan within the meaning of s. 19(1) now s. 24(1)1 of *The Planning Act*.[104]

Therefore, the courts, depending on the plan itself, seem predisposed to interpret conformity quite loosely, in keeping with the non-regulatory nature of official plans in Ontario.[105]

The case of *Holmes v. Halton (Regional Municipality)*[106] indicates that where an official plan is very clear in its provision, the plan will be used to prevent municipal action. In that case, the Regional Municipality passed a by-law adopting and confirming a number of resolutions which, *inter alia*, confirmed the selection of a certain site for a future landfill operation, authorized an application for approval by the Environment Review Board for use of the site, and authorized the commencement of hydro geological investigations on the site. The official plan and zoning by-laws of the area municipality designated the lands as agricultural, precluding waste disposal or landfill sites. The Regional Municipality had no official plan. The Court held that the regional by-law was contrary to the official plan of the area municipality and was therefore illegal.[107]

Even where a plan appears to be clear in its provisions or designation, however, a by-law which seems inconsistent on its face may still be interpreted to conform in spirit with the plan, particularly where the relevant

---

104 *Ibid.* at 31-2.

105 See also *Bele Himmell Investments Ltd. v. Mississauga (City)* (1983), 13 O.M.B.R. 17 (Div. Ct.) at 27, where the Court notes that, "Official Plans are not statutes and should not be construed as such. . ..the Board should give to the Official Plan a broad liberal interpretation with a view to furthering its policy objectives."

106 (1977), 2 M.P.L.R. 153, 16 O.R. (2d) 263 (H.C.).

107 Note that s. 24(3) of the *Planning Act*, R.S.O. 1990, c. P.13 enables municipalities to take into consideration a public work which does not conform to an official plan and to apply for approvals of the work and to take preliminary steps in respect of it such as carrying out investigations or obtaining reports. This section was enacted to overcome in part the effect of *Holmes v. Halton (Regional Municipality), supra* note 106. The Court in the second *Holmes* case, (1978), 5 M.P.L.R. 158 (Ont. H.C.), quashed municipal by-laws which approved a capital budget and the expenditure of funds for the disposal site, a levy on area municipalities for the development of the site and the seeking of approval from the appropriate provincial agencies for acquisition, operation and financing costs of the site. In order to compare the effect of s. 24(1) on a private work that is for the use of the public, see *Southwold (Township) v. Caplice supra* note 85, where the Court held that a waste disposal site proposed by a private corporation was not a public work.

statutory scheme envisages that this determination be initially resolved on the opinion of some planning authority or official.

This liberal approach to the interpretation of conformity appears to have been affirmed by the majority of the Supreme Court of Canada in the case of *Old St. Boniface Residents Assn. Inc. v. Winnipeg (City).*[108] In this case a developer sought to redevelop land in the City of Winnipeg. Some of this land was designated under the Greater Winnipeg Development Plan (Plan Winnipeg) as regional park and some as older residential neighbourhood, and under the more specific area plan, as future residential and residential. The land in question was zoned mainly residential but also partly light industrial. In order to effect the redevelopment, the developer proposed to purchase part of the lands from the City, which had acquired this land years before for park purposes, and to have the assembled land rezoned to allow two high-rise condominiums.

The City Council approved the sale of its land and the rezoning. Before the rezoning by-law was passed, the Residents' Association brought an application seeking an order prohibiting the council from passing the rezoning by-law on the basis that the rezoning by-law did not, as required by s. 599 of the *City of Winnipeg Act*,[109] conform with Plan Winnipeg.

The application was successful on other grounds, and the Residents' Association obtained an order prohibiting the passing of the rezoning by-law. On appeal, the Manitoba Court of Appeal reversed the Court below and further considered whether the rezoning by-law conformed to Plan Winnipeg. The Court reviewed Plan Winnipeg, characterized it as a "long-term planning document consisting of a mixture of policy statements, long-term objectives, general proposals and a land designation map" and concluded, notwithstanding that part of the lands in question were designated "regional park" on the Plan Winnipeg map,

> ... that new zoning need not fit the designation of that land on the map. What is important is that the zoning conformed to the spirit of the text and map in terms of what our civic elected representatives hope for the future for that particular area

and inclined to the view that the rezoning by-law did conform with Plan Winnipeg.[110]

Besides showing substantial difference of opinion on the substantive issue, the Court of Appeal indicated that the issue of conformity was one that was not appropriate for the Court but rather, as contemplated by the statutory

---

108 [1990] 3 S.C.R. 1170, (1990), 2 M.P.L.R. (2d) 217 (S.C.C.), affirming (1989), 43 M.P.L.R. 101 (Man. C.A.), reversing (1988), 39 M.P.L.R. 271 (Man. Q.B.).

109 S.M. 1971, c.105, s. 599, now *City of Winnipeg Charter*, re-enacted S.M. 2002, c. 39, s. 227.

110 (1989), 43 M.P.L.R. 101 (Man. C.A.) at 119.

framework, this issue was to be resolved by the designated commissioner and the committee of council.[111]

On appeal, the majority of the Supreme Court of Canada acknowledged the difficulty in determining whether a proposed rezoning by-law conformed with general statements of policy and principle. Rather than dealing with this "difficult" issue, the Supreme Court chose to affirm the decision of the Court of Appeal on the basis that the question of conformity to an official plan was primarily a planning decision based on fact and policy, and in such circumstances the opinion of those statutorily empowered to make this determination should not be disturbed except in the most exceptional circumstances.[112]

In contrast to the majority, who can be said to have resolved this issue on the basis of judicial deference, the minority concluded that since there was no privative clause, the reviewing official was not independent of council and, perhaps more importantly, since the matter of conformity did not involve complex planning issues in this case it was not appropriate to squarely face this issue.

This issue, it was suggested by LaForest J. speaking for the minority, was centered on the question of

> what is meant by the requirement in s. 599 [now s. 604] that the City "conform" to Plan Winnipeg. Does it mean that the City must follow the exact scheme set out in the policy area map, or should "conform" be interpreted in a more flexible manner, to permit council to enact zoning by-laws which may not represent an exact fit with the map, but comply with the general direction of the articulated policies?[113]

The resolution of this issue depended on the purpose and function of Plan Winnipeg in the planning process. Plan Winnipeg, it was suggested, was a "quasi-constitutional" document, which had a dual purpose. First, it was a document articulating long-term general policy and objectives in respect of the development and use of land in the city. Secondly, it was also, in light of the conformity provision of the *City of Winnipeg Act*, a limiting document which served to constrain the planning and more specifically the parameters of the land zoning powers of the council, and must be given that legal effect. If the city were not so constrained it could, without recourse to the more onerous plan amending provisions which included ministerial approval, change the essential character of future development in the city.

Accommodating the dual nature of this "quasi-constitutional" document necessitated a flexible interpretation, one "which reflects a balance between its general long-term nature, and its statutorily mandated function as the foundation of the planning process." The degree of nonconformity tolerated in any given case would, therefore, depend on balancing the long term ob-

---

111 *Ibid.*

112 *Supra* note 108.

113 *Ibid.* at para. 11.

jectives of the plan, which were to be liberally and flexibly interpreted, against the need to ensure that council did not exercise its powers in such a way as to inhibit the ultimate implementation of these objectives.

Resolving the issue of conformity in light of these principles could, it was acknowledged, be difficult in some circumstances particularly where the question of conformity required extensive planning expertise and direct knowledge of local land use dynamics. In this case, the issue of non-conformity was not of such a nature. The land in question was clearly designated "regional park" and a rezoning by-law authorizing a high-rise condominium development was clearly inconsistent with Plan Winnipeg as it then stood. Only if the Plan were amended would such a by-law be permitted.

While judicial deference should be a guiding principle in the judicial review of political planning decisions, the degree of deference appropriate in any given case should be related to the concerns underlying the need for deference, namely, that courts do not usurp the policy-making function of elected council, or involve themselves in planning matters for which they are unlikely to be institutionally competent. Such concerns manifest themselves most clearly where the courts are called upon to review the appropriateness of a plan or particular development. Where, however, the planning issue is one of non-conformity, these concerns should not be overriding. In such circumstances the courts are not called upon to review the appropriateness of the plan or proposed development, but are (at least theoretically) only called upon to determine whether a planning authority, having made a studied political decision that is then embodied in the plan, is now attempting to implement a different political choice while avoiding the substantial public and political scrutiny that would normally accompany such a change.

Admittedly, even such an inquiry requires a court to determine what the initial planning choice was, and given that plan policies are likely to be broadly phrased, the interpretive process offers the courts, who are neither politically responsible, nor expert in the field, an opportunity to substitute their opinion of what the appropriate policy should be. In such circumstances, deference, as expressed through a liberal and broad interpretation of the plan and by-law, is clearly appropriate, and findings of non-conformity should be few. However, when the plan, liberally interpreted, provides specific policy or land use designation, the courts are institutionally competent to face the issue of conformity squarely and should give effect to the plan's important purpose of restraining municipal planning authority that is inconsistent with the plan.

Given the preceding analysis and the statutory and factual context in the *Old St. Boniface Residents Assn.* case, the purposive approach taken by the minority is preferable. The issue of non-conformity, simply stated, was whether a seven-storey condominium high-rise development conformed with the Plan Winnipeg designation of regional park. As noted by the minority, this could not be said to involve a subtle issue involving great planning expertise or knowledge of local land use dynamics. The issue of non-conformity did not, therefore, involve concerns of policy substitution or institutional incompetence, and the majority should have given effect to the purpose of Plan Winnipeg (which, besides providing general long-term objectives, was to constrain the city from implementing development inconsistent with the Plan) and should have found the rezoning by-law to be non-conforming. The City, having gone through the onerous plan approval procedures, which included obtaining ministerial approval, should not be able to circumvent the plan amending procedures when it wished to implement new policies and approve new developments that were clearly at odds with the land use designation in the approved plan. Such a decision, it must be remembered, would not have precluded the development from occurring, but rather would have required the City to amend Plan Winnipeg, thereby subjecting this change in planning policy to active public and political scrutiny. Considering the nature of the planning change, from regional park to high-rise condominium, arguably this process would have been the more appropriate one.

4. Planning in Two-Tiered Systems

Another example of the courts giving official plans a substantial enough impact to directly affect land uses can be found in *Campeau Corp. v. Gloucester (Township).*[114] That case involved a situation where an area municipal zoning by-law designated certain lands as commercial and thus allowed the construction of a shopping centre. Two developers, Cadillac and Tartan, wished to develop a regional shopping centre on the site while another developer, Campeau, wished to construct a similar centre about one half mile away. The area would support only one regional centre.

The regional official plan approved on August 30, 1976 designated the lands of Cadillac and Tartan residential. In a move that clearly indicates that planning is concerned with competing interests, Campeau, approximately two years later, sought an injunction to restrain the issuing of a building permit for a shopping centre by Cadillac and Tartan. The argument was that the *Regional Municipality of Ottawa-Carleton Act*, which provided that every official plan and every by-law in effect in the planning area shall be amended to conform to the regional official plan forthwith,[115] meant that there was a statutory obligation on the township to amend its by-laws since the area in question was designated as residential in the regional official plan. As the by-law had not been amended, there was an obligation on the area municipality not to issue a building permit which would thwart the regional official plan.

The Court accepted the argument in spite of the fact that, traditionally, plans have not directly controlled land uses and in spite of the fact that the

114 (1978), 6 M.P.L.R. 290 (Ont. H.C.), affirmed (1979), 8 M.P.L.R. 147 (Ont. C.A.).

115 R.S.O. 1980 c. 439, s. 96(7), formerly s. 68(7), now repealed.

legislation was not as clear as that of Saskatchewan, which provides that any zoning by controls that are inconsistent with the plan shall be of no effect[116] or that of Vancouver, prohibiting development contrary to the official development plan.[117] The Court in *Campeau*[118] held that there was a statutory obligation on the area municipality to amend its by-laws and, in the interim, the municipality should refuse any application for a building permit even though the application complied with its by-law, since the by-law did not conform to the official plan of the region. An appeal from the decision was dismissed.[119]

The decision is an important one because it enabled regional municipalities to control, in effect, the zoning of area municipalities in Ontario; there is no definition of a regional plan in the legislation, so that the plan can be as detailed as the region desires. The case is also significant because it is an example of an official plan directly controlling land uses in the absence of some other local regulation — notably a zoning by-law to carry out the effect of the plan. The regional official plan has in law become more than a policy instrument and can be used to directly regulate the use of land. This effect may have been tempered by the enactment of s. 27 of the *Planning Act*.[120]

The Courts at both levels did not consider the view that the provisions in the regional acts in Ontario regarding conformity between the regional official plans and the local official plans and zoning by-laws were largely an attempt at a political compromise. This view is substantiated by the legislation, which provided for the predominance of the regional official plan and for local official plans and by-laws to be amended forthwith but did not provide a remedy for failure to amend. At the same time there is little protection in the legislation in Ontario (aside from Ontario Municipal Board review and Ministerial approval), since the scope and nature of regional official plans are not defined, to prevent small area municipalities from being dominated by large area municipalities in the region through the adoption of a very detailed regional plan. Section 27 of the *Ontario Planning Act* can be seen as an attempt to restore the compromise in part. Area municipalities are required to amend their plans to conform with regional plans within one year and if they fail to do so, regional municipalities may enact the amendment.

However, notwithstanding this apparent legislative solution to the problem, the issue of whether a regional plan operates to directly control land uses when it conflicts with a local zoning by-law, has not been conclusively resolved by the courts. In *Csele v. Pelham (Town)*[121] the chief building officer

116 See *The Planning and Development Act*, R.S.S. 1978, c. P-13, s. 38(3), and *The Planning and Development Act, 1983* S.S. 1983-84, c. P-13.1, ss. 50 and 62.

117 See the *Vancouver Charter*, S.B.C. 1953, c. 55, s. 563(2).

118 *Supra* note 1114.

119 See *Campeau Corp. v. Gloucester (Township)* (1979), 8 M.P.L.R. 147 (Ont. C.A.).

120 First enacted S.O. 1983, c. 1, s. 27; now R.S.O. 1990, c. P.13, s. 27, as amended.

121 (1985), 29 M.P.L.R. 188 (Ont. Dist. Ct.).

refused to grant a building permit on the basis that the proposed development, while conforming to the local official plan and zoning by-law, did not conform to the regional official plan. An appeal pursuant to s. 15 of the *Building Code Act*[122] was taken, and the issue was whether the regional plan was "applicable law" justifying the refusal of a building permit, for under the *Building Code Act*, an applicant was entitled to a building permit unless the development would not comply with the *Building Code Act*, the Building Code or "any other applicable law."

The Court reviewed the current statutory scheme in light of earlier jurisprudence and concluded that official plans were only statements of intention outlining the long-term objectives of the municipality and that, in light of s. 27(2) of the *Planning Act*, which provided the regional municipality with the authority to amend conflicting zoning by-laws, the regional official plan did not constitute "applicable law." The Court ordered the issuance of a building permit.

On the other hand, a contrary result was reached in the case of *J. & R. Rite Holdings (Oshawa) Inc. v. Oshawa (City)*[123] where once again the issue was whether nonconformity with the regional official plan justified the refusal of a building permit. The Court, relying on the case of *Campeau Corp. v. Gloucester (Township)*[124] and s. 27 of the *Planning Act*, found that the refusal was justified.

The result in *Csele*, it is suggested, is preferable in that it more accurately reflects the legislative intent as to both the legal status of official plans in Ontario, and the solution of non-conformity between regional plans and zoning by-laws. In Ontario, official plans are usually broad, general statements of policy, which lack the certainty that the law should have and are therefore inappropriate to directly regulate land use. This has been recognized by both the courts[125] and the legislature which, by virtue of ss. 24(1) and 27(1) of the *Planning Act*, has limited the effect of official plans to restricting municipal actions.[126]

The legislature has also envisaged the problem of nonconformity between regional plans and local zoning by-laws and has under s. 27(2) of the *Planning Act* provided a solution that involves neither the invalidation of the nonconforming zoning by-law, nor the direct regulation of land use by the regional plan. If the legislature had intended that the regional official plan should directly regulate the use of land or invalidate zoning by-laws when

122 R.S.O. 1990, c. B-13, now S.O. 1992, c. 23, s. 25.

123 (1988), 38 M.P.L.R. 97 (Ont. H.C.)

124 *Supra* note 119.

125 *Woodglen & Co. v. North York (City)* (1984), 26 M.P.L.R. 40 (Ont. Div. Ct.), leave to appeal refused (1984), 12 C.L.R. xli (Ont. C.A.).

126 *Planning Act*, R.S.O. 1990, c. P.13 as amended.

they were nonconforming, the legislature could have so provided, as indeed other provinces have done.[127]

E. CONCLUSION

Plans, realistically, are political documents. They can allocate power to regional municipalities over area municipalities (and to the area municipality dominating the region); they can allocate power to those whose interests are protected or advanced by the plan in functioning as a quasi-constitutional document protecting the *status quo*; or they can, by providing little guidance or policy direction, leave political decisions out of the public arena and largely in private hands. Municipal and regional plans are important, therefore, not merely in the control and direction they provide over local land use regulatory decisions and over local land uses in some cases, but also as documents that indicate local political choices that have been made. In spite of this fundamental utility at the regional or municipal level it is largely the province that controls local planning through the requirement of provincial approval of local or regional plans and through provincial "policy."[128] The rationale for provincial approval and policy setting is the need to co-ordinate planning on a scale larger than a municipal or regional one. The judicial trend towards greater deference to municipal decision-making powers is again evident in the planning field, as illustrated by the recent *Equity Waste* and *Goldlist* decisions.

---

127 See for example the *Planning and Development Act, 1983*, S.S. 1983-84, c. P-13.1 as amended, ss. 45(2), 50, 59 and 62.

128 See for example the *Planning Act*, R.S.O. 1990, c. P.13, s. 17(1); and the *Planning and Development Act*, 1983, S.S. 1983-84, c. P-13.1, s. 46.

8

Land Use Regulation

A. INTRODUCTION

The traditional basis of planning, as indicated above, was that official plans were to set overall policies and that those policies were to be implemented by other land use controls. The most important method of general implementation of plans was the zoning by-law, a process copied from American legislation first enacted in 1922, the *Standard State Zoning Enabling Act,*[1] whereby the entire municipality was divided into districts or areas with uniform regulations or restrictions in each area. It is a system of land use control now common to all Canadian provinces.

The basic premise of this method of implementing a plan is that rational separation of conflicting uses is desirable and is one of the main goals of the planning process. Pure zoning emphasizes the distinctions between uses rather than any relationship that ties them together. Indeed, its advocates years ago assumed that "landowners could be protected from the injurious effects of other land uses by dividing up the city — with houses here, businesses over there, and industry somewhere else."[2] However, with changes in technology and the economy, such separation of uses may no longer be necessary, or indeed beneficial. Planning should encourage the combining of compatible uses, such that people can live where they work and play.

Zoning developed with the view that the local legislature was to establish rules to govern development into the distant future, perhaps 20 or 30 years. The legislation was to be designed so that development could occur without further state intervention either through amending by-laws or through the administrative discretion of officials. Development was to occur automatically along the lines of the zoning by-laws. The concept was static, rather than dynamic, land use control. The plan was drawn, the by-laws passed and, slowly but inevitably, the city would fill out according to plan. The consolidations of zoning by-laws for cities in Canada show that this ideal is far from dead. The zoning by-laws generally cover the entire city, setting out districts

---

1 Reprinted in *A Model Land Development Code Tentative Draft No. 1* (Philadelphia, 1968) *supra* Chapter 7, notes 80 and 81.

2 Dukeminier and Stapleton "The Zoning Board of Adjustment: A Case Study in Misrule" (1961-62), 50 Ky. L.J. 273 at 339.

according to use and density in order to achieve the ends of the legally adopted plan.

The theory of zoning closely follows the rule of law value in that it seeks to provide certainty and predictability by limiting discretion. The rules are set in advance for all to see and everyone within a given zoning area is subject to the same rules.

Traditionally, zoning as a system of planning implementation in Canada was not intended to control the detail of the form or nature of development. Architectural quality was seen as beyond its purview; something for the private market to deal with. Zoning was limited to attempting to prevent conflicting uses by imposing prohibitions. In undertaking this task, it can be seen to have its roots in the common law doctrine of nuisance and in the equitable doctrine of restrictive covenants. Zoning is related to nuisance because both attempt to prevent unreasonable interference with the use of land.[3] It is related to restrictive covenants because it attempts by prohibition to prospectively prevent the use of land. Both nuisance and restrictive covenants have severe limitations as land use devices and zoning in part can be seen as an attempt to remedy those limitations.

B. NUISANCE

The tort of nuisance is found to exist where a person unreasonably interferes with the use and enjoyment of another's land. Nuisance is primarily retrospective in nature. Although there is the possibility of a *quia timet* injunction,[4] the relief, usually in the form of damages, is awarded only after there has been a physical interference with the use of land by another. Unlike intentional torts or negligence, the interference in question does not have to be caused intentionally or negligently. Instead, in deciding whether to find that a nuisance exists, the courts are required to make a determination depending on, *inter alia*, such factors as: the gravity of the harm; the character of the neighbourhood in which the land is situate; any abnormal sensitivity of the plaintiff; the utility of the defendant's conduct; the length of time the nuisance has continued and whether the person bringing the action came to the nuisance; and the effect of the nuisance on the value of the property affected.[5] In making such an assessment, the courts must balance the rights of the landowner against the rights of the person causing the interference; a

3 See for example *Walker v. McKinnon Industries Ltd.*, [1948] O.W.N. 537 (H.C.); *Walker v. McKinnon Industries Ltd.*, [1949] 4 D.L.R. 739 (Ont. H.C.), varied [1950] 3 D.L.R. 159 (Ont. C.A.), affirmed [1951] 3 D.L.R. 577 (Ontario P.C.).

4 The Latin "*quia timet*" roughly translates to "because he fears." This remedy is sought to prevent some likely future injury.

5 *St. John's (City) v. Lake* (2000), 191 D.L.R. (4th) 616 (Nfld. C.A.) at 628; *Walker, supra* note 3.

determination which involves a high degree of judicial discretion due to the open-ended nature of the "unreasonableness" standard.

The determination of whether to grant an injunction or damages also involves considerable judicial discretion. For example, in the case of *Bottom v. Ontario Leaf Tobacco Co.*,[6] the Court held that tobacco smoke and fumes coming from a factory saturating the plaintiff's clothing and furniture and causing him and his wife to become ill constituted a nuisance but that it could not be remedied by an injunction; only damages were given. The Court had to balance the injury to the plaintiff against the public good. In this case, the public good was the employment of some 200 people. Similarly, in *Mandrake Management Consultants Ltd. v. Toronto Transit Commission*,[7] the owners and occupiers of an office building complained of noise and vibration from the operation of the Toronto subway system. The Court of Appeal emphasized the substantial weight that should be given to an essential public service that benefited thousands of members of the public. Although the Court of Appeal overturned the trial judge's finding of a nuisance, the Court also stated that if there had been a nuisance, damages were the appropriate remedy when the safety and convenience of the public would be affected by an injunction.

The use of a broad and flexible test for nuisance may be defended on the basis that actual harm can often only be determined with reference to a known context, but the facts that give rise to a nuisance claim may vary considerably and would be difficult to anticipate through rigid standards. However, as a basis for determining appropriate uses for land, nuisance has a number of shortcomings. Firstly, predictability is diminished as the courts weigh a number of competing factors, including the "public interest." The absence of objectively determinable standards and the retrospective nature of nuisance results in uncertainty, which in turn may discourage investments being made to improve land.

Secondly, the "public good," may not be adequately presented to the courts, since, in most cases, there are only two parties appearing. The need for employment may have to be balanced against the evils of smoke and pollution and the parties may not be able or prepared to bring forward that kind of evidence. The adjudicative process is not suited to collecting and evaluating this type of evidence. Moreover, because of the inherent requirement to balance community objectives in a determination of a nuisance suit, courts are invariably involved in policy decisions, which in turn raises separation of powers issues.

The public nature of nuisance is exemplified by the rules respecting public nuisance. Public nuisance is distinguished from private nuisance by having effects that impact the community as a whole. In such cases, only the Crown, as represented by the Attorney General has standing to bring an

---

6 [1935] O.R. 205, [1935] 2 D.L.R. 699 (C.A.).

7 (1993), 102 D.L.R. (4th) 12 (Ont. C.A.).

action.[8] It is only where an individual plaintiff can show special damages, unique from other members of the community, that they themselves may bring a nuisance suit. In cases of public nuisance, the ability to enforce and seek compensation for community based property interference is actually removed from the community and placed in the hands of a provincial official.

The defence of statutory authority, which provides some protection from liability for nuisance arising from activities undertaken by public bodies (including municipalities) and authorized by statute, can also be seen as a statement of the public interest or public good, as it provides a defence to claims of nuisance arising out of such works; the rationale being that to allow claims of nuisance for activities carried out in accordance with a statutory mandate would in effect deny the mandate.[9] Although the majority of the Supreme Court of Canada attempted to narrow the defence of statutory authority in *Tock v. St. John's (City) Metropolitan Area Board*,[10] the Court later confirmed the judgment of Sopinka J., upholding this traditional view of the defence.[11] It should be noted that the standard that must be met for the defence to apply is a high one: the courts will not casually reach the conclusion that private rights are intended to be sacrificed for the common good. The defendant authority must show that there are no alternative ways to carry out the work. If only one method is practically feasible, it must be shown that it was practically impossible to avoid the nuisance.[12]

Zoning schemes are, in part, a legislative reaction to some of the shortcomings of regulating incompatible land uses through nuisance. Firstly, zoning, by determining the appropriate location for uses in advance, is proscriptive in nature. Landowners have some assurance through zoning that incompatible uses will not locate adjacent to their own use, creating greater certainty that their use of land will not be interfered with. In addition, because decisions respecting the location of uses are made by municipal councils, the process is democratized, allowing local communities to determine the relative benefits of economic activity and freedom from loss of property amenity. Zoning is not a substitute for nuisance actions and, as a result, locating an activity in a properly zoned area is not a defence to a nuisance claim. However, in weighing the factors to determine whether a nuisance exists, the zoning status of the land will be relevant to the character of the neighbour and the reasonable expectations of the plaintiff to be free from interference.

8 See *Cairns v. Canada Refining & Smelting Co.* (1913), 25 O.W.R. 384, 5 O.W.N. 423 (H.C.), reversed (1914), 26 O.W.R. 490, 6 O.W.N. 562 (C.A.), for a discussion of the difference between private and public nuisance. The court also pointed out that an individual could sue in respect of a public nuisance only if he could show some grievance apart from that suffered by the general community.

9 *Tock v. St. John's (City) Metropolitan Area Board*, [1989] 2 S.C.R. 1181, at 1225.

10 *Ibid.*

11 *Ryan v. Victoria (City)*, [1999] 1 S.C.R. 201.

12 *Supra* note 9 at 1226.

C. RESTRICTIVE COVENANTS

The regulation of land uses has also traditionally been accomplished through the rules respecting restrictive covenants. Here a landowner could, upon the sale of a piece of property, include as part of the assignment contractual provisions restricting how the purchaser may use the land. Such a contractual arrangement may be desirable where the vendor retains adjacent lands and wants to ensure that the uses put to the sold land do not interfere with the vendor's continued enjoyment of his land. The restrictions were enforceable against the purchaser as a matter of contract law. However, often the vendor would want the restrictions to apply to subsequent owners of the burdened property. As a matter of contract law, because there was no privity of contract between the owner of the benefiting lands and the new owner of the burdened land, the benefiting owner could not enforce the restriction. Similarly, the benefiting owner could not pass on the benefit to a new owner of the benefiting lands for the same reason.

Under the common law, the benefit could pass with the transfer of the benefiting lands where it was the intention of the original parties that the benefit could pass and the covenant "touched and concerned" the land. However, the common law rules would not allow for a transfer of the burden of the covenant, as this was seen as an intolerable restriction on the free alienation of land. As a result under common law, if an owner whose land was subject to a restriction respecting use, (for example, to only use the lands for a single residential use), sold the lands, under common law, the new owner would be under no such restriction.

Tulk v. Moxhay,[13] a decision made under the equitable jurisdiction of the courts, changed this situation by enabling the burden on land to run under certain conditions. In this case, which has clear parallels to modern planning considerations, there existed a covenant requiring the burdened owner to maintain certain lands as a park. Upon the sale of the lands, it was held that the purchaser, who had notice of the restriction, was bound by the covenant, as the covenant created an equitable interest in the land. The law, as it currently stands, allows for a restrictive covenant to run with the land (that is, bind future owners) where it meets the following conditions:

1) the covenant must touch and concern the land;[14]
2) the burdened lands and benefiting lands must be ascertainable on the face of the instrument creating the covenant;[15]
3) it was intended that the burden run with the lands;

13 (1848), 2 Ph. 774, 41 E.R. 1143 (Ch. Div.); see also *Parkinson v. Reid*, [1966] S.C.R. 162.

14 *Galbraith v. Madawaska Club Ltd.*, [1961] S.C.R. 639, 29 D.L.R. (2d) 153. See also *R. v. York (Township)*, [1960] O.R. 238, 23 D.L.R. (2d) 465 (C.A.); *Kirk v. Distacom Ventures Inc.* (1996), [1996] B.C.J. No. 1879, 1996 CarswellBC 1878 (C.A.).

15 See *London County Council v. Allen*, [1914] 3 K.B. 642 (C.A.).

4) the covenant must be negative in nature, which is to say that it cannot require the owner of the burdened land to take some affirmative step or spend money to comply with its terms;
5) the purchaser must have prior notice of the covenant.[16]

A variation on restrictive covenants in common usage today is the "building scheme" which involves a number of lots rather than just two. A building scheme exists when restrictive covenants are imposed during the course of development, with the intention that once the scheme has "crystallized" on the sale of the first lot, the vendor will be bound, and subsequent purchasers will be able to enforce the restrictions.[17] The purpose of a building scheme is to ensure that landowners within a development area maintain their residence in a similar architectural style or maintain a certain level of upkeep. In order for a building scheme to be in place, there must be: (1) a common vendor from which the plaintiff and defendant derive title; (2) prior to the first sale, the vendor had a scheme in mind that the lots would be subject to restrictions which, though varied in detail as to particular lots, are consistent with the general scheme of development; (3) the restrictions are intended to be for the benefit of all the lots sold, whether or not the restrictions are also intended to be for the benefit of other land retained by the vendor; and (4) both the plaintiff and defendant, or their predecessors in title, purchased the lots based upon the assumption that the restrictions were to enure for the benefit of the other lots included in the general scheme, whether or not they were also intended to enure for the benefit of other lands retained by the vendor.[18] In Ontario, it has also been held that a building scheme must be registered pursuant to s. 119 of the *Land Titles Act*.[19] Finally it should be noted that the removal of restrictive covenants even after the expiration of their usefulness is difficult. The case law has indicated that they should not be removed unless the condition or restriction is "spent or so unsuitable as to be of no value and under circumstances when its assertion would be clearly vexatious."[20]

Yet, despite the beneficial uses to which restrictive covenants can be put, the device of controlling land uses through restrictive covenants is a very limited one. Restrictive covenants are to be strictly construed, and any ambiguity is to be resolved in favour of non-enforcement[21] – in keeping with

---

16 For a general discussion, see Bruce Ziff, *The Principles of Property Law*, 2d ed., (Toronto: Carswell, 1996) at 351-58.

17 *Berry v. Indian Park Assn.* (1999), 174 D.L.R. (4th) 511 (Ont. C.A.).

18 *Ibid.* at 519.

19 *Ibid.* R.S.O. 1990 c. L.5.

20 See *Beardmore, Re,* [1935] O.R. 526, [1935] 4 D.L.R. 562 (C.A.), at 569 [D.L.R.]. For another example of an unsuccessful application to remove a restriction even though the proposed use was reasonable, see *Beardsley's Application, Re* (1973), 25 P. & C.R. 233 (Eng. Land Trib.).

21 *Kirk*, *supra* note 14.

the view that land should not be unduly encumbered. The restrictions must be negative, which involves examining whether money will have to be expended or court supervision needed. In addition, case law suggests that the restrictions must be precise and not variable[22] and they must relate to the use, not the users, of the land.[23]

In many ways, restrictive covenants are similar to zoning. Indeed, one of the purposes of enforcing such covenants as set out in *Tulk,*[24] was to protect the value of property and to prevent unjust enrichment. The Court in that case stated that the covenant should be enforced or else "it would be impossible for an owner of land to sell part of it without incurring the risk of rendering what he retains worthless ..." and that "the price [of the land] would be affected by the covenant, and nothing could be more inequitable than that the original purchaser should be able to sell the property the next day for a greater price, in consideration of the assignee being allowed to escape from the liability which he had himself undertaken ..."[25]

Zoning can be seen in part as a protective device to prevent the use of land in a way that will decrease the value of neighbouring lands, shift part of the cost of undesirable uses to unwilling neighbours and thus unjustly enrich the undesirable user. More importantly, zoning functions traditionally in the same way as restrictive covenants by placing negative restrictions on the use of land to prevent undesirable uses. Also, zoning restrictions must relate to the use and not the user of property.[26]

Traditional zoning, however, is an improvement on restrictive covenants. First, as seen earlier, it attempts to deal with land uses on a broad scale, although it can also be site specific. The entire municipality may, and usually does, come under its regulation. This is an important difference from restrictive covenants which affect two parcels of land or building schemes which require common ownership. Zoning, therefore, is seen as a major improvement in that it is comprehensive in scale and unaffected by land ownership. The technical requirements of ascertainable land, of benefits and burdens and lack of notice are totally removed, although others, as will be discussed, remain. Zoning can, therefore, be useful in implementing comprehensive rational planning.

A second improvement over restrictive covenants can be seen in zoning's public nature. Since it is legislatively imposed, usually at the municipal level,[27] it divorces land use control decisions from private ownership, and

22 See *Sekretov v. Toronto (City)*, [1973] 2 O.R. 161, 33 D.L.R. (3d) 257 (C.A.).

23 See *Galbraith supra* note 14.

24 *Supra* note 13.

25 *Ibid.* at 777-8 (Ph.), 1144 (E.R.).

26 See *R. v. Bell* [1979] 2 S.C.R. 212, (1979), 9 M.P.L.R. 103, 26 N.R. 457, 98 D.L.R. (3d) 255 (S.C.C.), reversing (1977) 2 M.P.L.R. 39, 15 O.R. (2d) 425, 75 D.L.R. (3d) 755 (C.A.), reversing (1976) 12 O.R. (2d) 487, 69 D.L.R. (3d) 375 (Div. Ct.).

27 In Ontario, however, there is a provincial power to zone. See the *Planning Act*, R.S.O. 1990 c. P.13, s. 47.

enables all interest groups in the political arena to have the potential of affecting land uses. Decisions respecting land uses are made, and benefits and burdens (in the sense of increased and decreased values of property) are distributed as under restrictive covenants, but the community can influence the distribution of those benefits and burdens. In keeping with its public nature, enforcement is undertaken by the state. Thus the burden of enforcing restrictions is not only removed from the individual but it is no longer restricted to the property owner. Zoning in this way has revolutionized land ownership and control. It has democratized the nuisance doctrine by transferring determinations from the courts to local legislatures and it has democratized restrictive covenants by enabling society to impose restrictions regardless of land ownership, although it is clear that restrictive covenants are still available for private landowners and will prevail even in the face of zoning by-laws. They are, therefore, still an important private method of land use control.

D. THE SCOPE OF THE ZONING POWER

While significant improvements over the regulation of land use have been realized through zoning, the municipal power to regulate land uses through zoning is not unqualified. As a species of municipal by-law, zoning regulations are subject to the same limitations respecting the general exercise of municipal power discussed above. A central determinant of the scope of the zoning power as conceived by the courts has been the court's understanding of the purpose of zoning.

The purpose of zoning regulation was examined by the U.S. Supreme Court in *Village of Euclid v. Ambler Realty Co.*,[28] a case which upheld the constitutionality of a zoning by-law dividing the municipality into different use and density districts against an attack which argued that the by-law deprived the respondents of property without due process of law and deprived them of equal protection under the law. The Court draws an explicit parallel between the law of nuisance and zoning provisions, noting that as American society has urbanized there is a greater need for laws respecting the use and occupation of private lands, and, like nuisance, the assessment of whether zoning constitutes an unreasonable interference with private property is dependent upon the circumstances and conditions present.[29] In holding that the zoning power was a justified exercise of the state's regulatory authority (referred to as the "police power"), the court concluded that the zoning regulation had a rational relationship to public health, safety and general welfare objectives.[30] In discussing how zoning achieved these ends the Court

28 272 U.S. 365 (S.C., 1926).
29 *Ibid.* at 387.
30 *Ibid.* at 395.

focused on the regulation of the physical impacts of land uses on surrounding lands. However, unlike nuisance, where actual interference with another's enjoyment of property is required to sustain a claim, zoning distinctions are made on the basis of potential and predicted impacts. One strength of the *Euclid* decision is that the court turns its mind to whether the underlying assumptions respecting impact are valid. The approach is functional not formalistic.

In the Canadian context, zoning does not have the same constitutional dimension, but the regulation of the physical impacts of land uses remains the touchstone of valid zoning regulation. While the validity of a zoning enactment should not turn on whether there is an actual impact, the extent to which the courts are willing to go behind the wording of the enactment, to assess whether there is a rational connection between the restriction and the prevention of some undesirable impact, has clearly influenced the court's interpretation of the zoning by-law and its validity.

The manner by which courts assess zoning regulation and its impact on judicial outcomes is exemplified in the cases of *R. v. Brown Camps Ltd.*,[31] and *Barrie (City) v. Brown Camps Residential & Day Schools*,[32] both decided by the Ontario Court of Appeal within several years of one another. In the first *Brown Camps*[33] case, Brown Camps Ltd., a company that owned and operated group homes for children in the care of Children's Aid, was charged with using a premisis as a commercial house for the treatment of children contrary to the municipal by-law which designated the premisis for use as a single family detached dwelling. The by-law defined "family" as one or more persons living as a housekeeping unit and provided that a house could be occupied only by a housekeeping unit. The defendant argued that the group of four children and the staff members caring for them constituted a housekeeping unit but the Court disagreed. It held that this group was not a family as it was composed of staff and "inmates" (the Court's term), the latter of whom were passive in their placement and there at the whim of the defendant. There was no special relationship between them and they did not agree to live there. The Court reasoned that personal election was necessary to establish a housekeeping unit. Ultimately, the Court focused on the commercial nature of Brown Camps and characterized the use as a commercial one.

In the second *Brown Camps*[34] case, a house was occupied in the same way and the municipality argued that the use was for the business of carrying on a nursing home or medical clinic and not a family dwelling unit. Under the by-law in this case, the area was designated for one-family detached dwelling units and dwelling unit was defined as separate living quarters for an individual or one family. "Family" was further defined as one or more

---

31 [1969] 2 O.R. 461 (C.A.).

32 (1973), 2 O.R. (2d) 337 (C.A.), leave to appeal refused (1974), 2 O.R. (2d) 337n (S.C.C.).

33 *Supra* note 31.

34 See *supra* note 32.

persons inter-related by bonds of consanguinity, marriage or legal adoption, or not more than five unrelated persons. Here, however, the Court of Appeal, viewed the use as being in essence of a residential character, looking at how the property was used, including the physical characteristics of the property.[35]

From a substantive point of view, the second case is clearly the more just outcome, with the Court appearing to be more sensitive to the objectives of the defendant to provide some semblance of family life to children under state care and supervision. While the first *Brown Camps* case purports to be concerned with the commercial nature of the use, it never examines whether any of the externalities that one might associate with commercial uses in residential areas, such as increased traffic, disturbances to neighbours, and the like, were in fact present or even likely to occur. The second case is an improvement in the sense that the Court was alive to the relevance of the actual impacts of the use, noting at one point that the properties in question have the same physical characteristics, internal and external of a residential home. The most satisfying reasons actually come from the trial judge who explicitly considers the objectives of separating residential from commercial uses:

> I can find in the evidence no serious inconvenience or detriment to the neighbours, and I am quite unable to conclude that the character of the zone is being changed, or that the objective of the by-law is being frustrated.

In neither of the *Brown Camps* cases was the validity of the by-law called into question. But in *R. v. Bell*,[36] a case with similar overtones, the ability of a municipality to favour families over other living arrangements was put squarely before the court. Here, the by-law restricted the premises to single "family" use and family was defined as two or more persons related by bonds of consanguinity, marriage, or legal adoption, non-paying guests and servants, the owner and two other persons and not more than three foster children. In this case, the house was occupied by three unrelated persons (none of which were the owner), and on the face of the by-law were in clear contravention of its terms. The Supreme Court of Canada, in holding that the prohibition was not a valid one, found that the by-law, in restricting occupancy to "family," was "not regulating the use of the building but who used it." The Supreme Court also quoted with approval from a lower court decision that stated that personal qualifications of this type or other personal characteristics or qualities were not a proper basis for the control of density or for any issue relevant to land use or land zoning.

Like the second *Brown Camps* case, the result reached by the Supreme Court of Canada appears sound enough, but the reasoning behind the result is obscure because the court adoption of the invalidity of "land zoning by

35 *Ibid.* at 343.

36 See *supra* note 26.

people zoning"[37] is not sufficiently elaborated on. The Supreme Court of Canada, in support of its decision, only notes the effect of the by-law in precluding the sharing of rented accommodation by two adult persons unrelated by blood or marriage. College students were mentioned as one of the "endless" examples that led the Court to the conclusion that the regulation of families could not have been within the contemplation of the provincial legislature when it empowered municipalities to pass zoning by-laws. No attempt is made to assess the purpose of restricting the allowable use to families or a minimum of unrelated persons.

A better approach in all cases, it would seem, would be to consider the purpose of the *Planning Act* and zoning, and to interpret the by-law and the scope of the zoning power in the context of that purpose. The zoning power is intended to prevent nuisance and physical interference with land and ensure that uses are physically compatible. In order to accomplish this, the Ontario legislature granted authority in the *Planning Act*[38] to regulate through zoning such matters as uses, densities, servicing and frontages on highways. At a minimum, the courts should look at the zoning power in that context and relate their interpretation to those kinds of zoning and planning considerations. Such an approach is consistent with the Supreme Court of Canada's decision in *Ottawa (City) v. Royal Trust Co.*,[39] where Mr. Justice Judson examined whether there was a rational basis for the enactment of a by-law respecting levies on new buildings for increased burden on sewers. He concluded that the categories established by the by-law of residential, non-residential, and combined residential and non-residential buildings were "natural and sensible" given the statute. This approach would also be consistent with the more recent jurisprudence of the Court requiring "that statutes be construed purposively in their entire context and in light of the scheme of the Act as a whole with a view to ascertaining the legislature's true intent."[40]

The Court of Appeal came closest to this approach noting that "the limitation of the use to 'families', as defined, may be based on such things as school, traffic, sewer or water requirements, or on a host of other needs, problems and concerns within the responsibility of the municipality."[41] However, even here there is no analysis whether such a limitation could possibly impact the provision of services. Had they done so, one may expect that such evidence would be difficult to find.

Blind adherence to the user versus use distinction should be avoided, for surely the distinction itself is a functional one. Zoning with reference to

---

37 The phrase is from the Court of Appeal decision (1977), 2 M.P.L.R. 39 (Ont. C.A.), quoted *ibid.* at 112.

38 R.S.O. 1990 c. P.13.

39 [1964] S.C.R. 526, 45 D.L.R. (2d) 220.

40 *Nanaimo (City) v. Rascal Trucking Ltd.* [2000] 1 S.C.R. 342, (2000), 9 M.P.L.R. (3d) 1 (S.C.C.) at 12; see Chapter 4, D (3) for general discussion.

41 (1977), 2 M.P.L.R. 39, 15 O.R. (2d) 425, 75 D.L.R. (3d) 755 (C.A.), at 47 [M.P.L.R.], 432 [O.R.] and 763 [D.L.R.].

the user will in many instances be improper because the personal qualifications of a user are unlikely to impact on the types of matters zoning is intended to control. Given the historic use of restrictive covenants to bar certain racial and ethnic groups from communities,[42] the Courts should be rightfully sceptical of zoning distinctions that appear to discriminate on the basis of personal characteristics. However, a rigid distinction between use and user is perhaps unwarranted. For example, it is not uncommon for developers to market housing schemes at retirees, such schemes would likely not generate the same demand for schools and parks (or at least certain kinds of parks) as a regular plan of subdivision. They may even generate lower demands on services due to lower average household size. Zoning by-laws that make such distinctions are rationally connected to the purposes of zoning.

The courts in these cases, as mentioned earlier, are rightly concerned about discrimination against various groups in society that might be adversely affected by zoning by-laws. In trying to prevent this from happening the Supreme Court of Canada has inhibited municipalities from zoning with respect to the users of property. The result is that a substantial limitation may have been placed on municipal zoning powers without any guarantee that such discrimination will not occur. Clearly, municipalities can discourage or encourage family uses by zoning with respect to unit size both in terms of floor space and number of rooms per unit. The establishment of minimum lot sizes, frontages and unit sizes can severely discriminate against the poor without zoning directly against the users of property. There is a need for the courts to be much clearer about the purposes for which zoning can be used and about what constitutes discrimination in zoning. While later cases have tried to circumvent the decision in *Bell*, none provide a satisfactory analysis of the purpose of the zoning by-law, resulting in the unpredictability zoning is meant to remedy. [43]

While it is easy to argue that aesthetic zoning to protect streetscapes, to ensure attractive buildings or to prevent shadows should be upheld in the absence of specific reference to such matters in legislation because such matters relate to physical use of land and thus are closely related to nuisance and safety concerns, the zoning of land for social welfare purposes is another question. The regulation of land uses for the building of low income housing,

---

42 See for example *Wren, Re,* [1945] O.R. 778, [1945] 4 D.L.R. 674 (H.C.), where a covenant precluding "Jews or persons of objectionable nationality" was found void on public policy grounds.

43 Since *R. v. Bell*, the courts have considered zoning in relation to families on several occasions including: *Smith v. Tiny (Township)* (1980), 107 D.L.R. (3d) 483 (Ont. H.C.), affirmed (1980), 114 D.L.R. (3d) 192 (Ont. C.A.), leave to appeal refused (1980), 114 D.L.R. (3d) 192 (note) (S.C.C.); *Faminow v. North Vancouver (District)* (1988), 61 D.L.R. (4th) 747 (B.C. C.A.); and *Canmore Property Management Inc. v. Canmore (Town)* (2000), [2000] A.J. No. 1117, 2000 CarswellAlta 1066 (Q.B.), all of which upheld the distinction. But see *Brendon v. ClubLink Properties Ltd.* (2001), [2001] O.J. No. 3904, 2001 CarswellOnt 3520 (S.C.J.).

for example, could easily be struck down on the user, as opposed to use, principle although, as indicated above, that distinction is inappropriate. A similar fate would befall by-laws zoning land for senior citizen housing and municipal legislation designed to make those homes more acceptable to the community.[44] In the absence of the user-use distinction, can it be argued that social welfare matters are an appropriate subject for zoning? Certainly most planning acts, as indicated earlier, in setting out the parameters of planning, include references relating to social and economic matters of a general nature. However, zoning provisions are generally related to the physical use of land.

In the absence of taking an approach that looks at the purpose of the legislation and the relationship of zoning with that purpose, the courts are interfering with the policy decisions of municipal governments on the basis of their own views. There are of course important areas where courts should interfere to prevent real discrimination — in cases where zoning does not relate to proper planning purposes or where, although it does relate to planning, it so substantially interferes or potentially interferes with the interests of minorities that it should be struck down. Where this is the case the courts should clearly state their reasons and indicate to all the reason for the interference. To give guidance to municipal decision-makers, the courts should face directly the issue of how broad the zoning power will be.

There may be increased willingness by the courts to allow "user" zoning since the advent of the *Charter*.[45] Where zoning is perceived as ameliorating the situation of the disadvantaged, for example, zoning requirements that include age or health requirements, then it may be allowed.[46] Both the *Charter* and the provincial human rights codes allow this type of "affirmative action" discrimination, and zoning to advance the cause will be allowed as long as it fits within the definitions in the *Charter* and the codes. The *Charter* does not, however, change the zoning powers with respect to zoning at "undesirable" users, and this still cannot be done.

E. DISCRIMINATION

The application of the general prohibition against discrimination to zoning by-laws also warrants special attention. Unlike the above discussion, we are speaking here of discrimination in the generic, non-pejorative sense – the prohibition against making unauthorized regulatory distinctions. Zoning is centrally concerned with making distinctions, as the very creation of a particular zone which restricts uses differentiates between landowners – those within the zone and those outside of it – at the discretion of council. On a

---

44 See *Toronto (City) By-Law 413-78, Re* (1979), 9 M.P.L.R. 117, 10 O.M.B.R. 38 (M.B.), where a zoning by-law permitting a senior citizens residence was struck down as being "people zoning" or zoning as to "user."

45 Schedule B to the *Canada Act 1982* (U.K.) 1982, c. 11.

46 *Goth v. Oakville (Town)* (1996), 32 O.M.B.R. 388 (M.B.).

broad basis, the creation of such distinction is clearly authorized by statute, but it is less clear whether council has the authority to zone lands on an individual, parcel-by-parcel basis, a process sometimes referred to as spot zoning.

In the early case of *Toronto (City) v. Mandelbaum*,[47] the City passed a by-law which provided that no lumber yard, wood yard, or planing mill shall be established in any place within the City "unless a permit therefore is first obtained from the committee on property, said permit to be approved by the city council before being issued."[48] The by-law was found to be *ultra vires* because of the provisions respecting the permit which, according to the Court, made the by-law not one of general regulation or application but rather one which was discriminatory in its application. When the municipality is given the power to regulate, it can pass only general regulations and cannot discriminate by giving permission to one person and refusing it to another.[49]

This argument was considered in the case of *Scarborough (Township) v. Bondi*,[50] where a municipality rezoned one piece of land owned by one property owner in order to prevent that owner from circumventing the general provisions of the zoning by-law respecting frontage because his land was a corner lot. Mr. Justice Judson upheld the by-law although it related to only one parcel. In his view, the intent and effect of the by-law was "to compel the respondent to fall in with the general standards of the neighbourhood." Far from being discriminatory, the amending by-law was seen as an attempt to enforce conformity with the standards of the original by-law. Mr. Justice Judson, however, went on to deal with the definition of discrimination and the view that a municipality cannot discriminate by giving permission to one and refusing it to another. Of this, he said:

> I ... doubt ... whether it can ever afford a guide in dealing with a restrictive or zoning by-law. The mere delimitation of the boundaries of the area affected by such a by-law involves an element of discrimination. On one side of an arbitrary line an owner may be prevented from doing something with his property which another owner, on the other side of the line, with a property which corresponds in all respects except location, is free to do. ...[51]

In the case of *North York (Township), Re*,[52] the Court dealt with the issue of zoning individual lots: "Small areas may be zoned as well as large ones and facts as to their ownership or control should have no bearing when consideration is being given to the question of whether or not the area sought

47 [1932] O.R. 552, [1932] 3 D.L.R. 604 (S.C.).
48 [1932] 3 D.L.R. 604 (Ont. S.C.) at 605.
49 Here the court relies on *Forst v. Toronto (City)* (1923), 54 O.L.R. 256 (C.A.).
50 [1959] S.C.R. 444, 18 D.L.R. (2d) 161.
51 *Ibid.* at 166 [D.L.R.].
52 [1960] O.R. 374, 24 D.L.R. (2d) 12 (C.A.).

to be zoned complies with the general purpose and intent of the legislation."[53] The courts in the *Bondi* and *North York* cases were willing to allow zoning on a case-by-case, lot-by-lot basis if it were done by the passing of a by-law. Spot zoning, to the Canadian courts, is not an evil. The parcel of land zoned can be any size. What is important is that there exists a credible planning rationale for the distinction. A fact which distinguishes the *Mendelbaum* case because the decision to issue a permit was entirely discretionary.

This approach of overruling municipal action on the basis of discrimination only where a by-law leaves room for further municipal restrictions or where no actual by-law is passed can be justified on the basis that the passing of by-laws is generally controlled by municipal plans and thus the exercise of municipal discretion is still structured by the plan.[54] The passing of a resolution or requiring some additional permit may not be so controlled.

Conversely, the mere passing of a zoning by-law for a large area is not sufficient to avoid the problem of substantive discrimination. In *H.G. Winton Ltd. v. North York (Borough),*[55] the applicants agreed to sell property to the Zoroastrian Society of Ontario. The land was zoned residential at the time of the agreement and the building commissioner confirmed in writing that the use of the property as a temple was permitted under the by-law. Within one week of the signing of the agreement, the municipality re-zoned the property and the surrounding area to prohibit church uses. The zoning by-law was passed without any materials or studies from the Planning Board; preparation of such studies was the usual practice in considering passage of a zoning by-law.

The Court in the case stated that the attempt to show that the zoning was of a wider area than one property was untenable. It found that the "council was not concerned about or interested in rezoning any property other than the applicant's." The Court further concluded that the by-law was discriminatory. However, that conclusion was not on the grounds of the zoning of one property but on the grounds that the by-law lacked any discernable planning rationale. The Court stated:

> ... there must be proper planning grounds or standards to warrant discriminatory distinctions between property owners in the same position, classification or zoning category. Here, no planning purpose has been shown to explain, let alone justify, the selection of a single spot in the borough as the subject of this amendatory zoning by-law. There is no rhyme nor reason, in a planning sense, for it.[56]

---

53 (1960), 24 D.L.R. (2d) 12 (Ont. C.A.) at para. 20.

54 See the *Planning Act*, R.S.O. 1990 c. P.13, ss. 34(11) and (19), which provides for O.M.B. review of by-laws only upon appeal by any person including the Minister or an agency.

55 (1978), 6 M.P.L.R. 1, 20 O.R. (2d) 737, 88 D.L.R. (3d) 733 (Div. Ct.). See also *Roman Catholic Episcopal Corp. for the Diocese of Toronto in Canada v. Barrie (City)* (1997), [1997] O.J. No. 2536, 1997 CarswellOnt 2261 (Gen. Div.).

56 *Ibid.* at 12 [M.P.L.R.].

In the case of *Petro-Canada v. North Vancouver (District)*,[57] the District passed a by-law which amended an existing zoning by-law by dividing gas stations into two categories: "gasoline bars" and "gasoline service stations." A gasoline service station was required to include a service bay for the servicing and repair of vehicles; a gasoline bar *may* contain a service bay. Both required service at a "full service pump" in addition to self service pumps for a specified minimum number of hours per day. The by-law divided the commercial zone into two zones, with gasoline bars which did not have a service bay only permitted in one of the zones. The B.C. Court of Appeal stated that zoning by-laws are by their very nature inherently discriminatory. They are only invalid if they are unreasonably discriminatory. Here the amendment applied equally to all gasoline stations in each zone, apart from the non-conforming status of existing stations. The stated reasons for the by-law were the retention of service bays for repairs in local communities and full service pumps for those who wish or need that service. The court found these to be legitimate municipal objectives that were not unreasonable.

Can it be concluded that the doctrine of discrimination has no application to zoning by-laws because of their inherently discriminatory nature? In answering this question, it is best to recall that the general application of this rule is moving away from a formal approach towards one that examines whether the distinction made has some rational purpose. A municipality's exercise of discretion in the creation of zones will not be disturbed where it has some foundation in proper planning principles. In this regard, courts must be careful to respect municipal policy decisions, even where those decisions shift public burdens on private landowners. Such allocations of burdens and benefits are part and parcel of the planning process. Such an approach does not in any way authorize arbitrary or unjustifiable decisions. Discretion is not the same as whim or caprice and the courts are properly exercising their supervisory function by looking behind municipal zoning decisions to critically examine their planning purposes.

F. BAD FAITH

As with the review of the exercise of other municipal authority, the doctrine of "bad faith" also raises unique concerns in the context of municipal zoning powers. Bad faith has been defined as occurring where "municipal councillors have abandoned all honest attempts at legislation and are corruptly seeking by the prostitution of their legislative powers to advance the ends of some member of council or some favoured individual ..."[58] Such a definition would seem to be so restrictive as to be limited to outrageous situations where

57 (2001), 17 M.P.L.R. (3d) 1 (B.C. C.A.), leave to appeal refused (2001), 2001 CarswellBC 2072, 2001 CarswellBC 2073 (S.C.C.).

58 See *Howard v. Toronto (City)*, [1928] 1 D.L.R. 952, 61 O.L.R. 563 (C.A.), at 956 [D.L.R.], at 580 [O.L.R.].

the council has acted with improper motive or illegally. It has also been emphasized that the courts "should be slow to find bad faith in the conduct of democratically elected representatives acting under legislative authority, unless there is no other rational conclusion."[59]

In *First National Properties Ltd. v. Highlands (District)*,[60] a developer who owned a large parcel of land attempted unsuccessfully to obtain planning and rezoning approval from the municipality for proposed residential development. The Nature Conservancy of Canada expressed interest in purchasing a portion of the property from First National. The Mayor of Highlands sent letters to the Nature Conservancy advising them of the plans of First National and what the District may do with the applications. Copies of these letters were also sent to the Ministry of the Environment, which was assisting the Conservancy with its negotiations. When it became apparent that the Conservancy could not purchase the lands, the province took over negotiations. The province purchased the majority of the property to develop some of the land into residential lots in order to recover some or all of their expenses in acquiring the property. Subsequently, the province applied for and obtained the rezoning that had been sought unsuccessfully by First National. First National again applied for rezoning similar to that obtained by the province on the land it had retained, and was again refused. The Court found that the mayor was motivated by an interest in preserving the lands in their natural state, and that this was a proper municipal purpose, even where lawful actions carried out in furtherance of that purpose adversely affect the interests of one or more property owners.[61]

Similarly, in the case of *Wall & Redekop Corp. v. Vancouver (City)*,[62] the Court refused to accede to an application to quash a by-law passed by the Council of the City of Vancouver based on the grounds that the by-law was passed in bad faith. In this case, the Council had rezoned certain property to permit a development and issued the applicant a permit for the development. A civic election was subsequently held and the new majority of Council was composed of those opposed to the development. The new Council in substance rezoned the property and the value of the property was diminished as a result of the development becoming a non-conforming use. The Court held that the Council had acted in what it conceived to be the public interest when it decided to rezone the property. This could not be impugned as bad faith. There was no suggestion that the action was founded on fraud or oppression

59 *MacMillan Bloedel Ltd. v. Galiano Island Trust Committee* (1995), 10 B.C.L.R. (3d) 121 (C.A.), leave to appeal refused (1996), 20 B.C.L.R. (3d) xxxv (S.C.C.); see also *First National Properties Ltd. v. Highlands (District)* (2001), 17 M.P.L.R. (3d) 80 (B.C. C.A.), leave to appeal refused (2001), [2001] S.C.C.A. No. 365, 2001 CarswellBC 2807, 2001 CarswellBC 2808.

60 *Ibid.*

61 *Ibid.* at 102.

62 (1974), 47 D.L.R. (3d) 155 (B.C. C.A.), affirmed (1976), 16 N.R. 435 (S.C.C.).

or improper motives, or that the members of Council were seeking to attain private ends or the gratification of private desires.

These two cases would appear to support the view that bad faith is a restricted doctrine. However, there have been a number of attacks on municipal zoning power on the basis of bad faith, and some have been successful. Part of the reason for this success may be that planning powers are always enacted for the benefit of certain groups in society, as discussed earlier. A further reason is that bad faith has not been limited to the serious situations suggested by the case law.

In *Wall & Redekop Corp.*, what the Council was in fact doing was supporting the interest of other private individuals in society, those opposing the project, over the interests of the developer. Moreover, the above two cases stand in stark contrast to other cases where bad faith has been used in a much broader way, such as *Winton*,[63] which was referred to earlier. There the Council rezoned lands to prevent the use of a mansion as a Zoroastrian temple. The Court refers to the fact that the by-law was pushed through with inordinate speed, that it was designed to give the pretence of being operative in a larger area, that usual Borough practices and procedures were set aside and that the two parties most affected were kept in the dark. The Borough gave public notice of the by-law and held an open meeting on it only after proceedings in the Court were well advanced. The finding that on "these facts the council acted unreasonably, and arbitrarily, and without the degree of fairness and openness and impartiality required of municipal government" indicates that a finding of bad faith can also rest on inappropriate process.

This use of "bad faith" by the courts would appear to be a most appropriate one. It is similar to the "fairness" doctrine that is discussed in Chapter 10 and that has been developing in the case law. It is a use of bad faith that is less likely to result in judicial review on the merits than a use which considers whether a public or private purpose has been served.

It should be noted that in the *Winton* case,[64] the Court also found that the municipality acted in bad faith in that it discriminated by singling out only one property. It has already been argued that the zoning of one property is not necessarily discriminatory. Rather it is whether the zoning by-law bears any rational relationship to the purposes of planning or whether instead the action substantially interferes with the interests of minorities.

In the case of *Pedwell v. Pelham (Town)*,[65] the Town of Pelham passed a by-law which froze development on the plaintiff's lots. The Court was not persuaded by the Town's submission that they were acting in the best interests of the municipality. The Court held that that kind of motivation was not

---

63 See *supra* note 55.

64 *Ibid.*

65 (1998), 47 M.P.L.R. (2d) 222 (Ont. Gen. Div.), additional reasons at (1999), 1999 CarswellOnt 634 (Gen. Div.), varied (2003), 37 M.P.L.R. (3d) 161 (Ont. C.A.); see also *Hollett v. Halifax (City)* (1975), 13 N.S.R. (2d) 403, 66 D.L.R. (3d) 524 (C.A.).

enough when their activities had not been frank and impartial. Meetings had taken place with no notice to the plaintiff with the view to stopping the development. No report was ever made. As a result of these meetings, an interim control by-law was passed to freeze development. A letter was sent to the applicants which set out phony concerns and non-applicable considerations. An in camera meeting was held, again without notice to the plaintiffs, at which time the interim control by-law was passed. The Courts found that Council had acted in bad faith, even though they did not "technically offend any requirements contained in the legislation with respect to the giving of notice."[66] The court stated:

> [A] municipality cannot cloak itself in the pubic interest veil and hope to escape scrutiny on the issue of the good faith brought to bear on the resolution of the issues. In these days of increasing accountability of governments to the citizens who have voted them into office, I have no doubt that it would be considered only normal to insist that a municipal corporation act in the public interest but as well that in doing so it demonstrate good faith to the parties affected by its decision.[67]

The Court suggested that the sole motive of the municipality was the frustration of the developers. This was exactly the motive of the Township of Scarborough in the *Bondi* case,[68] in which the Supreme Court of Canada upheld the by-law. In addition, contrary to *First National,*[69] the Court was less concerned with whether the municipality was acting in the public interest.

The case of *Rodenbush v. North Cowichan (District)*[70] is a further indication of the importance of improper process as a grounds for bad faith. In that case the municipality led Rodenbush, who was going to apply for a permit, into delaying formal application in the belief that the application would be approved. In the meantime, the municipality amended the by-law to prevent the development. The by-law was struck down.

G. PROHIBITING ALL USES

The *Rodenbush*[71] case raises another ground for the overturning of municipal by-laws. In that case, the by-law initially prevented all use of Rodenbush's land through a rural restricted zoning classification. The Court held that the municipality had acted to reserve private land for a public purpose and thus acted in a discriminatory manner against the owner. The Court stated that the action amounted to confiscation since the land was left with no other

---

66 *Ibid.* at 234.
67 *Ibid.* at 236.
68 See *supra* note 50.
69 See *supra* note 59.
70 (1977), 3 M.P.L.R. 121, 76 D.L.R. (3d) 731 (B.C. S.C.).
71 *Ibid.*

proper use. The municipality was entitled to acquire land by sale or expropriation, but not by zoning by-laws.

Case law in the U.S. provides a useful comparison as to how the courts will treat zoning that deprives a land owner of the use of his or her land. Contrary to Canada, property rights are constitutionally protected in the U.S., and private property cannot be taken for public use without just compensation.[72] In Canada, compensation depends on the existence of a statutory right. No owner of lands is entitled to compensation for expropriation or other damage to the value of land unless he or she can establish a statutory right.[73] The courts in the U.S. are, therefore, more willing to find that zoning that has had a significant adverse effect on land and is not reasonably necessary to effect a substantial public purpose is to be considered a "taking" warranting compensation.[74]

The U.S. Supreme Court has recently considered when zoning will be considered a regulatory "taking" and therefore subject to compensation in *Tahoe-Sierra Preservation Council Inc. v. Tahoe Regional Planning Agency*.[75] The respondent planning agency imposed two moratoria, akin to interim control by-laws in Canada, totalling 32 months. The applicant claimed that the agency's actions constituted a taking of their property without just compensation. The Court stated that a distinction must be made between physical taking and regulatory taking, wherein the latter requires a complex factual assessment of the purposes and economic effects of government actions. Moratoria, or interim development controls, are an essential tool of successful development; a rule which required compensation could force officials to rush through the planning process or abandon the practice altogether. With a temporary development ban, there is less risk that individual landowners will bear a special burden that should be shared by the public as a whole. The Court noted that a moratorium lasting more than one year should be viewed with scepticism, however, the delay in this case was not considered to be unreasonable.

In Canada, a similar assessment is made of the purpose of the government actions. In *Russell v. Toronto (City)*,[76] the City of Toronto passed a ravine control by-law that permanently prohibited all uses on four ravine lots. The purported intention of the by-law was to protect ravines from development. The Court of Appeal affirmed the decision of a review panel of the Ontario Municipal Board, that the subject property should be exempted from the by-law. This decision was based upon a long-standing Board policy that land cannot be sterilized unless the municipality can justify such a drastic

72 U.S. Const. amend. V.

73 *Sisters of Charity of Rockingham v. R.*, [1922] 2 A.C. 315 (Canada P.C.), at 322.

74 *Penn Central Transportation Co. v. New York City*, 438 U.S. 104 (S.C., 1978); *Goldblatt v. Town Hempstead*, 369 U.S. 590 (S.C., 1962).

75 535 U.S. 302 (2002).

76 (2000), 52 O.R. (3d) 9 (C.A.), leave to appeal refused (2001), 2001 CarswellOnt 2778, 2001 CarswellOnt 2779 (S.C.C.).

result.[77] The review panel stated that planning decisions must not allow the concerns of the public good nor private interests to become exclusive goals. Planning is a delicate balance between these two competing objectives. The review panel stated that although a municipality can re-designate or re-zone for the public benefit to arrest a trend that is harmful or undesirable:

> Where the health and safety of existing future inhabitants are involved, where there are patent and imminent hazards to the well being of the community, the municipality should have the unfettered discretion to sterilize the use of lands, without the additional burden of compensation.[78]

In this case, the City of Toronto did not present evidence that the development of the applicant's lands would attract such considerations, and could therefore not justify such drastic action.

There seems to be a strong basis on which to overturn municipal by-laws where virtually no uses are permitted. The reasoning behind this aspect of the case law, aside from a traditional statement that such by-laws are *ultra vires*, appears to be that a total prohibition makes land worthless, resulting in an expropriation for public purposes without compensation.

H. PLANNING AND LAND VALUE

A number of interesting problems arise with respect to the rationale behind overturning by-laws which prohibit all uses. First, it is clear that the mere diminution of land value by virtue of a planning decision will not result in the by-law being struck down or compensation being paid.[79] In *Steer Holdings Ltd. v. Manitoba*,[80] the *City of Winnipeg Act* was amended to prohibit the issuance of a building permit for any construction that would span a watercourse. The appellant had been negotiating with the province and the municipality regarding sale of the land. Once the amendment was enacted, negotiations stopped. The Court held that although there was a "taking away" in the sense that the uses for the land had been limited, there must be more than a mere limitation of land use for compensation. There must also be a corresponding acquisition by the governmental authority. This principle was also enunciated in *A & L Investments Ltd. v. Ontario (Minister*

---

77 *Nepean Restricted Area By-law 73-76, Re* (1978), 9 O.M.B.R. 36 (M.B.), varied (1979), 10 O.M.B.R. 76 (M.B.)

78 Cited in *Russell*, *supra* note 76 at para 25.

79 See *Steer Holdings Ltd. v. Manitoba* (1992), 13 M.P.L.R. (2d) 64 (Man. C.A.); see also *Belfast (City) v. O.D. Cars Ltd.*, [1960] A.C. 490, [1960] 1 All E.R. 65 (H.L.).

80 *Ibid.*

of Housing),[81] where the Court stated that for compensation to apply, the state must acquire the property taken from the plaintiff.

There is support for the view that the down-zoning of property, with the result that its value is decreased and with the result that the municipality might purchase it at some future date, cannot be a basis for an action for damages or to quash the decision. In the case of *Vancouver (City) v. Simpson*,[82] the Supreme Court of Canada dismissed an application to quash the decision of an approving officer whereby the officer refused to allow the subdivision of land. The subdivision would have permitted more intense development of the land than was permissible under the existing zoning. The approval was not granted on the ground that the proposed development would be contrary to the public interest in view of the municipality's long term plans and that a subdivision would permit a more intense use of the land and would render it more costly for the municipality to acquire in the future. While the reasoning of the Court is not entirely clear, it did, however, conclude that the officer did not act in bad faith, that there was no discrimination and that there was no issue as to the legal power of the officer to do what he did. The case seems to suggest very strongly that a municipal decision of this type is not invalid although the Court specifically stated that this was not a case of an expropriating municipality refusing consent for the express purpose of containing the value of land which it was expropriating.

The case of *Hauff v. Vancouver (City)*,[83] is an interesting contrast to *Simpson*. In that case, the City passed a zoning by-law which reduced the maximum development potential of certain lots by reducing the area to be taken into account for the purpose of calculating permissible building floor space. One of the major purposes of the by-law was to restrict or limit land values so that the municipality could more easily acquire the properties for park purposes in the future. The Court quashed the by-law because it was passed for the purpose of adversely affecting land value, and thus facilitating the public acquisition of land, rather than regulating its occupancy or use. A by-law passed for a *bona fide* planning purpose may adversely affect property values. However, the use of governmental powers to deliberately limit the value of property with a view to its transfer to the state at a lower price is quite different, the Court stated.

It is hard to reconcile the *Simpson* and *Hauff* cases — the purpose of the land use decisions was the same. Although the mechanism for making those decisions was different in that it was a decision of an officer in the former case and a by-law in the latter, there does not appear to be any legal signifi-

81 (1997), 152 D.L.R. (4th) 692 (Ont. C.A.), leave to appeal refused (1998), [1997] S.C.C.A. No. 658, 227 N.R. 281 (note), leave to appeal refused (1998), 227 N.R. 282 (note) (S.C.C.). See also *Mariner Real Estate Ltd. v. Nova Scotia (Attorney General)* (1999), 177 D.L.R. (4th) 696 (N.S. C.A.).

82 (1976), [1977] 1 S.C.R. 71, [1976] 3 W.W.R. 97, 7 N.R. 550, 65 D.L.R. (3d) 669.

83 (1980), 12 M.P.L.R. 125 (B.C. S.C.), affirmed (1981), 28 B.C.L.R. 276 (C.A.). See also *North Vancouver Zoning By-law 4277, Re* (1972), [1973] 2 W.W.R. 260 (B.C. S.C.).

cance in that difference. The deciding factor may lie in the imminence of the expropriation. In the *Simpson* case, the Court suggested that expropriation was not occurring. On the facts of *Hauff* however, it was to occur in the near future.

The traditional view seems to be that down-zoning for the purpose of expropriation is not valid (which is why such by-laws are ignored in expropriation cases in the assessing of market value).[84] The Supreme Court of Canada stated in *British Columbia v. Tener*,[85] that ordinarily, compensation does not follow zoning either up or down, however, the device of zoning cannot be used to depress the value of property as a prelude to compulsory taking of the property for a public purpose. It can, however, be argued that there is no need to treat such a down-zoning differently than any other form of zoning as long as it is for the purpose of ultimately providing services (park land) or preventing nuisances (a green belt buffer). Such a by-law would prevent the entire municipality from bearing the whole cost of the particular benefit, be it park or playground, because a certain portion will be borne directly by the owner as a result of the down-zoning, but this is the case in all zoning matters. Moreover, it can be argued that the unlimited ability to zone in this way will lead to inefficient decisions since a part of the cost of the decision is borne by the owner and not those who benefit from it. But this is also the case with all zoning decisions. Benefits and burdens are not necessarily allocated as the market dictates but instead in accordance with the community views as to how benefits and burdens should be allocated. Part of the cost of a park may be borne by an owner of the property instead of all the taxpayers of the municipality. The owner, it is fair to point out, may gain the benefit of other planning decisions while others suffer the burden and not all taxpayers may gain benefit from the park, only the surrounding community.

It seems, therefore, that the basic position outlined by the Supreme Court of Canada in *Simpson* is the most practical. Planning decisions should not be overridden only because of an attempt to shift burdens. Shifting burdens is the essence of planning and should be done by municipal councils to which the powers are given. The difficulty in starting to provide protection against such decisions is determining where to stop providing the protection. Preventing down-zonings where expropriation proceedings have commenced may be a clear category. Preventing them where proceedings are about to commence, or are imminent may be problematic. Similarly, any attempt on the part of the courts to quash the by-laws because of a total prohibition could cause difficulty if the courts moved down a "slippery slope" beyond an absolute prohibition of uses. The present case law indicates protection against total prohibition and at least a strong case against invalidating zoning for

---

84 *British Columbia v. Tener*, [1985] 1 S.C.R. 533; *Kramer v. Wascana Centre Authority*, [1967] S.C.R. 237.

85 *Ibid.* at 557.

financial reasons. Although there is some conflicting case law, particularly with respect to zoning for financial reasons, the courts would be well advised to remain true to their traditional approach, which is in keeping with the general assumptions of no compensation for planning decisions and of allowing municipalities to allocate the benefits and burdens of planning.

I. LIMITATIONS OF ZONING AND SUBSIDIARY METHODS

It can be seen from the above analysis that although planning brought about a revolution in land use decision-making, the courts are, in some respects, a check on that change. The doctrines referred to enable them to review municipal decisions on their merits and often replace council decisions with their own. On the whole, however, the courts appear relatively anxious to limit their own role. And although the case law indicates examples of inappropriate judicial analysis and intervention, a more clear-cut approach on the part of the courts respecting the purpose of planning legislation, the protection of minority rights and the process of municipal decision-making could well clarify and improve that role. Such an approach would ensure that Canadian courts do not, in an arbitrary and unpredictable way, replace the legislative judgment of municipal councils with their own.

Although zoning was originally thought to be a method of setting out in advance where development would occur and where uses would be located with minimal interference, new purposes for planning and zoning have arisen over the years. Municipalities have often wanted to phase in development over time so that the municipality can gradually expand the provision of services. Often municipalities wish to recover the costs of servicing lands and wish to control the siting and form of individual developments on a case-by-case basis to preserve streetscapes, to prevent substantial overshadowing in open areas, to reduce wind or to enhance vistas. These goals are difficult to accomplish through traditional zoning, which sets out identical rules for uses of the same type in advance. The use of zoning revolves around the allocation of land for certain uses subject to limited general regulation.

The criticisms of this approach are readily apparent. Perhaps the most obvious is that the system is not based on realistic assumptions since the implementation of zoning by-laws does not lead to the complete segregation of uses. However, complete segregation of uses may not be as necessary today, or indeed beneficial. As technology improves, the threat of nuisances is diminished. For example, in *Hamilton Harbour Commissioners v. Hamilton (City),*[86] the Ontario Municipal Board was faced with a zoning by-law which purported to ban all animal rendering plants from its industrial zones. The Board found that a modern rendering facility does not create the same impacts as plants of old and has "come some way from the conditions in

86 (1998), [1998] O.M.B.D. No. 802, 1998 CarswellOnt 6155 (M.B.).

which it was done even in the recent past."[87] The complete separation of uses isolates the different activities that people normally engage in, with a resulting increase in demands for transportation. It then becomes difficult to develop a community that integrates uses, maximizes existing infrastructure and efficiently moves goods and people. As communities grow, greater attention is being paid to growing traffic congestion and the loss of open space. Therefore, new strategies to promote and manage growth are being advocated across North America under the catch phrase of "Smart Growth."[88] In order to achieve these goals, a move away from zoning's traditional focus on the separation of uses is required.

Traditional zoning also does not lead to development which is of a quality that could be achieved with more complete control. It is too cumbersome a tool to deal with the form of development — architectural design, streetscapes, shadows and landscaping. Zoning regulation is too centred on land-use allocation. As a result, its standards become minimum standards. It cannot ordinarily impose conditions or positive obligations since it is prohibitive in nature. It cannot easily be used to set up temporary controls or distribute the cost of servicing development. It does not provide different parts of municipalities with different types of land use controls and regulations.[89]

The results of zoning regulations, where they are effective, can be seen only too well by driving through city streets where setbacks, lot sizes, designs and heights are uniform throughout an area. Monotony and sterility can be the result of zoning which sets minimum standards (that become in fact maximum limits), and much variety is lost. For example, if a by-law sets a requirement of a certain number of parking spaces per unit in apartments, pressure might be brought by a developer to lower that ratio and if that did not succeed the developer would certainly not exceed the requirement. Similarly, although the density could be the highest which the municipality thinks desirable, pressure would again come from developers to raise it. In short, zoning only restricts to prevent the worst and frequently inhibits the best or better.

The forces of development are many and varied. Patterns of development do not occur simply as a result of zoning by-laws. Economic forces are obviously the basis of any decision to develop land. The ability of an area to attract investment is important and this is in turn affected by neighbourhood amenities, location and transportation facilities. The size of lots, presence of vacant land and physical attributes of property can also have an important

---

87 *Ibid.* at 4.

88 See for example "Creating More Livable Communities", *Summary of the Smart Growth Conference Proceedings*, Smart Growth B.C., June 6-9, 2001; *Listening to Ontario: Ontario Smart Growth*, (Queen's Printer for Ontario, 2001); *Smart Growth*, (Northeast Midwest Institute, 2002), <www.nemw.org/smartgrowth.htm>.

89 Makuch, "Zoning: Avenues of Reform" (1973-74), 1 Dal. L.J. 294.

impact.[90] To expect development to occur strictly on the basis of zoning regulations is therefore unrealistic, as traditional zoning is too blunt an instrument to consider and address these factors.

The Ontario zoning powers and judicial interpretation of those powers perhaps show best the inadequacy of zoning. The *Planning Act* (Ontario) provides authority for a certain amount of control through zoning over height, bulk, location, size, floor area, spacing, external design, character and use of buildings.[91] Under those powers, municipalities are unable to include control over landscaping, individual design and individual location. Manitoba and Nova Scotia[92] have provisions for zoning the architectural design of buildings but even these, it can be argued, are meant to cover all buildings in a particular zone and thus are too general in nature. Although zoning of individual lots is possible, as seen earlier in the *Bondi*[93] decision, the process of zoning on a case by case basis is still suspect and very cumbersome.

Judicial interpretation of zoning powers has reflected the historical origins of zoning and the negative nature of those origins. It has also reflected the legislative origins of the American Acts and their general rule of law values. For example, the Ontario Court of Appeal in *Mississauga Golf & Country Club Ltd., Re*[94] denied municipal councils in Ontario the authority to impose positive duties on developers. Kelly J.A. disallowed certain conditions set out in a by-law as beyond the authority of the municipality. The case concerned the zoning of a lot for the purpose of a gas station, in part, upon the following conditions: (a) that the stations be of "Van Horne" design and of Credit Valley stone; (b) that parking be limited to two commercial vehicles, both of which were to be owned or leased by the operator of the station for use in breakdown and emergency cases; and (c) that the land be suitably landscaped at a cost not exceeding $1,000.00 and furthermore that it be fully maintained to original standards.[95]

Condition (a) was disallowed on the grounds that, in addition to limiting land use, it attempted to define the nature of the building by specifying the nature of material, not its height, location, bulk or use. Condition (b), the Court believed, went too far in that it defined the types of vehicles to be parked. The last condition relating to landscaping was simply held to be "not a valid provision for inclusion in a zoning or land use by-law."[96] Although

90 See Bourne *Private Redevelopment of the Central City: Spatial Processes of Structural Change in the City of Toronto* (Chicago, 1967).

91 R.S.O. 1990 c. P.13, s. 34(1)4.

92 See the *Municipal Government Act*, S.N.S. 1998 c. 18, s. 220, and *The City of Winnipeg Act*, S.M. 1989 c. 10, s. 589(2)(j) for examples of zoning legislation enabling municipalities to exercise architectural control along with the non-legislative techniques to be discussed later.

93 See *supra* note 50.

94 [1963] 2 O.R. 625, 40 D.L.R. (2d) 673 (C.A.). The case actually concerned the power of the O.M.B.

95 [1963] 2 O.R. 625 (C.A.).

96 *Ibid.* at 632.

the Court did not dispute the zoning of one lot only, the case was in keeping with the approach of earlier decisions in essentially allowing only minimum standards for the development of the community.

J. EXTRA LEGAL TECHNIQUES IN ZONING

The limited scope of zoning is not its only drawback. It should be noted that in its actual implementation the main values of zoning — certainty and predictability — have been lost. Because of an ability to spot zone and because of the need for zoning to respond to market forces, rezonings occur very frequently on a case-by-case basis. Although zoning was intended to allocate uses in a definite and visible way, so that everyone could simply look at the by-law and be certain as to the permitted use in a particular place, such is not the case. There is little certainty and predictability provided by zoning.[97]

Numerous techniques have been developed in order to provide more flexibility and control through the use of zoning. Often municipalities will force developers to enter agreements to do more than the basic zoning by-law requires if the developer needs to buy municipal property or have a road closed. This technique is very limited of course, and can be used only when the appropriate circumstances arise.

The granting of a minor variance from the requirements of a zoning by-law is one technique which can be used in order to provide greater flexibility. In Alberta, the *Municipal Government Act* provides that, upon an application for a development permit, a permit may be issued even if the proposed development does not comply with the land use by-law if it would not interfere with the amenities of the neighbourhood, or the use, enjoyment or value of neighbouring lands, and it conforms with the use prescribed in the by-law.[98] In British Columbia, municipalities are required to establish a board of variance to provide variances or exemptions to relieve hardship.[99] Variances may be granted if they would not:

> (i) result in inappropriate development of the site;
> (ii) adversely affect the natural environment;
> (iii) substantially affect the use and enjoyment of adjacent land;
> (iv) vary permitted uses and densities under the applicable bylaw; or
> (v) defeat the intent of the bylaw.[100]

---

97 See Makuch *supra* note 89 at 305-6.

98 S.A. 1994, M-26, s. 640(6); See also the New Brunswick *Community Planning Act*, R.S.N.B. 1973, c. C-12, s. 35; in Nova Scotia, the *Municipal Government Act*, R.S.N.S. 1998, c.18, s. 235; and in Saskatchewan, the *Planning and Development Act*, 1983, S.S., 1983-84, c. P-13.1.

99 *Local Government Act*, R.S.B.C. 1996, c. 323, Part 26, Division 6.

100 *Ibid.* at s. 901(2)(c).

In Ontario, the legislation provides the following test for determining whether to grant a minor variance: (1) that the variance be in fact "minor"; (2) the land, building or structure, or the use thereof, is desirable for the appropriate development or use of land; and (3) the intent and purpose of the zoning by-law and the official plan will be maintained.[101] These legislative provisions for allowing some relief from strict compliance with zoning by-laws demonstrate the recognition that zoning has its limitations. These provisions apply a purposive approach to development, recognizing that what is important is overall consistency with the intent of the by-laws and provincial plans.

The bonus is another technique that has been used to get away from the "minimum standards" lock. Under this approach, the municipality through its plan or by-law may provide for specific increases in density where a development meets certain additional requirements pertaining, for example, to landscaping, setbacks, or siting.[102] This technique has the problem however, of being uniform in application. A schedule is generally set out and the bonus granted to developers and the benefits received by the municipality are the same in every case. Therefore, all apartment buildings built under a bonus tend to look the same. For example, minimal landscaping with a fountain and open space may be required under the bonus. Flexibility is, therefore, not really enhanced and positive obligations cannot be enforced on subsequent owners in the absence of legislation.

Perhaps the most common way of increasing the scope and nature of the zoning power is the use of re-zonings and holding zones. If a developer wishes to proceed with a development which needs rezoning and the proposal does not meet the requirements of the existing by-law, negotiations can occur and an agreement may be entered into imposing numerous controls and obligations on the developer that could not be accomplished under a zoning by-law. The holding zone technique functions in the same way but there rezoning is required because the municipality deliberately zones the land as a "holding" zone, severely restricting land uses, and then rezones the property when a developer has entered into an agreement setting out conditions and obligations to be met.[103]

The cases of *Soo Mill & Lumber Co. v. Sault Ste. Marie (City)*[104] and *Sanbay Developments Ltd. v. London (City)*[105] are two examples of holding zones upheld by the Supreme Court of Canada. The technique used in each case was similar. In the former, the zoning by-law designated specific uses for the land and the official plan of the municipality provided for a holding category — H — to be placed on the specific uses. When the H was in place,

---

101 *Planning Act*, R.S.O. 1990, c. P.13, s. 45(1).

102 *Ibid.* at s. 37.

103 Under the *Planning Act*, R.S.O. 1990, c. P.13, s. 36, holding by-laws are specifically authorized.

104 (1974), [1975] 2 S.C.R. 78.

105 (1974), [1975] 1 S.C.R. 485.

only current uses were allowed in addition to certain agricultural uses, and home occupation and accessory uses. Under the plan, the H was to be removed by the municipal council by a zoning by-law amendment only if: (a) there was no adverse affect on neighbouring land; (b) future development would not be imperilled and would be in accordance with the official plan designation; and (c) the services were appropriate. The system operated so that the council would receive an application and, if it approved of the application and the developer entered into an agreement, the council would rezone the land, removing the H without the necessity of amending the official plan. This process was upheld by the Supreme Court of Canada primarily because the H by-law was still in conformity with the plan, a rezoning was required in conformity with the plan and was subject to Ontario Municipal Board approval, and some use of the land was allowed. Mr. Justice Laskin, as he then was, concluded that this was a legitimate form of development control.

The *Sanbay* case dealt with the use of the same technique. The land in question was zoned "multi-family residential," which included apartment uses. The H category restricted building to three units or less until the by-law was amended, and the amending by-law was to include appropriate schedules and appendices defining and illustrating the permitted building areas, parking areas, usable open space areas, and external design, together with regulations governing the size of floor area, character, and use of such building or structure. It can be seen from this technique that it was specifically designed to overcome the problems of traditional zoning. In upholding the by-law, the Court held that this by-law prohibiting certain uses was not the exercise of administrative authority as in the *Mandelbaum* case.[106] There was no regulation outside of the by-law and the passing of a by-law was used to control land uses. The Court stated that there were no other *ad hoc* requirements to satisfy in order to carry out development.

These two cases indicate the wide authority that municipalities can exercise through the use of holding zones. They are a natural extension of the *Bondi* case[107] in allowing the zoning of individual lots and they are a natural extension of the approach in *Mandelbaum* where the Court looked at the legal method by which the land use regulation is imposed. In that case, permission without resort to a by-law was required while in *Soo Mill* and *Sanbay*, a by-law regulated the land and an amendment was required before development could occur.

The surprising aspect of the second decision is the Court's statement that no "*ad hoc*" requirements were imposed. In fact, an agreement relating to every aspect of the development including siting and design was required on an individual case-by-case basis before development could occur. The Court allowed the detailed control of virtually all aspects of a development without specific authorization in the *Planning Act*. It is rather ironic that the

106 See *supra* note 47.

107 See *supra* note 50.

courts have attempted in many ways to limit municipal authority[108] and yet, in these situations, allow very broad control. If the introduction of zoning can be seen as the first revolution respecting the control of land uses, this series of cases can be seen as the second. They allow municipalities to enter into agreements requiring landscaping and floodlighting to the municipalities' satisfaction, certain entrances, express payment of levies, certain services and architectural approval of plans on a case-by-case basis before development can occur. This is indeed far removed from the 1922 *Standard State Zoning Enabling Act*.[109]

It should be noted, however, that in spite of these decisions there was still difficulty with this form of extra-legislative development control in Ontario. The process involved the rezoning of each individual parcel of land which, as a technique, was slow and cumbersome. Also, it was dubious that, given the law of restrictive covenants, any of the positive conditions in the agreements would run with the land. Finally, it was doubtful whether the municipalities had any authority at all to enter into development agreements. Even though the holding by-law itself had been upheld, the cases made no mention of agreements and the *Sanbay* case specifically stated that there could be no *ad hoc* obligations. Moreover, there was case law which indicated that municipalities had no authority to enter into or require such agreements absent specific statutory authority.[110] In addition, there was the example of other provinces in Canada where development control had been provided for directly by legislation.

K. LEGISLATED DEVELOPMENT CONTROL

In 1973 Ontario passed legislation to provide for development control and thus overcame the problems associated with the extra-legal techniques referred to above. Other provinces, for example, Alberta, Manitoba and Nova Scotia, had provisions for development control long before the legislation was passed in Ontario. The essence of all these schemes, is that development can be approved on a case-by-case or discretionary basis without the need to pass a by-law for the approval of the development. In addition, conditions can be imposed as a prerequisite to approval of the development. The legislation of these provinces, including Ontario, accommodates the use of not only zoning and the adaptations of zoning such as bonus provisions and holding zones, but also the use of development control.

---

108 See for example *Winton, supra* note 55 and *Bell, supra* note 26.

109 *Supra* note 1.

110 See *Walmar Investments Ltd. v. North Bay (City)* (1969), [1970] 1 O.R. 109, 7 D.L.R. (3d) 581 (C.A.), additional reasons at [1970] 3 O.R. 492n (C.A.); see also *Pacific National Investments Ltd. v. Victoria (City)*, [2000] 2 S.C.R. 919, reconsideration refused (2001), 2001 CarswellBC 523, 2001 CarswellBC 524 (S.C.C.) at 947.

Alberta has had development control for the longest period of time although its *Municipal Government Act* dates only from 1994. Under that Act, cities must pass a land use by-law which may prohibit or regulate and control the use and development of land and buildings.[111] A land use by-law divides the municipality into districts of such number and area as the council considers appropriate and sets out, with or without conditions, the permitted uses and the discretionary uses. The by-law can provide for development permits, conditions to be attached to such permits, the appointment of a development officer and the discretion that a development officer is to exercise with respect to the issuing of the permits.[112] Under the legislation, therefore, development can be approved on a discretionary basis with conditions.

The Alberta Act goes further and provides that councils that have adopted a general municipal plan may designate areas as direct control districts. Where a district is so designated the council may regulate and control the use or development of land or buildings in the district in such a manner as it considers necessary.[113] This section clearly avoids the problems and restrictions of the zoning technique. The council is not bound to approve by by-law, and any technique of control, including agreement, can be used. Virtually the whole municipality could be designated under such a provision although it appears that the underlying rationale of the Act is to allow traditional zoning to be in place in slow growth areas where the municipality wishes the *status quo* to be protected and to have development control through special districts and discretionary approvals elsewhere.[114]

The *Vancouver Charter* is very broad in its terms, empowering council to designate zones in which there shall be no uniform regulations and in which any person who wishes to carry out development must submit plans and specifications and obtain the approval of Council.[115] The *Charter* also enables Council to require a development permit and to impose conditions upon the issuing of the permit.[116] "Development" in the *Charter* is defined widely to include changes of use and carrying out of construction, engineering or other operations.[117]

The *Municipal Government Act, 1998* (Nova Scotia), similarly grants power to zone[118] although conditional and discretionary zoning is not generally allowed as it is in Alberta. However, regulation of the architectural design, character and external appearance of buildings is permitted. The Nova

111 See *The Municipal Government Act*, S.A. 1994, c. M.26.1, as amended, ss. 639 and 640.

112 *Ibid.* at s. 640.

113 *Ibid.* at s. 641(2).

114 See also *The Municipal Government Act*, S.A. 1994, c. M.26.1, s. 640(6), which allows approval of prohibited uses by the development officer.

115 S.B.C. 1953, c. 55, s. 565(f).

116 *Ibid.* at s. 565A.

117 *Ibid.* at s. 559.

118 S.N.S. 1998, c. 18, s. 220.

Scotia Act, moreover, not unlike the Alberta Act, enables the municipality to establish comprehensive development districts where the municipal planning policy so provides.[119] For such districts, the municipality is obliged to identify the classes of uses permitted in a district, developments or uses in a district that are permitted without a development agreement, the area or areas where a district may be established, and matters that the council shall consider prior to the approval of an agreement for the development district.[120] The council can pass by-laws specifying conditions for development in such districts and, most importantly, shall grant approval subject only to an agreement containing such terms and conditions as the council may direct.

The Nova Scotia Act, therefore, provides a mechanism for circumventing the limitations of zoning. Like the Alberta Act, the discretion granted to the municipality is very wide. Both pieces of legislation place no limits on the conditions which may be imposed. Although both require municipal development plans to be in place before a district can come under development control, it is unlikely that such plans will be detailed enough to limit the discretion of the municipality in its imposition of conditions and its exercise of powers of approval. Of all provinces, Nova Scotia and Alberta appear to have moved furthest from traditional zoning. They have moved dramatically from a system based on knowing in advance the rules that are imposed, to one that allows wide discretion in approving the imposition of conditions.

These Acts do not spell out the kinds of conditions that can be imposed. Nor do the Acts, unlike those of Ontario, Manitoba and British Columbia, set out that conditions or agreements may relate only to a certain set of matters. It is possible to argue, then, that conditions of payment of levies could be upheld and that requirements regarding services, design, siting and schools would all be possible. The only limit on the municipality would be that the conditions reasonably relate to the development.[121] It should be noted, however, that arguments can be made against certain conditions. The application of the *expressio unius* rule of construction means that it can be argued, for example, that specific legislative provisions allowing lot levies upon approval of plans of subdivision prevent levies under development control provisions.

Other questions can arise: are the personal circumstances of the applicant relevant; should permission be granted because a previous application was unsuccessful? The answers are unclear. The courts in Canada have not provided any precise definition as to the scope of the considerations which planning authorities can properly take into account.[122]

---

119 *Ibid.* at s. 226(1).

120 *Ibid.*

121 See *Zorba's Food Services Ltd. v. Edmonton (City)* (1970), 12 D.L.R. (3d) 618, 74 W.W.R. 218 (Alta. C.A.).

122 See *Campeau Corp. v. Calgary (City)* (1978), 8 M.P.L.R. 88 (Alta. C.A.); *Campeau Corp. v. Calgary (City)* (1980), 12 Alta. L.R. (2d) 379, 22 A.R. 572, 112 D.L.R. (3d) 737 (C.A.).

Similarly, in England, the limits of the kinds of conditions that can be imposed have not been precisely delineated. The House of Lords in the *Fawcett Properties Ltd. v. Buckingham County Council,*[123] case upheld a condition that any cottage constructed could only be occupied by members of the agricultural population, in order to maintain the green belt character of the area in which they were situated. Lord Denning stated with respect to the local authorities discretion to impose conditions:

> The local planning authority is empowered to grant permission to develop land 'subject to such conditions as they think fit'. But this does not mean that they have an uncontrolled discretion to impose whatever conditions they like. In exercising their discretion they must, to paraphrase Lord Greene's words in the *Wednesbury* case [1948] 1 K.B. 223, 233-234, have regard to all relevant considerations and disregard all improper considerations, and they must produce a result which does not offend against common sense; or to repeat my own words in the *Pyx* case [1958] 1 Q.B. 554, 572, the conditions, to be valid, must fairly and reasonably relate to the permitted development...[124]

His Lordship continued that planning conditions should be evaluated by the courts in the same way that local authority by-laws are.

The legislation of some provinces attempts to limit the breadth of discretion available in approving development applications and imposing conditions upon the granting of permission. In Manitoba, for example, this is done through legislative standards and through requirements for detailed planning. *The City of Winnipeg Act* provides for the establishment of development control areas by by-law within which zoning ceases to operate.[125] Development is very widely defined[126] and development permission is required before development can occur.[127] Conditions can be imposed and an agreement entered into regarding those conditions.[128] In granting development permission the council is to have regard to any material consideration, the Greater Winnipeg development plan, the provisions of the district plan, and the relevant provisions of the action area plan (a very detailed local plan), if any, for the area in which the land, building or structure in respect of which the application for development provision is made:

> Where a person makes application for a development permit in respect of a development, the designated employee shall, where the application conforms with the Plan Winnipeg by-law, a secondary plan by-law and development by-laws, issue a development permit.[129]

123 [1961] A.C. 636 (U.K. H.L.).

124 *Ibid.* at 678.

125 S.M. 1989-90 c. 10, s. 589.

126 *Ibid.* at s. 574.

127 *Ibid.* at s. 596.

128 *Ibid.* at s. 591.

129 *Ibid.* at s. 596(2).

The Act thus attempts to structure municipal discretion by the requirement of a sub-city plan of some detail. Elimination of discretion within the plan would defeat the purpose of development control.

In addition, the Act sets out legislative restrictions on the imposition of conditions. It provides that conditions may only concern one or more of the following:[130]

(a) the use of the land and any existing or proposed building;
(b) the timing of construction of a proposed building;
(c) the siting and design of a proposed building, including the materials to be used for the exterior of the building;
(d) traffic control and parking facilities;
(e) landscaping, open space and the grading of the land;
(f) the construction by or at the expense, in whole or in part, of the owner, of

(i) a system, works or equipment to provide electricity and water, and facilities for the collection of surface water and sewage, and
(ii) lighting for parking lots and streets, surface treatment of highways, pavement modifications, gate structures, walkway improvements, sidewalks, riverbank, stabilization, and dyke construction;

that are beneficial to or necessary for the development, or to serve the development; and

(g) the conveyance of land or payment of money, or both, to the city by the owner, where the application is for a classification to permit commercial use, industrial use, or a residential use of three or more dwelling units.

These limitations on the imposition of conditions define the authority of the municipality to impose such conditions and again attempt to redress the balance in favour of certainty and predictability in the development control system, retaining some of the value of a zoning regime.

The Ontario scheme is perhaps the most limited form of reform in Canada. It does not abandon zoning at all and merely grafts onto the zoning system the ability to impose certain conditions and require agreements with respect to those conditions in areas designated as "site plan control areas." The Ontario development control legislation[131] has had a difficult history since it was first enacted in 1973. A by-law passed by the City of Toronto pursuant to it was struck down by the Supreme Court of Canada[132] because, in part, it did not set out standards in advance that were to be imposed as a condition of development, so landowners did not have certainty as to what was required of them. The decision was indeed an unexpected one given the

130 *Ibid.* at s. 591(1).

131 See the *Planning Act*, R.S.O. 1990 c. P.13, s. 41.

132 See *Canadian Institute of Public Real Estate Cos. v. Toronto (City)*, 7 M.P.L.R. 39, [1979] 2 S.C.R. 2, 8 O.M.B.R. 385, 25 N.R. 108, 103 D.L.R. (3d) 226.

Court's upholding of development control in the absence of specific legislative authorization in the *Sanbay* and *Soo Mill* cases.[133] It was also unexpected because the view that certainty and predictability are required in a by-law designating a development control area runs completely counter to the purpose of such legislation: to introduce flexibility into the zoning system.

Under the Ontario Act, a municipality with an official plan may by by-law designate the whole or any part of the municipality as a site plan control area. The provision then prohibits any person from undertaking any development in the area unless approval has been given to plans showing the location of all buildings and structures to be erected, plans showing the location of all facilities and works to be provided, and/or drawings showing plan elevation and cross-section views for each industrial and commercial building and each residential building containing 25 or more dwelling units[134] to be erected. These drawings must also show: (a) the massing and conceptual design of the proposed building; (b) the relationship of the proposed building to adjacent buildings, streets, and exterior areas to which members of the public have access; and (c) the provision of interior walkways, stairs, elevators and escalators to which members of the public have access from streets, open spaces and interior walkways in adjacent buildings; but need not show the layout of other interior areas or the colour, texture, and type of materials, window detail, construction details, architectural detail and interior design.[135] The municipality is also empowered to require the owner to provide for the widening of highways abutting the land, access to and from the land, off-street loading and parking, walkways and pedestrian access, lighting, landscaping, waste storage, easements for water and sewage, and grading, and to enter into an agreement respecting these matters and the plans referred to earlier.[136] The agreement can be registered and will bind subsequent owners. Provision is also made in the Act for the dedication of parkland or payments in lieu of such a dedication.[137]

It can be seen that the Ontario legislation on-site plan control is much more limited than it is in other jurisdictions. The designation of a site plan area does not mean that zoning ceases to have effect. Indeed, the Act provides that height and density cannot be controlled under the section.[138] What the section purports to do is grant the municipality the authority to control limited aspects of design, excluding colour, material and windows, and impose certain restricted obligations through an agreement. The plans and elevation of

---

133 See *supra* notes 105 and 104.

134 Under the *Planning Act,* R.S.O. 1990, c. P.13, s. 41(5), drawings for residential buildings of less than 25 dwelling units can be required for buildings in areas specifically designated in the official plan.

135 See the *Planning Act,* R.S.O. 1990 c. P.13, s. 41(4).

136 *Ibid.* at s. 41(7).

137 *Ibid.* at s. 42; see also s. 51.1 wherein parkland dedication or payment in lieu can be required as a condition of sub-division approval.

138 *Ibid.* at s. 41(6).

residential buildings under 25 units generally cannot be reviewed and there is clearly no unbridled scope to impose conditions; discretionary power is thus substantially limited. This approach is an attempt to maintain the rule of law benefits of zoning by maintaining zoning controls in the important areas of height and density with the discretion of development control. However, the matters subject to such control are very limited. The section would appear to substantially reduce extra-legislative authority granted by virtue of the *Sanbay* and *Soo Mill* cases. The legislation does not attempt to structure municipal discretion by requirements of detailed planning as in Winnipeg. It attempts instead to reduce the possibility of abuse of discretion by limiting the amount of authority granted to the municipality and by providing an appeal to the Ontario Municipal Board.

L. MINIMUM STANDARDS BY-LAWS AND DEMOLITION CONTROL

The movement from the private control of land and uses to development control may be thought of as a complete revolution with respect to the control of land uses. Private control under court supervision has been replaced by municipal control which has become less and less structured with the movement from zoning to development control. It is important to remember that the land use controls discussed here only limit private initiative. In the absence of an attempt to develop land, these controls have no effect. It is interesting to note that there are other possibilities for control in the absence of development or positive action being taken by an owner of property. An example of authority to control land uses in the absence of development occurring can be found in Ontario's *Planning Act.*[139] There, provision has been made for municipalities to prevent the demolition of residential buildings. A demolition control area can be designated so that no residential building can be demolished without a permit. The provisions of the section attempt to strike a balance between the right of the owner to demolish his building at will and the need of the municipality to prevent "block busting" from occurring by homes being destroyed leaving lots empty and destroying streetscapes.

M. SUBDIVISION CONTROL

One final form of land use regulation, subdivision control, should be considered. This technique is used for land that is to be divided from large lots to smaller ones. It is essentially a technique which relates the imposition of land use controls to the creation of new interests in land. *The Municipal*

139 *Ibid.* at s. 33. See also *The City of Winnipeg Act*, S.M. 1989-90, c. 10, s. 472, which gives council the power to regulate the demolition of buildings.

Government Act (Alberta),[140] for example, provides that, with certain exceptions, an instrument which has the effect, or that may have the effect of subdividing a parcel of land shall not be accepted for registration unless the subdivision has been approved by an appropriate subdivision approving authority. Similarly, Ontario's *Planning Act* provides in part that no person shall convey land by way of deed or transfer, or grant, assign or exercise a power of appointment with respect to land, or mortgage or charge land, or enter into an agreement of sale and purchase of land, or enter into any agreement that has the effect of granting the use of a right in land directly or by entitlement to renewal for a period of 21 years or more, unless the land is described in accordance with and is within a registered plan of subdivision.[141] There is also provision in the legislation for the creation of a small number of lots on consent where a full plan would not be required.[142]

For subdivision control to come into effect there must be the creation of a new interest in land, that is, the subdivision of it. Subdivision control thus contrasts dramatically with zoning and development control — these latter techniques bear no relationship to land titles. Tying subdivision regulation to the passing of an interest in land has resulted in innumerable problems with title in property and the creation of schemes to circumvent the controls.[143] It is obviously more desirable to impose land use controls without consideration of title, but the technique, also stemming from the 1928 *Standard City Planning Enabling Act*,[144] seems so ingrained that it is unlikely to be abolished. The system has the advantage of not placing land under controls unless it is being subdivided: in the absence of any development through the creation of new interests in land, the controls do not come into force. Since subdivision control largely comes into play in rural and semi-rural developing areas where large lots are being divided into small ones, it leaves agricultural areas under a minimum amount of control through zoning.

Subdivision control operates in a way that is not dissimilar to development control. An applicant must submit a plan for the subdivision of property showing such matters as the roads within the subdivision, the lots and the purposes for which they are to be used, the services, the natural features of the land, and the existing zoning. The approving authority, provincial or municipal (this varies from province to province, and within provinces), is given the discretion to approve the plan. There is no development as of right, as would occur under zoning once the provisions of the by-law are met. Under

---

140 See *The Municipal Government Act*, S.A. 1994, c. M-26.1, as amended, s. 652(1).

141 R.S.O. 1990 c. P.13, s. 50(3)(a).

142 *Ibid.* at s. 53(1).

143 For an account of the problems caused by subdivision control, see Reiter, McLellan and Perell, *Real Estate Law* 4th ed (Toronto, 1992), Chapter 9. Numerous schemes such as "checkerboarding" and simultaneous conveyances were carried out to avoid the legislation. Several amnesties for past defective titles were also granted as the legislation was stiffened.

144 *Supra* note 1 at 210.

the Alberta Act,[145] for example, the approving authority may refuse an application unless the land is suitable for the purpose for which the subdivision is intended, the subdivision conforms to any statutory plan and land use by-law, as well as the Act and regulations, and taxes have been paid or arrangements have been made for payment.

Similarly, in Ontario, there is no obligation to approve a plan. The Act merely provides that in considering a draft plan of subdivision, regard shall be had, among other matters, to the health, safety, convenience and welfare of the future inhabitants and to conformity to the official plan and adjacent plans of subdivision; the effect of development of the proposed subdivision on matters of provincial interest; whether the subdivision plan is premature or in the public interest; the suitability of the land for the purpose for which it is to be subdivided; highways within the vicinity of the subdivision; the dimension and shape of lots; restrictions and proposed restrictions on the lands, buildings and structures within and adjacent to the subdivision; conservation of natural resources and flood control; adequacy of utilities and municipal services; adequacy of school sites; area of land within the subdivision to be dedicated for public purposes; and the physical layout of the plan having regard to energy conservation.[146] It can be seen therefore, that approving bodies, as discussed earlier with respect to development control, have virtually unlimited discretion in deciding whether to grant an approval or not. The major difference appears to be a lesser focus on the form of the development, and more on lot shape and size, service distribution and the physical layout of the area.

The other aspect of subdivision control which makes it akin to development control is that there is provision for the imposition of conditions and the entering into of an agreement respecting the subdivision.[147] The Alberta Act, for example, refers to conditions necessary to ensure compliance with plans, by-laws and the Act, and to a condition that the subdivider enter into an agreement with the council respecting construction of, or payment for, public roadways and pedestrian walkways to give access to the subdivision; installation of utilities necessary to serve the subdivision; the construction of, or payment for, off-street parking areas and loading and unloading areas; and the payment of an off-site levy or redevelopment levy imposed by by-law.[148]

In Ontario, the Minister, or regional municipality exercising the authority of the Minister, in approving a plan of subdivision may impose conditions respecting the dedication of lands for public purposes including highways and the widening of abutting highways (s. 51(25)(b), (c)). Furthermore, the Ontario Act has a very broad provision that the Minister, as a condition of approval, may require the owner to enter into one or more agreements with

---

145 S.A. 1994, c. M-26.1, s. 654(1).

146 See the *Planning Act,* R.S.O. 1990 c. P.13, s. 51(24).

147 *Ibid.* at s. 51(26).

148 See also *The Municipal Government Act,* S.A. 1994, c. M-26.1, as amended, s. 655.

a municipality dealing with such matters as the Minister may consider necessary, including the provision of municipal services (s. 51(25)(d)). The Ontario legislation, in contrast to that in Alberta, provides for the broader imposition of conditions at least through requiring that an agreement be entered into with a municipality. The Minister's condition is a standard one which states: "that the owner agrees in writing to satisfy all the requirements, financial or otherwise, of the Municipality concerning the provision of roads, installation of services and drainage." Section 51(26) of the Ontario Act further enables municipalities to enter into agreements imposed as a condition of approval of a plan of subdivision.

N. DEVELOPMENT CHARGES

The major issues with respect to the imposition of conditions are the purposes for which they can be imposed and the legal limitations on imposing such conditions. For example, most provinces require subdividers to install services. It is a proper planning purpose that costs are imposed on subdividers, rather than other ratepayers through increased property taxes.[149] Historically, uncertainty with respect to what the courts will allow has arisen frequently in Ontario, particularly in the context of the imposition of levies under such agreements by the municipalities. As has been mentioned, the scope of the legislation in Ontario is very broad. Section 51(25)(d) of the *Planning Act* merely states that the approval authority can require agreements with municipalities regarding such matters as the approval authority considers necessary. The *Municipal Act* (Ontario), although not authorizing agreements, previously provided that where a municipality receives monies with respect to subdivisions, the money is to be used only for work done in the subdivision, for the benefit of the occupiers of the subdivision, to meet expenditures incurred in whole or in part by reason of a subdivision, for a special purpose to meet expenditures for that purpose, or for any other purpose where it is not needed for any of the above purposes.[150] The section allows a very wide use for the monies received pursuant to subdivision agreements.

Due to the breadth of both s. 51(25) of the *Planning Act*, and s. 166 of the former *Municipal Act*, the courts and the Ontario Municipal Board attempted to limit the scope of these sections.[151] Not only was it required that the levies be fairly and reasonably related to the subdivision but detailed evidence was required about the relationship of levies to the capital costs of

---

149 *Homex Realty & Development Co. v. Wyoming (Village)* (1979), 23 O.R. (2d) 398 (C.A.), affirmed [1980] 2 S.C.R. 1011, (1980), 13 M.P.L.R. 234 (S.C.C.).

150 R.S.O. 1990, c. M.45, s. 164.

151 See *Steel Co. of Canada v. Nanticoke (City)* (1976), 6 O.M.B.R. 278 (M.B.); *Pinetree Development Co. v. Ontario (Minister of Housing)* (1976), 14 O.R. (2d) 687 (Div. Ct.); see also *Frey v. Phi International Inc.* (1977), 2 M.P.L.R. 1 (O.M.B.).

specific capital works necessary either for the development of a subdivision or as a result of the approval of a severance or condominium conversion.[152]

However, as lot levy practices varied among municipalities, both developers and municipalities in Ontario pressed for a standardized framework. On November 23, 1989, the *Development Charges Act* was introduced to bring greater uniformity to the widely varied lot levy practices. Development charges have replaced lot levies as the primary way to raise funds for services and improvements to infrastructure that are necessary as a result of development. Increased uniformity, certainty and accountability were sought by requiring municipalities to justify costs. In addition, developers were given an appeal process against unfair charges. [153]

In Ontario, development charges are governed by *the Development Charges Act, 1997*.[154] A municipality may, by by-law, impose development charges against land to pay for the increased capital costs required due to the increased need for services as a result of development.[155] A development charge is payable upon the issuance of a building permit, unless otherwise agreed to.[156] A municipality is entitled to deny a building permit unless the development charge has been paid.[157]

Before passing a development charges by-law, a municipality is required to complete a development charge background study, which determines the anticipated amount, type and location of development, increased need for services and the long term capital and operating costs for capital infrastructure. Municipalities may not impose development charges to pay for so called "soft services" such as museums, art galleries, tourism facilities, parkland, etc,[158] which is something that municipalities have tried to do in the past.[159] When the legislation was first introduced on November 25, 1996 as Bill 98, municipalities were required to pay 10% of the cost of hard services such as roads and sewers, and 30% of the cost of soft services. However, due to tremendous opposition, the province watered down these provisions. Currently developers are required to fully fund the cost of hard services such as water supply, waste water, storm water drainage and control, highway, electrical power, police and fire protection.[160] Other capital costs, such as for libraries and community centres, are discounted by 10%.[161]

---

152 *Ibid.*

153 *Development Charges Act, 1997*, S.O. 1997, c. 27, ss. 13-19. A similar appeal mechanism is contained in the Saskatchewan legislation, for an appeal to the Saskatchewan Municipal Board, *Planning and Development Act, 1983*, R.S.S. 1983-84, c. P-13.1, s. 55.6.

154 *Ibid.*

155 *Ibid.* at s. 2(1).

156 *Ibid.* at ss. 26 and 27.

157 *Ibid.* at s. 28.

158 *Ibid.* at s. 2(4).

159 *Steel Co. of Canada, supra* note 151.

160 *Supra,* note 153 at s. 5(5).

161 *Ibid.* at s. 5(1)8.

Similar legislative authority for the imposition of development charges can be found in British Columbia, Alberta, Saskatchewan and Nova Scotia. In British Columbia, the by-law for imposing development charges must be approved by an inspector.[162] Although municipalities are not required to conduct formal studies, as in Ontario and Saskatchewan,[163] in determining whether to approve a development charges by-law, the inspector is to consider whether the municipality took into account, among other things, the future use of land, the phasing in of works and services, whether the charges are excessive in relation to prevailing standards and whether the charges will deter development or discourage the construction of reasonably priced housing.[164] This is always a concern, as the cost of development charges imposed on residential development is passed onto the home-buyer.

As in Ontario, other provinces also grapple with the issue of what services development charges should encompass. In British Columbia, development charges are to cover the costs of such services as sewage, water, drainage and highway facilities (not including off-site parking), and park land.[165] Nova Scotia is perhaps the most restrictive, as it includes water systems, wastewater systems, stormwater systems and streets, which includes intersections, traffic signs and signals and transit bus bays.[166] Park land, recreational facilities or other cultural facilities are not covered, and these "infrastructure charges" only apply to subdivisions, and are contained in a subdivision by-law.[167] In Alberta, where land to be developed is within a "redevelopment area,"[168] charges can be imposed for land for parks, schools and recreational facilities; otherwise, the charges are limited to water, sewage and storm water.[169]

As discussed in Chapter 3, municipalities are limited in how they can raise revenue, and are prohibited from engaging in indirect taxation. The Ontario Home Builders' Association launched a challenge to the former Ontario *Development Charges Act*, arguing, among other things, that the levies sanctioned by the Act are indirect taxation and thereby contrary to the division of powers under the Constitution.[170] While the focus of the challenge

---

162 *Local Government Act*, R.S.B.C. 1996, c. 323, Part 26, Division 10, s. 937.

163 *Planning and Development Act*, 1983, R.S.S. 1983-84, c. P-13.1, s. 55.1(2) requires specific engineering studies on servicing requirements before council may establish a by-law which imposes a development levy.

164 *Supra* note 162 at s. 934.

165 *Ibid.* at s. 933.

166 *Municipal Government Act,* S.N.S. 1998, c. 18, s. 274.

167 *Ibid.* at s. 274(2). In Saskatchewan, parkland and recreational facilities are also included, *supra* note 163, s. 55.1(2).

168 *Municipal Government Act*, R.S.A. 2000, M-26, s. 634 defines a redevelopment area as an area created for such purposes as preserving or improving land and buildings, establishing, improving or relocating roads, public utilities or other services and to facilitate development.

169 *Ibid.* at s. 648(2).

170 *Ontario Home Builders' Assn. v. York (Region) Board of Education*, [1996] 2 S.C.R. 929.

concerned education development charges, the reasoning of the Supreme Court of Canada is applicable to other charges. The majority of the court held that while these charges involve features of both direct and indirect taxation, they are not true land taxes. The majority of the court adopted a purposive approach, stating that the purpose of development charges is to defray the costs of infrastructure necessitated by new residential development. As such, these charges are *intra vires* the province as ancillary to a valid regulatory scheme, namely land use planning, pursuant to ss. 92(9) (licences to raise revenue), (13) (property and civil rights) and (16) (matters of a local nature) of the *Constitution Act, 1867*.

9

The Rights of Landowners

A. INTRODUCTION

Central to the move towards comprehensive zoning schemes and away from common law approaches to land use regulation is the increased ability of municipalities to promote community values and the public interest through regulatory means. However, it is perhaps not surprising that the rights of landowners remain important considerations for both the legislature and the courts. Here, the rights of landowners are examined directly in the context of their right to a building permit and of their right to continue uses that do not conform to a newly enacted zoning by-law. In addition, the right of municipalities to freeze development in the face of public concerns through interim control measures will be addressed. The central question here is at what point in the planning process are the rights of landowners found to take precedence over the public interest in altering unsuitable land uses.

B. THE RIGHT TO A BUILDING PERMIT

As was outlined earlier, fundamental to land use regulation through zoning is that land uses and process rules are set out in advance so that owners of property know what they can and cannot do with their property and the means by which the land use regime can be altered. Based on this information, landowners can make reasonably informed choices regarding investment in property and future usage. The right to develop land in accordance with the zoning by-law is, of course, subject to the right of the municipality to alter those by-laws in accordance with procedural requirements. As will be seen in the next section on non-conforming uses, once a landowner has developed in accordance with the by-law, those rights are in essence deemed to have vested and subsequent rezonings cannot affect the legality (from a land use perspective) of the existing uses and structures. However, where an owner has taken certain steps to constitute its right to build, such as prepare and submit an application for a building permit, both the legislation and the courts' application of it have been less than clear regarding the legal status of a right to build.

The conditions under which a landowner has a right to a building permit vary in detail from province to province, but generally all provinces require that proposed buildings and structures conform to the regulatory requirements of the jurisdiction. In the case of Ontario, s. 8 of the *Building Code Act* requires that the Chief Building Official issue a building permit unless the proposed building will contravene the *Building Code Act*, the Building Code (a regulation setting out detailed building standards and requirements), or "any other applicable law."[1] The term "applicable law" includes federal and provincial regulatory instruments, as well as municipal by-laws,[2] but does not include common law rights of action,[3]official plans,[4] or development agreements.[5] In other provinces, the requirements are along similar but often narrower grounds requiring, for example, conformance to building and zoning requirements only.[6]

The statutory requirement to issue a building permit under defined conditions has traditionally been viewed as a non-discretionary obligation. That is, so long as the application meets the regulatory requirements, the municipal building official must issue the permit.[7] Where a permit issuance is refused, a landowner may make an application to the courts for a writ of mandamus (or judicial review) compelling the municipal official to exercise his or her statutory obligations to issue the permit. While this may involve the judicial interpretation of municipal by-laws, it does not normally involve controversial second-guessing of municipal decision-making, as the question in dispute is not one of policy, but rather interpretation.

However, difficulties arise when the municipality, upon learning of an application for a permit, decides that it does not wish to allow such a development and seeks to rezone the land in advance of the issuance of the permit. Once a permit is issued, the landowner's right to develop is protected from subsequent rezonings, which is to say that the right to develop vests upon issuance of the building permit.[8] As a consequence, the municipality often seeks to delay making a decision on the building permit until the new zoning is in place. In these cases, the courts have been required to adjudicate between

---

1 S.O. 1992, c. 23, s. 8(2)(a).

2 The term "applicable law" is defined in the Building Code, O. Reg. 403/97, s. 1.1.3.2 as "any general or special Act and all regulations and by-laws enacted thereunder, which prohibit the proposed construction or demolition of the building unless the Act, regulation or by-law is complied with."

3 *Alaimo v. York (City) Chief Building Official* (1995), 26 M.P.L.R. (2d) 69 (Ont. Gen. Div.).

4 *Woodglen & Co. v. North York (City)* (1984), 47 O.R. (2d) 614, 26 M.P.L.R. 40 (Div. Ct.), leave to appeal refused (1984), 12 C.L.R. xli (Ont. C.A.); *Woodglen & Co. v. North York (City) Chief Building Official* (1994), 23 M.P.L.R. (2d) 219 (Ont. Gen. Div.) at 225.

5 *Rotstein v. North York (City) Chief Building Official* (1995) 29 M.P.L.R. (2d) 305 (Ont. Gen. Div.).

6 See Quebec *Land Use Planning and Development Act*, R.S.Q., A-19.1, s.120; Alberta, *Safety Codes Act*, R.S.A. 2000, c.S-1, s. 40.

7 *Woodglen, supra* note 4 at 46-47 [M.P.L.R.], where the Court noted that the Chief Building Official is under a duty to issue a permit where the proposed construction would not contravene any law.

8 See *infra* section C, note in particular building permits maybe revoked under certain conditions.

the rights of landowners to rely on existing land use regulations and the rights of the municipal council to prevent a land use that is contrary to what they believe is the public interest.

Consider, for example the facts of *Toronto (City) Roman Catholic Separate School Board v. Toronto (City)*.[9] Here a separate school board sought to establish a school on a residential street and to that end bought several properties. Upon learning about the proposal, which was permitted under the existing zoning by-law, local residents asked council to enact by-laws prohibiting the use. Thereupon, the school board immediately made a building permit application to alter and extend the building in order for it to construct a building suitable for its purposes. Subsequent to the granting of the building permit application, City council rezoned the lands and the by-law was duly approved (by the Railway and Municipal Board). An action for *mandamus* was then brought by the school board compelling issuance of the permit. On appeal to the Privy Council, the writ was denied on the grounds that once the by-law had passed, there was no obligation to issue the permit, notwithstanding that such a right did exist prior to the passing of the by-law.

When dealing with the issue, the Privy Council indicated that a by-law can be passed any time up to the issuing of the permit. The Lords stated:

> [t]he whole object and purpose of s. 399A [the zoning section] is to empower the city authority, acting in good faith, to put restrictions upon that right [to a permit] with a view to the protection of neighbouring owners against that "grave detriment and hardship" to which the learned trial judge referred; and the "status" or proprietary right of the owner is limited by the powers of the city to be exercised for the protection of his neighbours ... where plans have been deposited but not yet approved ... the operation of the by-law is not excluded. There may be a prima facie right to have the deposited plans approved; but if so, that right is negatived by the passing and approval of the [subsequent] by-law.[10]

The Privy Council decision indicates that once a building permit application has been filed, the landowner has a *prima facie* right to the receipt of a building permit, but that right can be defeated by a subsequent rezoning, where that rezoning occurs prior to the actual decision being made by a municipal building official, or in the case of a *mandamus* application, by the petitioned court.

This approach is one that favours the broader public interest over the interests of landowners. By holding that the right to a permit does not vest until a decision has been taken, the court tacitly seeks to privilege the rights of municipal councils and surrounding landowners over the rights of individual landowners. This approach may be justified on the basis that, like in the *Toronto (City) Roman Catholic Separate School Board* case, often a munic-

---

9 (1925), [1926] A.C. 81, [1925] 3 D.L.R. 880 (Ontario P.C.).

10 *Ibid.* at 86 [A.C.].

ipality will not be aware of a problem until an application for a permit is made. Consequently, to prevent effective regulation after the discovery of the difficulty severely limits the ability of the municipality to grant protection. Moreover, the potential externalities stemming from such a use may continue for a long time and affect many people, which again favours curtailing private property rights in favor of public regarding regulation. The municipality, it can be seen, may need the maximum period within which to interfere and cannot be expected to know of and plan for every eventuality and problem in advance.

On the other hand, it can be argued that granting municipalities the ability to interfere at such a late date is inappropriate. The zoning power, as has been pointed out, is founded on the value of the rule of law, which includes knowing the rules in advance. To allow interference after an application is made is to subvert that value. It enables municipalities to delay approvals under false pretenses while by-laws are amended. It ignores the reliance that developers have placed on the existing by-law and thus it may render worthless investments made on the basis of the by-law. In this regard, protecting individual landowners may have a broader public purpose in that by respecting existing land uses, the courts would create a more stable environment for property investment and development. Moreover, there is a concern that by allowing municipal councils to alter zoned uses subsequent to an application may invite decisions made on the basis of political expediency, as opposed to good planning grounds.

As it was clear that the rights of the parties were being determined as of the date of the *mandamus* application, in cases, such as in Ontario, where zoning by-laws came into effect only after approval by the Ontario Municipal Board,[11] municipalities sought adjournments of the court proceedings until the new zoning by-laws were in effect. The result was that the rights of the parties were effectively determined by the decision to grant the adjournment. Here the situation differed from the decision in *Toronto (City) Roman Catholic Separate School Board* because in the absence of an adjournment there would be no effective by-law in place at the time the matter came up before the court. In addressing this situation, the Supreme Court of Canada in *Ottawa (City) v. Boyd Builders Ltd.* formulated a three part test for determining whether an adjournment should be granted in these circumstances. In order for an adjournment to be granted, the municipality had to demonstrate that it had a pre-existing intent to zone the property, that it acted in good faith and that it acted with dispatch in zoning the property.[12] The Court emphasized in its judgment the *prima facie* right of a property owner to do with her land what she will, subject to common law rights and validly enacted zoning by-

11 Prior to 1983 all zoning by-laws required approval of the Ontario Municipal Board. However, the *Planning Act* has been amended so that zoning by-laws come into force on the date of passage, unless appealed to the Ontario Municipal Board, s. 34(21).

12 (1965), 50 D.L.R. (2d) 704 (S.C.C.), at 705.

laws. The Court, it seems, saw the lack of an effective by-law as the means to reverse in part the decision in the *Toronto (City) Roman Catholic Separate School Board* case and provide more protection for the developer of land. However, in doing so, the court did not directly address the central problem regarding when a right to building permit vests, rather its approach was more functional, seeking instead to draw a balance between the rights of the landowner and the public interest.

In certain respects, the functionality of the *Boyd Builders* test was a helpful improvement on the position in *Toronto (City) Roman Catholic Separate School Board*. By providing some balance between the opposing rights of landowners and municipalities, this test could be used to curb abuses by councils who were simply responding to political pressure, by looking to specific expressions of prior intent to rezone. In order to satisfy this requirement, municipalities have passed resolutions expressing an intent to rezone land and have thereby circumvented to some extent the provisions of the case. Since the courts have upheld such statements of intent,[13] municipalities were in fact able to regulate land by the mere passage of resolutions rather than a zoning by-law, as the resolution would result in the adjournment being granted and a subsequent by-law being effective subject to Ontario Municipal Board approval. Such a situation does not enhance the rule of law value of zoning. In other situations, however, the courts have not been clear as to what is a sufficient statement of intent. In *R. v. Barrie (City)*[14] the decision was based, in part, on the view that an official plan provision was not a sufficient statement of intent. While in *Donald Bye Excavating Co. v. Peterborough (City)*,[15] an official plan provision was found to be sufficient.

The tests for good faith and dispatch also have provided the courts with considerable discretion. The case of *Hall v. Toronto (City)*[16] perhaps illustrates this best. In that case, the applicant wished to construct two townhouses on a lot in a residential neighborhood and called a meeting of his neighbours to inform them of his plans. The development was in conformity with the zoning but required certain other approvals. A neighbor then requested a committee of the City to initiate an amendment to the by-law to increase the minimum lot size so as to prevent the construction of the townhouses, on the grounds that they would be inconsistent with the character and aesthetics of the area. The committee recommended the change and the City council declared its intent by resolution to enact such a by-law and requested a report on the proposed by-law without informing the applicant, who received no notice of the matter. Until the approval of the resolution, the applicant had

---

13 See *Overcomers Church v. Toronto (City)* (1973), 39 D.L.R. (3d) 491, 1 O.R. (2d) 123 (Div. Ct.).

14 (1969), [1970] 1 O.R. 200, 8 D.L.R. (3d) 52 (C.A.).

15 (1972), [1973] 1 O.R. 139, 30 D.L.R. (3d) 415 (C.A.).

16 (1979), 23 O.R. (2d) 86, 94 D.L.R. (3d) 750, 8 M.P.L.R. 155 (C.A.).

been assured that the project conformed to the by-law. His plans submitted after the passing of the resolution complied with the by-law.

The Court of Appeal held that no adjournment should be granted and that an order in the nature of *mandamus* should issue. The Court concluded that the City's resolution did not demonstrate a clear zoning plan prior to the application. The committee and Council had not acted in good faith, showing an absence of frankness and impartiality by acting hastily and acceding to pressure to defeat the applicant's *prima facie* right to a permit without granting him a hearing. The object of the exercise was not planning but was, instead, the blocking of the application. In addition, the Court held that the granting of an adjournment also involved a balancing of the equities and here the equities favored the applicant. He purchased the property on the basis of the existing zoning, he proceeded with dispatch and divulged his plans to his neighbours. The municipality had no general plan to rezone and they did not show that the applicant's buildings would change the character of the neighborhood.

The distinction the court draws between planning and mere obstruction is difficult to maintain. Planning, by its very nature, involves the blocking of applications and courts must be careful to avoid substituting their own ideas of what constitutes good planning for those of the municipality. The court's assessment of the municipality's intentions are the stronger basis for the decision. The court may have been rightfully concerned about the less than forthcoming behavior of the municipality, as compared to a landowner who was candid about his plans for the land. To hold in favor of the municipality would have in essence rewarded the municipality for its lack of candor in a process that is premised on transparent decision-making.

The unpredictability of the case law under the *Boyd Builders* test raised problems regarding the instrumentality of such an approach. The determination of rights was largely left up to the courts, with the result being that the courts had considerable influence over land use decisions in these circumstances. Because both the decision to grant an adjournment and the decision to grant mandamus are discretionary ones, the approach has been a sort of contextual balancing similar to an exercise of equitable jurisdiction. This functional approach, however, undermined the rule of law values and predictability that one might expect where property rights are being interfered with.

The *Boyd Builders* case has been followed in a number of provinces and as such the three-part test continues to be considered and applied from time to time.[17] However, courts and the legislatures appear to be moving away from the balance struck in *Boyd Builders*, albeit in different directions. In Ontario, it is now clear that *Boyd Builders* is of no application. In *McDonald's*

17 *Venture 4th Inc. v. St. John's (City)* (1996), 31 M.P.L.R. (2d) 84 (Nfld. T.D.); *2858-5750 Québec Inc. c. Laval (Ville)* (1992), 14 M.P.L.R. (2d) 79 (Que. S.C.).

Restaurants of Canada Ltd. v. Humm[18] and then in *Woodglen & Co. v. North York (City)*,[19] it was held the existence of a statutory right of appeal respecting a decision regarding building permit issuance under the *Building Code Act* provided an alternative remedy to *mandamus*.[20] The authority of the court was restricted under the new right of remedy to only those remedies available to the building official. As a result, it was argued that the Court's power to consider the *Boyd Builders* test, which was premised on the Court's discretionary power to grant an extraordinary remedy, no longer existed. As a result, the Ontario Courts have ceased to apply the *Boyd Builders* test. It has also been suggested that the introduction of interim control by-laws, which allow municipalities to temporarily freeze development pending further study has also obviated the need for adjournments since these by-laws may be enacted and come into force without advance notice.[21]

Under the current Ontario regime, most courts suggest that the landowner's rights should be assessed as of the Building Official's decision.[22] Thus, only those by-laws in effect at the time of the Building Official's consideration of the application are relevant. On a number of occasions, the courts have indicated that the right to a building permit vests upon the filing of an application,[23] notwithstanding the clear position of the higher courts in *Boyd Builders* and *Toronto (City) Roman Catholic Separate School Board* that an application only gives rise to a *prima facie* right to a building permit. The better view remains that the filing of an application gives rise to a *prima facie* right that can be defeated by the subsequent passing of an interim control by-law, which unlike regular by-laws in Ontario take immediate effect. The passing of the by-law remains subject to the requirement of good faith, but this requirement must be viewed in light of the more stringent test for the finding of bad faith set out in the *Equity Waste* case.[24] Delay in considering the application may be indicative of bad faith, but such a determination will require courts to look at the entire context of the municipality enactment.[25]

---

18 (1983), 24 M.P.L.R. 103 (Ont. Co. Ct.).

19 *Supra* note 4.

20 S.O. 1992, c. 23, s. 25.

21 See *infra* this chapter.

22 *Woodglen, supra* note 4 at 225 [M.P.L.R.]; *Summit Glen Development Corp. v. Toronto (City)* (1989), 44 M.P.L.R. 50 (Ont. Dist. Ct.) at 52-54.

23 In both *Wolfond v. North York (City) Building Commissioner* (1990), 1 M.P.L.R. (2d) 189 (Ont. Dist. Ct.) and *Sixteenth Avenue Warden Ltd. v. Markham (Town) Chief Building Official* (1993), 12 O.R. (3d) 653, 18 M.P.L.R. (2d) 70 (Gen. Div.), the courts indicate that the right to a bulding permit "crystallizes" upon the filing of a complete application.

24 *Equity Waste Management of Canada Corp. v. Halton Hills (Town)* (1997), 40 M.P.L.R. (2d) 107 (Ont. C.A.), discussed *supra* Chapters 4, 8.

25 A central difficulty with the Ontario regime is that there are no defined time limits for the consideration of a building permit application by a building official. Consequently, it is often difficult for the courts to distinguish between unnecessary delay and administrative processing.

In British Columbia, the response to *Boyd Builders* was also to reject its application, but for different reasons. Here it has been held that the central distinguishing feature between the then Ontario regime and the British Columbia scheme was that in British Columbia zoning by-laws took immediate effect and thus there was no need for adjournments. The assumption is that the *Boyd Builders* test related solely to the adjournment and not to the *mandamus* considerations as a whole, which is technically true, but seems to ignore the underlying purpose of the three-part test. On this basis, B.C. Court of Appeal, in the *Monarch Holdings* case, reverted back to the test as originally articulated in *Toronto (City) Roman Catholic Separate School Board*.[26] Significantly, in British Columbia, the municipal legislation provided that council may withhold the issuance of building permits for up to 30 days pending changes to the existing planning regime.[27] This section provides explicit permission to municipalities to delay consideration of a building permit where changes to the land use regime are contemplated. This section was found not to have been resorted to in the *Monarch Holdings* case, although the reasoning for ignoring this section is not clear.

As a prerequisite to the operation of this section as it currently stands, the preparations of the new plan or zoning by-law must precede the application date by seven days. This scheme has been taken as a complete code replacing the conditions in *Boyd Builders*.[28] A municipality must avail itself of this process and meet its requirements, or the by-laws in force at the date of application are the operative by-laws.[29] Consequently, the B.C. legislature has come down clearly on the side of landowners since it is only where the rezoning process predates the application that a building permit can be held up. Although, the legislative scheme accounts for the most problematic threat to the public interest, which is where a landowner upon learning of a municipal intent to rezone seeks to undermine that intent by securing its rights through the application of a building permit. In this situation, where the municipal intent can be shown to have existed in advance of the application, it can maintain the integrity of that process.

A number of other provinces have legislation similar to that found in British Columbia, which specifically allow municipalities to delay the issue of a building permit pending the enactment of a new zoning by-law.

---

26 *Monarch Holdings Ltd. v. Oak Bay (District)* (1977), 4 B.C.L.R. 67, 79 D.L.R. (3d) 59, 4 M.P.L.R. 147 (C.A.).

27 *Municipal Act,* R.S.B.C. 1960, c. 255 as amended, s. 705.

28 *Municipal Act,* R.S.B.C. 1979, c. 290, s. 981; *Cheung v. Victoria (City)* (1994), 25 M.P.L.R. (2d) 184 (B.C. C.A.).

29 *Ibid.*

C. NON-CONFORMING USES

The existence of non-conforming uses raises a similar tension between the rights of landowners and those of the public at large. Here, the situation to be confronted is how planning regimes should treat existing land uses that no longer conform to the prevailing zoning requirements because of a subsequent change in the zoning requirements. Unlike the situation respecting building permit issuance, where the lands were not being used for the now prohibited purpose, here the change in zoning potentially deprives a landowner of existing uses. Traditionally, common law rules respecting the non-retroactive application of regulatory instruments would prevent the new zoning provisions from actually depriving the landowner of the right to continue to use the land in the same manner.[30] In Quebec, a similar concept, referred to as "acquired rights" was recognized by the *Civil Code*.[31] Under both civil and common law systems, the rationale for preventing interference with existing uses flows from the general principle that vested property rights cannot be interfered with without compensation. Although, at the present time, the right to maintain non-conforming uses has been codified in provincial legislation, except in P.E.I. and Newfoundland, where reliance remains on the common law rules.[32] The legislative provisions provide that municipalities cannot prevent the use of land or structures, where such land or structures were lawfully used for that purpose prior to the new zoning restriction coming into force. Thus, such uses, while not conforming to the by-law, remain allowable, and are, therefore, referred to as "legal non-conforming" uses. In this regard, the statutory provisions mirror the common or civil law requirements.

A central difficulty with respect to non-conforming uses is determining how broadly the protected use should be interpreted. A wide-ranging interpretation of what constitutes a protected non-conforming use would be in keeping with the concern over the confiscatory nature of zoning by allowing an affected landowner to exercise a significant degree of flexibility with respect to his or her land. On the other hand, municipalities often voice a concern that a broad interpretation of the rights of landowners with legal non-

30 *Toronto (City) v. Wheeler* (1912), 4 D.L.R. 352 (Ont. H.C.).

31 Discussed in *Saint-Romauld (Ville) c. Olivier* [2001] 2 S.C.R. 898 (2001), 22 M.P.L.R. (3d) 1 (S.C.C.) at 15 [M.P.L.R.].

32 Nova Scotia, *Municipal Government Act*, S.N.S. 1998, c. 18, s. 238; New Brunswick, *Community Planning Act*, R.S.N.B. 1973, c. C-12, as amended, s. 40 (1); Ontario, *Planning Act*, R.S.O., 1990, C. P.13, s. 34(9); Quebec, *An Act Respecting Land Use Planning and Development*, R.S.Q., c. A-19.1, s. 113(18); Manitoba, *The Planning Act*, R.S.M. 1987, c. P80, s. 48; Saskatchewan, *Planning and Development Act, 1983*, S.S. 1983-84, c. P-13.1, s. 113; Alberta, *Municipal Government Act*, R.S.A. 2000, c. M-26 , s. 643; British Columbia, *Local Government Act*, R.S.B.C. 1996, c. 323, s. 911; In some instances, the zoning by-laws themselves will recognize non-conforming uses, see *Prince Edward Island Museum & Heritage Foundation v. Charlottetown (City)* (1998), 45 M.P.L.R. (2d) 281 (P.E.I. T.D.).

conforming properties undermines the intent of the prevailing zoning prohibition. It is with these two competing views of non-conforming uses in mind that the courts' analysis of non-conforming uses may be examined.

The use that is granted protection is generally widely defined, so that in the case of *Toronto (City) v. Central Jewish Institute*,[33] a use of property for school purposes which took place in a garden and one room in the basement of a house was seen as a use of the entire building. There was no narrow examination of exactly where the physical activity took place. Here the Supreme Court focused on the fact that the statutory exemption was aimed at the "building" not the use itself. Consequently, so long as the use was the same and was contained within the building, an intensification of such a use was protected by its legal non-conforming status. More broadly, in *R. v. Rutherford's Dairy Ltd.*,[34] property which was used for parking vehicles related to a dairy and under which services passed to the dairy was considered to be used for the purpose of the dairy and thus the dairy building itself could be expanded on the property so used. Clearly, part of the reasoning is pragmatic. In the *Central Jewish Institute* case, the Supreme Court realized that the intensity of the use may expand and contract over time and it would be difficult to contain a use within certain parts of a building. Likewise, viewing the dairy operation as an integrated whole, as opposed to separate non-conforming parts, the court in the *Rutherford's Dairy* case recognized the need to allow a level of flexibility in respect of commercial operations.

In *R. v. Cappy*,[35] the Court examined whether the use of a stadium for stock car races, rather than track and field and other sports events for which the stadium was built, was a protected use. Notwithstanding that there were also some physical changes in the stadium to accommodate the racing, the Court held that the original use continued. In discussing the nature of the use and whether it changed or part of it was discontinued, the Court held that the use must be assessed in light of its purpose. Mr. Justice Laidlaw continued:

> In my opinion that purpose was a general one. It comprehended the use of the stadium for public amusement and entertainment and for public exhibitions and performances of all kinds. The purpose must be regarded collectively as a whole and cannot properly be divided into parts. Thus it cannot be said the purpose for which the property was used on the day of the passing of the by-law was for football games or for foot races or for any other particular kind of public entertainment, exhibition or performance. It was for one and all of that kind of activity.[36]

The alterations of the stadium did not indicate a change in use since use had to be looked at in a general way. The Court here by abstracting the use

---

33 [1948] S.C.R. 101, [1948] 2 D.L.R. 1.
34 [1961] O.W.N. 146 (H.C.), affirmed [1961] O.W.N. 274 (C.A.).
35 (1952), [1953] 1 D.L.R. 28, [1952] O.W.N. 481, 103 C.C.C. 25 (C.A.).
36 *Ibid.* at 35 [D.L.R.].

beyond what was in essence actually in existence at the time the use became non-conforming, seemed to tacitly accept that legal non-conforming uses could belong to a broader category of uses, i.e. general purpose stadiums, as opposed to track and field stadiums. However, legal non-conforming uses protect the actual use not some future potential use. Here, the court by defining the use broadly favoured the rights of the private land owner over those of the municipality. What is perhaps surprising is that the Court gave little consideration to the potential for increased impacts the change in use would have on surrounding landowners.

In trying to maintain a principled approach to the determination of the scope of legal non-conforming uses, the courts have made a distinction between a change in the type of use and a change in the intensity of use, the latter falling within the scope of legal non-conforming uses. Thus, for example, in *Magdalena's Rest Home Ltd. v. Etobicoke (City)*, an owner of a 15 bed rest home that had legal non-conforming status sought to increase the number of beds without external alterations. While the municipality argued that the legal non-conforming use was limited to the actual number of beds, the Court held that the protected use was a rest home and the increase was simply an increase in intensity.[37]

This distinction is elaborated on by the Supreme Court of Canada *Saint-Romauld (Ville) c. Olivier*[38] where an owner of a bar that was protected from the prevailing zoning (disallowing "cabarets") by acquired rights (legal non-conforming status) introduced nude dancers as the principal form of entertainment, which was previously provided by country and western singers. The issue for the Court's determination was whether this change went beyond what was protected by the bar's acquired rights. The decision of the Supreme Court, which was split on the outcome, illustrates the continued difficulty and value-laden nature of these determinations. In both the majority and minority opinions, the approach presented was more nuanced than previous considerations of the scope of the non-conforming uses exemption. For example, both Binnie J. and Gonthier J., speaking for the majority and minority respectively, rejected a categorical approach to the determination of the scope of exemption, whereby use would be defined in reference to a broader category of uses within which the actual use corresponded under the previous zoning by-law. Moreover, both accepted that intensification of uses was not a valid basis for objection. On this point, Binnie J. elaborates, noting that an intensification could be so significant as to affect the use's "character," although this may be a distinction without a difference. (For example, Binnie J. notes that increased traffic or noise from an intensified use should not

37 (1992), 12 M.P.L.R. (2d) 316 (Ont. Gen. Div.). This case and other cases involving the use/intensity distinction are discussed in Ira Kagen, "But I Do Not Want To Be Legal" (1993), 13 M.P.L.R. 252, who notes that in certain circumstances there are distinct advantages to having legal non-conforming status, as opposed to an allowable use.

38 [2001] 2 S.C.R. 898, (2001), 22 M.P.L.R. (3d) 1 (S.C.C.).

normally take it outside its exempt status.[39] A person or business should not become the victims of their own success, as it were.) Ultimately, if a use is to lose its non-conforming or acquired status, it must be of a different type.

In considering whether the type of use has changed, Binnie J. sets out two relevant considerations. Firstly, the new activity must not be too remote from the actual use. But this again, as Binnie J. concedes is largely determined by how broadly the existing non-conforming activity is defined. Secondly, the new activity should not create an undue additional or aggravated problem for the municipality. This consideration of "neighbourhood effects" is a significant development, as it allows courts greater freedom to balance the rights of landowners with the rights of the municipality and the public more generally. These factors must be considered together, along with the intensity of use.[40] Consequently, a relatively innocuous, but more remote activity, may be as likely to be considered within the scope of the acquired right as a more disruptive, but less remote activity.

Gonthier J., although he expresses his opinion in different terms, adopts an approach that is much the same as the majority. For Gonthier J., the central consideration is whether the new activity falls within the "real and natural expectations" of the user.[41] It is these expectations that the doctrine of acquired rights protects. In this regard, it is appropriate to assess the expectations in light of the overall purposes of the zoning regime, since activities that are contrary to these purposes are not reasonable expectations. Ultimately, Gonthier J., like Binnie J., looks to both the remoteness and impacts of the activity to determine whether it falls within the scope of the acquired rights, but Gonthier conflates the two considerations under the rubric of "expectation."

Where the opinions diverge is in the consideration of the effects themselves. Gonthier J. is much more willing to take a broad view of the impacts of erotic entertainment, noting that it is clearly seen in a different moral light than country and western singing. To some degree Gonthier J. situates his analysis in the context of the differential treatment municipalities often give adult entertainment venues, noting the case law upholding the distinct treatment of adult entertainment venues within planning regimes. The effects for the minority are more implied than proven. In contrast, Binnie J. specifically notes that those claiming neighbourhood effects have an onus to bring forth evidence of the impacts. In considering the evidence, Binnie J. finds no convincing evidence of undue impact, but his analysis appears focused on physical impact. In the end, despite the Court's attempt to place the determination of the scope of uses on objective grounds, the decision appears to turn on the differing views of the members of the Court on the moral turpitude of the activity in question.

---

39 *Ibid.* at 18 [M.P.L.R.].
40 *Ibid.* at 20 [M.P.L.R.].
41 *Ibid.* at 33 [M.P.L.R.].

A separate issue that often arises with respect to non-conforming uses is the requirement that in order to maintain a non-conforming use, the use must be continued without interruption. This arises from the basic purpose of the exemption, which is to maintain the *status quo*. However, where the use is not maintained, there can be no expectation that the exemption from the prevailing zoning should continue. This requirement has again been incorporated in many instances into the statutory scheme. In Quebec, for instance, a period of abandonment or interruption of least six months is required.[42] Other provinces have included similar elaborations on this requirement.[43]

In assessing whether a use has been discontinued, the central consideration is the intention of the landowner to abandon the use.[44] While seemingly straightforward, the courts' decisions on this point have been unpredictable. For example, in the case of *Gayford v. Kolodziej*,[45] the renting of a tourist house to one family for a summer resulted in the loss of a "tourist home" status because the "use" was discontinued. The case does not make clear why the length of tenure should have such a profound impact on the determination of a use. Conversely, in the case of *O'Sullivan Funeral Home Ltd. v. Sault Ste. Marie (City)*,[46] the use of funeral home was held not to be discontinued although no funerals had occurred for at least six months on the premises and they were occupied as a residence. The Court, however, did state in this case that the payment of business tax was an important consideration.

D. INTERIM CONTROL

Because of the ability of planning enactments to constrain the right of landowners to use their lands as they see fit, all planning statutes incorporate procedural safeguards to ensure that landowners and other interested parties have notice of changes to planning documents that may affect land uses and provide for opportunities to participate in the decision-making process. Consequently, changes to land use rules, even when strongly supported at a local level, cannot be effected without often time-consuming consultation proceedings. Given that landowners often reasonably rely on existing land use rules to guide investment decisions, or similarly, residents may look to these

---

42 *An Act Respecting Land Use Planning and Development*, R.S.Q. c. A-19.1, s. 113(18).

43 Newfoundland, *Urban and Rural Planning Act*, S.N.L. 2000, c. U-8, s. 108(2); New Brunswick, *Community Planning Act*, R.S.N.B. 1973, c. C-12, as amended, s. 40 (2); Manitoba, *The Planning Act*, R.S.M. 1987, c. P80, s. 51 (1); British Columbia, *Local Government Act*, R.S.B.C. 1996, c. 323, s. 911(1)(b).

44 *Toronto (City) v. San Joaquin Investments Ltd.* (1978), 18 O.R. (2d) 730 (H.C.), affirmed (1979), 11 M.P.L.R. 83 (Ont. Div. Ct.), leave to appeal refused (1980), 26 O.R. (2d) 775 (note) (S.C.C.).

45 [1959] O.W.N. 341, 19 D.L.R. (2d) 777 (C.A.).

46 [1961] O.R. 413, 28 D.L.R. (2d) 1 (H.C.).

rules in deciding where to reside, the procedural safeguards found in planning legislation are eminently desirable.

However, as seen in relation to the issuance of building permits, there are occasions where unforeseen consequences of existing land use policies or novel planning situations, may give rise to concerns that continued land development under existing policies may so negatively impact the public interest that more immediate attention to those policies and rules is required. For example, the advent of retail warehouse type development in the 1980s and 1990s, the existence of which was simply not contemplated in the planning documents of many jurisdictions across Canada, but which had potentially dramatic land use consequences, could result in a justifiable desire to prevent such development until its consequences were properly understood by planning authorities. Moreover, in cases where a planning authority, be it the province or a municipality, is currently engaged in reviewing or enacting new planning policies, it may undermine those policies, if development were to proceed prior to the finalization of new policies or contrary to a proposed policy direction.

In recognition of this, and understanding that initiating policy changes may in fact motivate landowners to secure their rights under the existing policies before the policies change (by securing a development or building permit), planning legislation in the majority of provinces permits municipal councils or in some instances provincial authorities, to control development on an interim basis, pending a review or study of existing planning policies.[47] Thus, an interim control by-law allows municipalities to freeze development temporarily by suspending the operation of existing development control mechanisms. The most significant difference with interim control measures is that unlike common planning enactments, interim measures take immediate effect and often do not require prior notice. In this regard, interim control by-laws are more prominent in Ontario where zoning by-laws may be subjected to long appeal processes. In most other provinces the ability to enact interim control measures is highly circumscribed and is often under direct provincial control. For example in Newfoundland, Nova Scotia and Manitoba, only the Minister may make interim development regulations.[48] In other cases, councils may enact interim control measures, but these are subject to provincial

47 Newfoundland, *Urban and Rural Planning Act, 2000,* S.N.L. 2000, c. U-8, s. 12; Prince Edward Island, *Planning Act,* R.S.P.E.I. 1998, c. P-8, s. 10; Nova Scotia, *Municipal Government Act,* S.N.S. 1998, c. 18, s. 198(2); New Brunswick, *Community Planning Act,* R.S.N.B. 1973, c. C-12, as amended, s. 71; Manitoba, *The Planning Act*, R.S.M. 1987, c. P80, s. 57; British Columbia, *Local Government Act*, R.S.B.C. 1996, c. 323, s. 911(1)(b); Ontario, *Planning Act*, R.S.O. 1990, c. P.13, s. 38; Quebec, *An Act Respecting Land Use Planning and Development*, R.S.Q. c. A-19.1, s. 61; Saskatchewan, *Planning and Development Act, 1983*, S.S. 1983-84, c. P-13.1, s. 105.

48 Newfoundland *Urban and Rural Planning Act*, S.N.L. 2000, c. U-8, s. 12; Nova Scotia, *Municipal Government Act*, S.N.S. 1998, c. 18, s. 198(2); Manitoba, *The Planning Act*, R.S.M. 1987, c. P80, s. 57.

approval.[49] The legislative purpose underlying interim control by-laws is described by the Ontario Court of Appeal in the following terms:

> An important purpose of interim control by-laws is to permit a municipality to change its mind, to reconsider its land use policies. Whether an area is suitably zoned, whether development should be suspended in the public interest, and whether proposed projects are compatible with a municipalities long range planning objectives are matters to be decided by municipal councils, not by courts.[50]

Under the Ontario *Planning Act*, the only prerequisite to passing an interim control by-law is that council must have directed that a review or study be carried out in respect of land uses policies within the municipality or part thereof. The interim control by-law may only be in effect for a one-year period, but this may be extended to a further year.[51] While interim control by-laws are subject to appeal to the Ontario Municipal Board, but unlike zoning by-laws enacted pursuant to s. 34 of the Ontario *Planning Act*, interim control by-laws take immediate effect and are in effect during the appeal period. A number of Ontario Municipal Board decisions respecting interim control by-laws have noted their extraordinary nature and have counseled caution in their use.[52] In light of this extraordinary nature, a strict and narrow approach to a municipality's power to enact interim control by-laws has sometimes been articulated.[53] In these cases, the Ontario Municipal Board has suggested that only urgent and unforeseen circumstances may justify the enactment of an interim control by-law. However, the better view, and the view subscribed to by the Ontario Court of Appeal, is that s. 38 of the *Planning Act*, which authorizes interim control by-laws, should be given a liberal interpretation in accordance with the purpose of the section and recognizing that protecting the public interest should take precedence over the rights of individual landowners.[54]

---

49 i.e. PEI and Quebec.

50 *Equity Waste Management of Canada Corp. v. Halton Hills (Town)* (1997), 35 O.R. (3d) 321 (C.A.).

51 *Planning Act*, R.S.O. 1990, c. P.13, s. 38 (1),(2).

52 *Scarborough (City) Interim Control By-law 22169-81, Re* (1988), 22 O.M.B.R. 129 (M.B.); *North American Life Assurance Co., Re* (1993), 29 O.M.B.R. 300 (M.B.).

53 See for example, *Corbeil v. Hamilton (Township)* (1993), 29 O.M.B.R. 129 (M.B.); *1281504 Ontario Ltd. v. Orangeville (Town)* (1999), 5 M.P.L.R. (3d) 289 (O.M.B.).

54 *Equity Waste Management, supra* note 50; see also *715113 Ontario Inc. v. Ottawa (City)* (1987), 63 O.R. (2d) 102 (H.C.); *893472 Ontario Ltd. v. Whitchurch-Stouffville (Town)* (1991), 7 M.P.L.R. (2d) 296 (Ont. Gen. Div.).

E. JUDICIAL INTERPRETATION OF ZONING BY-LAWS

The final area where the rights of landowners tend to collide with the interests of the municipality concerns the interpretation of zoning by-laws themselves. On the whole, courts have acknowledged that where a by-law is clear and unambiguous in its meaning, the by-law shall be interpreted in accordance with the "plain meaning" of the words contained within the by-law. That is, "in their popular, rather than their narrowly legal or technical sense."[55] However, where ambiguity arises the courts have recognized two competing approaches to the interpretation of zoning by-laws. Firstly, noting the restrictions a by-law places on an owner's right to use his or her property, the courts have articulated a strict interpretation in favour of the landowner:

> I have come to this conclusion realizing that a by-law restricting the use of land must be strictly construed and that any doubt as to the application of the by-law to prevent the erection of a specific building should be resolved in favour of such proposed uses. No authority need be cited for each of these propositions. These principles, however, need only be applied when upon the reading of the whole by-law there is ambiguity or difficulty of construction.[56]

On the other hand, the courts have also recognized the remedial nature of zoning enactments and have counseled that such by-laws must be interpreted in light of their purposes. This approach is exemplified by the following statement of the Ontario Court of Appeal:

> On this account, I consider the by-law to be remedial and one to be accorded a liberal interpretation to the end that it may afford to the people of the community protection against departures from or encroachment upon the standards adopted by the municipality as expressive of these purposes.
>
> Such an approach is, I believe, compatible with the proven necessity for the employment of external controls for the preservation of a fair standard of housing and land use and the expressed will of the people for a universal application of orderly planning to that end, I am not unmindful that it has not been uncommon for by-laws dealing with the use of lands and the use and erection of buildings to be referred to as restrictive by-laws and to be accorded a strict interpretation due to the fact that they have been approached as infringements on the freedom of choice of the owner and the use to which he may put his land.
>
> Notwithstanding this, it is my belief that Ontario Courts now accept that the obligation imposed on the municipal council to plan for the growth and devel-

55 *Haldimand-Norfolk (Regional Municipality) v. Painter* (1997), 43 M.P.L.R. (2d) 147 (Ont. Gen. Div.) at 149.

56 *Jones v. Wilson*, [1968] S.C.R. 554 at 559; see also *Bayshore Shopping Centre Ltd. v. Nepean (Township)*, [1972] S.C.R. 755, at 764.

> opment of the community demands recognition of the necessity for means to compel the observance of the rights of the community to determine and enforce the direction in which the community should be shaped, and that in this regard the rights of the community are paramount to the rights of the owner.[57]

The Courts have continued to apply both approaches, notwithstanding their apparent incompatibility.[58] If, however, these decisions are viewed in light of the broader approach to the balancing of the rights between landowners and municipalities, an approach which favours the private rights of individual landowners at the expense of the broader public interest appears to be out of step with the broader trend towards recognizing the legitimate role of municipalities in protecting the public interest through land use regulation and the need to give municipalities a degree of flexibility and autonomy in carrying out those duties. This is an approach which is largely recognized with respect to the interpretation of municipal by-laws generally and is consonant with the public regarding and democratic nature of local government.

---

57 *Bruce v. Toronto (City)*, [1971] 3 O.R. 62 (C.A.), at 66.

58 Examples of courts applying a narrow interpretation in favour of landowners include, *Miramichi (City) v. Duthie* (1997), 38 M.P.L.R. (2d) 23 (N.B. Q.B.), and *Ultimate Relaxation Inc. v. Coquitlam (City)* (1995), 30 M.P.L.R. (2d) 245 (B.C. S.C. [In Chambers]). The liberal approach has been applied in *Galway & Cavendish (United Townships) v. Windover* (1995), 30 M.P.L.R. (2d) 109 (Ont. Gen. Div.) and *Haldimand-Norfolk (Regional Municipality) v. Painter*, *supra* note 55.

10

Process Requirements and the Municipality

A. INTRODUCTION

This chapter addresses the legal requirements for open and transparent local government and the provision of fair procedures for those who are affected by municipal decision-making. The reasons for such requirements fall into two broad categories; process as a means to improve substantive decision-making, and process as an end in itself. First, given that a central purpose of local government is to ensure local political control over service provision and policy-making in a local area, rights to information, notice of decisions and the ability of affected persons to present their views on issues are integral to ensuring that local decisions reflect local public values and needs. The importance of this function in the municipal context is magnified because policy positions are less likely to be defined through electoral platforms, given the relative absence of party politics at the local level. Moreover, the use of special purpose bodies and the existence of multiple tiers of local government can also erode direct electoral accountability and responsiveness, the effect of which can be mitigated by imposing procedural obligations of local decision makers. Transparency of municipal decision-making processes also aids in deterring fraud and corruption by ensuring that local government decision-making is subject to public scrutiny. Conflict of interest regulation, which prevents municipal councilors from having a special or personal interest in matters they are charged with deciding, is similarly aimed at producing decisions that reflect public, as opposed to private or personal, interests.

Procedural requirements may also help to provide more accurate factual information to decision-makers and to the public. For example, planning decisions often require careful consideration of the particular context and the impacts on adjacent land owners. In this regard, notice and pubic participation requirements can facilitate an enhanced understanding of local planning conditions and potential impacts. Minority interests can also be protected in this manner by ensuring that particular interests that may not have a strong voice on municipal councils still have an opportunity to be heard.

Second, as municipalities are granted more extensive policy making powers, as well as broader discretion to exercise those powers, procedural obligations are important factors in enhancing local government legitimacy. Here process has a less instrumental role, but rather is desirable because it contributes to the functioning of democracy at the local level. The very notion of subsidiarity is premised on the idea that democracy is most effective and responsive at the level of government closest to the people. In this regard, procedural requirements provide citizens with a greater understanding of local issues and council decisions, opportunities for reducing conflict between competing interests, and promote the ongoing accountability of elected officials.

This chapter will view process requirements from the point of view of (a) common law provisions, the rules of natural justice and procedural fairness, (b) open meetings and access to information and (c) conflict of interest legislation.

B. COMMON LAW PROVISIONS

In putting the procedural obligations that are placed on municipalities into perspective, it is helpful to look briefly at the broader common law requirement that public decision-makers exercise their powers in accordance with a general duty to act fairly. In Chapter Four, the trend towards judicial deference of municipal decision-making was examined in relation to the substance of the municipal actions and by-laws. Municipal decisions cannot be attacked on the basis of whether they are substantively unreasonable, instead judicial review tends to focus on whether a municipality has exceeded the jurisdictional limits placed on it by its enabling legislation or common law restrictions. However, the courts have also recognized that under certain conditions municipalities, like other administrative bodies, owe procedural duties to those persons who are affected by their decisions.

Traditionally the source of procedural duties has arisen out of the components of the principles of natural justice; *audi alteram partem* — the right of a person to know and answer the case against them, and *nemo judex in sua causa* — the rule that a decision-maker must not be the judge in their own cause.[1] In determining whether a municipality in making decisions must extend procedural rights to those affected by a pending decision, the courts have traditionally looked to whether the decision in question involves the municipality acting in a legislative or quasi-judicial manner. The distinction being drawn here is elusive and appears to turn largely on the kind of interests the municipality's decision implicates.

---

1 See generally, Jones and de Villars, *The Principles of Administrative Law*, 2d Ed., (Toronto: Carswell, 1994), at 178-187.

For example, in *Howard v. Toronto (City)*,[2] the Ontario Court of Appeal held that, notwithstanding that the municipality was exercising a discretionary power (to enact a by-law), because the decision involved the municipality resolving a conflict of interests between private individuals, it was acting in a quasi-judicial manner and was thus required to extend procedural rights, such as affording the affected parties the opportunity to be heard.[3] Here the court frames the municipal council's duty in the following terms:

> In performing that duty councils are bound, like Courts of Justice, to see that every person interested is afforded full opportunity of presenting his views and contentions. The powers conferred on the council carry with them an obligation to see that every one affected gets British fair play, not only from the council itself when passing by-laws, but from its officers and committees in the preliminary steps leading up to the final result.[4]

The cases of *Wiswell v. Winnipeg (Metropolitan)*,[5] *Campeau Corp. v. Calgary (City)*[6] and *Homex Realty & Development Co. v. Wyoming (Village)*[7] all indicate that there is a duty to act fairly in considering certain zoning and subdivision matters. In the *Campeau* case, the Alberta Court of Appeal held that a municipal council acted unfairly in considering matters which were not raised at a public meeting and which were unrelated to staff recommendations. In the *Homex* case, Mr. Justice Estey stated, with respect to the deregistration of a plan of subdivision, that as a general proposition, wherever a statute authorizes the interference with property or other rights and is silent as to whether or not the agency in question is required to give notice prior to intervention in such rights, the Court will supply the omission of the Legislature and require the agency to afford the affected person an opportunity to be heard.[8] The Supreme Court of Canada held that in passing the deregistration by-law, Council's actions were not in substance legislative, but rather were quasi-judicial in character so as to attract the principle of notice and the consequential rule of *audi alterem partem*. The statute did not displace the common law rule by providing for the filing of a copy of the bylaw with the Minister, its registration in the registry office and the mailing of a copy to the registered owner of the land affected. The Council was acting in effect as the judge of its own actions in determining the outcome of its dispute with Homex.[9] While Homex had every reasonable opportunity to explain its refusal to install services, (a position which lead the municipality's decision to

2 [1928] 1 D.L.R. 952 (Ont. C.A.).
3 *Ibid.* at 966.
4 *Ibid.* at 969.
5 [1965] S.C.R. 512, 51 W.W.R. 513, 51 D.L.R. (2d) 754.
6 (1978), 8 M.P.L.R. 88, 7 Alta. L.R. (2d) 294, 12 A.R. 31 (C.A.).
7 [1980] 2 S.C.R. 1011, 13 M.P.L.R. 234, 116 D.L.R. (3d) 1, 33 N.R. 475.
8 *Ibid.* at 247 [M.P.L.R.].
9 *Ibid.* at 253 [M.P.L.R.].

deregister the plan of subdivision), it did not receive an opportunity to assess its final position on this matter in the face of the action of deregistration to be taken by the City, and it did not receive an opportunity to make known its position once fully aware of the Village's final position.[10] As a consequence, Estey J. found that the lack of notice requirements in the statutory framework did not serve to displace the common law requirements for notice.

These cases carve out one area where an individual has a right to notice and a hearing, if one is not provided by statute; that is, when individual rights are being affected by a decision of a local authority or when a quasi-judicial aspect of a decision can be found. They do not provide a right to be heard on all planning matters at the local level. For example, Estey J. notes that in the cases where the adoption of planning regulations "affecting a wide area comprising many different owners of land, [the planning authority] was acting in a purely legislative capacity."[11] Other kinds of municipal decisions that have also been found to require municipalities to act in accordance with the principles of natural justice include the issuance of licenses,[12] a by-law forfeiting a right of redemption respecting the payment of tax arrears,[13] and alteration of municipal boundaries.[14] All of these cases suggest that a central determinant of whether a municipality must act in accordance with the principles of natural justice will be the extent to which a municipal action implicates private rights, as opposed to those instances where the municipal decision is of a more general policy oriented nature.

What remains unclear is the content of the procedural rights that will be required. For example, where a municipality is said to be exercising a quasi-judicial function, what level of participatory rights will the affected party be accorded? The reliance by the majority in the *Homex* case on the distinction between legislative and quasi-judicial functions is noted by Dickson J., in a dissenting judgment, to be out of step with the Supreme Court's decisions in *Nicholson*[15] and *Martineau*[16] where the distinction between types of functions has been discarded in favour of a more flexible analysis based on a "duty of fairness." Here the level of procedural protection granted will depend very

10 *Ibid.*

11 *Ibid.* at 252 [M.P.L.R.], citing *Braeside Farms Ltd. v. Ontario (Treasurer)* (1978), 20 O.R. (2d) 541, 5 M.P.L.R. 181, 4 R.P.R. 165, 88 D.L.R. (3d) 267 (Div. Ct.) and *McMartin v. Vancouver (City)* (1968), 65 W.W.R. 385, 70 D.L.R. (2d) 38 (B.C. C.A.).

12 *Shields v. Vancouver (City)* (1991), 3 M.P.L.R. (2d) 48 (B.C. S.C.).

13 *Hershoran v. Windsor (City)* (1973), 1 O.R. (2d) 291, 40 D.L.R. (3d) 171 (Div. Ct.), affirmed (1974), 3 O.R. (2d) 423, 45 D.L.R. (3d) 533n (C.A.).

14 *Southampton (Village) v. Bruce (County)* (1904), 8 O.L.R. 664 (C.A.); see also *Barrick Gold Corp. v. Ontario (Minister of Municipal Affairs & Housing)* (2000), 193 D.L.R. (4th) 635 (Ont. C.A.).

15 *Nicholson v. Haldimand-Norfolk (Regional Municipality) Commissioners of Police* (1978), [1979] 1 S.C.R. 311, 78 C.L.L.C. 14,181, 23 N.R. 410, 88 D.L.R. (3d) 671.

16 *Martineau v. Matsqui Institution (No. 2)* (1979), [1980] 1 S.C.R. 602, 13 C.R. (3d) 1 (Eng.), 15 C.R. (3d) 315 (Fr.), 50 C.C.C. (2d) 353, 30 N.R. 119, 106 D.L.R. (3d) 385.

much on the nature of the rights at stake and the particular facts of the case.[17] Thus, even where a by-law has a broad public policy element, some level of procedural fairness may be required, if the actual effect of the by-law is to deprive a person of some pre-existing right or otherwise adversely affect them.[18]

The new approach incorporating the more contextual duty to be fair was applied in a municipal context by the Supreme Court of Canada in *Old St. Boniface Residents Assn. Inc. v. Winnipeg (City)*[19] Here the Court notes,

> The content of the rules of natural justice and procedural fairness were formerly determined according to the classification of the functions of the tribunal or other public body or official. This is no longer the case and the content of these rules is based on a number of factors including the terms of the statute pursuant to which it is seized and the type of decision it is called upon to make.[20]

As a result, the duty to act fairly is best seen as existing on a continuum whereby greater procedural protections shall be required for more intrusive municipal activity. There does remain in this formulation a strong bias in favour of the protection of private rights, particularly where municipalities are empowered to interfere with property rights.[21]

In this regard, it should be noted that the common law rules have been supplemented to a very large degree by statutory requirements for notice and opportunities to make representations. In some cases, statutory provisions give affected parties rights of a full hearing in front of council, with subsequent rights of appeal.[22] Otherwise, with respect to the legislative (public policy) functions of municipal council, the approach has been to mandate through legislation that municipalities conduct their affairs openly and provide the public with reasonable access to municipal documents. As these requirements are central to the democratic functioning of local government, they are examined in some detail below.

---

17 For criticism of the distinction between legislative and quasi-judicial functions see Jones and deVillars, *supra* note 1 at 185-193.

18 *Homex, supra* note 7, at 271 [M.P.L.R.].

19 (1990), [1990] 3 S.C.R. 1170, 46 Admin L.R. 161, 2 M.P.L.R. (2d) 217, [1991] 2 W.W.R. 145, 75 D.L.R. (4th) 385.

20 *Ibid.* at 236 [M.P.L.R.].

21 This privileging of property rights is particularly evident, for example, in Dickson's dissent in *Homex, supra* note 7, who notes that the procedural rights arise "from the fact that the by-law interferes, in particular, with private property rights of this one owner," at 268 [M.P.L.R.].

22 See for example, *Development Charges Act, 1997,* S.O. 1997, c. 27, ss. 12-18, providing for public meeting in front of council and right of appeal to Ontario Municipal Board respecting the passage of a Development Charges By-law.

C. OPEN MEETINGS AND ACCESS TO INFORMATION

Central to the common law duty of fairness is that the right to procedural fairness is premised on the existence of some particular effect on the right holder. As a consequence, where the municipality is acting in a legislative fashion and their actions are not directed or do not implicate the rights of a particular person, then the municipality owes no common law duty of procedural fairness. This absence of a duty to act fairly under certain circumstances is evident in situations where persons have sought information from the municipality or the right to attend council meetings. In these circumstances, the common law has afforded no remedy to those seeking disclosure or the right to attend council meetings. For example, in *Tenby v. Mason,*[23] a municipality sought to prevent a journalist from attending, without council's permission, meetings of the council. The Court held that the municipality was within its rights to do so, noting that the common law provides no right of access to council proceedings.

The *Tenby* case was adopted in Canada in *Journal Printing Co. v. McVeity,* where it was held that the right to information and to attend meetings at the local level is solely determined by statute.[24] Without legislation there is no public right to attendance at meetings of local authorities or access to any information.[25] With respect to attendance at meetings the courts have stated; "*Prima facie*, the constituent has no right of access to the meetings of the deliberative body."[26] Beyond statutory requirements, "the giving of information rests entirely in the discretion of the municipal authorities."[27] Therefore, without legislation, the decision of what is open or closed, available or restricted, is at the discretion of the municipality and various local authorities. In *McAuliffe v. Toronto (Metropolitan) Commissioners of Police*, which involved a request for access to internal police regulations, the court noted that the public interest in ensuring public scrutiny of municipal actions through access to information must be balanced with efficiency and the need, in this case, for police business to be held in confidence. However, the determination of that balance was a matter for the legislature, not the courts:

> In the absence of a statutory authority requiring that the desired information be made available to the public, there is no power in this Court to order it to be made available to the public. It is, perhaps, not superfluous to say that a board of commissioners of police can best retain the confidence of the public by

23 [1908] 1 Ch. 457 (Ch. Div.).

24 (1915), 33 O.L.R. 166, 21 D.L.R. 81 (C.A.), at 174 [O.L.R.], *per* Falconbridge C.J.K.B.

25 All local authorities are the creation of statute and any general requirement to disclose information or any general right to attend meetings, therefore, must be found in statute. See *McAuliffe v. Toronto (Metropolitan) Commissioners of Police* (1975), 9 O.R. (2d) 583, 61 D.L.R. (3d) 223 (Div. Ct.).

26 *Journal Printing, supra* note 24, at 172 [O.L.R.], *per* Middleton J.

27 *Ibid*. at 170.

> making available to members of the public all information relating to the government and operation of a police force except that with respect to which secrecy essential for properly carrying out the duties of such force.[28]

Here, despite the Court's recognition that transparency in government proceedings and operations is crucial to maintaining legitimacy, the Court felt that requiring open local government was a matter for the legislature not the courts. Ultimately, the provincial legislatures did respond to the demand for open government, resulting in statutory provisions mandating access to public meetings and providing for access to information held by municipal corporations.

1. Open Meetings

The statutory requirement for open municipal meetings in Ontario is typical. Section 239 of the *Municipal Act* (Ontario),[29] which is similar to what is found in the Acts of other provinces,[30] provides:

> 238 (1) In this section and in section 239,
>
> "committee" means any advisory or other committee, subcommittee or similar entity of which at least 50 per cent of the members are also members of one or more councils or local boards;
>
> "local board" does not include police services boards or public library boards;
>
> "meeting" means any regular, special, committee or other meeting of a council or local board.
>
> 239 (1) Except as provided in this section, all meetings shall be open to the public.
>
> (2) A meeting or part of a meeting may be closed to the public if the subject matter being considered is,

---

28 *Supra* note 25, at 596 [O.R.].

29 *Municipal Act, 2001*, S.O. 2001, c. 25.

30 See for example the *Municipal Government Act*, R.S.A. 2000, c. M-26, s. 198; the *Local Government Act*, R.S.B.C. 1996 c. 323, s. 242.1; *The Municipal Government Act*, S.N.S. 1998, c. 18, s. 22; the *Cities and Towns Act*, R.S.Q. 2003, c. C-19, s. 322; the *Urban Municipality Act, 1984*, S.S. 1983-84, c. U-11, s. 45; and the *Rural Municipality Act, 1989*, S.S. 1989-90, c. R-26.1, s. 37.

(a) the security of the property of the municipality or local board;
(b) personal matters about an identifiable individual, including municipal or local board employees;
(c) a proposed or pending acquisition or disposition of land by the municipality or local board;
(d) labour relations or employee negotiations;
(e) litigation or potential litigation, including matters before administrative tribunals, affecting the municipality or local board;
(f) advice that is subject to solicitor-client privilege, including communications necessary for that purpose;
(g) a matter in respect of which a council, board, committee or other body may hold a closed meeting under another Act.

(3) A meeting shall be closed to the public if the subject matter relates to the consideration of a request under the *Municipal Freedom of Information and Protection of Privacy Act* if the council, board, commission or other body is the head of an institution for the purposes of that Act.

(4) Before holding a meeting or part of a meeting that is to be closed to the public, a municipality or local board or committee of either of them shall state by resolution,

(a) the fact of the holding of the closed meeting; and
(b) the general nature of the matter to be considered at the closed meeting.

(5) Subject to subsection (6), a meeting shall not be closed to the public during a vote.

(6) Despite section 244, a meeting may be closed to the public during a vote if,

(a) subsection (2) or (3) permits or requires a meeting to be closed to the public; and
(b) the vote is for a procedural matter or for giving directions or instructions to officers, employees or agents of the municipality, local board or committee of either of them or persons retained by or under contract with the municipality or local board.

The structure of the open meeting requirements seeks to maintain the balance between the public's right to attend meetings and the municipality's right to maintain confidentiality of its proceedings where a lack of confidentiality would impede in some serious fashion the interests of the municipality. One important feature of the open meeting provisions is that committee meetings must also be held in public. This prevents councils from avoiding their responsibilities to conduct their affairs openly by discussing matters as committee of the whole in private session.[31] Moreover, the requirement that before a meeting can be held *in camera* council must state the nature of the matters to be discussed, clearly puts the onus on council to justify its decision to move into private session and creates a public record of the decision to do so.

Determining what constitutes a "meeting" that is subject to the open meeting requirements is not always straightforward. For example, when a municipal council held an off-site "retreat," but the matters dealt with at the retreat were considered to be within the scope of matters normally addressed by council, the closed nature of the meeting was found to have offended the open meeting provisions.[32] The failure to adhere to the open meeting requirements has the effect of nullifying the proceedings and making void any by-laws or resolutions enacted in conjunction with a flawed procedure.[33]

2. Access to Information

Like the open meeting requirements, access to information in municipal government and municipal bodies has been substantially changed by the enactment of statutory regimes respecting access to information. In Ontario, the law governing access to information is contained within the *Municipal Freedom of Information and Protection of Privacy Act*.[34] As the name of the Act suggests, in addition to providing the rules under which municipalities shall be required to disclose certain information in its possession, the Act also requires municipalities to keep certain personal information it may have confidential. The structure of the Act provides a broad right of access to "records" under control of the "institution."[35] Both the terms "record" and "institution" are broadly defined. A record means "any record of information however recorded," including computer records. The definition of institution

---

31 Earlier versions of this section only restricted the activities of council itself and, as a result, it was not uncommon for municipalities to resolve in a committee of the whole (a general committee which includes all members of council) to discuss matters *in camera*. See Stanley Makuch in "Freedom of Information and Local Government" in *Freedom of Information: Canadian Perspectives*, J.D. McCamus ed. (Butterworths, 1981).

32 *Southam Inc. v. Ottawa (City)* (1991), 5 O.R. (3d) 726 (Div. Ct.); see also *Economic Development Committee of Hamilton-Wentworth (Regional Municipality), Re* (1988), 40 M.P.L.R. 1, 33 Admin. L.R. 125, 30 O.A.C. 39 (C.A.), leave to appeal refused (1989), 102 N.R. 238 (note) (S.C.C.); but see *Vanderkloet v. Leeds & Grenville (County) Board of Education* (1985), 51 O.R. (2d) 577, 30 M.P.L.R. 230 (C.A.), leave to appeal refused (1986), 54 O.R. (2d) 352n (S.C.C.), where informal discussions among Board members were found not to offend open meeting requirements.

33 *Economic Development Committee of Hamilton-Wentworth (Regional Municipality), Re*, *ibid.*

34 R.S.O. 1990, c. M.56.

35 *Ibid.* at s. 4.

goes beyond the municipal corporation itself and includes school boards, police commissions, conservation authorities and the like.[36]

The Act also sets out a number of exemptions to the right of access.[37] Some of the exemptions are broadly drawn themselves leaving considerable discretion in the hands of municipal officials to determine whether access to a particular record should be granted. For example, the exemptions include records revealing "advice or recommendations,"[38] records that may reasonably be expected to interfere with law enforcement matters, confidential material received from other government branches, commercial information, information subject to solicitor and client privilege and personal information.[39] Many of the exemptions are also subject to a broad public interest test, whereby the exemption can be overridden "if a compelling public interest in the disclosure of the record clearly outweighs the purpose of the exemption."[40] The Act also prescribes a detailed access to information procedure, including a right of appeal to a provincially appointed Commissioner.[41] While all provinces, except Prince Edward Island, have access to information legislation, only Alberta, British Columbia, Manitoba, Quebec and Saskatchewan extend access obligation to municipal corporations under their provincial access to information legislation[42] or, in the case of Saskatchewan, by specific legislation.[43] In all cases, the open meeting and access to information requirements are cross-referenced so that access can be denied to material subject to an authorized closed meeting.[44]

3. Conflict of Interest Rules

As noted in the introduction to this chapter, traditionally the rules of natural justice also include a general rule against bias in decision-makers, (captured by the latin maxim, *nemo judex in sua causa*). This rule, in general administrative law, requires a high standard of impartiality on the part of

36 *Ibid.* at s. 2.

37 *Ibid.* at ss. 6-15.

38 *Ibid.* at s. 7, although here there are also exceptions to the exemption to limit the broad scope of this exemption.

39 *Ibid.* at ss. 8-14.

40 *Ibid.* at s. 16.

41 *Ibid.* at ss. 17-23, and Part III.

42 *Freedom of Information and Protection of Privacy Act (Alberta),* R.S.A. 2000, c. F-25; *Freedom of Information and Protection of Privacy Act (British Columbia)*, R.S.B.C. 1996, c.165; *Freedom of Information and Protection of Privacy Act (Manitoba)*, S.M. 1997, c. 50; *An Act Respecting Access to Documents Held By Public Bodies and the Protection of Personal Information (Quebec)*, R.S.Q., c. A-2.1.

43 *Local Authority Freedom of Information and Protection of Privacy Act*, S.S. 1990-91, c.L-27.1.

44 See for example *supra* notes 34, 42 and 43, Alberta, s. 23; British Columbia, s. 12(3),(4); Ontario, s. 6; Saskatchewan, s. 15.

decision-makers as part of the requirement for procedural fairness.[45] Here the law respecting bias was often said to involve two distinct considerations. Firstly, a decision-maker would be disqualified where he or she had a direct pecuniary interest in a matter to be decided. Secondly, flowing from the idea that justice be seen to be done, there must also be no "reasonable apprehension of bias."[46] In both cases, the test is an objective one, in the sense that reviewing courts are not making an inquiry into whether the decision-maker was in fact biased, but rather, whether certain conditions or circumstances were present such that a reasonably well-informed person would conclude that the interests of the decision-maker might influence the exercise of his or her duty.[47]

This is another way in which the process of municipal decision-making is regulated. Legislation in this area can be seen as a deterrence to corruption. Equally important, however, it has been seen as an attempt to ensure decisions are free from bias, and "fair" in the sense of responding appropriately to the concerns of the electorate.

There are a number of ways in which conflicts of interest are regulated at the municipal level. The common law governs municipal office holders, as does the *Criminal Code*[48] and, most importantly, conflict of interest legislation. The latter legislation varies from province to province, and in some cases from municipality to municipality, in both stringency and complexity. While some provinces have enacted specific conflict of interest legislation, other provinces have included provisions dealing with conflict of interest within the general municipal statutes. At the heart is the view that a local political decision-maker should not be influenced in his voting by having a personal interest in the matter being voted on. While a councillor has a right to express his or her ideas, and members of Council and the public have a right to hear these ideas, the conflict of interest provisions place reasonable restrictions on members of council for the protection of society, and as such, are demonstratively justified in a free and democratic society, and therefore do not conflict with the *Charter of Rights and Freedoms*.[49]

Both the *Criminal Code* and conflict of interest legislation are superimposed on the common law; as a result, the law relating to fiduciaries forms part of the law relating to municipal councillors. Councillors are not only "directors" of the municipal corporations but they are also public trustees,

---

45 See for example, *Energy Probe v. Canada (Atomic Energy Control Board)* (1984), 8 D.L.R. (4th) 735 (Fed. T.D.), reversed (1984), 15 D.L.R. (4th) 48 (Fed. C.A.), leave to appeal refused (1985), 15 D.L.R. (4th) 48n (S.C.C.) ("I have no doubt that the duty to act fairly as enunciated by the Supreme Court in the *Nicholson* case must include a requirement for an unbiased decision-maker. Any other conclusion would undercut the whole concept of the requirement of a duty of fairness," per Reed J., at para. 14).

46 *R. v. S. (R.D.)* (1997), 151 D.L.R. (4th) 193 (S.C.C.); see also *Committee for Justice & Liberty v. Canada (National Energy Board)* (1976), [1978] 1 S.C.R. 369.

47 *Old St. Boniface Residents Assn., supra* note 19.

48 R.S.C. 1985, c. C-46, as amended, ss. 121-126.

49 See *Stubbs v. Greenough* (1984), 25 M.P.L.R. 26 (N.S. T.D.).

and therefore owe fiduciary duties to their corporation and their community.[50] Members of local boards are in a similar position. A municipality can, as a result, seek an accounting of any profit made but no constructive trust for an improper profit can exist unless the profit was made "by reason and only by reason of the fact" that the councillor occupied a public office.[51]

Where a public official's personal interests may, or may appear to, conflict with his public duties, there is a breach of fiduciary duty notwithstanding the lack of any actual bias or improper motive. There is also the rule of equity that a trustee cannot profit from his position. This profit rule is analogous to the conflicts rule[52] and is especially forceful in a public official's case since that position is conferred by the public for public purposes only.

The *Criminal Code*, as indicated, also regulates municipal conflict of interest through the creation of certain offences. These include bribery or the acceptance of bribes, fraud or breach of trust by a public official in connection with his or her public duties, the selling or purchasing of offices, and the influencing or negotiating of appointments.[53]

In addition to common law and *Criminal Code* provisions there are legislated conflict of interest provisions for local governments. As indicated, the rationales for additional legislation are fairly clear. There are general notions of justice, such as the principles that no one can be a judge in his own case[54] and that no one can serve two masters,[55] but another perhaps more important consideration is the value of public confidence in local public officials and institutions.

The local politician has traditionally been free from the checks of political party affiliation and has, at least theoretically, retained greater discretion in voting than provincial or federal politicians. The confusion and lack of focus of power at the municipal level and the rule against delegation mean, as has been seen, that all important decisions are made at the council, board or commission level and yet there is little review or scrutiny, through the local political process, of those decisions; conflict of interest rules are of crucial importance at the local level. Moreover, local council or board members usually have other sources of income to supplement their municipal

---

50 See *Toronto (City) v. Bowes* (1858), 11 Moo. P.C. 463, 14 E.R. 770 (Canada P.C.); *Hawrelak v. Edmonton (City)* (1975), [1976] 1 S.C.R. 387, [1975] 4 W.W.R. 561, 54 D.L.R. (3d) 45, 4 N.R. 197.

51 *Hawrelak, ibid.* at 572 [W.W.R.], quoting Lord Russell of Killowen in *Regal (Hastings) Ltd. v. Gulliver*, [1942] 1 All E.R. 378 (H.L.), at 389.

52 McClean, "The Theoretical Basis of the Trustee's Duty of Loyalty" (1969) 7 Alta. L. Rev. 218.

53 *Supra* note 48.

54 *Benedict v. Ontario* (2000), 193 D.L.R. (4th) 329 (Ont. C.A.); see also *Winnipeg Child & Family Services (Central Area) v. W. (K.L.)* (2000), 191 D.L.R. (4th) 1 (S.C.C.); *R. v. Bow Street Metropolitan Stipendiary Magistrate*, [1999] 1 All E.R. 577 (H.L.).

55 *Moll v. Fisher* (1979), 8 M.P.L.R. 266, 23 O.R. (2d) 609, 96 D.L.R. (3d) 506 (Div. Ct.), at 269 [M.P.L.R.] *per* Robins J.

remuneration, particularly in smaller communities, which increases the potential for conflicts of interest.

There are basically two ways in which the legislated conflict of interest provisions deal with the problem. One is to disqualify anyone with a conflicting interest from seeking or holding public office. This is basically a codification of the law relating to fiduciaries. An example can be seen in the case of *R. v. Wheeler*,[56] involving the *Moncton Consolidation Act* which provided in part, "a person shall be disqualified from being elected and from being a councillor, if and while he ... had directly or indirectly, by himself or his partner, any share or interest in any contract or employment with, by, or on behalf of the council."[57] The other is to allow such persons to hold their positions as long as they comply with rules compelling disclosure of their conflict and that they abstain from discussing or voting on the matter.

The latter approach, relatively recently adopted throughout Canada,[58] has been in effect in Britain since 1933[59] and also in many American jurisdictions.[60] The basic tenets are timely disclosures of the interest, abstaining from discussion and from voting on the matter out of which the conflict of interest arose, and penalties such as vacating seats and prohibitions from running for office for a certain number of years. In the Ontario Act, a prohibition from holding office may be imposed for up to seven years.[61]

In the Alberta *Municipal Government Act*, both approaches are evident.[62] Under s. 174(1)(h), a councillor is disqualified from council if he or she "has a pecuniary interest in an agreement that is not binding on the municipality under section 173," which means any agreement, unless the agreement is for work in an emergency, is for the sale of goods or services at a competitive price by a dealer in those goods or services that is incidental to or in the ordinary course of the business, the agreement is approved by council before being signed by the municipality, or entered into before the term of the councillor.[63] However, there are also obligations of disclosure and abstention from voting and participation in respect of matters where a councillor has a pecuniary interest.[64] Therefore, a councillor is automatically disqualified for conflicts of interest of the narrower kinds in s. 173, but may escape disqualification in respect of more general interests as listed in s. 170(1), if disclosure provisions are complied with.

---

56 [1979] 2 S.C.R. 650, (1979), 9 M.P.L.R. 161 (S.C.C.).

57 *Moncton Consolidation Act*, S.N.B. 1946 c. 101, s. 12.

58 Beginning with Ontario in 1972 in the *Municipal Conflict of Interest Act*, S.O. 1972, c. 142.

59 *Local Government Act, 1933* (1933, c. 51).

60 See "Privacy Limits on Financial Disclosure Laws: Pruning *Plante v. Gonzalez*" (1970) 54 N.Y.U.L. Rev. 601; and Freilich and Larson, "Conflict of Interest: a Model Statutory Proposal for the Regulation of Municipal Transactions" (1970) 38 U.M.K.C. L. Rev. 373 at 384-390.

61 *Municipal Conflict of Interest Act*, R.S.O. 1990, c. M.50, s. 10(1)(b).

62 *Municipal Government Act*, R.S.A. 2000, c. M-26, ss. 171-172, and 174(1)(h).

63 *Ibid.* at s. 173.

64 *Ibid.* at s. 172.

The disclosure approach to conflict of interests allows people with possibly conflicting interests to sit on council as long as they comply with disclosure and abstention from discussion requirements. This approach is more workable for both councillors and electors. Minor or narrow interests, if properly disclosed, will not disable a member from the whole range of duties entrusted to him or her by virtue of public office. The publicity will enable electors to make an informed judgment and express their tolerance or intolerance of the interest held by the local member. The publicity of disclosure replaces disqualification as a check on conflicts of interest.

The Ontario *Municipal Conflict of Interest Act* (enacted in 1972) is the oldest example of this British approach in Canada.[65] In it, the nature of the interests covered is widely defined, but the means of avoiding a conflict, through a declaration and abstention, are simple. Moreover, there is wide discretion given to the court in the imposition of penalties to reflect that wide definition. The Act, therefore, appears to balance the imposition of a very wide definition of conflict of interest with suitable methods to avoid a conflict and prevent harsh penalties.

The scope of the Act is determined by the definitions of "council," "local board" and "municipality" found in s. 1. It includes virtually any body exercising statutory authority over municipal affairs. A few other jurisdictions have rules applying only to councillors or other boards, while some also include municipal employees. The wider coverage is desirable since many local boards carry out important functions and make important decisions.[66] Furthermore, high-ranking administrative officers or employees of the municipality also exercise important powers justifying their regulation as well. It is these officials who may exercise a disproportionately high level of power and discretion without being subjected to public exposure as a result of the under inclusive legislation.[67] It can be argued that their position of "trust" can be regulated by their employment contract or by by-laws passed by council and that different rules and sanctions should be tailored for them since they carry out their functions differently from councils and local boards. However, even this is not done as a matter of practice.

The Ontario Act[68] covers direct as well as indirect pecuniary interests. A duty is imposed by s. 5 to disclose any pecuniary interest, direct or indirect,

---

65 Now, R.S.O. 1990, c. M.50. This Act was to be repealed and replaced by the *Local Government Disclosure of Interest Act*. However, on April 13, 1995, a proclamation was issued revoking the previous proclamation which would have repealed the *Municipal Conflict of Interest Act*, just two days prior to the date of repeal.

66 See for example, *Edmonton (City) v. Purves* (1982), 18 M.P.L.R. 221, 19 Alta. L.R. (2d) 319, 37 A.R. 376, 136 D.L.R. (3d) 340 (Q.B.), where the Court held that s. 30, the conflict of interest section of the *Municipal Government Act, Alberta,* governs only council meetings and not board of commissioners meetings.

67 Currently Prince Edward Island (*Municipalities Act*, R.S.P.E.I. 1988, c. M-13) limits regulation to members of council. Alberta regulates councillors and members of the Assessment Review Board, *Municipal Government Act*, s. 169 and s. 480.

68 *Supra* note 61.

in any matter where the member is present at a meeting of the council or local board at which the matter is the subject of consideration. A definition of indirect pecuniary interest is found in s. 2 of the Act:

> 2. For the purposes of this Act, a member shall be deemed to have an indirect pecuniary interest in a matter in which a council or board is concerned, if,
>
> (a) the member or his or her nominee,
>
> (i) is a shareholder in, or a director or senior officer of, a corporation that does not offer its securities to the public,
> (ii) has a controlling interest in, or is a director or senior officer of, a corporation that offers its securities to the public,[69]
> (iii) is a member of a body, that has a pecuniary interest in the matter; or
>
> (b) the member is a partner of a person or is in the employment of a person or body that has a pecuniary interest in the matter.

Section 3 of the Act broadens the application even further, providing that the pecuniary interest of a parent or spouse, same-sex partner or any child of the member shall, if known to the member, be deemed to also be a pecuniary interest of the member. [70]

The courts have struggled with the basic issue of whether an interest is pecuniary or not. It would appear that any matter which can affect the member's (or his associate's, as the case may be) financial assets or income can give rise to a pecuniary interest. A pecuniary interest has been found concerning the creation of an access road to land owned by the son of a council member, in which the member was a co-mortgagor.[71] As well as for an application for the establishment of a recreational facility, when the neigh-

---

69 A "controlling interest" is defined in s. 1 as:

> In subsection (3), "controlling interest" means the interest that a person has in a corporation when the person beneficially owns, directly or indirectly, or exercises control or direction over, equity shares of the corporation carrying more than 10 per cent of the voting rights attached to all equity shares of the corporation for the time being outstanding.

70 Similar consideration of the interests of family members is contained in s. 5(1)(b) of the British Columbia *Financial Disclosure Act*, R.S.B.C. 1996, c. 139; s. 90.2 of the New Brunswick *Municipalities Act*, R.S.N.B. 1973, c. M-22; s. 207(d) of the Newfoundland *Municipalities Act, 1999*, S.N.L. 1999, c. M-24; s. 170(1)(b) of the Alberta *Municipal Government Act*, R.S.A. 2000, s. M-26; s. 5(1) of the Manitoba *Municipal Council Conflict of Interest Act*, C.C.S.M. c. M255; and s. 31(b) of the Saskatchewan *Urban Municipality Act, 1984*, S.S. 1983-1984, c. U-11.

71 *Russell v. Toney* (1982), 137 D.L.R. (3d) 202 (Alta. C.A.).

bouring business was owned by a councillor.[72] However, the mere fact of making a campaign contribution is not enough to create an indirect pecuniary interest. In *King v. Nanaimo (City)*,[73] the British Columbia Supreme Court found that a council member had a pecuniary interest in respect of voting for projects being undertaken by companies that had made contributions to his election campaign, even though he did not expect any financial gain as a result of the vote. The court held that an "indirect connection between the donation and the votes," even though it was a past contribution and a later vote, was sufficient for finding the existence of an indirect financial interest. In overturning this decision, the British Columbia Court of Appeal held that the contribution did not, in and of itself, create a pecuniary interest although there could be circumstances in which the contribution and the "matter" could be so linked as to justify a conclusion that the contribution created a pecuniary interest in the matter.[74] Such a clear link is important because developers frequently make contributions to more than one candidate, or even to all candidates. If the interpretation of pecuniary interest is too broad, an entire council could be prevented from dealing with particular matters.[75]

Interests of spouses often trap local members and have led to many of the cases; two cases which involved teachers' contracts reached opposite results. In *DeVita v. Coburn*,[76] a councillor whose husband was a high school teacher did not participate in negotiations for a new contract but voted in favour of the general municipal budget, which included teachers' salaries, without disclosing her interest. The judge noted that the fact of her husband being a teacher was well known and found that her vote on the budget had no effect on her interest since the salaries were determined before the budget meeting. He stated that an elected representative should not be lightly unseated and the Act was not contravened.[77] Alternatively, it was a technical contravention committed through inadvertence and no penalty should be imposed. It was also pointed out that the applicant wished to unseat the councillor in order to run himself for the vacant seat.

In *Moll v. Fisher*,[78] the reasoning was more detailed and satisfactory. Two school trustees who voted for a secondary school teachers' contract had spouses who were elementary school teachers. The Divisional Court relied upon evidence that there was a real connection between terms in elementary

---

72 *Cornwallis (Municipality) v. Selent* (1998), 47 M.P.L.R. (2d) 277 (Man. C.A.); see also *Costello v. Barr* (1998), 118 O.A.C. 145 (Div. Ct.) relating to the ownership of land adjacent to property proposed for waste disposal site; see also *Arbez v. Johnson* (1998), 159 D.L.R. (4th) 611 (Man. C.A.), leave to appeal refused (1998), [1998] S.C.C.A. No. 375, 236 N.R. 381 (note) (S.C.C.).

73 (1999), 50 M.P.L.R. (2d) 134 (B.C. S.C.), reversed (2001), 24 M.P.L.R. (3d) 1 (B.C. C.A.).

74 *Ibid.* at 6.

75 See G. Cockrill, "Campaign Contributions Create Pecuniary Conflict of Interest in British Columbia, (1999) 5 D.M.P.L. 17.

76 *DeVita v. Coburn* (1977), 15 O.R. (2d) 769, 77 D.L.R. (3d) 311 (Co. Ct.).

77 *Ibid.* at 772 [O.R.].

78 *Supra* note 55.

and secondary school teachers' contracts. It construed the Act broadly in a manner consistent with its purpose.

A common exception to the definition of pecuniary interest is those interests that are in common with electors generally.[79] This principle is also contained in the common law. The basic common law position was expressed in *L'Abbé v. Blind River (Village)*[80] and reaffirmed in *Blustein, Re*.[81] A councillor is disqualified from voting if he or she has a special and personal interest distinct from that of the inhabitants generally. In other words, there is no disqualification if the interest is shared with the public generally. It is not the matter that is to be considered, but rather the pecuniary interest in that matter which is considered in determining whether there is an interest in common.[82] Furthermore, the pecuniary interest must be different in kind and not merely in degree.[83]

In the case of *Ennismore (Township), Re*,[84] the municipality brought an application to determine whether a member of the municipal council, who owned property within a certain area that was the subject of a study and possible construction of a communal water supply system, had a conflict of interest. The Court considered the defense of whether the interest in the water supply system was different from that of other electors who where also affected by the issue and applied a two step test: (1) does the member of council have a pecuniary interest in the matter being considered; and if yes, (2) is it different in kind and not merely in degree, from any pecuniary interest that those electors affected by the matter have? In finding that the councillor did not have a conflict of interest, the Court referred to *Jackson v. Wall*,[85] which stands for the common law principle that where a project is of great community interest, it can override any coincidental interest or benefit that the member of council may have.

The whole issue of the scope of interests to be caught is an interesting one. The requirement that the interest be pecuniary recognizes that a presumption of bias can easily be made if the person has a private financial stake in the matter. Such a presumption may be equally justified in the case of sentimental or relational interests such as the pecuniary interests of close friends or relatives.

---

79 See for example in Ontario s. 4(j) of the *Municipal Conflict of Interest Act*, R.S.O. 1990, c. M.50; in Manitoba see s. 4(5)(a) of *The Municipal Council Conflict of Interest Act*, C.C.S.M. c. M255; and in Newfoundland see s. 207(4) of the *Municipalities Act, 1999*, S.N.L. 1999, c. M-24.

80 (1904), 7 O.L.R. 230 (C.A.).

81 [1967] 1 O.R. 604, 61 D.L.R. (2d) 659 (H.C.), affirmed [1967] 1 O.R. 609n, 61 D.L.R. (2d) 664n (C.A.).

82 *Ennismore (Township), Re* (1996), 31 M.P.L.R. (2d) 1 (Ont. Gen. Div.).

83 *Ibid.*

84 *Ibid.*

85 (1978), 21 O.R. (2d) 147 (Co. Ct.). See also *Edwards v. Wilson* (1980), 11 M.P.L.R. 171 (Ont. Co. Ct.), affirmed (1980), 31 O.R. (2d) 442 (Div. Ct.).

Bias can also result from purely personal interests not reasonably reducible to any financial gain. However, not all biases or appearances thereof are prohibited. After all, in a wide sense, candidates receive votes on the basis of their declared biases, such as a devotion to a certain political outlook,[86] or other interests such as a particular religion or a concern for working mothers. Such biases go beyond the private gain of the member though they may constitute a personal interest. The requirement of some pecuniary factor appears to draw a reasonable and workable line between "conflicts" which should be caught and those which should not. While there may exist some unacceptable biases which do not involve direct or indirect pecuniary, perhaps the most that can be done is to leave them up to the individual councillor to decide whether to disclose, being mindful of the adverse publicity which could result from a discovered concealment.

If the law is to extend further into the conduct of councillors and local board members, there must be an accompanying concern for the members' ability to learn of, and comply with the obligations. Section 209 of the Newfoundland *Municipalities Act, 1999* contains an interesting provision in which a councillor who is in doubt as to whether a conflict of interest exists must still disclose and let council decide.[87] Although this leads to certainty of obligations, it is a questionable manner of determining matters since the council may decide the matter for improper reasons.

The type of disclosure required is also an important issue. In Ontario, every declaration of interest and the general nature of the interest shall be recorded in the minutes of the meeting, or where the meeting is not open to the public, in the minutes of the next meeting that is open to the public.[88] In Manitoba, the disclosure of a pecuniary interest made during a meeting shall be recorded by the clerk of the meeting and filed with the clerk of the municipality.[89] The clerk of every municipality is required to keep a central record for this information, which is open to the public for inspection.[90] Many provinces require written disclosure of the interest, which enables the public to gain access to information on the frequency and nature of conflicting interests which may be held by its elected representatives. The rationale behind disclosure is the natural check which publicity provides.

British Columbia, New Brunswick, Newfoundland and Saskatchewan similarly require councillors to register a statement of their financial inter-

86 See, for example, the treatment of bias in the *Old St. Boniface* case, *supra* note 19, where the Court acknowledges that elected representatives have views and that this does not automatically constitute bias.

87 The *Municipal Act, 1999*, S.N.L. 1999, c. M-24. See also s. 90.4(4) of the New Brunswick *Municipalities Act*, C.S.N.B. c. M-22.

88 Section 6, *Municipal Conflict of Interest Act,* R.S.O. 1990, c. M.50; see also s. 208 of the *Newfoundland Municipalities Act*, 1999, S.N.L. 1999, c. M-24.

89 *The Municipal Council Conflict of Interest Act*, C.C.S.M. c. M255, s. 6.

90 *Ibid.*

ests.[91] Some cities have by-laws requiring registration of certain interests, especially real estate in the city.[92]

The countervailing argument against more disclosure is that privacy rights of councillors or board members must be protected. It may be too much to require disclosure of the specific details or dollar value of the interest. It is appropriate to ensure that the privacy rights of councillors is balanced with the right of the public to ensure unbiased decision-makers. Registration acts as a supplement to oral disclosure. It protects the councillor from allegations of cover-up and informs the public, and also serves as an advance check on potential improper action by the councillor. However, depending upon the nature of the disclosure required, it may be too great an invasion of privacy and it may deter potential candidates, especially in smaller communities. In response, perhaps those who seek or accept public office must be taken to accept the encroachment of public rights against their own private ones.

There are several listed exceptions to the disclosure requirements in the Ontario Act. These include the common sense one of interests arising solely from being a director or senior officer of a corporation incorporated for the purpose of carrying on business for the municipality or local board or by reason only of the member being a member of a board, commission, or other body as an appointee of a council or local board.[93] Such interests embody public duties similar to those of the member as a councillor or board member and any conflict must be accepted since private or personal interests are not involved.

Another necessary category of exception is one applying to voting on an election or appointment to fill a vacancy or position on the council or board and to voting on remuneration for the members,[94] as well as for interests which are so remote or insignificant that it cannot reasonably be regarded to influence the member.[95] In Manitoba, members are presumed not to have a pecuniary interest unless the value is $500 or more.[96] In the absence of an exemption to this effect, any interest, however slight, can disqualify a councillor, as the magnitude of the interest has been considered irrelevant.[97] A profit of $300 has been held sufficient for a significant interest.[98]

The majority of legislation provides for certain factors to be considered

---

91 See the *Financial Disclosure Act*, R.S.B.C. 1996 c.139, first enacted as the *Public Officials and Employees Disclosure Act*, S.B.C. 1974 c. 73; *Municipalities Act*, R.S.N.B., 1973, c. M-22 s. 90.4(1); *Municipalities Act, 1999*, S.N.L. 1999, c. M-24, s. 210; and *The Urban Municipality Act, 1984*, S.S. 1983-84, c. U-11, s. 32, which requires the disclosure of land and buildings holdings.

92 *Municipal Government Act*, R.S.A. 2000, c. M-26, s. 171.

93 *Municipal Conflict of Interest Act*, R.S.O. 1990, c. M.50, s. 4(h).

94 *Ibid.* at ss. 4 (g) and (i).

95 *Ibid.* at s. 4(k).

96 *The Municipal Council Conflict of Interest Act*, C.C.S.M. c.M255, s. 4(5)(c).

97 *Mino v. D'Arcey* (1991), 2 O.R. (3d) 678 (Gen. Div.), additional reasons at (1991), 2 O.R. (3d) 678 at 685 (Gen. Div.).

98 *Ibid.*

in sentencing, such as inadvertence, error, or honest mistake.[99] In *Cornwallis (Municipality) v. Selent*,[100] the Manitoba Court of Appeal considered the meaning of inadvertence and held that if a councillor is cognizant of the applicable legislation and recognizes the possibility of a potential conflict of interest, then the decision to participate in the proceedings cannot be considered inadvertence. In this case the councillor had concluded, wrongfully, that he was not in a conflict of interest position.

The Ontario Act, upon a finding that a member has contravened the Act, requires the member's seat to be declared vacant.[101] In addition, the judge may disqualify the member for a period of time, not exceeding seven years, as well as order restitution.[102] The majority of the conflict of interest legislation provides for disqualifying members, as well as the payment of fines or restitution. This has a strong deterrent effect but a correspondingly drastic impact on the councillor's constituency. When a seat is vacated, a by-election is usually needed, which can be very costly.

Restitution and fines represent a middle ground in which some flexibility exists. Another "middle ground" option is suspension from office for a short period of time. There is concern over the effect of long suspensions on quorum, especially in small councils or boards. The other obvious reason for concern is that with elected bodies, the citizens are entitled to representation, and suspension, no matter how short, infringes upon this right. In practice though, a new election will leave the constituents without a representative for a long time, too. It must be recognized, however, that suspension generally will not be a sufficient deterrent and would deprive the constituents without giving them a chance to get someone new in the position.

The effectiveness of the rules as a deterrent depends not only upon the nature of the sanctions but also upon how the force of the rules is initiated. Ontario's Act operates wholly on the basis of private enforcement,[103] as does the Saskatchewan Act.[104]

This private route recognizes that the rights of an elector are infringed when a violation of the Act occurs. The public prosecution route, such as in

99 In Ontario, see s. 10(2) of the *Municipal Conflict of Interest Act*, R.S.O. 1990, c. M.50; in Manitoba, see s. 22 of the *Municipal Council Conflict of Interest Act*, C.C.S.M. c.M255; see s. 33(5) of the Saskatchewan *Urban Municipality Act, 1984*, S.S. 1983-84, c. U-11; and see also s. 10(1) of the British Columbia *Financial Disclosure Act*, R.S.B.C. 1996, c. 139.

100 (1998), 166 D.L.R. (4th) 546 (Man. C.A.). See also *Sheehan v. Harte* (1993), 15 M.P.L.R. (2d) 311 (Ont. Gen Div.).

101 *Municipal Conflict of Interest Act*, R.S.O. 1990, c. M.50, s. 10(1)(a). This penalty is also provided in Saskatchewan (*Urban Municipality Act, 1984*, S.S. 1983-84, c. U-11, s. 33(5)(a)), and in Manitoba (*Municipal Conflict of Interest Act*, C.C.S.M. c. M255, s. 21(2)(a). See also s. 206(2) of the Newfoundland *Municipalities Act, 1999*, S.N.L. 1999, c. M-24, where a seat can be declared vacant by the resolution of council.

102 *Municipal Conflict of Interest Act*, R.S.O. 1990, c. M50, s. 10(1)(b) and (c).

103 *Ibic'.* at s. 9(1) .

104 Section 33(4) of the *Urban Municipality Act, 1984*, S.S. 1983-84, c. U-11.

New Brunswick[105] and British Columbia[106] may make the violation seem more like a criminal offence, but it is also consistent with the nature of the offence being an injury to the general public. In any event, the approaches can be combined. Having prosecutorial control come solely under the Attorney General may be too restrictive and frustrating for an elector who wishes to pursue an allegation.

105 Section 90.9 of the *Municipalities Act*, R.S.N.B. 1973, c. M-22.

106 Sections 9-11 of *the Financial Disclosure Act*, R.S.B.C. 1996, c. 139.

Index